Nothing to Hide

MENTAL ILLNESS IN THE FAMILY

Nothing to Hide

MENTAL ILLNESS IN THE FAMILY

Interviews by Jean J. Beard and Peggy Gillespie

PHOTOGRAPHS BY GIGI KAESER

Foreword by Kay Redfield Jamison, Ph.D.

Introduction by Kenneth Duckworth, M.D.

Afterword by David Maraniss

THE NEW PRESS
NEW YORK

In memory of Paul Gottlieb in appreciation for his extraordinary support, courage, generosity, and vision.

Photographs © 2002 by Gigi Kaeser
Text © 2002 by Jean J. Beard and Peggy Gillespie
Foreword © 2002 by Kay Redfield Jamison, Ph.D.
Introduction © 2002 by Kenneth Duckworth, M.D.
Afterword © 2002 by David Maraniss

Published in the United States by The New Press, New York, 2002
Distributed by W. W. Norton & Company, Inc., New York

LIBRARY OF CONGRESS CATALOGING-IN-PUBLICATION DATA

Beard, Jean J.
   Nothing to hide : mental illness in the family / interviews by Jean J. Beard and Peggy Gillespie;
photographs by Gigi Kaeser ; foreword by Kay Redfield Jamison.
      p. cm.
   Includes bibliographical references.
   ISBN 1-56584-721-0(hc.)
   ISBN 1-56584-786-5(pbk.)
   1. Family — Mental health. 2. Mentally ill — Family relationships. 3. Mentally ill — United States —
Interviews. I. Gillespie, Peggy, 1948 — II. Title.

RC455.4.F3 B39 2002
616.89 — dc21

2002019769

The New Press was established in 1990 as a not-for-profit alternative to the large, commercial
publishing houses currently dominating the book publishing industry. The New Press operates in the
public interest rather than for private gain, and is committed to publishing, in innovative ways, works
of educational, cultural, and community value that are often deemed insufficiently profitable.

The New Press, 450 West 41st Street, 6th floor, New York, NY 10036
www.thenewpress.com

Book design by Figaro

Printed in China

2 4 6 8 10 9 7 5 3 1

To Ashley Beard, my child of grace, and Leila Linen, my saving grace
—JEAN BEARD

To the memory of my husband, Gregory Gillespie
—PEGGY GILLESPIE

To the memory of my parents
—GIGI KAESER

CONTENTS

FOREWORD

KAY REDFIELD JAMISON, PH.D.
PROFESSOR OF PSYCHIATRY
THE JOHNS HOPKINS SCHOOL OF MEDICINE
AUTHOR, *AN UNQUIET MIND*

THERE ARE AS MANY KINDS OF STIGMA attached to mental illness as there are people, for each of us has his or her own set of beliefs, prejudices, and misunderstandings. Much of the stigma is ingrained in the ancient attitudes held by virtually every society on earth. These attitudes show themselves in the decisions that societies make and in the behaviors that societies allow. It is clear, for example, that newspapers and television stations can print or broadcast remarks about those with mental illness that would not be tolerated if made about any other minority group. Stigma also insinuates its way into policy decisions about access to competent health care, health insurance, job discrimination, and research priorities.

Those who have mental illness also stigmatize themselves: They do not demand of their lawmakers and healthcare systems that which they deserve. Their expectations of society are frighteningly low, and not at all consistent with the large voting block they represent. Self-stigma has many damaging consequences, including having an inhibiting effect on acknowledging one's illness and, indeed, in recognizing it; in seeking treatment for it; and in following treatment recommendations once they are made. The inability to discuss mental illness in an informed and straightforward way—to deal with it as the major public health concern that it is— is simply unjustifiable in the twenty-first century.

There is also stigma against mental illness that comes from the clinical community itself: the doctors, psychologists, nurses, and social workers who have had no great cause to examine their own beliefs seriously because their professional communities have not thought it important enough to see to it that they do. Most clinicians are compassionate and competent, but there are far too many who are not.

There is a large group that I think of as the "silent successful"—people who get well because they have had excellent clinical care and because they are the beneficiaries of a superb research enterprise, but who are afraid to speak out about their mental illnesses for fear of personal or professional retribution. This is understandable but unfortunate, for it perpetuates the misperception that people with mental illness do not get well. As a result, what remains in the public eye is the great mass of *untreated* mental illness—the newspaper accounts of violence and the homeless mentally ill. What is *not* seen is all of the people—the truck drivers, lawyers, teachers, secretaries, physicians, members of Congress—who have been successfully treated, who show up for work, who compete, and who succeed.

My interest in mental illness is both professional and personal. I first became ill with a severe form of manic-depressive illness when I was a senior in high school. Like most people who get psychiatric disorders, I had absolutely no idea what was happening to me. After years of no treatment and my illness getting much worse, I finally received medical care—more than ten years after my first breakdown.

I was fortunate in receiving excellent clinical care and fortunate in being able to afford it. As a result, I was able to benefit from the extraordinary advances in research. But it is not fair that I have had access to care when so many others have not. Everywhere I go in this country, in city after city and on college campus after college campus, I see the terrible suffering of those who do not have access to healthcare and who have been hurt by stigma. Mental illness is ruthless in the pain it causes.

The only way to counter this pain is to make mental illness more human and to show how it affects people and the people who love them. This is the great grace of *Nothing to Hide: Mental Illness in the Family,* a remarkable book that gives a face to those who have mental illness. The photographs and interviews give a dignity and humanity to patients and their families, as well as providing a real sense of the day-to-day difficulties of living with mental illness. This book is both wonderful and important.

PREFACE

JEAN J. BEARD AND PEGGY GILLESPIE
AMHERST, MASSACHUSETTS

NOTHING TO HIDE: MENTAL ILLNESS IN THE FAMILY introduces forty-four families whose lives have been changed by mental illness. These families are from diverse racial, ethnic, religious, and socioeconomic backgrounds. They live in areas both urban and rural, from Los Angeles to a small town in Tennessee. Clearly, mental illness knows no boundaries.

When a debilitating illness, either physical or mental, strikes a child, an adolescent, or an adult, it has an impact on the entire family. A diagnosis of mental illness, however, carries with it an additional challenge: the pervasive and destructive burden of stigma. Stigma gives rise to myths, stereotypes, and misunderstandings about people who have psychiatric disorders and their family members. The primary goal of *Nothing to Hide* is to dispel common misconceptions about mental illness in order to decrease stigma.

In 1997, we began the process of looking for individuals who have been diagnosed with a mental illness and who would be willing to participate with their family members in a photo-text exhibit. We were given many helpful leads by national mental health organizations and professionals involved in the mental health field. We were pleased that so many families were enthusiastic about being included in this exhibit, and we wish we could have included them all.

We traveled coast to coast to interview these families in their homes or their workplaces. We were always warmly wel-comed, and their hospitality and generosity of spirit never failed to touch us. In listening to their struggles and disap-pointments, as well as to their dreams and hopes for the future, we were profoundly moved. We admire their courage in stepping forward to share their private stories in a very public way.

In a few cases, family members did not participate in *Nothing to Hide,* either because they weren't able to come to the interview, chose not to, or were not invited by the individual who has a mental illness. In one case, a woman's family is comprised of her two closest friends because she is estranged from her family of origin. In every case, how-ever, the importance of family is acknowledged and explored.

After editing the transcripts of our conversations with the individuals and their families, each person had the oppor-tunity to carefully review their text in order to add or delete any material if they so wished. This process ensured that the stories in *Nothing to Hide* would be *their* stories, not ours.

In 1998, the exhibit began touring the country to ven-ues as diverse as public and private schools, universities, museums, libraries, medical schools, hospitals, mental health organizations, and statehouses. Currently, six copies of the touring exhibit of *Nothing to Hide* are still on the road, and the response to the exhibit continues to be overwhelmingly positive. In order to bring these photographs and stories to a wider audience, a decision was made to publish *Nothing to Hide* in book form.

We realize that the forty-four stories in *Nothing to Hide* do not reflect the entire spectrum of diagnoses and treatment modalities that exist in today's complex mental health field. Nevertheless, the families who grace the pages of this book are united by their courage and strength in the face of extraordinary and often devastating circumstances.

We appreciate and respect all the people we met while working on this book and are enormously grateful for their participation. It is our hope that *Nothing to Hide* will lead to a greater understanding and acceptance of all those affected by mental illness.

PHOTOGRAPHER'S NOTE

GIGI KAESER
CHESTERFIELD, MASSACHUSETTS

WHEN PEOPLE POSE FOR FAMILY PICTURES, they usually feel self-conscious and they try to look good. They often smile unconvincingly, or look serious. When I succeed as a photographer, I have interrupted these reactions.

Bartola Esparza looks at her son Trini with pride, Jean Beard and her daughter Ashley share a moment of affection and fun, and Norma Abney tells her son Tony that she loves him. Diana Wong peers lovingly into the face of the man she loves, just as her mother seated in front of her does, as the shutter opens and closes. Sandra Bey, bemused at her rambunctious grandson Corey, holds his arm to keep him in the picture. Molly Cisco and her friends crack each other up, as they always do. These are normal family moments caught by the camera. They are not candid pictures, but pictures of people being photographed for *Nothing to Hide.* In every case at least one person in the picture has a mental illness.

People sometimes ask, "Why are these people smiling?" I can't answer that question. But I know the question betrays a notion that most of us have about mental illness: that those who have it are different from us. Surely, we think, they don't feel what we feel; they don't express it in the same way. Now, please take another look.

INTRODUCTION

KENNETH DUCKWORTH, M.D.

I WONDER HOW *Nothing to Hide: Mental Illness in the Family* would have changed my life if this book had been available to my family in 1966. I was in the second grade that year, a tall kid who loved sports and tolerated school just fine. My friends were always around. I had never heard of psychiatry, never had a relative go to medical school—not even to college, for that matter. I knew nothing about psychiatric illness, and I thought I would grow up to be a baseball player. But everything was about to change.

My father, a playful and loving traveling salesman, became very ill. Suddenly Dad was talking real fast, hearing voices, acting erratically, and yelling a lot. I came to understand that my father had manic-depressive illness (now called bipolar illness). Unlike heart disease, about which people would have been understanding and sympathetic, there seemed to be no acceptable way to communicate that he had a psychiatric illness—not to other kids, not to other family members, not to our neighbors. When he went to the psychiatric hospital, friends stayed away for quite a while. I felt as if I had become invisible—invisible in school, in church, and even in the neighborhood. There were no friendly faces to support my having a dad with a psychiatric illness. The members of my family—mom, brother and sister, and I—were also afraid to face the truth, and so we suffered alone.

The damnedest thing was that after I'd get my dad back, his 100 percent old self, there'd be no space in which to talk about what had happened. Lightning struck, took him away to the hospital, then sunshine again. Over the years this was the constant threat: never knowing when the bolt would come.

It was never far from my consciousness, but my family still didn't talk about it. Silence and shame were the enemies that won out.

I assumed that my situation was unique, that no one else was experiencing the anxiety and fear that accompany a big and poorly understood condition like bipolar illness. Had I been able to imagine that millions of American kids were dealing with a variation on this theme, I would have felt less alone, less isolated. Looking at our own crisis through the lens of this book might have given my family the strength to deal constructively with the truth of what was happening to us and with the impact of this mysterious illness on a wonderful man whom we loved.

I never did become a ballplayer; nevertheless, my dad and I spent many fine afternoons at the ballpark as a very happy duo, enjoying the precious good times that can come as a reprieve during even the most difficult of illnesses. I became a psychiatrist in part because I knew I would always be proud of my work if I could help people with psychiatric illness—and their families—reclaim days like that as their due.

As a psychiatrist, I am regularly visited by people who have suffered from symptoms of psychiatric illness for two, five, even eight years without seeking help. This is the compounding tragedy of psychiatric illness. When people suffer from its symptoms, they often do so in shamed silence, not wanting to admit to their troubles because they anticipate being stigmatized as "different," or even "crazy." They are confused by their symptoms, even frightened by them, but have little social support for finding out what is wrong and seeking help.

This saddens me greatly because psychiatric illness is just that, *illness.* Although there is much that we do not yet fully understand about its causes and treatment, there is much that we do know and many ways in which we can help those who suffer from its manifestations. In *Nothing to Hide: Mental Illness in the Family,* a powerful and compelling book, you will become well acquainted with forty-four families affected by psychiatric disorders. You will see their faces; you will hear their individual stories; you will witness their struggles to recover as they learn how to navigate through the world of mental health treatment. And you will surely come to see that psychiatric illness is nothing to hide.

In order to dispel the stigma of psychiatric disorders among the general public, the families in this book speak urgently about the great need for education and understanding. For the readers of this book who are unfamiliar with the terrain of psychiatric illness, I'd like to offer some very basic perspectives on the way psychiatric illnesses are currently conceptualized, diagnosed, and treated.

A word on terminology: Over the years, the vocabulary we use to describe psychiatric illnesses has changed to reflect our changing perceptions and beliefs. This is often a source of contention. Although it is the label most commonly used in our culture, many people object to the term "mental illness" because it is broad and somewhat ill defined. They also feel that it contributes to stigma by implying that associated symptoms are "just in your head." I prefer the terms "psychiatric disorder" or "psychiatric illness" because I believe that they accurately reflect the central biomedical component of the processes at work. Psychiatry is a branch of medicine that looks at the whole person as a person, not just as a set of symptoms. A more recent term, "brain disorders," defines very biologically the conditions I am calling psychiatric. Some feel that using the label "brain disorders" oversimplifies a complex set of experiences and outcomes.

Words have great power. When talking about people who use psychiatric services, do I refer to them as "patients," "clients," "mental health consumers," or "consumer-survivors"? This dilemma arises most often in public forums, and I consistently try to use the vocabulary that others choose for themselves. I do the same in my office, asking people how they would like me to refer to them. They almost always choose a form of their own name—"Bob" or "Mr. Garvey"—but the point is that we come to that together.

Nothing to Hide illustrates this linguistic journey. Many people have a different take on their experiences and have their own language to describe themselves and their situations. The editors of this book don't take a stand on language, other than to choose the term "mental illness" to use in their title, because the term is still considered acceptable and it is the most common one in use today. Otherwise, the editors have allowed the individuals to speak for themselves, even if the language they use may be considered stigmatizing to other people. For example, some people in this book consider words like "nuts" and "crazy" to be just as offensive as racial epithets; others use these words with a sense of humor. The editors wanted the voices of the individuals to be authentic, and didn't censor language for political correctness. To me, that is the point of *Nothing to Hide* and of all good clinical work: to illuminate the personal.

WHAT IS A PSYCHIATRIC ILLNESS?

No one is spared life experiences that cause anxiety, fear, sadness, and even despair. Some of the clients I see come to me because they are feeling depressed or anxious in response to a crisis, a loss, or an adjustment in their lives. Their problems are causing them such intense anxiety and sadness that they may be overwhelmed and even temporarily disabled by them. They recognize that they need more help than they are getting from the people in their lives, and they have turned to a psychiatrist. Because psychiatric conditions exist on a spectrum, it is sometimes difficult for me to draw an exact line defining when a person with emotional suffering may be developing a clinical disorder. A person who is suffering with sadness and hopelessness about the future may be having a normal grief reaction, or may be developing a clinical depression. The distinction is rooted in the level of functional impairment the person has, as well as the intensity and duration of the symptoms. It is also difficult to predict the course of a condition when a person first seeks psychiatric treatment.

People who come to me describing symptoms of depression, anxiety, or disordered thinking that have disabled them for weeks or months or even years, without any obvious antecedent, might be suffering from a psychiatric disorder. They will probably need help over a longer period of time; that help might include medication and, even with the best efforts on both our parts, their symptoms may recur.

Why do some people develop a psychiatric illness and others do not? The most honest answer is that we do not know. We certainly cannot identify any single cause. We have learned that there is a genetic component to these conditions and that, like diabetes and some forms of cancer, they commonly run in families. Of course, that does not mean that everyone in a family will be affected. There are, for example, many sets of identical twins in which one of the twins develops schizophrenia and the other does not. The current consensus among doctors and researchers is that some people are born with a biological vulnerability to various forms of psychiatric illness, and that environmental influences or experiences can trigger the development of symptoms. Viral infection or birth trauma might raise the risk for one twin and not for the other. The significance of any particular environmental impact may never be known because, depending on the type of illness, psychiatric symptoms appear within different age ranges. The one condition for which we usually know the cause is posttraumatic stress disorder (PTSD). After the horrific terrorism of September 11 at the World Trade Center and the

Pentagon, many people developed PTSD. My colleagues in New York City and in Washington, D.C., confirm what I have seen in my work with traumatized people in Boston; the intensity of the trauma is the best predictor of who will develop PTSD and what the duration of their experience with it will be. With the support of family and friends, many people will begin to feel more like themselves within a matter of months. Others will benefit from psychiatric care. Though most people with PTSD return to a very high level of functioning, many of them will always have an added vulnerability to other stresses and losses.

Before we understood that genetic tendencies and biological vulnerabilities account for many of the manifestations of psychiatric illness, doctors used to blame parents, and particularly mothers, for the problems that their children developed. To this day I have women complain to me that their son's or daughter's psychiatric illness doubly traumatized them—first, by the diagnosis, and then by the blame they received from the mental health professionals. There are many examples of this damaging attitude in *Nothing to Hide.* When Katie Currier's young son Kevin was hospitalized because of severe behavioral symptoms, her family experienced this firsthand. She says, "Kevin's doctors thought that his acting-out behavior was a sign that my husband, Pete, and I had been abusing him. They were suspicious of us! We were so devastated and shocked that we could barely hold it together. Although we were never formally accused of child abuse, I'll remember this trauma for the rest of my life."

Appreciating that parents are not the root cause of psychiatric illness is important. It is just as important to appreciate that families have an impact on an individual's course of treatment. Families that offer clear support, encourage treatment, and are educated in the causes and courses of psychiatric illness are often essential to a person's recovery. Conversely, a family that shames a member for their symptoms can worsen an outcome.

Approaching someone who is ill with an open and nonjudgmental heart is not always easy. It takes sophistication to know when someone who is sad can pull herself up by her bootstraps or when more intervention is needed. Marco Chan, who has major depression, describes in this book a common reaction to his diagnosis of depression: "Lots of people said to me, 'You look fine and you seem fine. Why aren't you functioning? Just get over it! Get on with your life.' It was hard for me to explain to them that it wasn't quite that easy."

In some cases, it can be hard for the individual who is sad to even know that they need psychiatric help to recover. Some people who have serious symptoms lose the perspective that they are ill—they lose insight—and families who are able to hang in there and respond constructively to what can be a very difficult and upsetting situation are invaluable.

In the 1950s, when there was little understanding of the biological component to psychiatric illness, treatment emphasized the "talking" therapies. This approach is based on the assumption that if patients can understand the damaging experiences of their past, that understanding will free them from the effects of those experiences. This insight-driven form of therapy is sometimes called "insight-oriented" therapy or, when it conforms to the kind of in-depth analysis Sigmund Freud practiced beginning in the 1930s, it is called "psychoanalysis."

Psychotherapy has developed many subtypes. These subtypes include various one-to-one talking therapies, (cognitive, insight, behavioral), and group, couples, family, and occupational therapy, in which the therapist works with more than one person. The development of these variations represents our ongoing progress in matching the individual (or group) to the best possible form of treatment. However, we have also learned that, by itself, psychotherapy is an inadequate way of dealing with many serious illnesses. Antipsychotic medications that help people with schizophrenia organize their thinking were introduced in the mid-1950s. The first generation of antidepressants became available in the 1960s, and lithium, a medication that stabilizes mood for people with bipolar illness, was introduced in the 1970s. Though rarely enough alone

to treat people successfully, each of these medications, and the newer medications that have been introduced since, have greatly enhanced the treatment options for many clients.

WHAT ARE SOME OF THE MORE COMMON TYPES OF PSYCHIATRIC DISORDERS?

According to the National Institute of Mental Health, mental disorders are common in the United States and internationally. An estimated 22.1 percent of Americans ages eighteen and older—about one in five adults—suffer from a diagnosable mental disorder in a given year. When applied to the 1998 U.S. Census residential population estimate, this figure translates to 44.3 million people.

Schizophrenia

The term "schizophrenia" is commonly misunderstood to mean "split personality." In fact, the term was coined at the turn of the twentieth century and, though "schiz" does come from the Greek for "split," it refers to the split between thought and emotion that sometimes characterizes the condition.

Approximately 1 percent of the population in the United States suffers from schizophrenia, and both males and females develop this illness in equal numbers. For that 1 percent, symptoms usually develop between the late teens and early thirties. We do not know the cause of schizophrenia, but we think that its delayed onset is the culminating effect of the failure of certain cells in the brain to develop or migrate to their proper sizes and spaces within the brain. Advances in the technology for viewing the brain offer great hope for the future. When we understand the brain better, we will be better able to intervene in the course of the illness.

When someone is diagnosed as having schizophrenia, they have commonly experienced at least six months of difficulty with what psychiatrists call "testing reality." That is, they have been hearing, thinking, or believing things that have no basis in reality. Someone suffering from schizophrenia may experience delusions (fixed false beliefs), auditory hallucinations (hearing things or voices that are not real to an outsider even if they are clearly so to the individual), and paranoid thinking (when one believes that others are out to "get" him or her). Not surprisingly, such difficulty with testing reality is usually accompanied by a decline in normal functioning, and people often withdraw. They may stay in their room, begin to do poorly at school or work, and lose interest in relationships. Unfortunately, difficulty testing reality is also commonly associated with poor insight and self-awareness. People who suffer from schizophrenia, for example, might have difficulty accepting that their auditory hallucinations are not real, or that there is not—could not be—someone tapping their telephone.

The treatment for schizophrenia is advancing with each year. There is a consensus in the scientific literature that medications can successfully reduce the severity and frequency of symptoms. Although drug treatment for schizophrenia has been available since the 1950s, newer medications do not cause movement disorders—known as tardive dyskinesia—at nearly the same rate that the older medications did. They are also more effective, particularly in helping patients with their activity level and motivation. The newer medications are widely used and can keep symptoms under control most of the time for most of the people who take them. They are not, however, a panacea. Some people do not respond to them, and the newer antipsychotic medications have a new profile of side effects, including weight gain and the risk of diabetes.

Even with treatment, managing a serious and persistent illness such as schizophrenia can be a full-time job, and patients can get discouraged. There is a serious risk of suicide, particularly in the early stages of the illness, but with treatment, many people can live successfully with schizophrenia. Some people have the hardest time in the early years of their illness, but can accommodate better later in life. Most people who have schizophrenia can live outside a treatment facility and many can have relationships and find a place in society. Fred Frese, PhD, a psychologist, mental health advocate, husband, and father who has paranoid schizophrenia, illustrates this point when he talks in *Nothing to Hide* about his long journey with psychiatric illness:

I was diagnosed with paranoid schizophrenia when I was only twenty-five years old. For the next ten years, I was in and out of various mental hospitals. I was told many times that I was insane, and I was given little hope that I could ever lead a dignified or reasonably normal life.

Today, I am the Director of Psychology at Western Reserve Psychiatric Hospital, a state hospital in Ohio. Ironically, I used to be a patient in the Ohio State mental health system. Traditionally, it has been taught that you don't recover from schizophrenia, that it is a degenerative brain disorder. I was told over thirty years ago that the symptoms of schizophrenia only get worse, not better. The thing is, people do recover, but because there is such a stigma against mental illness, people who get better often are reluctant to acknowledge that they have ever been sick.

I have seen similar outcomes in my own practice. After we found the medication that did the best job of controlling his symptoms, one of my patients with schizophrenia was able to return to a job that he liked and develop a rewarding relationship with a woman. These successes were the result of much hard work on his part, hard work made possible by the foundation (as he described it) that the medication provided.

Mood Disorders

Mood disorders, also referred to as "affective disorders," comprise a range of psychiatric conditions that impair or distort an individual's sense of well-being. The most common of these disorders are *major depression* and *bipolar disorder*. The latter is also known as "manic-depressive" illness.

Major Depression

Approximately 25 percent of all women and about 10 percent of all men will experience a major depression over the course of their lifetimes. These numbers appear to remain consistent across demographic groups in the United States. Everyone experiences feeling sad, but we say someone has a clinical depression if the sad feelings persist for more than two weeks and are accompanied by many of the following: hopelessness, concentration difficulties, suicidal thoughts, sleep disturbance, or appetite changes. The sad feelings might also be accompanied by: a loss of interest or pleasure in activities that had previously been enjoyable; noticeable restlessness; loss of energy; appearing to be "slowed down"; and difficulty functioning. A first episode of major depression is usually precipitated by a stressful experience, but recurring bouts of depression often have no obvious cause or trigger.

We do not understand the underlying causes of major depression. Affective illness does tend to run in families, and depression may be a biologic response on the part of at-risk individuals to stressful experiences. We do know that treatment for depression—psychotherapy coupled with antidepressant medication—has a good response rate. Even when depression recurs (and it will, a substantial percentage of the time), patients almost always improve with support, medication, and psychotherapy.

Bipolar Disorder

Bipolar disorder occurs in approximately 1 percent of the population, and men and women have bipolar illness in about equal numbers. Most people who develop a bipolar disorder begin with an episode of depression that is followed by a mood swing that takes them in the opposite direction. These moods, often described as "manic" episodes, are characterized by the feeling of being "high" and full of energy. During a manic episode, which can be as short as a few days or as long as weeks and months, people often sleep very little; have racing thoughts; make impulsive decisions; and feel as if they have all of the answers. People who have bipolar illness often have manic episodes alternating with depressive episodes or, less commonly, they can have sequences of the same types of episodes. Some of the most creative people in the history of Western civilization may have had bipolar illness—enjoying bursts of creative energy during their manic periods. In a mild form, a manic episode can be quite functional, but for those whose episodes become increasingly severe, mania can be destructive. On many occasions the person's judgment deteriorates; he or she can become quite hostile, and eventually even lose touch with reality—perhaps hearing voices or imagining that someone is out to get him or her.

We do not know what causes bipolar disorder, but like depression it appears to involve a chemical imbalance in the brain. Though it tends to run in families, bipolar disorder is thought to be genetically distinct from depressive disorder. People with bipolar disorder have an even greater tendency to misuse drugs and alcohol during active episodes of the illness than do people who have schizophrenia or major depression.

Bipolar illness is particularly challenging to treat because people who suffer from it often like feeling high and don't accept that they are ill. It is easier for a doctor to form a treatment alliance with a patient when the manic episode has ended and he or she may be having regrets about what they may have said or done. A thoughtful doctor can help a patient anticipate future warning signs of the illness. This alliance is of great value because, since the introduction of lithium in the 1970s, we have had medications that are effective mood stabilizers, protecting patients from the highs and the lows of bipolar disorder. Some individuals respond to treatment very well and function at a very high level. My experience is that most patients are relieved to have the extreme highs and lows of their moods modified by treatment; however, choosing that treatment is an intensely personal decision. It must be made over and over if the patients are to successfully protect themselves from serious manic or depressive episodes.

Obsessive-Compulsive Disorder

Obsessive-compulsive disorder (OCD) is considered an anxiety disorder in somewhat the same category as panic attacks and posttraumatic stress disorder. OCD affects approximately 3 percent of Americans—children and adults—and appears to impact people across demographic lines. People with OCD have intrusive, preoccupying thoughts that make them anxious, and they try to relieve their anxiety with compulsive or ritualized behaviors. A person with intrusive and preoccupying thoughts of contamination, for example, might wash his hands obsessively or take extreme measures to keep his house clean. Unfortunately, the obsessive thoughts recur frequently, and the behaviors used to relieve the anxiety become compulsive.

People with OCD almost always feel that their fears are at least exaggerated—if not completely irrational—so not only do they feel trapped by their cycle of compulsions, but they are also ashamed of their "nonsensical" behavior. Difficulties with OCD can so dominate a person's life that they interfere with relationships and work. A person who needs to check hundreds of times whether they have turned off the stove will have difficulty making social plans and perhaps meeting deadlines. Someone who is preoccupied with fears of contamination might not only have significant and visible skin problems from washing their hands over and over, but also might be too anxious about cleanliness to join friends for dinner at a restaurant.

Fortunately, the treatment of OCD has improved substantially in the past two decades. For me, the first step is education—that is, explaining to people with OCD (and, when appropriate, to friends and family) that what often seems like simply weird and annoying behavior is a true psychiatric illness. They need to know that behavioral therapy and medication can probably make a significant difference for them. Behavioral therapy is different from insight-based therapy because, instead of dealing with the underlying causes of a problem, it helps a person manage their current difficulty. For OCD sufferers, this means help shaping their thinking and their environment in ways that will minimize triggers of obsessive thinking.

The course of OCD is variable, and difficult to predict. As with most psychiatric illnesses, OCD may be chronic—even lifelong—but it is treatable, usually with good results. People who have supports in place have a much better chance to live a full and productive life, even if the condition stays with them.

HOW DO WE DIAGNOSE AND TREAT PSYCHIATRIC ILLNESS?

Unfortunately, there are no simple blood tests, CT scans, or psychological tests that can diagnose psychiatric illness. The best we can do at this time is understand a person's symptoms over time and organize them into patterns, and appreciate that the symptoms may have meaning for the person. This is not categorizing for the sake of categorizing. These patterns of symptoms often predict the most effective treatment approach. It is important to understand that a single interview may not get the diagnosis right. A person who is hearing voices might be suffering from a number of different conditions. Auditory hallucination is a common symptom of schizophrenia, but it can also be a component of severe depression, bipolar illness, drug use, or a seizure disorder in a specific part of the brain. Following the longitudinal course of a person's condition is essential to diagnosis.

Proper diagnosis is further complicated by the fact that different conditions appear most typically at different stages of life. For instance, if a child in the first grade has great difficulty paying attention, is very distractible, and often acts impulsively, we might judge that he or she has attention-deficit/hyperactivity disorder (ADHD). For an adult, these symptoms could be signs of ADHD, but he or she may also be developing bipolar illness. The patterns of onset of an illness are very helpful in diagnosis, but we must be careful. They can also limit our ability to "see" illness.

In the 1960s, psychiatrists thought that children couldn't get depressed in a clinically significant way. Our concept of depression was that people became depressed when they were critical of themselves, or when they had an overactive conscience. Children were not thought to have those capacities, so they were not diagnosed with depression. In the late 1970s, the move was made to rely more on symptoms to organize diagnoses, and children were looked at more objectively. We saw that they could suffer from significant depression. Today some researchers feel they have identified children who have bipolar illness. This is controversial because it flies in the face of the patterns we have observed; patterns that tell us bipolar illness usually develops in one's late teens to thirties or forties. Time and further research will tell on this important question. The important point is that once we can "see" symptoms for what they are, we are able to intervene more thoughtfully and effectively.

Treatment and Recovery

The purpose of my work with patients is to help them recover and maximize their functioning. I learn from person to person what works best for that individual. In some cases, what works best might be medication and job training, or participation in a self-help group. For other patients, a brief hospital stay is necessary to stabilize them after an episode of symptoms such as those caused by a severe depression, a suicide attempt, an intense episode of mania, or a psychotic break. Although an even smaller number of patients may require long-term care in a psychiatric hospital or a treatment facility, there is little disagreement in the field that, with adequate support and proper medication, most people can and should do well living in their community. This is an important departure from a much older practice of locking people away in "mental hospitals," which contributed to the stigma surrounding psychiatric disorders.

Beginning in the 1800s, people who were diagnosed with psychiatric illnesses were often relegated to the long-term custodial care of state-owned "asylums." The treatment concept was that patients had a greater chance of recovery if they were removed from the stresses of modern life. The unintended (or perhaps intended) consequence of this practice was to warehouse people with odd or undesirable behavior away from the rest of society, reinforcing the idea that these individuals should be shunned. Those who were discharged from a state hospital found it smart to conceal that they had ever been there as a patient. Although insurance companies today are making it difficult to keep patients in the hospital long enough to even stabilize them, the practice of long custodial hospitalizations was common as recently as the 1960s and 1970s. Unfortunately, ending this practice—sometimes called deinstitutionalization—has hardly had a uniformly happy outcome. Most communities have failed to invest in adequate community-based care as an alternative to state hospital care, which often releases to the streets those with the most severe manifestations of psychiatric illness—thus, those who are most in need of help, but who reject their family's and doctor's support precisely because they have such difficulty "testing reality," often wind up homeless and untreated.

Many of the stories you will read in this book describe how difficult it often is to get proper psychiatric care within the public health system. Although I have also seen the public sector be life-saving and creative for some individuals, there often just isn't enough money to provide good treatment to everyone who needs it.

Media Myths/Crystallizing the Stigma

The main source of information most Americans have about psychiatric illness is the media. Reading the newspapers and tabloids, watching TV, or going to the movies gives the false and deeply entrenched impression that people who have a psychiatric condition are dangerous. If a crime is committed by someone with a history of psychiatric illness, any news reporting is likely to reveal this and to imply that the illness is a contributing factor—even a cause—of the criminal behavior. But the overwhelming majority of Americans who are violent do not have psychiatric illness, and psychiatric illness, by itself, is not a trigger for violence. Best estimates are that people with psychiatric illnesses commit approximately 5 percent of all violent acts in America. A narrow range of psychiatric symptoms—including extreme paranoia and certain kinds of auditory hallucinations coupled with active substance abuse—are associated with a *risk* of violent behavior, but with ongoing treatment and proper medication, the majority of even the subgroup of people with these illnesses are no more dangerous than people in the general population. According to the American Psychiatric Association, recent research has shown that the vast majority of people who are violent do not suffer from mental illnesses. In fact, those who have psychiatric illnesses are more commonly the victims of abuse and violence than its perpetrators.

The stigma attached to psychiatric illness has a profound effect on individuals and their families, and it also affects our ability to make progress in the field. Less shame and fear result in better recognition, which supports better research. Progress is possible. Cancer was once regarded as a disease that was so mysterious and scary, it could not be discussed with patients. Now it is the subject of public fund-raisers that take their inspiration from cancer survivors who speak openly about their struggle to recover. The process has benefited cancer patients everywhere and has increased the support they can enjoy from friends and family.

Nothing to Hide presents equally inspiring people who have had the courage to go public about their experiences with psychiatric illness for the benefit of us all. As Mike Campbell, the father of a young woman who has schizophrenia, says: "It's a struggle [to have a mental illness] and it's a real test of your faith and your ability to survive, but getting through it proves that the human spirit can endure." As both the son of a father who had a psychiatric disorder and as a psychiatrist, I applaud the spirit of endurance and compassion exemplified by all of the courageous individuals who share their stories in this inspiring and, ultimately, hopeful book.

FAMILY

PORTRAITS

—————

We tell stories, build

From fragments of our lives

Maps to guide us to each other...

—Pat Schneider
from the poem "Going the Longest Way Around"

Standing: Winzer, Brandon, Vivian *Seated:* Brandi, Eddie

THE YOUNGBLOOD / ANDREWS FAMILY

SHREVEPORT, LOUISIANA

WINZER ANDREWS / BRANDI ANDREWS / BRANDON ANDREWS
EDDIE YOUNGBLOOD / VIVIAN ANDREWS

EDDIE

WHEN I FIRST GOT SICK, I FORGOT HOW TO WASH MYSELF. I got to the point where I couldn't eat or sleep. I even forgot how to write. I didn't know how to do nothing. I was hospitalized in a mental institution, where I was diagnosed with schizophrenia.

After I was discharged from the hospital two months later, I was referred to a local mental health center. The doctor prescribed lithium for me. Whatever the cause, I became lithium intoxicated and I got sick. I went into a coma for two weeks, and they had to take that medicine out of me. The doctors thought that I would pass on, but by the help of the Lord, I'm still here.

I guess there were several reasons for my mental illness. My mother committed suicide in 1969 when she walked into a river and drowned herself. That hurt me terribly. My aunt, who was like a sister to me, died of cancer when she was only thirty. I didn't have much affection or companionship in my life because I was divorced, and I felt all alone. I withdrew, and unless I had to go somewhere, I just stayed in the house. I went to work and to church, but then I would come right back home and go to bed. That was it. I felt an emptiness in my soul, and there wasn't much joy in my life. At times, I still feel a deep loneliness that is hard to describe.

I'm doing pretty good now. I'm able to do all my affairs, like work and driving. I'm also more interactive with people, and I enjoy the kids I work with at Pizza Hut. I tell them, "Y'all keep me young." They be jiving and teasing me.

As far as I know, until you get in a difficult situation, you never know who your real friends are. The people who really know me can usually tell if I'm upset. All they have to do is look in my eyes, because my eyes talk.

I love everyone in my family. When my grandkids, Brandi and Brandon, come over, they feel relaxed with me. Whatever they feel comfortable doing is all right with me. I give them space to let themselves go. I tell them if they want to watch a movie, watch a movie. If they want to bang on

Like I say, mental illness is nothing to hide. I'm not "crazy" as some people might say; I simply have a mental illness. I'm going to be all right until God gives me a call.
— EDDIE

the piano until I say, "That's enough," it's fine with me. Before I went into the hospital, my grandkids were still in high chairs and they just looked at me funny. Now if they want to ask me something, they just come and ask me.

In the midst of all my trials and tribulations, I still tried to serve the Lord. I joined my church when I was eight years old, and I started playing the piano there when I was only twelve. I've continued to play at the church for forty-six years. With the help of God and the mental health system, I'm doing just fine. I like sharing my experiences with others. As the song goes, "If I can help somebody as I pass along, then my living will not be in vain."

Like I say, mental illness is nothing to hide. I'm not "crazy" as some people might say; I simply have a mental illness. I'm going to be all right until God gives me a call.

VIVIAN

I got a phone call at work and was told that Momma was suicidal and talking about death. It hit me then that she was in really bad shape. I went to a doctor for advice, and he felt that she needed to be institutionalized. We had to wait for weeks for a room to open up in a hospital. In the meantime, my husband, Winzer, and I made sure that Momma was included in family activities.

The hardest thing I ever had to do was put Momma in the hospital. I remember that day distinctly because it was around the first birthday of my twins. Momma had been depressed for a while, but she was particularly depressed that day. Her house had just burned down, and she was living with her aunt. I called my brother and sister to tell them that something bad was happening with Momma.

Momma didn't want to go to the hospital. My aunt, my cousin and I had a minister come over to help persuade her. We finally got her in the car and we drove for several hours with Momma telling us what she was and was not going to do. When we arrived at the hospital, a doctor convinced her to sign herself in.

It was real hard for my sister and brother to accept that Momma was so sick that she needed professional help. They had been telling me, "Do whatever you have to do. Help Momma in every way you can." When my sister, Diane, called, wanting to know how everything went on the day Momma was admitted, I said, "Everything's okay. I got Momma into a hospital." Diane went to pieces and said, "I hate that Mom had to go to the crazy house!" I told her, "Well, it's not a crazy house. It's a place where Momma can get some help." When Diane visited Momma a few days later and saw what the situation was, she accepted the fact that our mom was really sick and needed to be there.

Momma was in the hospital for two months and I saw her every weekend. When she was discharged, she came home on medication. She wasn't eating right and she wasn't taking enough fluids. She became incoherent, and couldn't really function at all. When a doctor examined her, he discovered that Momma's lithium level was so high, it was off the charts. Her brain could have been fried! She was in critical condition for two weeks and almost died. At one point, her heart even stopped beating. They worked on her, and then she screamed. That was the best scream we ever heard! It was a miracle that Momma survived.

We've had a lot of support over the years from my church family. Momma played the organ at church for many years, so it's like she's been there all her life. The people there really love her. When she first came home from the hospital, everyone at church got involved and tried to get her out of her depression. They talked to her, encouraged her, and let her know that she was worth something. We all tried to give our mom space so that she could do the things that she liked. She preferred to stay in the house, and we never forced her to come out.

This was a hard time for me because I had twins to cope with. They were only babies when all of this was going on. I was trying to work and take care of them and my Momma, too. But we all got through it.

In time, I began to read more and more about mental illness, particularly when our son, Brandon, was diagnosed with

ADHD. After our experience with my mom, I was able to say, "Okay. We've got to do something." We dealt with Brandon's issues right off the bat, and this got him further along than if we had had no previous experience with mental illness or disability.

When I was promoted to benefits consultant at my office, I worked with the Employee Assistance Program in mental health. I learned a whole lot about mental illness and the different treatments for it. This helped me understand that mental illness in the family does not need to be a terrible experience. My mother is not the only person who is sick; there are a lot of people in this world, diagnosed or not, who have problems.

When people at work call me to ask about the mental health program, one of the first questions they ask me is, "Will the company find out that I'm going to counseling?" There is a lot of stigma out there and people feel, "Oh this is terrible. I'm going to lose my job if people know that I'm going for help." I try to assure them that if they get help, it will help the company. I say, "If you are at peace with yourself, then you're going to be more productive. So why would the company fire you for getting some help?"

WINZER

In our house, we've come to realize that every family tree is like a real tree. There are short branches; there are long branches; there are branches in the shade that don't grow as well as the ones in the sunshine. When you do come to that point of understanding, you can learn how to accept and deal with anything.

When my wife, Vivian, told me, "We've got a problem with Momma," I replied, "Okay, what are we going to do about it?" Vivian and I worked together right from the beginning to help Granny.

It's hard to accept that someone you love needs help. But the morning Granny walked down the hall in her birthday suit, that was it. We had to do something. From that point on, we accepted her illness and just rolled with the blows. If Granny is having a good day or a good week or a good month, then we go with it. If she's having an off week or an off month, we just give her space.

When Granny came home from the hospital, Vivian and I tried to make her be a grandmother to our kids, but she wasn't ready for it. She could just have the twins around her for a little while before she would say, "Y'all getting on my nerves. You have to go!" We accepted this and said, "Well, let's give Granny some time and she'll come around. Let's give her a chance to grow, too."

The last two years have been just wonderful because Granny is able to be a grandmother again. The kids like to go over to her house now. They like to be around her. Granny picks Brandi up on Friday evenings from ballet. She also sneaks out and watches the twins get off the school bus after school and then checks on them if they're home alone. The twins talk about her all the time. Granny has made a big difference in their lives.

The church family comes in and helps Granny. Sometimes Vivian and I are criticized because some people think we aren't helping Granny enough. We say, "Granny's got to do things for herself now. She's still young. She's only in her fifties! If she gives up and throws in the towel, she's never going to grow and move back into the mainstream."

When we all get together as a family, it's really a fun thing. When we get stressed out with one another, we back off and give each other space. You can soar like an eagle in your profession, but when all is said and done, family is all you've got.

BRANDI

My brother, Brandon, and I visit our grandmother every week. Usually she's happy. Sometimes she's tired, but she's still happy. We mostly talk and sing. She lets us do whatever we want when we are over to her house. I try to call Granny every day to make sure she's all right.

In our house, we've come to realize that every family tree is like a real tree. There are short branches; there are long branches; there are branches in the shade that don't grow as well as the ones in the sunshine. When you do come to that point of understanding, you can learn how to accept and deal with anything.

— WINZER

Beth, Dan, Leslie, Emma, and Conor

THE HENNESSEY FAMILY

SOUTH HADLEY, MASSACHUSETTS

BETH HENNESSEY /DAN HENNESSEY / LESLIE HENNESSEY
EMMA HENNESSEY / CONOR HENNESSEY

LESLIE

WHEN I WAS A TEENAGER, I HAD ALL SORTS OF FEARS. I didn't want to take a shower, and I didn't want to go outside. I couldn't fall asleep at night because I was afraid I was going to die. I even stopped eating at one point, because I thought that the food would stick in my throat and I would choke. I saw a psychiatrist who told my parents that I was simply afraid to grow up.

My parents didn't have any idea about what was going on with me. We lived on an air force base, and they took me to lots of doctors who didn't have a clue about what might be causing my strange behavior. I remember one doctor in particular who asked me why I wouldn't eat. I said, "Well, if I eat, I'm going to choke and die." This seemed very clear to me, but it wasn't to him. He only wanted to know about our family relationships and whether or not I got along with my mother and father. I didn't have a problem with my parents that made me resist eating or going to sleep at night. We were a very loving family.

I lost so much weight that I was hospitalized. I was given a lot of medical tests, which proved that there was nothing blocking my throat. My doctors would tell me over and over again that there was no reason for me to be afraid of choking. They began treating me for anorexia nervosa, which was not what I had at all! One of the doctors said, "You're only doing this for attention. You've got to start eating now." It was a very frustrating time for me.

When I was keeping everybody in my family up at night, my sisters got angry at me because they had to get up early and go to school in the morning. My youngest sister remembers yelling at me, "Just eat! Why can't you just eat!" I got a lot of attention and special treatment back then. My sisters understand this now, but at the time, they both felt that it wasn't fair.

Things were very tough in our family because no one understood me. During my teenage years I saw social workers, therapists, psychiatrists, and psychologists. They all tried to figure out what was going on with me, but no one came up with an answer. My parents were told to wait it out; that

When I went to college, my symptoms got worse again. I had new fears and compulsions. I could manage on the outside, but back in my apartment, I would fall apart and worry about everything. I saw a social worker who thought that I was afraid of graduating and having to enter the real world. He told me that I should just get married and have ten kids, so that I wouldn't have time to worry. That was his advice!

—LESLIE

it was just something I would have to outgrow. Despite all the help my parents were trying to get for me, nothing was actually working.

I had so many fears that, at one point, I couldn't be around other people. I didn't even want to go to school. My parents threatened to send me away to boarding school, which was a horrible idea to me. Instead, I attended a local program for kids who needed a different atmosphere from the regular high school, and it was just perfect. I fit in there very well. Within a year, I was able to return to my high school and graduate.

When I went to college, my symptoms got worse again. I had new fears and compulsions. I could manage on the outside, but back in my apartment, I would fall apart and worry about everything. I saw a social worker who thought that I was afraid of graduating and having to enter the real world. He told me that I should just get married and have ten kids, so that I wouldn't have time to worry. That was his advice!

I kept most of my worries to myself because they were very scary. I thought I was either going to go crazy or that people would think I was crazy if I told them what was in my mind. If I were to tell somebody that I worried about running over someone when I was driving my car, I was sure they would think I was nuts.

I met my husband, Dan, when I was in college. I purposely didn't tell him about my symptoms. In fact, I hid them from him. I did tell him about my fear of driving, though, and that I needed to check and recheck that I hadn't run over someone with my car. I was worried that Dan would say, "Leslie, I think you're crazy," but he has never been like that.

A few years later, I finally figured out what was wrong with me. One day at work, I was reading a *Time* magazine article about obsessive-compulsive disorder. I was just like the person described in the story! I remember leaving the office with the magazine, thinking, "This is it! I'm not crazy. I have OCD." I still have that wrinkled-up magazine. I wish I had looked for another therapist right then and showed her the article, but it would be another five years before that happened.

Dan and I got married and we had three children. I had a very bad bout of OCD a year after our second child was born. At the time, no one besides Dan knew that I had this illness. Things got so bad that I finally called my mother and said, "Please come up. You've got to help me take care of the kids." I even said to Dan one day, "You can't go to work tomorrow. I need your help." I had hit rock bottom. I tearfully told Dan that I thought I might need to tell someone the truth about what I was struggling with, and that maybe I should start taking medication.

I met with yet another therapist, and this time, I cried my heart out to her. She said, "You're not crazy," and she gave me some literature about OCD. She was the first mental health professional in all those years who gave me a diagnosis. This was the first time I felt safe enough to actually talk about my obsessions and compulsions and rituals with a therapist. I had held back about all that stuff with my previous therapists. I was afraid that they would say, "You're incapable of taking care of your children. You can't be a mother if you're having these crazy thoughts." My ultimate fear was that I would lose my children. My kids are my life.

After I was diagnosed, Dan kept urging me to tell my family about my OCD. He would say, "They love you and they'll help you with this." I didn't want anyone to know about my illness because I still felt that in some way I wasn't made of the right stuff. I was afraid that people, even my family members, would relate to me differently if they knew about my OCD. When I finally did tell my mom and my sisters, all they wanted to know was how they could help me. My diagnosis explained so much about my strange behavior back when I was a teenager. My sisters apologized for the things they had said to me in the past, even though I told them there was no need to. It took me much longer before I told Dan's family that I had OCD.

It's hard to explain what OCD is. It's not like saying to a friend, "I have diabetes." I didn't tell any of my friends about my illness for a long time because I wanted people to see me as capable of caring for my children, of having a good marriage, of joining the PTA. I didn't want the fact that I have OCD to hurt the kids or to make it harder for them in school. I wanted what's best for them. At the same time, if one of my kids were to develop OCD, I would have been the first to say, "It's okay! OCD is a disorder of the brain. It's not all of who you are."

I have the kind of OCD where I do a lot of checking. For instance, when I leave the house in the morning, I have to follow a certain pattern. I have to check the stove, the coffeepot, the toaster, and the oven. Even if I know that I haven't used the stove, I still have to make sure that it's turned off. The coffeepot and the toaster are another matter because I know I've used them. Sometimes I have to check these appliances three or four times.

When I was at my worst a few years ago, I would have checked maybe five, six, or seven times, left the house and locked the door, gone down the steps, and then unlocked the door, gone back into the kitchen, and made sure yet again that everything was unplugged. Even then, in my mind, I would doubt whether I had really checked everything or not. Had I actually unplugged all the appliances? Was I thinking about something else when I was checking so that I didn't check everything carefully enough? Now, with the help of my behavioral therapy, I only let myself check twice. That's on a really, really good day. Some people with OCD will check for hours and hours. They lose their jobs, their families, and their independence.

I wash my hands more often than the average person does, but then again, I have three little kids so I ask myself, "Is this my OCD or is this real life?" The only thing I do that's kind of quirky is that I have to rinse the kids' cups out especially carefully before I put juice in them. Not their bowls or spoons, just their cups. I'm stuck with the cups! Lately I've said to myself, "Okay, Leslie, this is something you're going to have to work on and nip in the bud."

I went on an antidepressant about three years ago because I was having a tough time taking care of the kids. I was very lucky, because it brought my symptoms way down. I could do things that I hadn't been able to do for years without so much as a worry. I sometimes wonder why I waited so long to go on medication. I don't take it now, and my symptoms have stayed more or less the same. When I begin to feel that I need to check the coffeepot more than twice, I do a certain breathing exercise, which is part of my behavioral modification program. I can make behavioral changes on my own. I still go through debilitating periods at times, but for the most part I can stay on top of my symptoms and keep everything else going. I'm really proud of that.

My kids help me with my behavior modification, too. When I'm driving away from the house and worrying about whether or not I unplugged the toaster, I inevitably hear them begin to argue over which music tape to put on. By distracting me, they help me forget what might be going on in the kitchen. The kids give me something else to focus on.

Dan and I have a very strong marriage. I know that he is committed to me and to the kids, and I'm committed to him. My behavioral therapist has taught Dan how to help me with my OCD. Dan's job is to say to me in a very clear way, "Leslie, remember that we agreed that I'm not going to check such and such for you." In the beginning, I got really mad when he would say that. I used to rely on Dan to check things for me and make sure that everything was all right. But now he holds out firm, and that's what he's supposed to do. Even though we've gone through some real tough times, Dan is my best friend. I can tell him anything.

After I was diagnosed, I read about OCD, but for a long time, I never met or talked to anybody else who had it. My family kept saying, "It's really going to change things for you if you can just meet someone else with OCD." I decided to join a support group for people who have this illness. When I went to my first meeting, Dan went with me. We rode up in the elevator, and then we rode right back down. I milled around in the lobby for a while. I knew I wanted to meet other people with this illness; I just didn't know if I wanted them to meet me! Finally Dan and I rode back up, and the leader of the group saw me. She came out of the room and

I didn't tell any of my friends about my illness for a long time because of my kids. I wanted people to see me as capable of caring for my children, of having a good marriage, of joining the PTA. I didn't want the fact that I have OCD to hurt the kids or to make it harder for them in school. I wanted what's best for them. At the same time, if one of my kids were to develop OCD, I would have been the first to say, "It's okay! OCD is a disorder of the brain. It's not all of who you are."

—LESLIE

I've always loved Leslie for who she is. I never felt that she was crazy. OCD is just one part of her. It's no different from having a physical illness. OCD is a condition, and once you know what your condition is, you deal with it. And that's what we've been doing.

—DAN

asked me, "Are you looking for the OCD meeting?" I pointed to Dan and replied, "I think he is."

Dan and I met with a small group of eight people. I didn't say much that night, but I felt really good about going. I left the meeting feeling high and excited. About a year and a half after attending my first meeting, Dan and I were asked to facilitate the group.

Just today somebody from the support group asked me, "Can I call you if I'm having a bad time of it?" And I said, "Oh, yes. Anytime. Please call me." It feels really good to have someone want to talk to me about *their* problems with OCD. It feels good to say to someone else, "You're not alone." The group is good therapy for me, and helping others has helped my self-esteem.

Mental illness tends to run in families. It's been in my family and in Dan's. I'm beginning to think that it's been in almost everyone's family. My mother had a very bad depression about ten years ago and was hospitalized. She went from being a "take charge" kind of person to someone who couldn't decide whether or not to have a glass of water, or even whether or not to get out of bed in the morning. She didn't really care about anything. This was hard for my father to understand, and it was a very tough time for both of them.

Mental illness doesn't just happen to strangers; it can happen to your mother or your father or your sister or a friend or your child's teacher. It can happen to anyone you know.

The more I understand about OCD and other mental illnesses, the more compassion I feel for others who suffer from these disorders. I have compassion for the person living on the street who has lost his support system and is so isolated that either he doesn't want help or people just aren't coming to help him.

Sometimes I think about how different my life would have been if I didn't have OCD. But despite all the problems it has caused, I've pretty much decided that having OCD is not the worst thing that can happen to you.

My priorities have shifted from secrecy about my illness to educating others, and from living with the stigma to fighting the stigma head-on. I began by finally telling Dan's family and then I told our friends. I had underestimated all these people. The support Dan and I have received has been incredible.

Over the years, I began to see my illness in a different way. I've now gotten to the point where I can talk publicly about having OCD. I work as an advocate for the local branch of the National Alliance for the Mentally Ill. Last spring, our family appeared in the local Sunday newspaper in order to help educate the public about the symptoms and treatments for OCD. If anyone told me three years ago that I was going to speak out about mental illness, I would have answered, "When cows fly!"

DAN

I've always loved Leslie for who she is. I never felt that she was crazy. OCD is just one part of her. It's no different from having a physical illness. OCD is a condition, and once you know what your condition is, you deal with it. And that's what we've been doing.

Before Leslie was diagnosed, I kept trying to coax her into seeing a good counselor. We finally got lucky when she met a therapist she trusted enough to open up to. Leslie knew she had reached a point where she had to talk openly and honestly about her symptoms. Leslie was relieved when she was finally diagnosed, and she felt much less alone when she met other people who also have this illness.

Leslie and I would sometimes drive to Cape Cod for vacation. Before we would leave the house, we had a routine. Leslie would check that all the appliances were unplugged and she would leave the house first. Then I would have to go back inside and check everything again for her. She would still have doubts that I'd really checked things thoroughly, so we'd have to go back in and check together. Sometimes we would drive two hours and get halfway to the Cape and we would have to turn around and drive all the way back home because Leslie was afraid that our house might be on fire.

At first, I tried to make sense of Leslie's behavior, but I couldn't. I would give her all sorts of rational reasons about why she shouldn't worry about things, but this never brought her anxiety level down. It was frustrating for me. I understand much more now about OCD, but her behaviors can still be frustrating.

Leslie's dependency on me was quite challenging. There were times when she didn't want me to go to work, so I stayed home with her. Part of me knew that staying home didn't really help her that much, but I didn't know what else to do. We're in a much better position now because we both understand OCD. We've both worked hard to arrive at the point where we are today, and there are benefits from this. We feel satisfaction and happiness with our lives right now.

In the past, I didn't know what I was supposed to do to help Leslie, and I was torn in many different directions. It's hard to see someone you love feeling so anxious, but my step-ping in to help Leslie was only a short-term solution. It would only fix the problem for a few minutes. Now that I've learned from professionals that I'm not supposed to help Leslie with her checking, things are so much easier for me. My role is much more clearly defined now. Leslie and I have some new guidelines.

Leslie knows that her thoughts are irrational, but she can't always stop herself from going through her checking routines. It's hard to explain this to people. They say, "You already checked that! Get on with it." It's hard for most people to understand the irrational fears that come with having this illness. A situation, which might provoke only mild anxiety in one person, might feel like being in a war zone for somebody with OCD.

People do look at you differently when you have a mental illness or any other "abnormal" condition. Fortunately, I'm not one to worry about what other people think about my family or about me.

Standing: Raimundo   *Seated:* Auxiliadora and Salvador

THE LOPEZ FAMILY

WEST COVINA, CALIFORNIA

AUXILIADORA LOPEZ / RAIMUNDO LOPEZ / SALVADOR LOPEZ

SALVADOR

OUR FAMILY COMES FROM NICARAGUA. When my son, Raimundo, went to school there, he couldn't do reading and learning. My brother, a psychiatrist, thought that maybe Raimundo had some dyslexia.

The schools in our country were very tough. You had to learn a lot by heart, which is difficult for many students. I had to help Raimundo with his homework for hours almost every night.

When Raimundo was around fourteen, there was the Sandinista revolution in our country. Our family had to leave Nicaragua. Our children, Raimundo and Gabriela, came to Los Angeles and stayed there for a year with my brother-in-law. Then they moved to San Juan, Puerto Rico, where my wife, Auxiliadora, and I had settled. In San Juan, Raimundo had some treatment by a psychiatrist.

During Raimundo's high school years in Puerto Rico, he was the target of his classmates, who teased him a lot. This was very hard for him. Maybe that was one of the causes of his problems, but I also think mental illness is caused by chem-ical imbalance. My wife and I have learned a lot during the whole process of Raimundo's sickness, but at first we didn't understand what was happening to him. Our son would wake up at midnight and call out, "Help me. Help me." We did not know how to help him.

A psychiatrist told us that Raimundo has bipolar disorder. Sometimes he is depressed and sometimes he is high. After he had the diagnosis, we thought that this type of brain disorder could be cured. The doctor said, "I'm going to give Raimundo pills for a while, but then I'm going to stop. I don't want to make him dependent on his medication." Later on, when we learned that Raimundo's illness would be for his whole life, we felt depressed. Now that Raimundo's taking his medication, we know he's under control. We know he has to take medication for his whole life. One very good thing about our son is that he always takes his medicines.

Raimundo is taking three different kinds of medicine every day, but he doesn't know how to take his medicine on his own. My wife and I have to give it to him. The doctor told me that if I feel he needs more medicine, I can give him more. That's something that the doctor has trusted me with.

I like all of Raimundo's doctors. I can talk to them anytime. I take him twice a month to see his psychologist and once a month to his psychiatrist. They are pros. Raimundo also likes to talk to the doctor. Sometimes I don't want to go with him into his sessions because I think he would be more open with just the doctor there, but my son likes me to go in with him. Sometimes it's okay with Raimundo if I stay in the waiting room.

Raimundo has never been hospitalized. Even when he is out of control, he takes his medicine, so in half an hour or so, he's under control again. When he gets out of control, we don't have to call the hospital. Auxiliadora and I have had to call the police only once.

The main problem for us is that Raimundo gets angry and aggressive, especially when we go to the supermarket or shopping. Sometimes we don't know why he gets so angry with some people. They push him or bump into him, and he doesn't like it. We worry when he gets violent. Raimundo is now a big man. If he gets violent at home, I take my wife someplace until he gets calm. Our son has never hurt us. Sometimes he pushes Auxiliadora, and we have to be careful. That can be very scary.

The violence is one problem, but Raimundo's bad judgment is also a problem. He says things that are not true, but he thinks they are true. Sometimes he gets some idea like we should move from our house and then he wants to go look for a new house. We don't want to go, but if he wants something, you have to give it to him right now! When he wants to buy something, it has to be in a hurry.

We tried to find day treatment programs for Raimundo, but they aren't good for him. He sleeps the whole morning, so what program can take him only for the afternoon? One time he went to a school for disabled people, where they taught him printing, but he got violent with someone, and so they don't take him anymore. Raimundo studied office work and typing on the computer, but the computer is very difficult for him. I had to go to the school to talk to the teacher, and she said she couldn't teach him anymore because he doesn't progress. We don't know what we can do. We have tried.

Raimundo prefers to live at home with us. In his room he has a lot of toys. He likes to go to the store and buy toys like G.I. Joe. We probably take too much care of him. Sometimes my wife and I are afraid and we worry about what's going to happen when we pass away. That's what we don't know. But we have our daughter, Gabriela. We hope that she will take care of Raimundo after we're gone. She's a good girl.

When I was working, the people at my job never knew about my difficulties with my son. I didn't say anything. Nothing. I wasn't afraid to tell them, but it wasn't easy to tell people. I never tried to get help from friends at work. When I went to work, I would forget about our problems with Raimundo for the whole day. At work, you have a different face and you have your concentration. When you get back to your home, you see what's going on.

Auxiliadora and I are pretty religious and we have believed in God ever since I can remember. We are Catholic, but we don't think there's going to be a miracle with Raimundo. We do know that as long as he takes his medicines, he will be under control. The main thing that sustains us is our belief in God.

My wife goes to a support group every week. Many other people there have the same problem as we do. That's not good, but it's support. We are all in the same boat. We are accustomed. We are adjusted. Yes, it is our life.

AUXILIADORA

Our son, Raimundo, has a mental illness. He lives with my husband and me. A friend of mine once say to me, "You are always taking care of Raimundo. This is not a life for you." I tell her, "My son *is* my life."

Auxiliadora and Raimundo

Our son, Raimundo, has a mental illness. He lives with my husband and me. A friend of mine once say to me, "You are always taking care of Raimundo. This is not a life for you." I tell her, "My son is my life."
—*AUXILIADORA*

When Raimundo was young, he wash his hands all day long. Over and over. I tell this to my husband's brother, who is a psychiatrist. He treat Raimundo and give him medicine. I think at first that Raimundo would get better with the medication and the doctor, but he didn't.

Raimundo don't have friends to come to talk with him. He have to eat with my husband and me, go to the movies, go to shopping, do everything with us. He can't drive because it makes him too nervous, so Salvador drives him everywhere.

My mother never understood Raimundo's illness. She thought he got too much nurturing from my husband and me. My brother also says we give Raimundo too much care. Our son's illness is very, very hard for people to understand. People who don't have mental illness at home don't understand the problem or how to help these people who have this problem. Some friends come here and talk to us a little bit and then they go. They don't see the problem. I tell them, "My son, he have a mental problem. He is not doing good."

*I don't blame anyone any-
more for the problems that
I have in my life. I say to
myself, "Life brings two
things. It brings you both
tragedies and good things.
Bad things and victories."*
— RAIMUNDO

When Salvador and I moved to California, we went to a support group. When I met the group, I feel relief because I learn that Raimundo is not the only boy who has so many troubles. When I listen to another person in the group talk, I think, "Oh my God, I know I'm not alone. It's not only my son. There are so many."

Raimundo is a very good boy. He doesn't smoke. Never. He doesn't drink. Never. He even went to a college and got a degree in tourism and travel because he likes to travel. He traveled with us when he was a child. We used to travel a lot. This year we didn't take a vacation because he wasn't doing so good.

We also have a daughter, Gabriela. We hope that she will take care of Raimundo when my husband and I die. Our son wants to stay living in our house. He likes the good life. He doesn't like the poor life. We were looking for a place for people like Raimundo, but most places are very, very bad. They are dirty and dark. My son wouldn't even have his own room.

RAIMUNDO

I grew up in Nicaragua. When I was fourteen, my Uncle Roberto diagnosed me with a mental illness. He didn't say what kind.

I flew to New York when I was fourteen in a student exchange program in order to get acquainted with the American way of life. Then I saw the pictures of the horrible war that was going in my country. I couldn't believe the war was happening or the killings, but it was shown on TV. I flew back to Nicaragua.

Our family decided to leave Nicaragua because we thought the rebels were going to get us. We left the country in a hurry. I flew to California with a neighbor and her children. Before the flight took off, the pilot said, "We are going to fly through the war zone, so we're going to take off at midnight when the plane is not visible, so they won't shoot us." We closed all the shades on the windows of the airplane and we had to be quiet so nobody would hear us when we were flying over the war zone. It was very scary. But we made it.

My father worked for the government for many years in Nicaragua. He is a civil engineer and urban planner. My father became a minister of urban development, and he traveled a lot because of his position. We had a house, but we lost it because of the war. My father lost his work. We lost everything we had.

We moved from California to Puerto Rico, where I went to high school. The kids at my school picked on me a little bit because they said I was too nervous or too tense. They knew I was a refugee from the war and they made fun of me because of that. I was timid. I was shy to girls. I was shy to people. I couldn't speak to people. I was afraid of people. After you see the killings and you see dead bodies, you get afraid of people. You think everybody is going to kill you or something. It's just the way it goes when you see things like that. War has that problem.

The mother in the student exchange family I had stayed with in America called me one day. She told me that her husband had died in a car accident. That shocked me a lot. The support I had gotten from him and his entire family during a very difficult time in my life had been very important to me. I needed that support, and it helped me to go on in life. When he died, it made me very angry and very sad.

My psychiatrist explained to me that people get sick. People die. Like my exchange family father died. President Somoza died. Other people in my family have died. That makes me very depressed because I knew and loved these people. They were important in my life.

I've been violent, but I'm dominating that. I dominate that because I don't feel that anger no more. I don't feel violent anymore. I don't feel that I hate people anymore. I don't blame anyone anymore for the problems that I have in my life. I say to myself, "Life brings two things. It brings you both tragedies and good things. Bad things and victories."

One of the things I love to do is walk. I go places and get lost. As a child, my mother would often say, "Where is my son?" My mom and dad would have to look to find me because I would walk everywhere. Or I would take a bicycle and ride on the bicycle, or take a bus and ride to the store or whatever. I've always been that way. I like to travel a lot. My parents and I have been through the Panama Canal. We've been to El Salvador, Guatemala, Mexico City, Puerto Rico, Orlando, and New York City.

I speak good Spanish and good English. I'm totally bilingual, and that helps me to continue my life because I had a good education. I went to a bilingual school and they helped me to speak good. That helped me to go through life. That was important to me.

My sister, Gabriela, is a big help to me. She is a very normal girl. She never became a mental patient like me. Everyone in my family loves me and accepts me the way I am, even though I am a mental patient.

I still hear voices sometimes. When I hear voices, it's like somebody is trying to talk to me. Sometimes when I go places, I hear them like a whisper. Or maybe I hear a lady speak to me when I'm listening to the radio. Sometimes I see people in the street and there's nobody there, or I see people in the street who have already died. But when I look back, there's nobody there. I see dead people in my dreams, too. I dream all these things. Once I said to my doctor, "Why do I dream all these things? Are dreams real or are they just fantasies?"

Clockwise: Clifford, Mallory, Verna, and Sarah

18

THE JOHNSON FAMILY

SALEM, NEW HAMPSHIRE

CLIFFORD JOHNSON / SARAH JOHNSON / MALLORY JOHNSON
VERNA JOHNSON

VERNA

OBSESSIVE-COMPULSIVE DISORDER IS CALLED THE "doubting" disease. Both of my·daughters have it. When our oldest daughter, Sarah, was diagnosed with OCD, I just sat there and cried. My best friend cried with me. When a trauma like this happens, it just blindsides you.

When Sarah was in the third grade, she had some odd behaviors. I took her to see a doctor, and he said that she showed signs of being obsessive. He also explained that her symptoms could wax and wane and that, in time, they might go away. He did caution me that Sarah might need medication down the road. After six months, her symptoms did go away.

When Sarah was in seventh grade, my husband, Cliff, and I started to notice strange things about Sarah's behavior once again. Her obsessions came back full blown. For instance, she would shut a door, hold on to the doorknob, and then stand there waiting. She seemed to be counting or thinking about something. She would take two-hour showers, and then do something strange with her bathroom light switch.

Sarah used to have a ritual at bedtime every night. She would close her eyes and hold her breath. I would think, "This girl's going to faint." It drove me up a wall! She also lost eight pounds because she couldn't eat without throwing up. There was a time when she couldn't type without touching each key twice. This made it very difficult for her to complete school projects. Over the years, her rituals have changed. For instance, when she walks by a microwave or a mirror, or anything with a reflection, she is compelled to look at herself.

After Christmas that same year, Sarah didn't put any of her gifts away. When the tree was taken down after the holidays, her presents were still under it. Around that time, Sarah also began to have an obsession about being popular and pretty. She started to hang around her younger sister, Mallory, all the time. In the past, they had fought like cats and dogs, but Sarah thought that maybe if she hung around Mallory, who was popular, it might bring her good luck. In fact, Sarah couldn't bear to be away from Mallory. If her sister would go upstairs, Sarah would go up with her.

Sarah stopped calling her friends. I would ask her, "Where's so and so?" She would answer, "I don't know. She's

When I told Cliff that Sarah had to go into the hospital, he said, "What do you mean?" I said, "She's suicidal." He said, "Are we just going to sign a paper and they'll keep her there forever?" He was worried that Sarah would never get out.
— VERNA

When Sarah was back at home but still very sick, Cliff was working every day. It almost seemed to me that going to work and driving an eighteen-wheeler might be easier than staying home and dealing with what might happen there. I was afraid something would happen to Sarah when I was all alone with her. I'd say to him, half-jokingly, "Can't I go to work with you?"
— VERNA

not my friend anymore." When Sarah came home from school, she'd put on the TV and go to sleep. That's not what a typical eleven-year-old does. They're always on the go.

Sarah's isolation from her friends made me recall a time when she was in kindergarten and her teacher described her to me as standoffish. I asked the teacher what that meant, and she said, "Sarah stands back and watches the other kids before she chooses who she wants to play with." Our daughter was only five years old and she already was "obsessed" with the fear that she would become unpopular. I wondered back then if she was a snob, but now I understand that Sarah was so afraid of not being liked that she couldn't look at or talk to kids who weren't popular. She was scared that being around someone unpopular would rub off on her. She's still afraid of this.

There were all these little clues that something might be wrong with our daughter. Cliff and I decided, okay, she needs a doctor. When we took her to see one, he put her on medication right away. Fine! After being on medication for three weeks, Sarah traveled with us to visit my parents in Florida. My mother said, "Sarah's manic," and my father said, "Sarah's catatonic." Sarah was way worse than she had been before she went on the drug, but I assumed that maybe she just had to get over a hump. I thought she should give the medication a try for one more week, but I knew something wasn't right.

After four weeks on medication, Sarah told her guidance counselor at school that she was having suicidal thoughts. When I was informed about this, I immediately made an appointment with a therapist, who recommended hospitalization. I asked him, "What is going on? Could it be the medication?" The therapist said, "No, not really." But I talked to people who told me they had friends who had gotten worse when they were on that particular medication. By this point, Sarah was manic all the time. She just wasn't the daughter I knew. As far as I was concerned, it had to be the medication!

When I told Cliff that Sarah had to go into the hospital, he said, "What do you mean?" I said, "She's suicidal." He said, "Are we just going to sign a paper and they'll

keep her there forever?" He was worried that Sarah would never get out.

On the first day of Sarah's hospitalization, Cliff decided to go to work. I thought, "I'm not alone in this. He should come to the hospital with us." It really bothered me at first, but then I thought, "Well, maybe this is the only way he can deal with it."

I was distraught when Sarah was hospitalized. She was in there for four days, and I still hadn't met her doctor. On the day of her release, the nurse sat down with us and I said, "Isn't the doctor going to come in and talk to us?" Well, in a perfect world, you would meet your daughter's doctor. Well, in a perfect world, my daughter wouldn't be in a psychiatric hospital.

When Sarah was back at home but still very sick, Cliff was working every day. It almost seemed to me that going to work and driving an eighteen-wheeler might be easier than staying home and dealing with what might happen there. I was afraid something would happen to Sarah when I was all alone with her. I'd say to him, half-jokingly, "Can't I go to work with you?"

When Sarah was rehospitalized four weeks later, her medication was changed and she was put on an antipsychotic drug. I thought, "My God, is she psychotic?" The doctor was standing at the nurse's station and he said, "Well, Mrs. Johnson, you know your daughter is psychotic and she has behavioral problems." I said, "Are you talking about Sarah Johnson? You need to talk to her school nurse and the principal. This is not what my daughter is like!" I realize that many parents don't want to believe that their child has a serious mental illness. But in Sarah's case, I was absolutely certain that her psychosis was caused by her medication. I tried to explain this to him, but he told us that parents often don't understand. He said that we just weren't accepting the situation.

A month later Sarah became depressed again and wanted to die. I told the doctor, "I'm not fooling around anymore. You better get her into that great children's hospital in Boston." You've got to watch out for your child because nobody else is going to do it. He did refer Sarah to Boston, and the doctors and staff there were wonderful. We wanted Sarah off all meds and to start clean because Cliff and I knew that it had to be the meds that were making her feel suicidal.

The staff listened to us and made changes in Sarah's treatment based on our recommendations. They immediately took her off all medication for the entire summer. Her OCD symptoms went sky-high, but her depression was much better. She wasn't suicidal at all. She was even able to go to a sleepaway summer camp for a week.

My parents were in Florida when Sarah first got so sick. My mom is a retired nurse and she was heartbroken that she couldn't be with us to help. I didn't tell my grandmother anything at first. She's eighty-seven, and I didn't want to upset her. After Sarah's third hospitalization, I finally told her that Sarah was sick. My grandmother said, "Why didn't you tell me earlier?" She wanted to know what having OCD means and why Sarah does what she does. I tried to explain as much as possible to her. Cliff's mother didn't know how to handle the situation. Once, she picked up the phone to call Sarah at the hospital, but she couldn't bring herself to even dial the number. She just didn't know what to say.

My youngest daughter, Mallory, also has fears and obsessions. I took her to Sarah's psychologist, and he said, "Mallory, make a list of your worst fears." She listed almost thirty things. She's afraid of everything! With Mallory, I sometimes wondered if it was just her imagination running away with her. It turns out that she has borderline OCD.

I've wondered if OCD is genetic, because I was also very fearful as a child. My mother tells a story of when I must have been only eight years old. I had an eyelash in my eye and I couldn't get it out. My mother said, "Just forget about it." I said, "Are you going to leave it in there?" She said, "Yes, because you won't let me help you get it out." I said, "Will I die?" I was afraid of dying, of being kidnapped, of going in the water. Fortunately, as an adult, I'm no longer afraid of the water or of getting an eyelash in my eye.

A friend of mine who was going through a horrendous divorce told me, "Nothing bad ever happens to you and Cliff." She calls us "Ken and Barbie." I said, "Come on, now, we all have our ups and downs." This was putting it mildly. But you just roll with the punches. My mom always said, "God fits the shoulders to the burden."

CLIFFORD

Sarah's illness snapped us out of a fairy-tale lifestyle.

Verna and I made so many mistakes dealing with Sarah's situation. There's so much you need to learn about mental illness. You really need to talk to other people who have the same problem with their kids and who have gone through similar experiences.

You should also investigate your doctor's background and whether or not he's worked with other adolescents who have the same illness as your child. You can't just take at face value what the doctor tells you. When Sarah was in the hospital, the psychologist wouldn't even talk to Verna or me. That's outrageous! There was no need for that at all.

There was a time when Sarah was addicted to her medication. It was as if she were drunk. This was not our Sarah; this was the medication. But the doctor said, "No, it's not the meds. Your daughter has behavioral problems." I was outraged by the way he handled the issues of Sarah's meds. It was an absolute nightmare.

The mental health system for kids needs to be changed. The biggest problem with some hospitals is that they combine all the kids into one unit. For example, kids who have tried to kill their families are put into the same unit as kids who have OCD. For their own safety, you shouldn't lock all these kids together in one place.

I once had to take a knife out of Sarah's hand and hold her down when she was suicidal. That just about broke me, and I'm not one of those people who cry easily.

Verna and I made so many mistakes dealing with Sarah's situation. There's so much you need to learn about mental illness. You really need to talk to other people who have the same problem with their kids and who have gone through similar experiences.

— CLIFFORD

SARAH

When I was three, I remember watching the movie *Pinocchio*. When Pinocchio lied, his nose would grow, and eventually he turned into a donkey. I was scared that my nose was going to grow, too. Whenever my parents thought I was lying, they'd joke, "Oh, your nose is growing, Sarah," and I'd scream and cry and run and look in the mirror to make sure it wasn't. My mom also used that old expression, "If you're lying, your tongue will turn black." Whenever she said that to me, I'd have to go to a mirror and check out my tongue.

When I was nine, I had these little things I did. Every time I'd trip or fall, I had to cover my mouth, and every time I'd blink, I had to cover my eyes. I did all these different things to make sure bad things wouldn't happen to me. I was afraid. I know it sounds kind of ridiculous, but I couldn't help it.

When I was about thirteen, I started to get real depressed because of all my fears and rituals. I was acting different and taking a much longer time to do things. Mama noticed this and kept questioning me. She said, "If you don't stop this behavior by the time we go to Florida for Christmas, then I'm going to take you to a psychiatrist." I said, "No," because I wasn't sure what was going on. I knew there was something weird about my behavior.

When I became suicidal, my parents had me admitted to a hospital. The first hospital I was in didn't really help because I don't think I wanted to be helped. I was put on medication, but then I got depressed again and had to go back into the hospital. This happened over and over again. It's been almost a year since I was hospitalized, so I guess I'm doing a lot better.

When I was depressed, I stopped talking on the phone with my friends. After school, I'd go upstairs to my room and spend all my time making collages. I'm making one now, but I do a lot of other activities as well. I play softball and basketball and I take dancing lessons. When I dance, my OCD goes away. All I think about is what my next dance step will be.

It's very hard to find the right medication because some of them have really horrible side effects. My psychiatrists kept trying different drugs on me, and nothing was working. One medication made me depressed. Another time, the doctors put me on a medication that made me so agitated, a girl at school kept staring at me. "What are you looking at," I yelled at her. I felt bad, but I was too agitated to apologize. That's not me. I'm a nice person. I don't usually go around yelling at people. Now I'm on a medication that's working pretty well.

I'm not depressed anymore, but I still have OCD thoughts. I can't make eye contact or talk to other kids who aren't popular. I'm scared if I do, it will increase the risk that I won't be popular, either.

Last year, I told too many kids at school that I have obsessive-compulsive disorder. I thought I could trust this one girl, but she told everybody, "Sarah's a psycho. Sarah's mental. She's been in a mental hospital. She tried to kill herself." Half the stuff she said about me wasn't true, and I was so mad at her. I asked her, "Why did you say all those things?" I told her that I didn't want to talk to her anymore and that she should leave me alone. This year I decided to get back at her. I made a little flip-book that made her look like a cow and I gave it to her. I said, "This is you, you crusty old cow." I went overboard. I couldn't help it because I was so upset.

I want people to know that I'm not "mental." There's nothing really wrong with me. This illness is just part of how my brain works. I'm a normal person.

I was sitting outside one day reading a book about depression. My cousin saw it and he goes, "Why are you reading that book? Do you want to grow up and live in a mental hospital and be a mental case?"

I'm in an OCD chat group on the Internet. I talk to other kids who have this illness, and they understand me. When I talk to my mom and dad, they're like, "Why did you do that?"

or, "How can you stop doing that?" It gets so confusing and frustrating. But when I talk to the kids in the chat room about things, they understand and give me advice.

I want other kids who have OCD to know that they're not alone. I was reading my e-mails today from my OCD chat group and one girl wrote that she feels like a freak and an outsider. We're not outsiders. There are so many kids who have OCD. I'm not the only one.

MALLORY

I might have OCD, too, but I don't need medication. I think I have some of Sarah's ideas and fears.

I say to myself, "If I did such and such, what would happen?" For instance, if I go past a street sign, I have to put my foot down on the ground. I also have to review in my head everything I know. This year I've even had to remind myself what my name is. When you get to school in the morning, you sit down in a small gym. I have to think, "I'm Mallory Johnson." I'm not afraid that I'll become someone else. I just think I'll forget who I am or where I am and I'll be embarrassed. It mostly happens when I'm in school or when I'm walking by myself. Sometimes I have to think about where all my friends are sitting because what if I sat with different people? I may forget and think they're my friends even if they're not, and I'll get embarrassed.

I have so many fears. I'm even afraid of being kidnapped when I'm walking home from school. If a car slows down, I get scared it will stop and I'll get kidnapped. So I walk faster and I get the shivers. I think of a scene in a movie I saw when the camera is on a dead body in the shower and I worry that a dead body is going to be in my bathtub. I have to leave the shower curtain open when I take a shower because I'm so frightened. If I shut the curtain, it will be sort of dark and shadowy and I'm afraid I'll see a dead body. At night I take our dog into the bathroom with me.

Sarah and Mallory

I want people to know that I'm not "mental." There's nothing really wrong with me. This illness is just part of how my brain works. I'm a normal person.

—SARAH

I want other kids who have OCD to know that they're not alone. I was reading my e-mails today from my OCD chat group and one girl wrote that she feels like a freak and an outsider. We're not outsiders. There are so many kids who have OCD. I'm not the only one.
—SARAH

I saw a television show once where a girl died and another girl was in her room looking for something and the dead girl appeared in the mirror like a ghost. I have a mirror on my bureau. I'm afraid when I look in it that I'm going to see someone bad. I'm also petrified of going over bridges with water under them. One night, I went to my grandpapa's house with my family. It was pouring rain, and there was thunder and lightning. When it's raining and I'm in the car, I feel trapped. I make sure all the doors and windows are shut. I was also afraid that the bridge would collapse and we would fall into the water. I spent that night at my grandpapa's house so I wouldn't have to go back over the bridge again.

There's a chair in my living room, which my great-grandfather always sat in. He wouldn't sit anywhere else. When he died, my great-grandma gave it to our family. My daddy said, "Great-grandpa might still be sitting in the chair." This scared me.

My mom and dad have a walk-in closet that I can see from my room. The door doesn't shut completely, so it's always open a little bit. I get scared that someone is in there looking at me and that he'll pop out and get me.

I don't like to sleep. I have a daybed, and it's up against the wall because I don't like to go to sleep with my head facing the headboard. I'm afraid I'll get attacked just like the boy did in the movie *Friday the 13th*. When I get real scared, I pull my covers up over my head so that only my face is showing. I don't even take the covers off in the summer. I can't have my feet near the edge of the bed because I'm afraid someone's going to come up and get me.

I'm in a singing group and we're going to perform in Washington D.C. One of my fears about this is that I might faint in the middle of the performance. Everyone will look at me, and I'll be embarrassed. There's one part where we have to turn around backwards in the dark. I'm afraid I'm going to fall off the stage or something like that.

I talk to two of my friends about my fears because they can understand. We tell each other a lot of stuff. I would never tell any of my other friends because they would never understand. One reason I don't want to tell them is because then they'd talk about it to other kids and make fun of me. I'd like to say to them, "Don't make fun of me, because a lot of people have OCD."

Standing: Tony and Ricky *Seated:* Robert, Alice, Randall, and Dolores

THE ENCINAS FAMILY

WEST COVINA, CALIFORNIA

ROBERT ENCINAS / ALICE SY / TONY PELAIS / RANDALL ENCINAS
RICKY ENCINAS / DOLORES ENCINAS

DOLORES

MY SONS, ROBERT AND RICHARD, ARE IDENTICAL TWINS. They both have schizophrenia.

Robert lives independently in his own apartment nearby. Richard is married and has a child, and he also lives close to us. Richard decided not to talk about his illness publicly because he's doing very well right now. We also have two other sons, Tony and Randy. Our oldest child is a daughter, but she lives in another state.

I first realized that Robert might be sick when he was a teenager. I came home from work one day and found him sitting in a chair holding his head in his hands. I said, "What's the matter, Robert?" He answered, "Oh, gosh, I'm really confused, Mama. I can't think straight. There's something wrong with my head." He began to talk about all these religious delusions he was having and then he said, "You know, if someone at school asked me where I live, I wouldn't know what to tell them." I thought, "Oh, my God! There's something really wrong here!"

Within weeks, I had Robert tested by a psychologist, who diagnosed him as having latent schizophrenia. Robert was admitted into a psychiatric hospital almost immediately. The afternoon that I was to drive Robert to the hospital, his twin brother came home from school for lunch, which was unusual for him. As I was backing the car out of the driveway, Richard stood there, saying, "What about me, Mama? What about me?" I knew right then and there that we were in real trouble.

Richard came home early one night from playing in a varsity football game. He said, "Mama, when I was out on the field, I had this delusion that I didn't have any clothes on. I tried to get hurt so that I could get off the field because I thought everybody was staring at me." It didn't occur to him to ask to be taken out of the game because he wasn't feeling well. Richard didn't want to tell anyone what was happening to him, and he soon followed Robert into the hospital. The twins were real depressed and sick, but they both got excellent care.

Richard and Robert got a pass from their psychiatrist to leave the hospital to go to their senior prom. He loved both the twins, and he even helped them pick out their tuxedos. Another time, the psychiatrist asked me, "What's this thing your sons have with older women?" I said, "What do you mean?" He replied, "Well, they have all the nurses at the hospital just charmed!"

The twins were hospitalized for six months. When they came home, my husband, Ricky, and I argued a lot over how to manage them. In every family there's a marshmallow and a hardnose. Ricky is very kind and generous and sweet, and I'm the hardnose. "Straighten up and fly right" is my attitude. Get your act together and get on with your life! In my view, my husband pampered and babied the twins. They were like little birds that wanted to grow up and jump out of the nest, but Ricky would go out there, grab those little birds, and throw them right back into the nest again!

We didn't realize at the time that the twins had been doing street drugs. Their drug of choice was marijuana, which complicated their treatment. If the boys were out on the street and needed money, Ricky would just give it to them. I'd say, "Don't give them a penny because they will just spend it on drugs." I didn't even want to hand over their Social Security money to them. Ricky and I had a big fight about this, and finally I said, "That's it! I'm not dealing with this issue anymore." I wrote a letter to our cousin and asked him if he would handle it. Ricky said, "You can't ask somebody else to take on this burden," and I said, "Watch me!" Our cousin said he'd be happy to help the twins take care of their money, and that took care of my fights with Ricky. However, the twins still came to Ricky and me and asked for extra money. There were times when I was ready to kill my husband because he was so soft. I was ready to kill all of them.

Robert worked as a security guard for a while and then he joined the navy. My husband encouraged him to go. "Maybe he'll do well," Ricky said. I wanted to tell the recruiters that Robert was sick, but Ricky said, "No, just let him go." So I waited for the ax to fall. One night I came home from work and my daughter told me that a naval hospital in Chicago had called to say that Robert was in their psychi-

atric unit. He had cracked up just two days after his enlistment. After they stabilized him, the navy sent Robert home with an honorable discharge.

Sometimes one twin would get sick and the other wouldn't. They got to a point where they would take care of each other. One time I came home from work and Richard said, "Mama, I'm tired. I had quite a day. I had to hospitalize Robert this morning. He couldn't talk and he couldn't get his shoes on; he was really out of it. I helped him get dressed and then I called his psychiatrist." Robert didn't have any medical insurance at the time, so Richard was planning to give the hospital his own ID if his brother couldn't get admitted. Since they are identical twins, Robert could get into the hospital by pretending he was Richard.

Having two sons who are sick is terrible, but if you think it makes life miserable for their family, look at what they had to go through! It was much worse for them. On the other hand, if the twins hadn't gotten sick, they might have been successful and moved away. But they aren't away. Ricky and I get to see both of them often. You've got to look at both sides of everything, and make the best of it. It's not easy, but you keep on going, anyway. Like I've always said, if you have a problem, you don't turn your back on it. For better or for worse, that's the way I think about life.

People have to get educated and learn about mental illness. With help, Ricky and I learned how to survive and even thrive with mentally ill kids. Now I give back what I've learned. I get a big thrill out of helping other people. We both go on panels to educate professionals about how families cope with mental illness. We tell them what they do wrong, and what they do right.

For me, the most important job of parenting is to teach my children to be independent, and I mean all of them! I want them to be able to think for themselves and to live their own lives. I want them to come visit me because they love me and care about me, not because they need to borrow money or ask me who they should marry. I don't need kids who call me every day and say, "What should I do today? How will I manage this?" Make your own damn decisions! If you make a mistake, well, that's your tough luck! If you raise your kids right, they're going to go out there and make good decisions on their own. They will learn to problem-solve by themselves and not rely on their parents to fix all their problems. I think Ricky and I have done a good job, because all my kids take pretty good care of themselves.

RICKY

It was very confusing when the twins got sick because Dolores and I had no idea what mental illness was. We had never encountered anything of the sort, and we had never even heard of schizophrenia.

When Robert first got sick, we couldn't believe he was feeling the way he was. We just didn't understand. At first, we thought that he was having a tough time dealing with high school. Robert was so confused, he couldn't explain what was going on with him. It was scary because there was nothing we could do to help him. And then Richard got sick, too.

The twins didn't want to take their medications at first. They would be released from the hospital, and Dolores and I would have them all set up in an apartment, and then they would forget to take their meds and end up right back in the hospital. It would be turmoil all over again trying to get them stabilized. There were always setbacks for us. It was so disappointing because when Robert and Richard started doing real good, you figured they'd be fine. Instead, they'd be back to square one. They finally learned to take their medication every day, and that's when everything kind of leveled off. They're both doing pretty well now.

I come from a small town in Arizona, and my family is very close. My brother and sister watch out for each other. My wife's family is close, too. I see the same thing in other Hispanic families. We are very caring people. We stick together! That's what helped our family get through all of this.

Some Hispanic families might be overly protective of a relative who is sick and keep him or her in the background. Some families, Hispanic or not, don't even want it known that they're coping with mental illness at all. They think they might be blamed for causing their relative's illness. This is the old way of thinking about things. It isn't the case at all.

RANDY

I was in the seventh grade when my brothers first got sick. I was still growing up, so their being sick became a way of life for me. It took my parents a lot of time and effort to take care of them, and this took their attention away from me. Even though I was at an age where it was kind of fun not having your parents on your back all the time, all of a sudden a lot of things kind of slowed down. It was frustrating for me, but for the most part it was fine.

A few years ago, I had quite an experience with the twins. I work for an airline, and I can get free plane tickets. I thought it would be fun to take them on a trip to Missouri to visit our relatives on the old family farm. Richard and Robert were both doing pretty well at the time, and I assumed that all I would have to do was keep an eye on them. In a way, I felt like I was traveling with two teenagers.

A friend of mine named Mike came with us on this trip. He had a problem going through airport security because the alarm kept going off. Mike has a real short temper, and he got frustrated and started cussing at the security guy, calling him a camel jockey and all kinds of stuff. I said, "Mike, just shut up and get over here." And then both Richard and Robert said, "Gosh, we're the ones who are supposed to be mentally ill!"

When we were waiting to make a connection in the Las Vegas airport, all of a sudden Robert just disappeared. Richard got all frustrated and pissed off at him. When we finally found him, he was gambling at a slot machine. We only had three minutes left to catch the flight. A similar thing happened when

> *Some Hispanic families might be overly protective of a relative who is sick and keep him or her in the background. Some families, Hispanic or not, don't even want it known that they're coping with mental illness at all. They think they might be blamed for causing their relative's illness. This is the old way of thinking about things. It isn't the case at all.*
> —RICKY

My whole world turned upside down when my brothers got sick. One minute, Richard and Robert are playing football, and the next minute, they're in a psychiatric hospital.

— TONY

In a Chinese family, if someone becomes mentally ill, the family members keep it to themselves. I saw this with my own relatives. If they had a child with a mental illness or a child on drugs, no one outside the family would know about it. There's too much pride. They don't want it to be known that mental illness is in their family. Everything is kept in the closet.

—ALICE

we got to Missouri. We were waiting for the bus to take us to the car rental place, and Robert disappeared again. By the time we found him this time, we had missed our bus.

My parents had given me only sixty dollars to spend on each twin during the trip, so I had to be careful that they didn't spend their money all at once. We'd go into an antique store, and Robert would say, "Oh Randy, I found this army helmet. I really, really want it!" And I'd say, "Look around first and see if you find something else you might like." In a few minutes, he'd come back all excited and say, "I found this really great jacket." Then Richard would come up to me, holding something, and say, "Randy, I want this!" Finally we'd all walk out with nothing and we'd go to the next store and do it all over again. Even though we had a good time on this trip, I'm not sure if I'd do it again.

I didn't grow up thinking that mental illness was supposed to be something bad. My brothers looked pretty normal and they didn't have any weird behaviors or do anything strange. There are so many different variations of schizophrenia, and we probably ended up with the luckiest one. Most people who meet the twins don't think that there is anything different about them. When people ask me about them, I'm the first to say, "Oh, yeah, both my twin brothers have schizophrenia. It isn't a big deal. Yada, yada, yada."

TONY

When my brothers first got sick, I was in my own little world. I was sixteen and I had always looked up to these guys. To see them break down so suddenly was awful. I couldn't believe it. They were so strong physically and mentally and everything they did was "all-American." I looked up to them; the whole school did. I was so proud to be the "little Encinas."

My whole world turned upside down when my brothers got sick. One minute, Richard and Robert are playing football, and the next minute, they're in a psychiatric hospital. When they went down, everybody was asking

me questions. I had to do a lot of explaining. I didn't know what to say because I didn't understand what was going on. One friend asked me, "What happened to your brothers? I heard they freaked out." I told him they had a chemical imbalance or something like that, and that they were in the hospital for a checkup. I told other people that my brothers had gone away for a while and would be back soon. It was a confusing time for me, and I missed them when they were gone. I had to grow up very quickly.

These days, I get together with the twins once in a while. If I have a barbecue, I'll ask them over. I've taken them camping and to the movies. If I need to move furniture or something like that, I'll ask them to help me. I know I can always count on them. We're still close, and they know I'll back them up no matter what. They do their own thing, and that's okay with me. I never get disappointed with them if they can't handle something, because I know it's just their mental illness.

I'm married to Alice, and we have a son and a daughter. When Robert and Richard are over, we're not afraid of them at all. I know they're not going to flip out. Both the twins have really good hearts, and this keeps them from doing bad things.

ALICE

The first time I met the twins, they seemed perfectly normal to me. When my husband, Tony, told me that his brothers were sick, I said, "Oh, they don't look like they have a mental illness." In the two years since I've known them, I've never seen them act abnormal. To me, they're normal. I once took a psychology class, and we watched videos of people who have schizophrenia. I remember thinking, "The twins don't look or act anything like that."

In a Chinese family, if someone becomes mentally ill, the family members keep it to themselves. I saw this with my own relatives. If they had a child with a mental illness or a child on drugs, no one outside the family would know about it. There's too much pride. They don't want it to be known that mental illness is in their family. Everything is kept in the closet.

ROBERT

People need to know what having schizophrenia is really like. Just the facts. The real version, not the Hollywood one.

With schizophrenia, when you're not on your medication, you have delusions. You have paranoia; your moods go up and down; you hear voices. You're pretty much out there. You just don't know what's going on. When you're mentally ill, you're living in a science fiction world that's come true.

I first got sick when I was about sixteen and a half. I was in high school. I had no idea what was happening to me, and even now, there's a lot I don't remember. For years, I was always in and out of the hospital every few months because I would stop taking my medication and would smoke pot instead. I'm thirty-seven now, and I've been off illegal drugs for ten years. I take my meds and I haven't been in the hospital for three years.

I've been married and divorced twice. I have a twelve-year-old son who lives with his mom. My twin brother and I are really close. Even though Richard is married now and has a two-month-old daughter, we've stuck together.

People need to know what having schizophrenia is really like. Just the facts. The real version, not the Hollywood one.
— *ROBERT*

Norma and Tony

THE ABNEY FAMILY

HADLEY, MASSACHUSETTS

NORMA ABNEY / TONY LINFIELD

NORMA

I'VE BEEN A SINGLE LESBIAN MOM FOR EIGHTEEN YEARS. My son, Tony, and I have a nice relationship, or at least I feel we do. We've done quite a bit of moving around, which Tony absolutely detests. Hopefully, we won't have to move again.

Tony knows that I have bipolar disorder. I was diagnosed with it when he was only fifteen. My mental illness has a lot to do with my inability to work and to function as a "normal" human being. Of course, this affects my son. When I'm manic, I have about thirty projects going on simultaneously around the house. Nothing ever gets finished. Tony has had to deal with my running around and being too busy to spend much time with him. I also get short-tempered. I try not to, but I do.

There's another side to my illness. Sometimes I get so depressed that I can't get up off the sofa. Tony saw me go through a really bad depression a few years ago, and he had to learn how to fend for himself. He did his own laundry and cooked all his own meals. I wasn't able to do hardly anything for him back then. He hasn't had much of a normal life, but

on the whole he's become a real good person, and he has some close friends. Tony is a big support to me.

The basis of understanding between Tony and me comes from the two of us just sitting down and talking together. We've always been able to communicate openly with each other. I think that most teenagers want to talk with their parents without arguing. When the yelling starts, nobody listens. When I was a kid, my parents would either shout at me or use the belt. It's not at all like that with my son and me.

I went through manic and depressive episodes for years before I was finally diagnosed. I just learned to live with them. It's like someone who has a physical disability—you learn to compensate. My partner back then was diagnosed with multiple personality disorder, and I went to therapy with her to learn more about her illness. When her therapist began to get to know me, she was able to see my bipolar illness. She said it was probably getting worse because I was getting closer to menopause and because it had been left untreated for so long. Bipolar disorder runs in my family. My grandmother on my mother's side had it, too.

There are all different aspects to being bipolar. There are even some real plusses to being manic. Before you get to that extreme state, you can have some real fun with it! You sure can spruce things up around the house with all that extra energy.

— NORMA

I've never been hospitalized for bipolar disorder, but my illness still presents quite a problem because the medications don't work well on me. I get so many bad side effects from them. One summer when I was manic, my doctor started me on a low dose of a medication and then raised it because it wasn't working. The medication was supposed to calm me down, but I spent the next two weeks almost sleepless because it had the totally opposite effect on me. I couldn't reach my doctor because he was on vacation. Now I'm on medication, which has helped stabilize the manic side of my illness to some degree. This, in turn, helps stabilize the depression side of it. One usually follows the other.

There are all different aspects to being bipolar. There are even some real plusses to being manic. Before you get to that extreme state, you can have some real fun with it! You sure can spruce things up around the house with all that extra energy.

I've been on disability for a couple of years now. I did have a job at one point, but it became excruciatingly stressful for me. My boss was extremely loud all the time. He yelled a lot, and I just don't deal well with people who yell a lot. We spoke about it, and he tried to tone it down, but it was just who he was. You can't expect someone to totally change, if that's who he or she is.

When things go bad for me, I suddenly don't exist anymore for some of my friends. I call them, and my phone calls don't get returned. Their response is to close the door. They don't understand my illness well enough to see beyond it.

If I were to tell people that I'm hearing voices, they would immediately think that the voices are telling me to do bad things. They would be afraid that I could potentially go off the wall. But actually when I hear voices, they're usually not telling me anything at all. Sometimes I just hear a lot of mumbo jumbo or someone calling out my name.

It's always been very easy for me to see people as who they are and to know that there are different aspects to each individual. Every person is a human being who needs to be accepted, loved, cared for, and respected. Everyone, whether

I don't have to deal with people who are judgmental and who say, "Well, Norma, have you stopped crying yet? Why don't you get up off the sofa? Look at you, just sitting there!" Sure, I can understand how people might think I'm lazy. It must be hard to see a healthy-looking person just sitting around doing nothing. No wonder people think, "Well, I can get up. Why can't you?" Well, I can't get up because things are going on in my mind that don't allow me that freedom. People who have a mental illness just don't have that freedom. It's different for us.

— NORMA

they have a history of mental illness or not, needs that. Unfortunately, some people don't understand this. I think that if people would just open up their eyes and their minds instead of being so judgmental of each other, things would be different.

My ex-partner is my best friend. There's not much about what goes on with me or Tony that I can't talk to her about. Even if I'm feeling like shit that day, she gives me a great deal of acceptance. I guess I'd probably be lost without her.

I don't really give a damn what most people think about me. If someone has a problem with my having a mental illness, well, I don't need anyone like that around me. It's their loss and my gain. They're history! I don't have to deal with people who are judgmental and who say, "Well, Norma, have you stopped crying yet? Why don't you get up off the sofa? Look at you, just sitting there!" Sure, I can understand how people might think I'm lazy. It must be hard to see a healthy-looking person just sitting around doing nothing. No wonder people think, "Well, I can get up. Why can't you?" Well, I can't get up because things are going on in my mind that don't allow me that freedom.

People who have a mental illness just don't have that free-dom. It's different for us.

I think it is up to the mentally ill to speak out in their own way if they can. For each one of us who does speak out, there are thousands who can't. Society needs to know that we are people, too. As we become more outspoken, the stig-ma of mental illness will slowly begin to fade.

My long-term hope is to be a happy person. That's all I want out of life—to be happy with who I am and with my life situation. Material things don't matter to me at all. If I had to walk out of this house today and leave everything I own behind, I would still be happy with who I am. To me, that's the most important thing. For now, I know that this might be as good as it gets.

TONY

There's never a dull moment in this house.

I pretty much learned to support myself at a young age and to help my mom. Things wouldn't get done if I didn't do them. When you're faced with something like this, you just have to do it.

In high school, I didn't know that much about my mom's illness. When she was working in the shed on wood projects till eleven o'clock at night, and getting up at six in the morn-ing, I would ask her, "What's going on?" I'd watch her spend most of her time working on all these projects and not fin-ish any of them. Until a couple of years ago, I didn't fully understand why she would do that. Mom ran into a real bad spell and was on the couch a lot. That's when I found out exactly what was going on with her and what I needed to do to help.

My best friend knows a few things about my family, but she doesn't know that my mom is gay and she doesn't know that my mom is bipolar. I never talked about my mother's illness with any of my friends in high school because they wouldn't have understood. If I told some of them now, they might understand, but not too many people go up to some-one and say, "My mom or my dad has bipolar disorder." Stuff like that just doesn't happen, but it sure would be nice if it did. I'm pretty sure a lot of other kids have problems like mental illness in their families. If they had somebody else to talk to, they would realize that they're not alone.

Most of the kids at my school who had family problems either did drugs or drank. I'm not the type of person who can hide behind drugs or alcohol. It's a road that I never went down because that's not the way I am. As for me, I usually keep most of my feelings inside. I don't talk about myself to people. It would have probably been easier for me if I could have talked to people about what was happening with my mom. It would have helped me to understand her problems.

I can talk to my mom about most anything. We have an understanding that I can go out with my friends and come home whenever I want to. I don't have to ask permission. Some of my friends can't stay out late because their parents set curfews for them. Even when I was under eighteen, I was allowed to stay out later than my other friends, as long as I didn't come home drunk or stoned. My mom never grounds me. She's always trusted me a lot. Most parents don't trust their kids, which is a shame. I feel real lucky! Most of my friends wish they had a mother like mine.

> *My best friend knows a few things about my family, but she doesn't know that my mom is gay and she doesn't know that my mom is bipolar. I never talked about my mother's illness with any of my friends in high school because they wouldn't have understood. If I told some of them now, they might understand, but not too many people go up to someone and say, "My mom or my dad has bipolar disorder." Stuff like that just doesn't happen, but it sure would be nice if it did.*
> —TONY

Yoeh Chiao, Tammie, and John

THE TSAI FAMILY

ROSEMEAD, CALIFORNIA

YOEH CHIAO TSAI / TAMMIE TSAI / JOHN TSAI

TAMMIE

MY BROTHER IS ONE OF MY BEST FRIENDS. John and I share a closeness many siblings never do, but it wasn't always this way. John has schizophrenia.

When I first realized that John was sick, I didn't tell our mother. She's blind, and I didn't want to worry her. She wouldn't know how to carry on, because every mother hurts for her children. When she moved to California from Taiwan, I had to tell her about John, but I encouraged her not to take it too seriously. I said, "John is okay. He can be a great man, but unfortunately he is sick. People get sick in different ways. Some people are sick in bed, but John can walk anywhere he wants to."

My mother was disappointed with my brother because she always wanted everything to be perfect. I said to her, "We all have five fingers, and each finger is different. In this world, nothing is perfect. Nobody has a perfect family. There are no perfect parents and no perfect children."

Through trial and error, I have learned how to guide John. I never let my failures with him discourage me. I learned that my tone of voice had an impact on him, so I would speak words of respect in a soft voice. I also found that my gestures and attitudes affected him. I sometimes played like a child with him, or I would talk silly to make him laugh and smile. Singing old songs with John made him feel comfortable. I demonstrated patience and my peaceful intentions. I learned to never give up. For instance, I would ask John to go hiking with me. Each time I asked, he would answer, "No!" One day, I asked him again in my warmest voice if he would go hiking with me. And he said, "Yes."

John and I joined the Chinese-American Outdoor Club. This group has been incredibly supportive to both of us. When my brother began to rock climb, he was afraid. The other members of the group encouraged him by telling him that he could do it. They applauded each time John reached the top. His confidence continued to grow as he accomplished small tasks during these hiking trips, such as carrying water from the river for everyone. All of these little things gradually built up his self-esteem. The physical exertion and natural serenity helps to release John's tensions and stress. The warmth of the group eases him because of the happiness and

> *My mother was disappointed with my brother because she always wanted everything to be perfect. I said to her, "We all have five fingers, and each finger is different. In this world, nothing is perfect. Nobody has a perfect family. There are no perfect parents and no perfect children."*
> — TAMMIE

Tsai family with friends from the Outdoor Club

laughter. He returns to the city with a memory of good times and happiness in the voice of the wind.

It was not easy for me to convince John to take his medicine, but it is vitally important for him to do so. At first, he refused because he didn't think he was sick. I had to be creative in getting him to take the medication prescribed by his doctor. I mixed his pills with his juice without telling him. I also told John that I took vitamins to stay healthy and that his medication served the same purpose. He takes his med-

ication regularly now, and he doesn't need my reminders anymore.

I also took John to see Chinese herbal doctors. Chinese medicine attempts to balance the yin and the yang of the whole person. Along with his regular medication, the herbal medicines help him remain calm and stable. John accepted these medicines more readily because they were familiar to him. My brother and I also go to Chinese exercise classes, which emphasize bringing harmony to the whole person.

Of all the things I do to help my brother, none of them compare with the support of family and close friends. When I learned that John would never be cured, my siblings and mother never questioned my decision to care for him. They give me the moral support to go on. We were fortunate to find a friendly church whose members care for John and me. An example of their caring was when John went to a religious retreat, the minister arranged to be his roommate. This open demonstration of acceptance and brotherly love helped my brother rebuild his faith and trust in other people. It touched both of us.

JOHN

I love to go hiking, climb mountains, and go camping with groups because that improves my health. The beautiful scenery helps me open my heart.

I have a good time talking with friends, and this helps me get away from aloneness. Sometimes I work as a volunteer to build and maintain mountain trails with my sister. I feel that I'm very useful and that all the activity is helpful for my illness.

In tree: Emily, Laquetta, and Megan *Standing:* Paul, Brianna, Jane, Angelina, and Paul Jr.

40

THE SCHNITTER FAMILY

<u>WESTERVILLE, OHIO</u>

JANE SCHNITTER / PAUL SCHNITTER / PAUL SCHNITTER JR.
EMILY SCHNITTER / MEGAN SCHNITTER / LAQUETTA SCHNITTER
ANGELINA SCHNITTER / BRIANNA SCHNITTER

JANE

PSYCHIATRIC ILLNESSES RUN IN MY FAMILY. My father had paranoid schizophrenia. I suffer from a cyclical depression, and five of my seven children have been diagnosed with mental illness.

Our family is a large, multiracial family. My husband, Paul, and I adopted five kids, and I gave birth to two. Paul Jr. was adopted first. A year later, we adopted Corey, and then I gave birth to Emily. Megan was born two years later. As time went on, Paul and I wanted even more children. We decided to adopt older children because there are so many who need homes. When the agency offered us the possibility of adopting three girls at the same time, we said, "Yes."

Brianna, Angel, and Laquetta were all living in the same foster family, and the agency wanted them to stay together. All three of the girls were crack babies; and two of them have fetal alcohol syndrome. Because they are African American and we are white, the agency was more concerned with the racial issue than with their psychological problems.

When our oldest son, Paul, began having trouble in elementary school, the school psychologists ran some tests on him. When the results came back, they told us, "Well, Paul has a low I.Q. He is slow and he will always fail." We said, "Well, we don't accept that." We were referred to a mental health professional who had a very good reputation. She talked with my husband and me for about an hour, but she never met our son. She never even shook his hand. She told us, "Okay, the problem is basically your parenting." She said that I wasn't organized enough! My husband and I laughed about this later, and I thought, "That was the end of that." Clearly, things wouldn't get any better if our son's problems were caused by my lack of organizational skills. I'm not a very good housewife in many ways, but that's just me. I can't keep up with it all. Still, I knew that my disorganization wasn't making our son throw fits.

When Paul was eight, he became seriously depressed. He had to repeat first grade, and some of the other students made his life miserable by teasing him unmercifully. It helped a lot that we moved from down south up to Ohio that year, but he still had lots of problems. After all, he had moved to a different state, a different neighborhood, and a different school.

> *We were referred to a mental health professional who had a very good reputation. She talked with my husband and me for about an hour, but she never met our son. She never even shook his hand. She told us, "Okay, the problem is basically your parenting."*
> —JANE

41

My husband and I fought with Paul every day of the week. He was often crabby and he couldn't handle stimulation very well. He certainly couldn't handle disappointments. One morning, I thought, "I can't do this for another second! I can't live with this child anymore." If I didn't get away, I was afraid that I would lose it. He was just so difficult. I decided to walk around the neighborhood and calm myself down. Paul followed me, throwing himself down on the sidewalk behind me. I begged him, "Please get away from me. Just give me some time to calm myself down. Please go back in the house!"

Paul said some things that frightened me terribly. For instance, one day we were riding in the car and he was upset about something. We were bantering back and forth, and he said, "I'm going to jump right out of this car while it's moving. You'd like that, wouldn't you?" Another time, he and his younger brother, Corey, were pulling the legs off of flies and setting them on fire. I said, "How would you like to be set on fire and have your legs pulled off?" Paul said, "You'd like to see that, wouldn't you? That's what you want for me."

My husband and I decided to take Paul to see another professional. He told us that our son had childhood depression and attention deficit disorder. After Paul was diagnosed and put on medication, we recognized that there had been something seriously wrong with our son for quite a while. We watched some old childhood videotapes, and in many of them, Paul was miserable and kicking at things. We realized that his illness hadn't appeared all of a sudden.

Paul was getting his medications, but not a whole lot of good therapy. He saw a series of psychiatrists because there was so much turnover. One therapist didn't seem to understand our son at all. We weren't sure if it was a cultural problem, because she had a heavy accent. I'd say to her, "Well, Paul's doing such and such," and she would tell him, "Okay, now, Paul, you shouldn't do that." I thought to myself, "We already tell him that!"

Paul still has problems handling excitement and disappointment. When things aren't going well, he can be very pessimistic. He's always expecting that the worst is going to happen. Sometimes he actually sabotages things so that it does. Paul is finally recognizing this pattern in himself.

Paul's real strength is his personality. He's well liked socially and he's very good with people, but he struggles academically. His school didn't help us until fifth grade when we got him tested privately and he was labeled learning disabled. He did well in fifth, sixth, and seventh grades, but then the school retested him. They decided he was just lazy, stupid, and spoiled, and they took away all his extra support. Eighth grade was a terrible year for him. When Paul went on to high school, one teacher finally recognized his problems, and they put him in a more appropriate and supportive program.

Paul has taken his medication off and on, but he's not taking any at the moment. He doesn't want to. He functions okay without it, but I personally feel it would make his life easier if he would take it. He's just not interested right now.

Megan suffers from childhood depression and anxiety. She has crying episodes and sometimes gets angry at small things. As an infant, she was very laid back, but as a toddler she threw fits in the car. One time, she kicked so hard that she knocked the car out of gear. During these episodes I would take her out of the car and sit in the grass with her until she calmed down. When Megan was in the fourth grade, her troubles got worse. She was sick a lot with migraines and stomach problems, which kept her out of school. We took her to a psychologist, who did biofeedback with her, and her physical symptoms decreased. Unfortunately, her high level of anxiety did not. Megan went on medication in the fifth grade.

When our three youngest girls arrived three years ago, they could be quite violent. They would hit, kick, swear, and bite. If we held them in passive restraints, they'd all try to bite us, and Angel would spit.

After a while, all three of them improved. Not too long ago, Angel was mad at her dad and she yelled at him, "You're just a mean awful old dad." My husband said to me, "I'm so proud of her. She didn't use one swear word. That was very appropriate anger."

Angel has never had a clear-cut psychiatric diagnosis. She is developmentally handicapped, with a low I.Q. At ten, her reading has still not clicked in, although she does know all her letters and her sounds. She can print anything you spell for her, but she cannot sit down and read a word except for her name. Angel takes many medications daily for her multiple problems, and she needs all of them. She was started on Ritalin, which helps because she has ADHD. Angel also takes a sedative to calm her down, an antipsychotic drug for extreme impulsiveness, and an antidepressant for depression and anxiety. At night, she takes Benadryl so she can sleep. Angel functions quite well with all these medications.

Our youngest child, Brianna, was a crack baby and she has also been diagnosed with a minor case of ADHD. She takes a low dose of Ritalin in order to function in school, although we don't always give it to her at home. We've found there isn't that much of a difference between when she takes it and when she doesn't. Sometimes I'll give it to her before she goes to gymnastics class to help her concentrate. She's very athletic and she participates in a lot of sports.

Laquetta's problem is that she's language impaired. I'm not sure yet whether she has a mental illness. She's in a learning disabled class due to fetal alcohol syndrome. Sometimes she can't get words out. Her speech teacher said that some wires in her brain were crossed that shouldn't have been.

There are times when I say, "This is too hard. What am I doing?" I have to keep reminding myself that although life is harder for me since the three girls arrived, their lives are much easier. When they arrived, they didn't know what cotton candy was or how to swim. They had never even been to a pool or a beach or an amusement park.

My husband and I often come from two different places about our children. Sometimes he feels that they should learn how to control their behavior and that all they need is better discipline. I feel that their behaviors are completely out of their control. Of course, I realize that it's always a mix of the two. Sometimes I tend to be too sympathetic, and he can

be too harsh. Over the years, we've kind of blended our approach to them.

When our children get out of control, a cold shower can stop their difficult behaviors from escalating. This may not work for everyone, but it works for our kids. We discovered this when we were at a wedding when the kids were much younger. Paul wouldn't go to sleep in our hotel room. He cried and screamed for hours. My husband and I kept putting him back into bed, but he wouldn't stop. We even tried putting him in bed with us, and that didn't work, either. Then we took him for a car ride, and he quieted down a bit. When we got back to our room, he started screaming again. When this kind of behavior happened again at home, we tried putting him in a cold shower. He was able to calm down because he wanted to get out of the shower so badly. Of course, we took him right out. Since then, we've used this technique with the younger kids as well. It works well with them. Brianna says, "I don't want a cold shower," and she will change her behavior in order to avoid taking one.

As for me, my depression comes monthly, almost like severe PMS. When I ovulate, I start to go downhill until my period comes. I have three or four days when I cry all the time and can't function very well. In fact, I'm pretty much incapacitated. After a few days, I feel better.

I teach preschool three afternoons a week. When I was talking with the director a few months after I was hired, I casually mentioned to her that I took Prozac. She kind of panicked and said, "Jane, please don't let any of the parents or the other teachers know about this. If I had known this before I had actually known you personally, I never would have hired you. It would have scared me too much."

PAUL SR.

I grew up in a family of nine siblings. Any problems we kids had were handled through family intervention or prayer. Apparently, this wasn't all that was needed because several of

I teach preschool three afternoons a week. When I was talking with the director a few months after I was hired, I casually mentioned to her that I took Prozac. She kind of panicked and said, "Jane, please don't let any of the parents or the other teachers know about this. If I had known this before I had actually known you personally, I never would have hired you. It would have scared me too much."

—JANE

When I'm feeling really down, I go to a special place. I need to get away when I have a lot of things on my mind. There's a place down by the Hoover Dam where I can see all the water coming out through the back of the dam and I can see the rest of the reservoir. I look at the water and I just sit and think. There's something very soothing about watching water.

—PAUL JR.

my siblings are currently on medication for depression.

I told Jane before we were married that I wanted nine kids. I thought we were done at four, but now we have seven! You never know what life is going to bring.

Initially, it was difficult for me to accept Jane's depression as a real illness. Luckily, I have a sister and a brother-in-law who are both very knowledgeable and outspoken about mental illness, and they've been helpful to me.

My friends at work know that my wife and many of my kids are on medication, but they find the fact that we have seven kids and are a blended multiracial family even more unusual.

I worry whether Jane and I are doing the right things for our kids, and whether I'm doing the right things for Jane. I guess all you can do is try your best. Learning about mental illness has been quite an adventure!

PAUL JR.

When I was in the first grade, the kids made fun of me constantly. They'd pick on me and stuff like that, just because I couldn't do certain things. I would scream at them.

Sometimes I get too excited, and that's a problem. I'm too loud. I'm too outgoing or something, and I've always expected the worst. The psychologists didn't do much to help me. Pretty much all I did with my therapists was to talk to them about how my day went. That was about it. They didn't really understand where I was coming from.

About four years ago, I decided that I wanted to be like everybody else, so I stopped taking my medication. I wanted to see what I could accomplish without it. Taking medication was a struggle for me. I especially felt embarrassed taking it at school.

I'm not always the best at dealing with my sisters, especially Megan. Sometimes it's difficult when she's crying or whining. I'm not always sympathetic. I have to remember that

I lose control at times, too. I have to be reminded that she can't help the way she acts.

When I'm feeling really down, I go to a special place. I need to get away when I have a lot of things on my mind. There's a place down by the Hoover Dam where I can see all the water coming out through the back of the dam and I can see the rest of the reservoir. I look at the water and I just sit and think. There's something very soothing about watching water.

EMILY

My siblings can be annoying, but not because of their mental illnesses. It's just because they are my sisters and brothers. Megan always bothered me the most because she's been my sister the longest and we've always had to share a bedroom.

People know that my sisters take medication, but they don't know why. My friends noticed that Megan was always crying in order to get attention, but it was no big deal to them. They're more interested in the fact that I have a large family. Everyone wants to come over and see my younger sisters. A friend said that coming over to my house is never boring because something is always happening.

MEGAN

A couple of weeks ago I was sick for a few days. I had homework that I hadn't had time to finish. I didn't know what to do. I didn't think I could finish it on time. All I could do was cry. I probably could have finished my work if I had stopped crying, but I never thought of that.

When I've gotten upset at school, my friends talk to me about it. They understand because they have their own problems. Knowing that my friends also have problems kind of calms me down.

My friends and I sit together at lunch and we usually talk about our problems. We probably talk a lot more than we actually eat. We try to help each other. It's comforting to know that my friends really care. I also have really good teachers; they understand everything.

My brother, Paul, used to protect me. If I came home from school crying, he'd tell me that he would beat up any kid who was making fun of me. It was kind of comforting to know that my older brother would help me. Paul also taught me how to protect myself. Knowing that somebody really cared about me helped me a lot.

ANGELINA

I have a dog named CJ and I like him. He likes to go for walks with me and he can open the door all by himself to go in and out of the house. Brianna and I share a room. My favorite book is *The Ugly Duckling.* I can read it all by myself. Sometimes I forget the words and I have to remember what the story is about.

Megan

Standing: Ashley and Jamie *Seated:* Anson H., Jean, and Anson M.

THE BEARD FAMILY

GREENWICH, CONNECTICUT, AMHERST, MASSACHUSETTS,
NEW YORK CITY, NEW YORK, AND BALA CYNWYD, PENNSYLVANIA

ASHLEY BEARD / JAMIE BEARD / ANSON H. BEARD
JEAN J. BEARD / ANSON M. BEARD, JR. / LEILA LINEN

JEAN

I DON'T THINK I CAN EVER DESCRIBE TO ANYBODY what it's like to have a daughter who has been so sick. There are just no words for it.

My daughter, Ashley, has been mentally ill since she was a little girl. She hasn't been able to live at home since she was thirteen, and she will never be able to function outside of a highly structured therapeutic environment. She lives with full-time staff and two other clients in a sweet little house on the grounds of a residential treatment facility in Pennsylvania. Ashley's house has a white picket fence, a garden, and a mailbox. To her delight, she also has permission to have a dog who sleeps under her bed at night. These may seem like insignificant things, but to Ashley they have all the importance in the world.

When I think back on all the years that Ashley was psychotic, I can't believe that our family got through those times and came out the other side. Now that she is doing so much better, it's tempting to think, "Oh well, it wasn't that bad." But actually, it *was* that bad. It was a nightmare for our entire family, but especially for Ashley.

I knew that there was something not quite right with Ashley by the time she was two. By the time she was five, I was walking around with a sense of dread. That feeling has never completely gone away. Ashley is thirty now, and when the phone rings at a late hour, I still worry that it might be bad news from her unit.

In the early years of Ashley's childhood, she didn't seem to take in information the way that she should. For instance, if I asked her to go down the hall and into her room and bring out her hat, her parka, and her mittens, she would come back in a few minutes with a puzzled look on her face. Then she would say, "I can't remember what you wanted me to do." Ashley also repeated herself constantly, asking me the

When I think back on all the years that Ashley was psychotic, I can't believe that our family got through those times and came out the other side. Now that she is doing so much better, it's tempting to think, "Oh well, it wasn't that bad." But actually, it was that bad. It was a nightmare for our entire family, but especially for Ashley.

—JEAN

same question over and over again. For a period of a few months when she was about four, she would follow me around the house, asking me nonstop, "Mommy, do you love me? Do you love me? Do you love me?" I didn't think this was normal. I was always worried about her. Her pediatrician thought I was just an overly anxious new mom, but I never thought so.

When Ashley was in kindergarten, her three-year-old brother, Anson, was already ahead of her in many ways. I used to ask myself, "What's the matter with Ashley?" It was obvious that at the very least she had severe learning disabilities, but I always sensed some sort of emotional confusion in her. She seemed fragile and extraordinarily anxious.

Ashley was hit by a car when she was five while our family was on vacation in Florida. She had no head injuries, thank God, but she spent months in traction at a local hospital. When she was discharged, I brought her home by train because she was encased in a heavy, plaster full-body cast. When the cast was finally removed two months later, my husband, Anson, and I became even more concerned about Ashley. She was terrified of the outdoors, of odors, of the scent of gasoline, of any sudden noise, and even of the wind. She was so frightened that she really couldn't function outside of the house. I suspected that her emotional difficulties weren't caused just by the car accident. I thought that she suffered from more than post-traumatic stress disorder.

Ashley saw a child psychologist twice a week for the next three years. This woman was very honest with us. She felt that Ashley would probably never be able to lead a completely normal life, and that she would always need structure and psychiatric help. She was not surprised when Ashley, by the time she was seven or eight, began to exhibit clear signs of mental illness. Ashley would wash her hands compulsively until they were raw and bleeding, and she would stand in front of a mirror for hours on end to make sure that her eyes were in the right place on her face. She was very reluctant to go outside because she thought that flies and even bits of grass would enter her body and damage her.

One summer, when Ashley was about nine, she wouldn't go outside at all. When she was ten, she could only go to school sporadically. By the time Ashley was eleven, she was psychotic. She would have episodes where she would be either extremely aggressive or catatonic. Many times her body would become as rigid as a board. Ashley would stand frozen and unmoving for hours with a blank expression on her face. She could hear us speak to her, but she couldn't respond. My husband and I would wet her lips with a washcloth and just wait it out because we couldn't get her in the car to take her to the emergency room without injuring her. There were also times when Ashley would break windows in the house or, in utter frustration, she would throw things.

I would come home from work thinking, "I wonder how Ashley did today?" I always worried about how her day at school had gone and whether or not she would be so unsettled that our entire evening would be ruined. The smallest things would set her off, and it would take me hours to settle her down again. If she misplaced something, even a tiny thing, everybody in the family would have to stop what they were doing immediately and look for it so that Ashley wouldn't "go off." We were always on pins and needles.

There was so little I could do to help my daughter. Ashley and I would sometimes cry together when she came out of a psychotic episode. She would be devastated and terrorized and in so much emotional pain. I would hold her and think, "Can this really be happening?"

Shortly before Ashley turned thirteen, it became clear that Anson and I could no longer take care of her at home. She was admitted to a psychiatric hospital on an emergency basis. Ashley was completely terrified, and I couldn't find the words to explain to her why she could no longer live with us. The situation was also very hard on her younger brothers. They worried that if they "misbehaved" down the road, they might be "sent away," too. To say that all five of us were devastated is an understatement. I still find it impossible to talk about the details of the day that Ashley left home.

Dealing with the institutional system in this hospital was incredibly difficult. My phone calls to Ashley's unit were often not returned, and suggestions that I made to her direct care staff weren't responded to. I was even told when I could or could not visit my own daughter. We Beards were completely shut out of the mental health system, and the message we got was that the medical professionals simply didn't care about the family. To this day, I still resent the lack of support that we got from those who took care of Ashley in those early years. Nowadays, families, ours included, are much more involved in the treatment of their kids. It's about time.

One particularly gruesome day about fifteen years ago when Ashley was home on a pass, she and I were shopping downtown. I could sense that her anxiety level was building rapidly. She suddenly bolted away from me and I couldn't catch up with her. She ran screaming down the street. A policeman helped me chase her, calling for backup. A squad car finally cornered her in a parking garage, and one cop straddled her because she was so out of control. The worst of it was that the police assumed Ashley was on drugs even though I was screaming, "Don't touch her! Don't touch her. She's psychotic." They threw her in their car anyway, and took her to the emergency room, where she was finally stabilized hours later. Ashley can talk about this episode now with a sense of detachment, but for many years afterward she wasn't comfortable with anybody who wore a uniform. As for me, just thinking about this incident is unbearably painful.

My parents grieved terribly about the situation with Ashley, but they would seldom ask me directly about her. It was easier for them to call my twin sister, Lee, to get news of how Ashley was doing. My parents weren't all that helpful even though they lived only a few miles away. For instance, they never offered to take Ashley to the park or out for lunch to give me a break. They didn't cope very well with their sorrow or with mine. My strongest ally over the years has been Lee. She was there for me right from the beginning, and she was always available to Ashley. Lee still calls and visits Ashley on a regular basis, and she continues to give me enormous

Leila and Jean

support and understanding. My younger sister and brother are not involved with my daughter. I can't remember the last time they asked about her, and they have never visited her at any of her residential placements or the several psychiatric hospitals she has been admitted to over the years.

In the early years of Ashley's illness, my friends would often ask me about her. But when she left home to live in residential treatment centers and various locked inpatient psychiatric units, the news about her was usually so grim that after a while a lot of them gradually stopped asking. This is understandable, but it was still painful for me. I would go out of my way not to share with them how much pain I was in. There didn't seem to be any point to it. I became isolated

I don't think that you grow from this particular type of pain. We may have gotten real close as a family, but it was a high price to pay. I think it's one thing to acknowledge that perhaps meaningful things come out of the horrific, but frankly, I really can't see any redeeming features to our family's situation.

—*JEAN*

from the world of happy people because I wasn't happy myself, and I just couldn't connect very well with those who were.

There are so many myths about the various treatments for mental illness. For instance, I cringe when people make jokes about electroshock treatment when they don't know what they're talking about. Ashley has had over twenty of these procedures, and each one was easy, quick, and painless. I would stay with her each time, and when she woke up, we would go have pizza together. It was actually a sweet routine. Another myth is the assumption that all brain operations on mentally ill patients are lobotomies, which turn them into zombies. When she was in her twenties, Ashley had two neurosurgical operations which made her life worth living. Her anxiety decreased dramatically, and she could think clearly for the first time in years. This freed her up to enjoy her life a lot more. Most importantly, Ashley started to smile and laugh again. This was a huge gift for all of us. Now, when I'm with this sweet daughter of mine, it is a joy to see her doing so well.

Ashley comes home on a pass once a month for four or five days. During one recent visit, she and I went out for breakfast to a local restaurant. I was preparing her medications when the waitress came over to take our order. When she saw the bottles of pills lined up on the table, the waitress joked with me and said, "What are you, a drug addict?" I replied, "Actually, no. My daughter is a psychiatric patient, and these pills are for her." Ashley immediately added, "I have a mental illness, and these pills make me feel better." The waitress was embarrassed, but I wasn't and neither was my daughter. Since Ashley doesn't fit the stereotypes so many people have about the mentally ill, this kind of thing happens all too often.

I worry about what will happen after my husband and I die, and so does Ashley. She asked me recently, "When you guys are gone, where will my home be?" I told her that she would stay with her two brothers on her passes, but she repeated, "Okay, but where will my home be?" She just couldn't envision a life without her mom and dad, and this broke my heart.

I don't think that you grow from this particular type of pain. We may have gotten real close as a family, but it was a high price to pay. I think it's one thing to acknowledge that perhaps meaningful things come out of the horrific, but frankly, I really can't see any redeeming features to our family's situation.

ANSON H.

I was seven when my sister got sick. I knew instinctively that there was something very wrong with Ashley, and having that kind of instability around was very disconcerting. It made me an anxious person, and I was a basketcase growing up. I had problems of my own, no question. Her illness affected me emotionally.

Unlike my brother, Jamie, I never wanted to have friends over when Ashley was around. I didn't like the uncertainty, because I was a control freak and Ashley was a variable I couldn't control. I didn't want to be in a position where she would "go off" or have a total meltdown. One of my most vivid recollections was when I was ten years old and three of my friends were over. Ashley had a bad psychotic episode and started throwing apples around the house and breaking windows. I was mortified.

I was always selfish in the sense that I felt embarrassed by my sister. I didn't even tell my close friends about her until I was in my late teens. I think they all knew, but it was a subject I didn't bring up because I didn't want anybody to feel sorry for me. If someone asked me if I had any brothers or sisters, I would always get a nervous feeling in my stomach. I hated that question. I would answer, "I have a brother," and then I'd quickly say, "How about you?" Or I'd say, "I have a brother and a sister," and right away, I'd talk about my brother Jamie and then say, "What about you?" I would throw it right back at them. I had the system down pat.

We walked on eggshells around the house when Ashley was still living at home. It was a no-win situation more often than not because something always happened to set her off. It was the ultimate catch-22. Even if you tried hard to be quiet, you couldn't be perfect. It was terribly frustrating. Simply having Jamie and me around was a source of discomfort for Ashley. In one sense, she loved being with us because we were her brothers, but our mere presence reminded her that she couldn't lead a normal life.

In recent years when someone asks me about Ashley's diagnosis, I usually say that she has schizophrenia, even though technically she doesn't. It's easier to say she has schizophrenia than explain that she has been diagnosed over the years with a complex variety of illnesses, including pervasive developmental disorder, atypical psychosis, OCD, and body dysmorphic disorder. Using the word "schizophrenia" is my way of saying, "Don't go there. Back off. Don't press me on the details." This usually stops people in their tracks, and they move on without asking for a long-winded explanation.

I thoroughly enjoy the time I spend with Ashley now. I'm always going to make time for her. I think she is the most impressive person in our family.

JAMIE

One Thanksgiving when I was about eighteen, the entire family was sitting around and talking about current events. We sort of lost track of Ashley for five or ten minutes. She was just sitting there and then, all of a sudden, the glow on her face just kind of trimmed down and she lost it. She totally lost control. We ended up having to take her to the emergency room. I think that what happened was that Ashley realized that her brothers were two grown men who led normal lives. We were conducting a normal, everyday conversation that she couldn't participate in because she didn't understand what we were talking about. It's got to be excruciatingly painful for her to know that her two brothers, who came out of the same womb as she did and were brought up in the same house, are completely comfort-

able in the world. Once Ashley was institutionalized, she missed a whole part of life. It's so sad.

I was never really embarrassed that my sister was mentally ill. Would I take Ashley to my junior prom? No, but I was never self-conscious when my friends met her. It was almost a relief to have them know what my sister was like. If she was psychotic or acted out, I'd feel so badly for her. The hardest thing for me was how to describe her illness to other people because she had so many different symptoms. When somebody would ask me about Ashley, I would say, "Well, she's severely emotionally disturbed," and I'd throw out a couple of examples of her behavior. For instance, I'd tell them about how Ashley would sit in front of a mirror for hours at a time checking to see if her eyes were in the right place. She was never sure that they were.

When I was a kid, I used to think that if Ashley were in a regular educational environment, instead of going to a special school, maybe she could learn proper behavior. I didn't realize then that Ashley's behavior wasn't her fault. I'd see something she was doing and I would want to say, "Stop it." It took me a while, but I eventually figured out that this was an irreversible, tragic situation that had to be accepted. None of it was Ashley's fault.

Ashley often has the ear-to-ear grin of a ten-year-old girl on Christmas morning. But this can change in an instant. All of a sudden, her face looks like her best friend was just killed in front of her eyes. It's such an extreme case of depression and confusion and anxiety. You see it and you wish you could do something, but there is nothing any of us can do to help her.

Mom and Dad are not the kind of people who would institutionalize their daughter and then forget about her, which is what some other families do. They are extremely special and loving parents, and they've been with Ashley every step of the way. Both of my parents give Ashley a great time whenever they are with her, but her illness has definitely had a huge impact, especially on Mom. Essentially, Mom spearheads this operation. She has made unbelievable sacrifices, and I think

We walked on eggshells around the house when Ashley was still living at home. It was a no-win situation more often than not because something always happened to set her off.
—ANSON H.

I was never really embarrassed that my sister was mentally ill. Would I take Ashley to my junior prom? No, but I was never self-conscious when my friends met her.
—JAMIE

The way I approach life, you have to play the hand you're dealt. You can't just run around wringing your hands, thinking, "Why did this have to happen? Why did lightning have to strike me?" That's the wrong way to go through life.
—ANSON M.

The issue of mental illness must be raised to the level of a national problem so that this country can allocate appropriate funds to help. Our family is privileged, and we've been able to give Ashley the best life we possibly can. I'm not covered by insurance for her care any longer. How many people in the world can afford the price of good mental health care? It's a fraction of one percent. This situation has to change.
—ANSON M.

Jean and Ashley

that's kind of sad. Ashley took so many years of energy from her. Mom's been there for her forever; she talks to Ashley all the time; she advocates for her; she plans all her passes home from the unit.

Ashley has been a distant part of my life because she left home so early. I only see her on holidays but I call her regularly. Whenever I talk to my mom, she always asks me, "When's the last time you called Ashley?" I call her just to tell her how much I love her.

ANSON M.

My daughter, Ashley, may have severe psychiatric problems, but if she's having a good day, she can be fabulous. She's got a great

sense of humor and shows unusual sensitivity to others. She can deal with her symptoms now in a better way. She no longer gets aggressive or psychotic like she did when she was younger. She used to throw things, hurt herself, or break windows out of frustration and terror. Her craziness got into the whole family. You're always thinking, "What's going to explode in your face next?"

For years and years, our family never had a joyful holiday. When Ashley was still living at home, things were always very tense, and when she was in various locked units, all of us would spend holidays with her there. It's only been in the last four or five years that all of us Beards have been able to celebrate relatively peaceful and happy holidays at home together.

It takes so little to please Ashley. If she wants something and we say, "No, you can't have it," she accepts it. She's never argumentative. And she is so thrilled by the simplest of things in life, like a candlelight dinner at home with just her and me. Being with Ashley is very refreshing. She and I have an incredible relationship, and I thoroughly enjoy it. I never say, "Oh, this is the weekend Ashley's coming home. I've got to take care of my sick daughter." Ashley can't wait to come home on her monthly pass, and I look forward to her visits, too. We have so much fun together.

The way I approach life, you have to play the hand you're dealt. You can't just run around wringing your hands, thinking, "Why did this have to happen? Why did lightning have to strike me?" That's the wrong way to go through life. The most important thing is to have a positive attitude and look for the good in things as opposed to the bad. Having a daughter like Ashley has probably made us a more caring family. It certainly makes you more respectful of other people who have problems.

I once read that more money is spent on the prevention of tooth decay in this country than on research for schizophrenia. These priorities don't seem straight to me. The issue of mental illness must be raised to the level of a national problem so that this country can allocate appropriate funds to help. Our family is privileged, and we've been able to give Ashley the best life we possibly can. I'm not covered by insurance for her care any longer. How many people in the world can afford the price of good mental health care? It's a fraction of one percent. This situation has to change.

ASHLEY

My mom and dad and two brothers write and call me often. I like hearing from them and I like being with them. When I go to sleep at night, I think about my family and how much I love them. I also have wonderful cousins. My mom has a twin sister, and I love her a lot. My Aunt Lee is like a second mom to me.

My life used to be scary and difficult, and sometimes it still is. But I know how to handle the rough times now. This makes me feel happy and proud of myself. For the most part, people have been kind to me. But some people have been mean to me by teasing me and being rude and making fun of me.

I wish I had never gotten sick. Maybe I could have gone to high school and college. I'm thankful that I'm much better now and that I have mostly recovered from my hard times. But I don't like living away from home. I miss my family. I'm happy that I come home a lot and that I can travel now with my family to our other home in Idaho. I also have friends and a dog named Angel Anne, who lives with me in my house.

Sometimes I'm unhappy because I haven't had an easy life. My brothers can do more than me, but someday maybe I can do some of the things they can, like drive a car and be more independent. I'm starting to do some of the things that my brothers do, like use a computer. I even have a job. I'm mostly all better now. I used to be depressed and scared and anxious and I didn't love myself. I love myself now. I think I'm a good person and I'm thankful for being me.

LEILA

My first inkling that there might be a problem with my niece, Ashley, came from my twin sister, Jean. When Ashley was only two years old, Jean asked me if I thought Ashley was unsophisticated for her age. I thought Ashley was right on target, but what did I know? My first child was only six weeks old at the time, and I had no reference point.

Jean was worried about the possibility that Ashley had developmental delays, but I was so preoccupied during those early years with my own growing family that I paid little attention to her concerns.

I have sweet memories of Ashley coming to our house and playing Barbie dolls with my two little girls. They played for hours on end in an upstairs bedroom. By then, certain things were difficult for Ashley. I remember getting ready to take all three girls to church one Sunday and Ashley had trouble getting her barrette in her hair correctly. She became very anxious. My youngest daughter eventually helped her, and off we went.

As the years went on, Ashley became very sick. I remember feeling that I had all the luck and that Jean had so much to deal with. I am sure in retrospect that I was selfish in my attention to my own family and in my inattention to my sister's worries. I still don't feel that I have a good track record either in terms of helping Jean or in doing enough for her daughter.

To this day, Jean has never complained to me about what her life has been like coping with Ashley's illness. She has never said to me, "How come you have all the luck and I have all the difficulties?" This is particularly remarkable given the fact that we are identical twins. A reasonable assumption would be that our lives and experiences would be similar.

I think that Ashley is a remarkable person and I know that her positive qualities stem from her parents and all that they have done for their daughter over the years. Ashley is thoughtful, loving, and empathetic toward others. She always tries to look on the best side of things. I respect her courage and her dignity. I love her dearly.

My life used to be scary and difficult, and sometimes it still is. But I know how to handle the rough times now. This makes me feel happy and proud of myself. For the most part, people have been kind to me. But some people have been mean to me by teasing me and being rude and making fun of me.
—ASHLEY

Trinidad, Frank, and Bartola

THE ESPARZA FAMILY

AZUSA, CALIFORNIA

TRINIDAD ESPARZA / FRANK ESPARZA / BARTOLA ESPARZA

TRINIDAD

I WAS WORKING AS A TAX AUDITOR when the symptoms of my illness suddenly appeared without warning. I became paranoid and thought that people were always watching me. I would walk by the TV set and think that the voices of the actors were talking directly to me. I would hear them say, "Well, there's Trini again. He's going back to his room." I thought they knew where I was, what I was doing, and even what I was thinking.

At work, things got very difficult for me. I was once totaling up some figures and they just wouldn't come out right. After doing the calculation several times, I asked a friend to do it with me. He said, "The reason it isn't adding up is that you aren't seeing this number," and he had to keep pointing to a particular number until I finally saw it. When that happened, I realized that something was wrong with me, but I didn't know what it was. I decided to see a therapist, but she couldn't figure out what was going on with me, either. I quit my job because I didn't think I was capable of doing my work anymore. The day I resigned, I went jogging and a policeman saw me acting strangely. He brought me home.

My dad and my older brother took me to a hospital, and that was the beginning of a long series of hospitalizations. I was initially diagnosed with schizophrenia and later on with schizo-affective disorder. I was in denial at first. Even though I knew something was seriously wrong with me, I didn't want to believe that I was mentally ill. It seemed as though nobody knew what I was going through, and I felt I was experiencing things that no one else had ever experienced. Until I began to meet people who had been through the same thing, I felt all alone.

I didn't stay in touch with any of my high school friends after I became ill, although I did decide to attend my tenth high school reunion. I got a pass from the hospital and I went for a couple of hours. It was scary. I felt completely out of place and I didn't have much to talk about. I do have one friend from college whom I correspond with, and he's been pretty supportive. I've also met new friends at the clubhouses I go to, and we have something in common. We are mental health consumers. I've also met lots of people over the years who have encouraged me and given me hope. Above all, my parents and my siblings have always been there for me.

Seeing my son put in restraints was the hardest thing that a mother could ever see their child go through. I couldn't bear it. My husband and I were both in tears. I know it's a normal procedure for the patient's safety, but it's very hard to see your son strapped down like that. When I got my first dosage of that sight, oh, that hurt me.

— BARTOLA

I first experienced the stigma of mental illness when I applied for a volunteer job. I was in a voc-rehab program, and my counselor arranged a job interview for me. After the interview, I was asked to step out of the room, and my counselor was told, "Sorry, but Trini is mentally ill and we don't believe in him. We don't think he would fit in here or be able to do the job." My counselor didn't give up. He used his personal connection to the director of the program, and I was hired as a data entry volunteer. Twelve months later, I was picked as Volunteer of the Year! It turned out I was more than capable of doing the job.

I've become an advocate for the mentally ill. When I first started working at a clinic, my doctor asked me if I had ever made a speech. I said, "No," and he replied, "Be prepared, Trini. We'll have you speaking all over the place." And I have! I average eight appearances a year at conferences and at law enforcement agencies. I explain that even an overachiever like me can become mentally ill. I tell the audiences that I was the student body president in high school and an excellent student all through college. Mental illness does not affect just one type of person.

After I spoke to one police department, they came up with the idea of making cards like driver's licenses that would identify a person as mentally ill. The purpose of these ID cards is to save people's lives. Folks who have mental illness are often jailed and then kill themselves there. The police don't usually realize that a prisoner is sick until after the fact. If the police were informed, these folks could be sent to a special place where they could receive treatment.

I hope there will be a cure for mental illness someday soon. It's just a matter of time and research. Maybe someday the whole mental health system will be out of business. I like to give people hope that if I can get well, so can they. I'm now able to work part-time at the clinic where I used to be a mental health consumer. Granted, I'm not working full-time yet, but I will sometime soon. I'm just not ready for that yet.

BARTOLA

When my son, Trini, first got sick, he was acting completely opposite to the way he had always been. As a teenager, he had never gone through a stage of arguing with his parents, so I thought he was just going through a delayed rebellious phase. He began to let everything go.

Trini stopped taking care of himself and his room. He wouldn't wash his hair and he wouldn't eat hardly anything. He even thought it was normal to hear voices. He just got worse and worse. Eventually, he stopped drinking water. When that happened, I was so concerned that I said, "Trini, you're sick." He argued with me and said it wasn't true. One day, I broke down in tears because I just couldn't take it anymore. Trini was so dehydrated and thin! My husband, Frank, and I knew we had to do something. It was very hard for us to take him to the hospital, but we did.

One of Trini's doctors advised us not to let him come home if he decided to walk out of the psychiatric hospital. The doctor said that Trini would go back to the hospital on his own if we didn't let him in the house. I just couldn't do that. One cold and rainy day, he hitchhiked home with all of his belongings. We let Trini come inside and we talked with him for a while. First he wanted to go back to the hospital, and then he didn't. He kept changing his mind. At one point he decided to return, and I called the hospital. Trini's bed had already been taken! We had to get him into another hospital until they had room for him on his unit. The police and an ambulance came to our house to get him. They handcuffed him and put him on a gurney.

Seeing my son put in restraints was the hardest thing that a mother could ever see their child go through. I couldn't bear it. My husband and I were both in tears. I know it's a normal procedure for the patient's safety, but it's very hard to see your son strapped down like that. When I got my first dosage of that sight, oh, that hurt me.

When our neighbors asked questions about Trini, I would answer them truthfully. Frank and I let them know right away that Trini was mentally ill. They weren't mean to him, and they didn't ignore him. They treated him just the way they used to. Many people won't tell anyone that someone in their family has a mental illness. They keep it to themselves and hibernate in a closet. I tell people like that to open up and let the world know. Treat the mentally ill as normally as anybody else. Don't treat them differently. I've treated Trini the same way I always did, and he's turned out beautiful.

I never thought about mental illness before Trini got sick. It never even crossed my mind, because our family hadn't ever experienced it. Everything was new to us. After Trini was diagnosed, I started reading books and watching television shows about mental illness. It's sad that the only way people will reach out and do anything about mental illness is when it hits someone in their own family. If it hadn't happened to my son, Frank and I wouldn't have become involved or listened to anything on this subject. It's sad to say that, but that's how it is.

The good news is that after trying many different drugs, Trini has finally responded to his medication. That's when his life started all over again. The medication brought him back, and he's still our Trinidad!

FRANK

Trini had a very good job, and then he started to go downhill. My wife had been observing what was going on with him, but she didn't tell me for months. She kept it to herself.

When Trini's behavior began to change, I didn't want to accept that he was mentally ill. He had been the student body president in his high school, a star athlete, and a graduate of California Polytechnic State University. All of a sudden, he was acting so strangely. I came up with all sorts of explanations for his behavior. For example, Trini's work required him to audit companies. I wondered if a businessman was angry with Trini because of the results of an audit. Perhaps he had put something in Trini's drink. Or I would think that maybe the fumes of the leaded gasoline from Trini's 1955 Chevy

weremaking him sick. Or, maybe he was partying too much and we didn't know about it. For the life of me, I couldn't figure out what was going on.

Before we learned about mental illness, Bartola and I were ignorant of the facts. I didn't even know what mental illness was. I thought that all people who were mentally ill had gone through bad experiences, which made them go over the edge. I had a neighbor back in the 1950s who was real athletic. After he returned from the World War II, he just hid under cars and didn't want to do anything. We all thought that his behavior was caused by something he had experienced in the army. So when Trini was diagnosed, Bartola and I assumed that maybe he had experienced something terrible that we didn't know about. I even blamed myself for Trini's illness at first. I thought I had done something wrong.

Trini couldn't tell us what was wrong. He had to write it down. I asked him once, "Do you want help?" He wrote, "Yes, I do." As soon as I saw that, Bartola and I took him to the emergency room and from there he went to a mental health unit.

The mental health professionals began to educate my wife and me about what was really going on with our son. We went to a series of ten sessions with the doctors. We repeated this course twice because we couldn't understand it all that well the first time around. Trini would say to us, "You don't have to go." His younger brothers looked up to Trini so much that they didn't want us to take the course, either. They didn't want to believe that their older brother was so sick.

Trini's recovery has been a slow process, but he is doing well now. For myself, I have learned a lot about mental illness. Now I know that there are many different illnesses, not just one. I'm also very grateful for all the caring doctors who are doing research and finding new medications.

What really gets me upset is when researchers find a medication that works well, but there aren't enough people who need it. Then the drug companies don't want to spend the money making it because they can't make a big enough profit. This is called an "orphan medication." I call it corporate greed.

Many people won't tell anyone that someone in their family has a mental illness. They keep it to themselves and hibernate in a closet. I tell people like that to open up and let the world know. Treat the mentally ill as normally as anybody else. Don't treat them differently. I've treated Trini the same way I always did, and he's turned out beautiful.
— BARTOLA

What really gets me upset is when researchers find a medication that works well, but there aren't enough people who need it. Then the drug companies don't want to spend the money making it because they can't make a big enough profit. This is called an "orphan medication." I call it corporate greed.
— FRANK

Back row: Meland, Annie, Mike, and Jaime *Seated:* Jodi

THE CAMPBELL FAMILY

ALBUQUERQUE, NEW MEXICO

MELAND CAMPBELL / ANNIE CAMPBELL / MIKE CAMPBELL
JAIME CAMPBELL / JODI CAMPBELL

ANNIE

MY OLDEST DAUGHTER, JAIME, FIRST WENT TO COUNSELING WHEN she was in her freshman year at the University of New Mexico. My husband, Mike, and I had a sense that something was wrong, but we assumed that her emotional problems were caused by the stress of adjusting to college. We thought that Jaime simply needed some support. We had no idea that she had a serious illness.

Jaime was found wandering around the campus one night, crying and hysterical. We got a phone call from somebody at the computer center who told us that our daughter was rocking back and forth outside on the lawn. Mike and I went over to the college and brought her to the university mental health center. The doctor on call felt that Jaime was having a temper tantrum because earlier that evening she had become frustrated while working on her computer. He also felt there were dynamics in our family that encouraged this kind of behavior. He thought we were not allowing Jaime to grow up.

Jaime attempted to stay in college, but after a month or so it was obvious that she couldn't continue. She had to drop out and move back home, where I took care of her full-time. It took almost six months before she was diagnosed with schizophrenia.

Whenever I left the house to go shopping, I gave Jaime the phone numbers of friends she could call if she needed to. I always tried to have some kind of a backup system of support in place for her. I would tell Jaime, "I'm going out. If you have a problem, this is who you can call." We'd have everything all lined up. We'd even go over it and rehearse it, but sometimes Jaime was so disoriented that she wouldn't remember to call anyone when she needed help. One hot summer day I left her at home alone. Jaime knew where I was and she had my phone number, but instead of calling me, she put on three layers of clothing and a long overcoat and started walking up the street to find me. She had all these clothes on, a pair of socks, and no shoes! When I saw her, I said, "Jaime, why didn't you call me?" All she could say was, "Oh."

Jaime did some silly and scary things when she was very sick, but she always knew what was going on. It must have been terrifying for her. On occasion, she would say, "I wish

A woman psychologist told me that bad parenting, particularly by the mother, caused schizophrenia. She basically said that I was the cause of Jaime's illness! That hurt, although there was a part of me that actually wanted this to be true. If it was my fault, then maybe I could change, and Jaime's illness would go away.

—ANNIE

Jaime's illness was devastating for all of us. We lost all of our dreams, and Jaime lost all of hers. She had worked so hard at school and she knew what she wanted to do with her life. We had to let all of that go.

—ANNIE

Jaime and friends at Gould Farm

I could just black out when these things happen. I just wish I didn't have to know."

When Jaime was living at home with us, she and I had some good times. We spent a lot of time together, trying to find a way to get through what was a very difficult situation. Sometimes, it was a matter of finding practical things to do. We went to craft shows, Jaime permed my hair, and we did things we never would have done had she been in college. One year, Jaime made Christmas wrapping paper by hand using garbage bags, grocery bags, and paint. We wrapped our presents that December in the paper that Jaime had made. This was special for all of us. Perhaps, at nineteen, Jaime should have been doing something else, but that's where she was back then.

A woman psychologist felt that the close and affectionate tie between Jaime and me was inappropriate. She told me that bad parenting, particularly by the mother, caused schizophrenia. She basically said that I was the cause of Jaime's illness! That hurt, although there was a part of me that actually wanted this to be true. If it was my fault, then maybe I could change, and Jaime's illness would go away.

As a mother, I tried to do everything I could to keep my daughter out of the hospital. When I was young, my aunt had schizophrenia and I remember visiting her in a hospital. She eventually hung herself. Naturally, the thought of my own daughter in a mental hospital really concerned me.

Mike and I looked at our values and what was important to our family, and we tried to keep things as normal as possible for Jaime. We worried that if she had to be hospitalized and sleep in a room with people she didn't know, she would really flip out. I looked at this scared child of mine and thought, "She's having a hard enough time of it as it is." Mike and I had her sleep in the bedroom next to ours, so we could hear her. Sometimes I even slept in the same room with her so I could keep track of her at night.

After a while, I decided to take a part-time job on weekends because Mike could stay at home with Jaime. It was hard for me to leave her because we had grown so tight, but it felt necessary so that Jaime wouldn't become dependent solely on me.

There came a time when Jaime needed residential treatment. She moved to Massachusetts into an innovative program. At first, Jaime would call us every day. I would tell her, "Just make it to the end of the week," and we'd hang up the phone and bawl our heads off. It was hard to get out of the role of caregiver and to break away from always having to be on call.

Our younger daughter, Jodi, was a real trouper. She was the baby of the family, but when Jaime got sick, Jodi grew up real fast. She was very responsible and she understood that there was something seriously wrong with her older sister. Jaime often behaved like a five-year-old, and Jodi would literally have to baby-sit her. That was quite hard for Jodi, who was only thirteen at the time. Mike and I were so proud of her.

Jaime's illness was devastating for all of us. We lost all of our dreams, and Jaime lost all of hers. She had worked so hard at school and she knew what she wanted to do with her life. We had to let all of that go. On the other hand, there is always hope. It used to be that when people had illnesses like this, you'd put them away forever and forget about them. There are many different kinds of medicines and treatments now, so being mentally ill is not the end of the world. Jaime still wants to become a teacher, and I have the utmost confidence that she will find a way to do this. It just might not be the way she had originally planned.

Mental illness is a part of Jaime's life. She has had to accept her limitations and take care of herself, just as if she had diabetes or a heart problem. But she's still Jaime. This hasn't changed, and I don't think it ever will.

MIKE

Before Jaime was diagnosed with schizophrenia, Annie and I went through a six-month period of not knowing exactly

what was wrong with her. The doctors tried many different medications, but no one really knew what was going on. Some doctors and counselors were real good about talking with my wife and me, but there were others who were pretty tight-lipped. Maybe they didn't want to alarm us until they knew what was really happening, but not knowing was hard for both of us.

There were times when life looked bleak. I used to wonder, "Geez, is it going to be like this for the rest of our lives?" I want people to know that there may be some fits and starts figuring out the right treatment, but schizophrenia is a treatable disease. From our experience and from what we have read, we know that many people can get through it. It's not always as bleak as it seems.

When Jaime left home for residential care, it was a separation that needed to happen, but it was tough for the whole family having her live so far away. In the beginning, we had doubts that she would make it. After the first few months, we started to feel more comfortable. When we visited Jaime, we could tell that she was doing better. This helped me get used to her being gone, just as if she were away at college. Annie and I had to learn to let go, which is what everyone has to do with his or her kids. It was a natural process that we would have had to go through even if Jaime hadn't gotten sick.

I've discovered that my life is much richer because of our experience with Jaime's illness. The insights that I've had are real valuable to me. Yes, it's a struggle and it's a real test of your faith and of your ability to survive, but getting through it proves that the human spirit can endure.

JAIME

I have schizophrenia and if anybody gets close to me, they're going to know about my illness. I always say, "I'm Jaime first, but Jaime has a mental illness." It's not all of who I am, but it is definitely a part of me.

Mental illness is a part of Jaime's life. She has had to accept her limitations and take care of herself, just as if she had diabetes or a heart problem. But she's still Jaime. This hasn't changed, and I don't think it ever will.
—ANNIE

I've discovered that my life is much richer because of our experience with Jaime's illness. The insights that I've had are real valuable to me. Yes, it's a struggle and it's a real test of your faith and of your ability to survive, but getting through it proves that the human spirit can endure.
—MIKE

My boyfriend was the only person out of my entire group of friends who stood by me when I got sick. My other friends would say things like, "You're just too weird." One friend even called me a "schizoid." I had been there for them when they were failing in school or having family troubles. Then, when I needed them the most, they were gone. That was the hardest part of my journey—losing my peer group when I most needed it. For me, this was the clearest example of the stigma of being mentally ill.

—*JAIME*

When I first got sick, I remember huddling in a corner of my room, crying. Mom came in and said, "What's wrong?" And I said, "I'm scared." She asked, "What are you scared of?" I said, "I don't know. I'm just really scared." A week later, Mom and I met for lunch and she said, "I'd really like you to go see a college counselor because I think you may need some help right now adjusting to being away from home."

After I was found wandering around the campus really out of it, I did see a doctor. He told me that I was essentially an emotional two-year-old who was just throwing a tantrum. He said I needed emotional parenting from someone outside the family. I was like, "Uh-oh, that's not good." I was so pissed!

I kept having these little fits. I'd feel dizzy and then I'd fall asleep, and then five minutes later I'd wake up and say, "Hi," and then I'd feel dizzy and go back to sleep again. I ran through this cycle every fifteen minutes. One night, Mom, Dad, my sister, Jodi, and I were at a local restaurant and I kept falling asleep. Each time I woke up, my family members would still be talking with each other, but they were making sure that I didn't fall asleep in my food. It could have been an embarrassing situation for them, but it wasn't. They didn't say, "Okay, Jaime, it's time to go home." Instead, they said, "Have you finished eating yet?" This helped me feel as if I could be "me," even if "me" at the time was someone who needed twenty-four-hour care.

I used to have terrifying thoughts like, "I wonder if my cereal is going to blow up in my stomach?" Everything was so strange for me, and I know that it had to be extremely hard on my family. It was painful for me to realize that although I could function most of the time, there were times when I couldn't function at all. I wondered why I couldn't stay in control all the time. Keeping up a facade was important to me. People would think that I was doing okay, but I really wasn't.

My boyfriend was the only person out of my entire group of friends who stood by me when I got sick. My other friends would say things like, "You're just too weird." One friend even called me a "schizoid." I had been there for them when they

were failing in school or having family troubles. Then, when I needed them the most, they were gone. That was the hardest part of my journey—losing my peer group when I most needed it. For me, this was the clearest example of the stigma of being mentally ill.

For me, having schizophrenia is a warning sign that I need to take good care of myself. It's part of me, and it's a lifestyle. It's a disorder that often causes me to be out of touch with what other people perceive to be reality, but I'm not about to say that it's not my reality. I feel that it's a different kind of reality. Actually, it's a different kind of living, and a different kind of life. It's not something that you can just walk into and then walk out of. Having schizophrenia is life-transforming. This illness will be with me all of my life.

I still have hallucinations. I hear birds calling me to them and I see fingers in trees. I see four little men that I call "mushroom men." This doesn't mean that these things aren't "real" for me, it just means that other people don't see them. The "mushroom men," for instance, have been a part of my reality ever since I first saw them. They have created a little space in my life. Sometimes I feel like they're watching me off in the distance. This is probably one of the most vivid hallucinations I've ever had. The first time I saw them, I was coherent enough to know that "mushroom men" shouldn't be standing next to a pine tree. They weren't scary, but not knowing where they came from was weird. I've actually become rather attached to all of my hallucinations because they are an integral part of me.

When my stress level got too high in the past, I tried to bite through my skin, bang my head on the cement floor, or pull out my hair. There were times when I would get violently angry. My mom would have me smash a pile of newspapers or do something physical to help me stop my behavior. Now I have to be careful to monitor how much stress I'm under because otherwise I might hear voices telling me that I'm a rotten person.

During all the years that I was really sick, my family helped me feel like I was still a person and not a burden or some-

Jaime at Gould Farm with a friend

I still have hallucinations. I hear birds calling me to them and I see fingers in trees. I see four little men that I call "mushroom men." This doesn't mean that these things aren't "real" for me, it just means that other people don't see them.
—*JAIME*

one who needed to be "fixed." They believed in me even when I didn't believe in myself. Mental health professionals definitely didn't believe in me. In my experience, it's uncommon in the mental health field for a patient to be treated as a person.

My mom and I have shared our lives together and we are very close. At times, that made things more difficult, but we've always had a good, solid relationship. She didn't make me go away from home when I first got sick, and that was very important to me. She did five-minute checks on me even when I was in the bathroom. If I stayed in there for too long, she would come in and say, "Are you doing okay?" What kept me out of the hospital was my family, especially my mom.

After a while, I felt it was time to leave home and learn to live more independently. At the age of twenty, I felt pressure from our society to be in school or at work, and not to live at home with my parents. I wanted a place where I could belong, a place where I could rediscover who I was. At the same time, I wanted a place that needed me. It was very hard to leave my family, but this was something I needed to do in

During all the years that I was really sick, my family helped me feel like I was still a person and not a burden or someone who needed to be "fixed." They believed in me even when I didn't believe in myself.
—*JAIME*

order to get well. I decided to go into a residential treatment program.

The staff there believed in me. They told me, "You're going to have to work thirty hours a week on our farm." This is close to full-time work in the "real world." It's probably one of the highest expectations you'll find in any mental health program, which was really important for me. It was also a strong draw for me that I would be living with forty other people who were also mentally ill. Soon after I arrived, I wrote to a friend and said that things were great because everyone there was like me. He wrote back saying that it must be boring. He didn't understand my need to identify with other people who were facing the same struggles as I was.

After I began to improve, I entered a transitional program in Boston. I took a job tutoring a couple of boys in math. I was reviewing algebra on the train on my way home one morning. I had a card that allowed me to get on the train for half-price, but I had forgotten to bring it that day. When I asked for a discount, the conductor asked me where my card was. When I told him I had left it at home, he asked me, "Are you a student?" I said, "No, I have a mental disability." He said, "People with mental disabilities don't do algebra." I felt like saying to him, "Excuse me, but I can do algebra! In fact, I can do calculus!" I was so irate that I wrote a letter to the editor of the *Boston Globe,* and it was published.

Our family can laugh now about what happened to me years ago. It's a genuine laugh. It's like we're saying, "Yeah, that was kind of silly." Even so, no one in my family devalues my experience or forgets how hard it was.

Since I've been on medication that has helped me, I'm much better than I was even a few years ago. My goal is to speak at high schools and colleges about my illness. I want students to ask me their scariest questions about mental illness. I also want to help train mental health professionals about what it's actually like to be sick. They may have a lot of book-learning, but that doesn't mean that they really understand how schizophrenia can affect someone. I want to help them understand that.

JODI

When my sister, Jaime, first became ill, I was in my last year of middle school. I was scared all the time because I never knew what was going on with her. None of us in the family knew what was wrong. At first, I tried to isolate myself from my sister. I didn't want to be around her because I didn't know what was going to happen. I struggled with every single emotion you can think of.

One day, I walked into the kitchen and found Jaime lying on the floor. When I called out her name and tried to get her up, she didn't move. She was totally out of it. I went and got my mom, and we all ended up spending the entire day at the hospital.

At first, I didn't want my friends to come over when Jaime was at home because I didn't know how they would react to her. I didn't want them to think that I had a psycho sister! When I told my best friend about my sister's illness, she was too frightened to come over when Jaime was there. I had a lot of friends who felt like that in the beginning.

A few years later, Jaime came to one of my eighth-grade science classes and talked to my classmates about her illness. I was worried that all my friends were going to look down on me, but they didn't. That year, I became very close with most of them, and I was eventually able to tell my best friend everything. She would sit and listen to me just like a therapist. This felt really good. It helped to have a group of friends who were willing to hear about Jaime and not just say, "Boy, your sister's crazy."

If Mom and Dad wanted to go out at night, I would stay home with Jaime. I was baby-sitting her as if she were my five-year-old sister. And she wasn't five! Jaime was nineteen and I was only fourteen. I'd get scared because I didn't think I could let her out of my sight. If she started walking toward the door, I would say, "Jaime, where are you going? Why are you going out?" There were a couple of times when I had a lot of trouble keeping her inside, but I always made sure that she didn't leave the house. My parents always gave me the phone numbers of friends I could call if I needed help.

In the beginning, I was mad at Jaime for getting sick and for taking my parents' attention away from me. I felt that her illness had ruined my life. In fact, I had no life at all, because when I wasn't at school, I was at home making sure Jaime was okay. I got to go out sometimes, but it wasn't enough for me.

I tried to distance myself from my family because I was mad. I was probably mad because I didn't know what was going on. I have to admit that it was kind of a relief when Jaime left home for residential treatment. It was enjoyable at first, but after a while I began to miss her. Our relationship improved when Jaime got better. I feel like she's my big sister again.

I want people to know that mental illness is not as bad as some people make it seem. If you're dealing with it in your family, you need to share your feelings and experiences with friends. You need to be open with them. It's much harder otherwise. It's not good to lock everything up inside you.

MELAND

My husband and I didn't know anything about mental illness before our granddaughter got sick. It was something totally foreign to us. At first we were both in total denial. Jaime had so much potential that we couldn't believe this was happening to her. We could see that she was not her usual self, but we tried to blame it on other things, including her boyfriend!

My husband and I didn't talk about Jaime with our friends. We mostly just talked between the family and ourselves. I started to read everything I saw in newspapers and magazines about schizophrenia, and gradually, I realized that we were wrong. Jaime was indeed mentally ill, and her problems were not something that would simply pass in time.

Before Jaime got sick, she used to drop by my house quite often and spend the night. After she became ill, I didn't see nearly as much of her. When she left home for residential treatment, I was glad that she would be getting the help that she really needed. We wrote each other often, and her letters to me were so good that I've saved all of them.

In the beginning, I was mad at Jaime for getting sick and for taking my parents' attention away from me. I felt that her illness had ruined my life. In fact, I had no life at all, because when I wasn't at school, I was at home making sure Jaime was okay. I got to go out sometimes, but it wasn't enough for me.
—JODI

Back row: Andrew, Bill, and Debbie *Front row:* Jake and Luke

THE McDOWELL FAMILY

WALTHAM, MASSACHUSETTS

ANDREW McDOWELL / BILL McDOWELL / DEBBIE McDOWELL
JAKE McDOWELL / LUKE McDOWELL

JAKE

SOME PEOPLE SAY THEY ARE "OBSESSED" with things like baseball. I have obsessive-compulsive disorder, and I used to be obsessed with germs.

I wouldn't let anyone other than my family members touch me. If they did, I would lick my hands and rub a certain spot on my face until it was raw. At home, I used to sit on my mom's lap and line my legs up perfectly with hers so that I wouldn't touch the furniture. I did this because I was afraid of lice. When I did go to school, I wouldn't sit near anyone because I was afraid they had lice.I was also scared of chemicals. I couldn't even walk on grass because of the fertilizer. My brother, Luke, had a Power Wheels car and he would ask me to play with him in the backyard. I would just say, "You go ahead without me."

There was a time when I wouldn't go to school because I couldn't put my socks on. The creases in them felt like rocks. My parents had a system where I would get a poker chip worth a certain amount of money for each time I would wear them. I could save up to buy myself a toy. It was bribery. It was like, "I'm going to wear my socks today so I can get paid."

The kids at school didn't understand me. One time I overheard a girl say, "What's with Jake? He licks himself!" When she asked me why I did that, all I could answer was, "I don't know." Kids gave me a real hard time at school. One of my classmates picked me up and said, "Look, he's trash," and then he put me in a garbage can. That really hurt my feelings.

I didn't talk much about my thoughts and obsessions because I didn't understand them. I couldn't figure out what was wrong; I was just being me. After a while, I thought I was completely insane. I would slam my head against the wall and say to myself, "I'm crazy and I want to die. I hate my life." When I was finally diagnosed with OCD, the doctor told me that I had a mental illness, but that I wasn't crazy. I was a bit happier after hearing that. I still worried and obsessed, but my fear that I was crazy was gone.

I am real open about having OCD. After I was diagnosed, I spoke about my illness to my class at school. A couple of other kids were diagnosed with it, too. It helped them to meet someone else who had OCD.

I met one kid who had OCD really bad. He wouldn't let anyone play with his LEGOs or go into his room at all. I asked him, "What are your obsessions and what do you need help

Kids gave me a real hard time at school. One of my classmates picked me up and said, "Look, he's trash," and then he put me in a garbage can. That really hurt my feelings.
—*JAKE*

When I was finally diagnosed with OCD, the doctor told me that I had a mental illness, but that I wasn't crazy. I was a bit happier after hearing that. I still worried and obsessed, but my fear that I was crazy was gone.

—*JAKE*

Some parents say, "I don't want to put my kid on medication and I don't want anyone to know about their illness." I tell them, "If your kid had diabetes, wouldn't you give him insulin? Wouldn't you tell his teachers that he might have a diabetic reaction in school?" In my view, keeping OCD a secret is absurd.

—*DEBBIE*

with?" He let me play with him and he let me go into his room. He trusted me. Now we hang out together.

I've gotten much better because I'm on medication and in treatment. My life was screwed up before, and I wasn't a happy person at all. Now I have a lot of things to live for. When I grow up, I want to help other people who have OCD.

DEBBIE

My husband Bill and I thought that our son Jake was trying to drive us nuts. His behavior made no sense to us at all. When Jake refused to put his socks on, I'd think, "Of course he can put his socks on if he wanted to." We had seen him wear them before, so it felt like Jake was simply being stubborn. It was awful.

I would often find about thirty pairs of socks discarded on the floor of Jake's room. One night, I put a pair on him while he was asleep. I figured that if they were on his feet in the morning, it would be okay when he woke up. But he took them off in the middle of the night.

Jake's teachers thought that his behavior was caused by some big family problem. They even suspected that we were abusing him, so they called the Department of Social Services. That sure was delightful! Here is this family that doesn't have a clue what's going on with their kid, and on top of everything else, the school thinks we're abusive parents. We saw a family therapist, and even he thought that there must be something strange going on in our home.

Many pediatricians and even mental health professionals aren't well educated about childhood OCD. It took over a year for Jake to be diagnosed, even though his was a classic case. He was eight years old before we finally found a psychologist who diagnosed him correctly. Bill and I felt better immediately because what Jake suffered from had a name. However, we had never heard of OCD. For all we knew, it could have been something that would send Jake away for a hundred years. The psychologist explained OCD to us and

then he told Jake, "It's my job to know what 'crazy' is, and I would tell you if you were. You aren't crazy."

The day after Jake was diagnosed, he went to school, sat down in his morning circle, and announced, "You know how I've been acting strangely? Well, I've just found out that I have something called OCD." Jake's doctor helped him understand from day one that there was no reason to feel ashamed of his illness.

As Jake got better, he wanted to feel like a normal kid. He was in school one day, and his class was dissecting a sheep's brain. Without even asking Jake, the teacher gave him a pair of rubber gloves so he wouldn't have to touch it. None of the other kids were given gloves, and this made him angry. He thought, "Why did she give the gloves only to me?" The teacher was trying to help him, but she should have asked Jake first. She just thought, "Oh, this is the kid with the germ thing." She could have given gloves to all the kids so none of them would think, "Oh, Jake is that 'different' child."

I wanted to make sure that Jake fully understood his diagnosis, so I suggested that the two of us write a book for children about OCD. Jake dictated it to me, illustrated it himself, and we sent it to the Obsessive-Compulsive Disorder Foundation and they published it. Ever since then Jake has been speaking at mental health conferences about OCD. He has even appeared on national television shows like *Inside Edition*.

I do a lot of education and outreach about OCD. I often talk to parents who don't want to acknowledge that their kids have this illness. I also speak to parents who know their kids have OCD but who are afraid to reveal the diagnosis to their children's teachers because they're so fearful of negative repercussions. Some parents say, "I don't want to put my kid on medication and I don't want anyone to know about their illness." I tell them, "If your kid had diabetes, wouldn't you give him insulin? Wouldn't you tell his teachers that he might have a diabetic reaction in school?" In my view, keeping OCD a secret is absurd.

Jake's struggle with OCD is no different than if he had diabetes or needed glasses. OCD is a biochemical imbalance in the brain. It should be treated no differently than any other illness. We are very open in our family, but sometimes people will still say, "What's that thing your kid has? CBS?"

In school, kids are taught to speak out against racist comments when they hear them. When people make bad comments about mental illness, like, "You're a crazy psycho," no one says anything. When I hear comments like that, I call people on it.

I know that many people turn to their clergy when times are difficult for them. I am Jewish, and as a child, the joys and rewards of my religion were focused on family and home. I think that's why my search for support during Jake's tough times was not focused on a rabbi or a synagogue. I had the sense that a rabbi would be no different than most people I encountered . . . though well meaning, ignorant of OCD. And rather than finding truly useful support, I would just be explaining the illness for the thousandth time.

As a Jew, I talked to God many times during Jake's struggles, but I didn't think that a trip to the temple or a chat with the rabbi was going to make a difference in our lives. I wish I could say that wasn't the case, but for me, my solace came in more private prayer.

Jake's psychiatrist is Jewish, and on several occasions he has suggested to Jake that finding a personal expression of faith might be helpful to him. The psychiatrist never said this in a "pushy" way, but simply as a suggestion to help Jake deal with his issues.

I sometimes wonder where this illness came from and whether anyone in my extended family might have had OCD. People can have some of the symptoms of OCD in a milder form. For instance, my dad has always been funny about how his clothes feel when he wears them. He's very particular about certain things and he's a true perfectionist, but he doesn't have any rituals that interfere with his life. My mom was also treated for depression, and supposedly there are links between OCD and depression.

My husband and I run a hotline for people with OCD who just need to talk. One guy called me in tears from his

Andrew, Bill, and Debbie *In air:* Jake *Center front:* Luke

office one day. He told me that his wife wouldn't admit that she has a problem, but she has contamination fears and makes him take off all his clothes before he enters their house at the end of each day. He said, "I don't want to go home from work anymore, and I don't know what this is doing to my three-year-old child." I gave him the name of a social worker and suggested that he get some literature on OCD for his wife to read. Hearing about this kind of situation just rips your heart out.

I thought that we had won our battle with mental illness when we got Jake back to a "normal" life. Bill and I found ourselves fighting this "bully" all over again when our youngest son, Luke, was recently diagnosed with bipolar dis-

In school, kids are taught to speak out against racist comments when they hear them. When people make bad comments about mental illness, like, "You're a crazy psycho," no one says anything. When I hear comments like that, I call people on it.
—DEBBIE

If people were to meet Jake, they would have no idea that a couple of years ago he couldn't even leave his room. It's important for people to understand that a diagnosis of OCD is not a death sentence. It doesn't mean that you will have to spend the rest of your life locked up.
—BILL

order. It's been very tough to garner the strength to go through this struggle all over again.

The medical side of Luke's illness hasn't been too rough because we've been through most of it before. The treatment he's received from his teachers, however, has been exceptionally difficult. Luke had to leave school four months ago, and he's being tutored at home. His principal has been wonderful in terms of keeping in touch with him and getting him the services he needs, but his teachers have not called, sent a note, or communicated with him at all. I told the principal that if Luke had a broken leg, pneumonia, or cancer, he would have been inundated with letters, cards, or phone calls. Luke has been ostracized because he's at home with a mental illness. This is a nine-year-old child who is hurting.

The people who supposedly care about Luke have sent him the message that they don't really care about him at all. I'm sure this happens all the time because of the stigma of mental illness, but when it happens to my kid, it makes me furious. I speak out against stigma so that maybe this type of thing won't happen to the next child. Sadly, I'm afraid there will always be a "next child."

BILL

From the time he was a toddler, Jake always insisted on wearing skinny pants. They had to be absolutely skin-tight and without any tags inside or he wouldn't wear them. When he was a young kid, there were so many nights when he couldn't go to sleep. What we called "bad thoughts" would keep him awake. All I could do was yell at him. I thought Jake was simply a stubborn child and that it was just a kid thing.

It got so bad that Jake and I had a code word to use when we were over the top with frustration. Jake would say the word "peanut" to me, and this would mean that he was completely fed up, and then I would say the same word back to him and he would know that I was fed up, too. Then we were able to give each other some space.

When I had to travel a lot for work, the doctors thought that my being away so much was causing Jake's strange behav-

iors. I canceled as many trips as I could, and I told my colleagues why. When there was an actual name for Jake's disorder, I was relieved. I could tell the folks at work what my son actually had, and even if I sometimes got a blank stare in return, I could explain it to them. Schizophrenia might be hard to understand for some people, but if you talk to them about someone who is obsessive about germs, they get it. They can identify with that.

Jake used to ask questions constantly about all sorts of things, and there were times that he never let up. For instance, he would ask, "Is Grandma going to be all right?" I'd answer, "Yes, she's going to be fine." Then Jake would say, "But she's got a heart problem. Are you sure she's going to be all right?" And I'd say, "Well, yes, the doctors are taking good care of her and she'll be okay." Then Jake would ask, "But is she going to die?" This type of questioning was unrelenting. When our son was finally diagnosed with OCD, Debbie and I began to understand that much of his repetitive questioning was simply because Jake was seeking reassurance. We learned not to get sucked into it. Realizing that this was a symptom of OCD helped all of us. We finally knew that we weren't nuts, that we weren't bad parents, and that we didn't have a dysfunctional family.

Our family was on a talk show once, and a guy in the audience thought that Debbie and I were just being permissive parents. He said, "Send Jake to me and the stick will stop him from doing this stuff." As if you could beat the crap out of a kid and that would stop his symptoms!

Jake is a normal kid. We've been through some horrible times, but he's fine now. His OCD is under control, and it's no longer interfering with his life. It's just a part of who he is. The obsessive side of his personality might even serve him well in the future.

If people were to meet Jake, they would have no idea that a couple of years ago he couldn't even leave his room. It's important for people to understand that a diagnosis of OCD is not a death sentence. It doesn't mean that you will have to spend the rest of your life locked up. Medication and behavior therapy can work.

Not everyone has as positive a reaction as Jake did to therapy and medication, but OCD can usually be treated. When you're slogging through the horrible you-can't-get out-of-the-bedroom days, it's hard to believe that things will ever get better. But they do get better. I think people need to hear that.

Debbie and I tell Jake that he's strong, that he's beaten this bully, and that he did it himself. Sure, the medicine helps and the doctors gave him the tools to fight his illness, but he has worked very hard to get better. Now I can say to him, "Are you obsessing, Jake?" And he can answer, "Yes." He knows what he has to do, and he does it.

ANDREW

I don't remember my brother Jake as "the OCD sufferer." I really remember very little about when he was sick. I knew that something was wrong with him because he was going to all these doctors. I don't remember exactly when I learned that he had OCD. It seems so long ago now.

I remember getting dragged to therapy, which I didn't like because it just went round and round in circles and Jake wasn't getting any better. He was screaming all the time, and his lips were raw from all the rubbing and licking. I withdrew because Jake's behavior was too painful to watch. I didn't deal with it. I couldn't talk about my brother with any of my friends. I just stayed up in my room and read my history books.

When I was in middle school, I got sick of all the negative crap I was hearing about mental illness. I said to myself, "Well, you know about this, so teach what you know." I chose obsessive-compulsive disorder as the topic for my class project. I explained OCD by saying, "You have to check the stove a hundred times to make sure it's off because you think that your house might burn down if you don't. Most people may check once, but if you have OCD, you might do it a hundred times or more."

I began my report on OCD with an exercise for the class to do. I asked them to write a few words with each letter shaped absolutely perfectly and everything laid out exactly right with the exact same amount of space in between each letter. Then I set a strict time limit to complete the assignment. This showed my classmates how frustrating having OCD can be.

When I mentioned to my class that OCD is a mental illness, a student lashed out at me. He started screaming, "No, it's just a nervous disorder! I can get five psychiatrists to say that it is." I knew he had OCD, because he had already told me. He wasn't keeping it a secret; he just didn't want to admit that he had a mental illness.

LUKE

Do I remember when Jake was having problems? Do I ever! He annoyed me because when we played outside with our wooden swords, he wouldn't step on the grass if it had fertilizer on it. Jake also kept me up at night. He kept rolling around in his bed trying to find a comfortable spot, and it was hard for me to fall asleep listening to this. We had to go to bed at different times so that I could fall asleep first. I also remember his problems with socks and that he wouldn't hold chemicals in a bottle even if it was plastic. I remember when he learned to hold a bottle of Drano for thirty seconds.

I know that OCD is a chemical imbalance in the brain, but I don't really understand it. I do know that if you take medication it will eventually calm you down. OCD is like a wave when it comes ashore. It gets lower and lower and it will stop. Well, for some people it will stop and for some people it won't, but it will be better in a couple of years for many people.

I just found out that I have bipolar disorder. It's hard for me to stay in one mood. For example, on my birthday I started to cry when I saw all my presents. I was happy and sad at the same time.

It's hard to be homeschooled. I miss my friends. I'm taking new medicine now and I'm doing a lot better. I hope I'll be able to go back to school. Sometimes I think I'm a different species than other people.

OCD is like a wave when it comes ashore. It gets lower and lower and it will stop. Well, for some people it will stop and for some people it won't, but it will be better in a couple of years for many people.

—*LUKE*

Paul

PAUL GOTTLIEB

NEW YORK, NEW YORK

PAUL

BIRTHDAYS WERE ALWAYS MARVELOUS DAYS FOR ME, and they were enthusiastically celebrated in my family. As my fortieth birthday approached, however, I was dreading it for no particular reason. It would have been normal for me to plan a big celebration, but I just didn't want to do it that year. It didn't feel right. My natural emotions were being affected by something I didn't quite understand. In retrospect, I now know that I was experiencing the onset of a severe depression, which lasted from 1974 until 1981.

I was in what I thought was a happy marriage at the time. I had two wonderful sons. I had a successful career in publishing, which was moving along well. Of course, I had certain frustrations, but they were the normal frustrations of everyday life.

I began to have certain experiences that were very strange and puzzling to me. For example, one day, I was talking to someone at work about a close colleague of mine and I just burst into tears. I remember thinking how odd that was. It wasn't the sort of behavior that was characteristic of me at all.

In thinking about my past, I don't remember demonstrating any symptoms of depression in my childhood or even in my adolescence, when all sorts of difficult things can happen. When I started college, I had just turned seventeen. I

was an erratic student, and eventually I got thrown out for being a completely irresponsible character. I had been pretty well-behaved at home, but when I hit college I got a little wild. I was kind of immature and I was drinking and partying more than I should have. But I don't think that was about depression. I think it was about busting loose.

During my college years, I had a roommate who battled with mental illness. He tried to commit suicide and wound up being hospitalized. I was fairly supportive of him, but his struggles didn't resonate or call up any echoes within me at the time. As a matter of fact, until I was hit by depression myself more than twenty years later, I was rather intolerant of people who were unable to deal with their own difficulties. I was the kind of person who would urge someone to pull up their socks and just get on with it. One of my closest friends struggled with depression for years, and I used to get very annoyed with him. I couldn't understand why he was making such a fuss about what I saw as no big deal.

After leaving college, I came home to New York City and got a job. The next year, I went back to school and studied political science. After I graduated, I decided I would go into the diplomatic corps. I'd always had wanderlust, so the idea of travel intrigued me. I went off to Europe and visited a girl I had known at college whose father was an American diplomat in Italy. I spent a week with her family and realized that

Over time, the simplest, most practical things became extremely difficult. Little things became major decisions. For instance, I had trouble picking out a tie in the morning, or I would look at my messy desk and it would terrify me. I would think, "How can I go on like this? How can I go on so ineffectively and inefficiently?" I was worried that everyone would find out I was an empty shell and everything was falling apart inside me. I won't say that every day was like that, but the frequency of days like that accelerated.

— PAUL

diplomacy couldn't be my career even though I had passed the foreign service exam. Things have changed in the diplomatic service since then, but at that time it was an absolutely WASP profession. Here I was a Jew without any money, which were not exactly qualifications that were going to get me very far in the foreign service.

I returned to New York and got a job as a literary agent at a major firm. Then I was drafted and shipped off to Europe, where I had an absolutely marvelous time. I lived for a while with a girlfriend in an army barracks in Stuttgart and worked in a unit called the Seventh Army Symphony Orchestra and Soldier Shows Company. I was just a private, but I was bouncing around, traveling all over Europe. It seemed a blessed life.

In 1959, I left the army and went to work for the American government in Russia as a translator and guide for the American National Exhibition in Moscow. It was the first time that there were a large number of young Americans in Russia, and we were showing the Russians the American way of life. I met an American girl who worked at the exhibition, and a year later, we were married. We went back to New York, where we lived the happy life of young marrieds. Good things were happening.

Many years went by, my wife and I had two sons, and all of a sudden it was 1974 and I was about to turn forty. That was when depression began to take over my life. It happened gradually, almost as if it were two steps down, one step back up. It wasn't a direct descent into something; it wasn't like plummeting out of a window.

I've always been a very proud person and a competent, take-charge kind of man. When my depression started, I was running a company in a rather authoritative way. People expected me to be the leader, and I was comfortable with that role. But all of a sudden, things became much more complex, confusing, and difficult for me. I've heard that depression sometimes hits people who seem particularly competent. When you begin to experience depressive periods, there's a sense of guilt and a worry that people are going to discover that you're not the strong person you seem to be. You become riddled with self-doubt.

In the first couple of years of my depression, I grappled alone with disturbing symptoms. I had this feeling of implosion, of everything being sucked in, of the walls closing in. It was as if there were plates in my head, similar to tectonic plates that are always moving and are not together as they should be. I began to lose my ability to easily manage the realities of my life.

Over time, the simplest, most practical things became extremely difficult. Little things became major decisions. For instance, I had trouble picking out a tie in the morning, or I would look at my messy desk and it would terrify me. I would think, "How can I go on like this? How can I go on so ineffectively and inefficiently?" I was worried that everyone would find out I was an empty shell and everything was falling apart inside me. I won't say that every day was like that, but the frequency of days like that accelerated.

I would enter dark periods of sleeplessness, of constant inchoate worry about nothing specific, and of increasing inability to function. My wife was somewhat aware of what I was going through, but I talked to no one about it in detail, including her. I was a responsible, self-sustaining person who did everything for myself. I didn't need anybody to help me. I was the strong one in the family, the "giver" in our marriage. In fact, I was the one who helped everyone else all the time. In a pinch, people called on me. I was reluctant to share my feelings even with my closest friends.

I kept hoping that I would feel better. Whenever my suffering would go away for a week or so, I'd say to myself, "I'm fine. I'm going to be just fine." But over the next four years, matters continued to grow worse. The darkness gathered, and I began to lead a sort of double life. Externally, I "acted" the part of myself in my personal and professional worlds. I knew enough of what my normal behavior had been like before I got sick to act it out. And I wasn't such a bad actor!

I finally got to a point where I was feeling so bad that I turned to my dearest friend, Jeffrey Kramer, who was a brilliant Freudian psychiatrist. I called him up one day and said, "I have to talk to you," and we went out and had lunch. Jeffrey was somebody with whom I had always shared all the adventures of my life, both positive and negative, and he knew more about me than anybody else, except perhaps my wife. Of course, he was upset when I told him what I had been wrestling with for so long. He felt he should have noticed what was happening to me, but I was such a good actor that even Jeffrey hadn't been able to see it. Certainly, he hadn't been looking at me with a professional analytical eye. His reaction was to put me in touch with a well-known Freudian analyst in New York. I saw this psychoanalyst on and off from 1976 until 1981.

Before I began therapy, I felt that I knew myself quite well in all the dark interstices of my mind. Although there were a couple of insights and cathartic moments in therapy, there were no surprises and nothing that I didn't already know. I already understood my relationship with different members of my family, and I sort of understood who I was and what I was about. My treatment didn't touch the core of my increasingly depressive condition. My analyst was baffled. He didn't understand my case. We examined this and that, but unresolved psychological issues didn't seem to be the cause of my problem. It was caused by something else, and neither he nor I knew what it was. Looking back on it all, psychoanalytic treatment was not a totally useless exercise, but it really had nothing to do with my particular kind of depression.

Jeffrey, in consultation with my analyst, would prescribe rather primitive medications for me. None of the drugs I tried helped me very much, and I felt increasingly worse. I sometimes suffered side effects such as sexual dysfunction and dizziness, so I stopped taking these drugs on a regular basis.

There were very few days when I couldn't make it to my office. Working was the one thing that somehow kept me moving, and I had to earn a living. As bad as it was sitting in the office and faking everything, it was better than just sitting at home and staring at the walls around me. But there were days when it was literally almost impossible to get dressed to go to work. I was frightened.

Because I'm in the field of art book publishing, I have always led a gregarious and sociable business life. You go to exhibition openings, you have lunch with people, and you attend meetings. I was finding these kinds of activities more and more difficult to do. There was a time at work when I would literally hide at lunchtime. I would buy a newspaper, go to a hotel, find the men's room, lock myself in a stall, and pass the hour reading the paper in order to stay out of the way of other people. And then I would have to make myself go back to work. I couldn't wait to get home at the end of the day and crawl into bed.

When my psychic pain became unrelenting, I began to have suicidal thoughts. At a certain point, you weigh the misery that you feel against the positive aspects of your life. I still had a wife and two children whom I loved, but it was as if the balance was shifting the other way. The desire to relieve myself of my pain became more and more intense. All the reasons for living—my sons, the rest of my family, my friends, my enthusiastic engagement with the world around me—were now outweighed by excruciating mental suffering. The pain had simply grown too great.

Even though I loved my sons, I began to think they would be better off without me because I was going to become a terrible burden to them. I never actually tried to commit suicide, but I played "toreador" with buses. I would cross the street in the most dangerous ways possible, sort of tempting fate to knock me down. When I was in my office, I would sometimes sit at my desk, stare out the window, and contemplate jumping.

Things got so bad that I could no longer hide the intensity of my condition from my wife, but she wasn't capable of dealing with it. Instead, she was frightened and angry and couldn't talk about it with me. I suppose from her perspective she felt cheated out of what she had learned to expect from her husband, which was a certain kind of behavior and a certain kind of reality. Our marital life was disintegrating.

The weird thing was that through all of this I was still running companies. In the earliest days of my illness in 1975,

Paul

I was the CEO of a company called American Heritage Publishing Company. Then I founded the U.S. branch of a British publishing company, a very successful enterprise, which I ran until 1979. In 1980, I was invited to come to Harry N. Abrams Inc. as editor in chief, and I accepted that post. It was a big job with new responsibilities, and yet, I was getting sicker and sicker. In spite of everything, I was still able to perform well enough to be appointed president of Abrams within the year. I felt as if I was digging my nails into the palms of my hands, continuing to function with a sort of stubborn determination.

Things continued to get worse for me emotionally. One day, I literally couldn't get myself to go to work. Instead, I rented a car and drove from Manhattan up to West Point and just walked around. I felt lost and separated from life. It was

ghastly. When I was driving back home to the city, I stopped on the New Jersey side of the Hudson River just above the George Washington Bridge and stood at the edge of the cliffs overlooking the river. I don't remember if I was seriously thinking of hurling myself down. I don't even know if I could have done it. But I started screaming hysterically. Screaming. Just screaming into the air. I was desperate.

I don't know how, but I managed to get through that fall and winter at work. By this time, I was the CEO at Abrams as well as the publisher. When you think about it, it's really crazy that you can be that sick and fool everybody. It was an act; a very effective acting job. Sometimes people who appear competent and accomplished find it very difficult to admit that they've become weak and disabled. If you have the means, as I did, to fake it, well, you fake it. You're in denial. But you don't even know exactly what you're denying.

On April Fool's Day 1981, I went to work as usual. By noon, I was in such a state that I knew I had to leave the office and that I couldn't come back. The pain had grown too great, and I was having constant suicidal thoughts. I was breaking down. I started walking across Central Park toward my analyst's office, and I remember feeling as if I were walking barefoot on broken glass. Every step I took was excruciatingly painful.

When I got to my analyst's office, I hammered on his door, and of course he was startled to see me show up there without an appointment. He took one look at me and immediately called my wife. He told her that I was having a complete breakdown and needed to be institutionalized. After my wife got off the phone with my analyst, she got a call from a friend of hers. My wife blurted out what was going on with me. By a miraculous coincidence, it turned out that this friend had a relative who was a psychopharmacologist. I was able to get an appointment to see this doctor the very next morning.

In the meantime, my analyst just wanted to get rid of me. He was finished. He couldn't do anything more for me. Whatever he'd been doing was like applying a Band-Aid to a severed aorta. I crawled out of his office, went to a phone, and told my wife that I would meet her at Jeffrey's house. I managed to get myself to his place, and I just lay down on the floor. My wife came to get me and somehow we made it home.

The next morning, I met with the psychopharmacologist, a knowledgeable scientist and sympathetic doctor. He gave me hope for the first time in six years. He explained that I had an endogenous depression, meaning that I was depressed for physiological rather than psychological reasons. He told me that he would find the right combination of drugs, which could cure my illness and end my misery. These were his words to me: "You're going to be fine. Your sickness is not unlike diabetes. It's as if something is wrong with your blood. I don't know what it is yet, but I'm going to find your insulin."

I told the doctor, "I can't go on. I've got to call my company and resign. I can't take the pressure of it. I can't cope anymore. I need to be institutionalized." He replied, "No you don't. Don't make any decisions yet. Do not resign." I decided to take his advice, but I didn't go back to the office. The doctor and I cooked up the notion that I had developed diverticulitis, and that I was going to be hospitalized for observation. No one except my wife was allowed to visit me.

I spent about a week in the hospital, where I sank into a kind of oblivion while my doctor experimented with various antidepressant drugs. He explained that with mental illness, you can't just draw a blood sample and say, "Ah-ha! You need this, or you need that."

People have many different kinds of experiences with mental illness. My doctor posited that at one end of the scale there are those who are suffering from psychological problems generated by relationship or parenting issues or whatever, and at the other end are people who are purely physiologically ill. I seemed to be in the latter category, because at the end of the period of experimentation the doctor finally mixed the right cocktail of medications for me. Miraculously, I was "myself" again, and after that, I never experienced a moment of the old depression.

I was basically cured and I went back to work. It was as if the mist had cleared and there I was again. During all those years of my illness, there was the reality of my internal mind and then there was my external performance in the world. The combination of drugs somehow brought my interior and exterior selves back together. There were no more tectonic plates shifting around in my head.

If I hadn't found a doctor who cured me, I would have died. I think I would have killed myself. Fortunately, human beings can't really remember pain, but we can sort of put ourselves back in the memory of the emotional state we were in. As I look back now on that time in my life, it was unbearable. When life becomes unbearable, people kill themselves. Even though there are all the reasons in the world to stay alive, there are also overwhelming feelings that you can't go on anymore. It's like drowning. You are suffocated by them.

Once the doctor felt that I was in good shape, he took me off all my medications and prescribed a very small dose of lithium as a maintenance drug. He thought it was necessary, and I accepted his decision. It was amazing to feel better again but at first it was scary, because I thought, "Will this cure last?" My doctor warned me to be on guard. "You could get into a depressed period again or you could become manic-depressive," he said. "You must not forget what happened to you."

After twenty-nine years of marriage, my wife and I divorced. I know that my illness had a destructive impact on our marriage, although her behavior and interests had a great deal to do with it as well. If she were a different kind of person, it might have turned out differently, but because my illness was so very frightening for her, she was not supportive of me in any important way. Instead of being responsive, my wife pursued her own interests even more vigorously than before, and her career became more and more significant for her. She and I never really faced what was going on with me, partly because neither of us understood it for such a long time. I certainly didn't understand it. She was neither able to understand it, nor was she of a mind to try very hard. Her escape from my illness was to escape from our marriage.

After my marriage ended, I soon fell in love with the compassionate, smart, and beautiful woman who has been my wife ever since. I've never been happier. I fell in love with her the first time we went out, and by our second date, I thought I had to tell her about my depression. After we came home that evening, I put out a bottle of port, most of which I drank, and I told her everything. Fortunately, she has a Zen-like kind of spirit and she accepts things as they are.

If I were to distinguish between two major groups of people, there are those who have endured some kind of adversity and there are those who haven't. The latter spend most of their lives worrying about how they will survive if something bad happens to them. If you are in the large group who has suffered some adversity, whether physical or mental, you may learn, as Roosevelt said, "There's nothing to fear but fear itself." In fact, there's nothing to fear but death itself. If you can make it through a really bad time and survive, nothing can get you.

I decided a few years ago that it might be time to go off the small maintenance dose of lithium I had been taking for sixteen years. I went to my psychopharmacologist and said, "Enough already. I feel great." I had felt great for years. That's not to say that I couldn't feel sad or depressed. I had lived through the death of a father I adored and the death of a marriage that I thought I was in for life, with appropriate feelings of grief and sadness that eventually evaporated. You go back to your life. It's not unlike the attack on the World Trade Center on September 11. You feel horrible, then you wake up one day and say, "I don't have an option. I have to keep on going." At any rate, my doctor said he didn't recommend going off lithium, because the fact was that nobody knew what could happen. He advised me not to fix something that was working so well. He thought that if I went off it, another problem might be triggered and he might not be able to pull me out the same way he had before. So I continued to take the medication.

In 1997, my publishing company was sold to a French corporation. I was under tremendous stress and I felt anxious and exhausted. All of a sudden, I developed a variety of symptoms, including blurred vision, insomnia, lack of physical coordination, mental confusion, slurred speech, and hand tremors. I even lost twenty-six pounds in six weeks. It was a nightmare. At first, I assumed the symptoms were related to the pressures of work. Well, they weren't.

Over the years, it never would have occurred to me that the small dose of lithium I was taking might be poisoning me. My doctor had never told me that when you take lithium your blood levels have to be monitored on a regular basis. I wasn't told that lithium is one of those drugs with a narrow "window" of effectiveness: Too little is useless, and too much can kill you. It's a very volatile drug. For whatever reason, in the spring of 1997, I had a severe toxic reaction to the lithium. Very few people had taken it every day for sixteen years, so it may have been a cumulative effect, or maybe my body chemistry had changed.

Perhaps I should have taken more responsibility for my own physical state. If you take any drug, obviously you should question its power, the reasons for its prescription, and insist on knowing all possible side effects on both a short- and a long-term basis. You should be warned to watch for specific symptoms and deal with them as soon as possible. I realize now that my childish faith in all doctors is a product of a different time.

By the time my blood levels were tested, I had lost two-thirds of my kidney function. As soon as I stopped taking the lithium, I recovered completely and began to feel better physically than I had in years. Fortunately, going off lithium did not plunge me back into the dark night of depression.

I haven't been on any medication since 1997. None. Zero. So far, so good. Who knows, I may be sailing through a benign period and then in a year, I may just crash off the face of the earth. But I will be watching out for this and I will not forget what it felt like to be so sick.

When I was ill, I would look at my friends who had some kind of spiritual and religious faith and envy them because

I haven't been on any medication since 1997. None. Zero. So far, so good. Who knows, I may be sailing through a benign period and then in a year, I may just crash off the face of the earth. But I will be watching out for this and I will not forget what it felt like to be so sick.

—PAUL

I saw that it gave them a certain solace or comfort. And yet, I've never been drawn to religion and I don't have any sense of a need for it. I grew up in a totally secular family. My mother, who is going on ninety-one, is an atheist. She came out of the old leftist philosophy that says, "Religion is the opiate of the masses." Although we're Jews, I grew up without any feelings of identification with any kind of religion. I do believe in the basic human tenet of "Do unto others." That makes sense to me. And I do have a belief in the possible goodness of men and women, and in the joy that life and the world can bring us.

My struggle with depression has made me available and sympathetic to people who are troubled. I can see them a mile away. There's an artist, a young woman, who came into my office one day with a project to discuss. I looked at her and asked, "Are you all right?" She just fell apart. It turned out that she had been struggling for years with depression and she couldn't talk to her parents about it. I was the first person who had identified something that was crushing her. She went on to get treatment, although she still struggles with the demon of depression.

People have learned an awful lot about mental illness in the past twenty years, but I still think it is highly stigmatized in the business world. When I was running Abrams, we were a subsidiary of a $4 billion corporation that installed a personnel policy for screening new employees for alcohol and drug abuse. I argued with the medical director of the corporation, saying, "I don't care if people are abusing drugs or alcohol, the real root cause for many of them is probably depression. They're self-medicating as a way of trying to mask something they don't understand. That is the problem you should be focusing on." When I disagreed with him about the company's policy, he had no idea that I was suffering from depression myself.

People say that more man-hours are lost in the work environment from unidentified and untreated depression than from all other illnesses combined. Where I worked, if you had a heart problem or cancer, you'd never find a more sympathetic, supportive group of people and medical programs. But for years I had to be secretive about my mental illness because I was in control of millions of dollars of the corporation's assets, and I couldn't run the risk of having my judgment mistrusted.

This past year, I was interviewed by the *Wall Street Journal* for an article about executives who suffer from depression. When the article ran, I didn't get any negative responses. Instead, I received many letters and messages applauding what I had done and telling me, "Yes, I have suffered from depression, too, and have never spoken of it." Some of the most amazing responses I've had were from colleagues and friends whose stories I never would have guessed. They were "acting" at the same time as I was "acting," and we never knew about each other's suffering.

The statistic I've heard is that something like 30 million people in this country suffer from depression, and thirty thousand people a year commit suicide. There's a huge population suffering from this illness.

In the business environment, it's very important to spread the notion that even people who are in the grip of this disease can and do function. Most people who are successful aren't likely to talk about a history with mental illness. First of all, there's the stigma. Second of all, there's a kind of hubris in one's success, and one doesn't want to redirect attention to something that is the antithesis of success. It's important to realize that mental illness is not a failure; it's a life horror.

Life is weird, isn't it? I had dinner last Saturday night with an old friend. We'd been through our "life wars" together, and I said to him, "Life is just a big soap opera. We're in it. We still have parts. And we can't change the channel."

People say that more man-hours are lost in the work environment from unidentified and untreated depression than from all other illnesses combined. Where I worked, if you had a heart problem or cancer, you'd never find a more sympathetic, supportive group of people and medical programs. But for years I had to be secretive about my mental illness because I was in control of millions of dollars of the corporation's assets, and I couldn't run the risk of having my judgment mistrusted.

—PAUL

Pearl, Audrey, and Theodora

THE JOHNSON FAMILY

COMPTON, CALIFORNIA

PEARL JOHNSON / AUDREY JARRETT / THEODORA JOHNSON

PEARL

BABY, FIFTY-ONE YEARS I BEEN IN THE PRISON SYSTEM. From the age of sixteen, I was in and out, in and out. The jails didn't have all these mental health programs they have now. When you got out of prison, they just gave you a few dollars to catch the bus. Nothing else.

Speaking as a black woman, my story begins back in the old days of the forties when I was coming up in the countryside near Shreveport, Louisiana. All we knew was how to sing praises and pray. When my family moved to California in 1943, I was an "A" student and I played music.

During World War II, blacks weren't allowed across Main Street in South Central, which is what my neighborhood in Los Angeles was called. Blacks was on this side, and the whites was on that side. The late mayor of Los Angeles, Tom Bradley, was a police sergeant back then. He would gather all us black kids after school and take us to the park on the white side of town. We would practice track, volleyball, and basketball. I was good at sports because I was from the country. In Louisiana, we ran barefooted all through the fields, and I

knowed how to play baseball with a broomstick and a tennis ball and how to fish with a string for some fatback. All this played a big part in pruning me. But when I came out to California at the age of thirteen, I got culture shock because you couldn't run the streets barefooted and you had certain limitations. Even so, Sergeant Bradley saw the potential that I had. According to him, I was going to become the first black female track star. I began to run track at the Coliseum and won a lot of medals and trophies.

I made my mistake by not telling my mama that I was in an after-school athletics program for kids in my neighborhood. I didn't tell her about this because I didn't think it was that important. So when she found out what I'd been doing, she took me to juvenile court on July 6, 1946, and told the judge that I was incorrigible. I winded up being incarcerated for the first time.

I hadn't done nothing. I had no boyfriends. I hadn't had no sex. I was only thirteen and I was still a virgin. I wasn't contaminated. The judge sent me to a place that was like a summer camp where there was only white girls. They was rich movie actors' kids who had gotten in trouble.

People believing in me made me start believing in myself. I began to believe that I was somebody, and that I was the most precious thing on this earth. No matter what anybody else says, I'm the greatest! And that's where I'm at today.

—PEARL

I didn't last long there because every time something went wrong in that place, I was accused. I used to have to get on my hands and knees and polish and wax the cobblestones. I became a slave.

A lot of my troubles started in this place. I sure cried a lot there. I had always been told by my mama that if you sing praises and pray, you can get out of your troubles. I did a lot of singing and praying, and I still winded up depressed. I think the staff called me "Major Depressed," which caused them to give me all sorts of medications that they don't even make anymore. To keep you quiet in those days, they gave you medication and knocked you out for two or three days at a time. I don't call that treatment. I call that mistreatment!

I had talent. Everyone in my family has some kind of musical background in them, and I had it, too. This place killed all of that. Being in there was a hardship for me, so I ran away when I was sixteen. I hitchhiked with another girl, and we got as far as New York State. I was arrested for white slavery because I had crossed state lines with a white girl who was only thirteen, a minor. We both got sent to jail in Utica, and then we were transferred to St. Anne's work convent in Albany.

By the time I was seventeen, I was emotionally sick and without no plans. I returned to California, where I got pregnant with my daughter Theodora. She was born when I was eighteen. I tried to go back to school after she was born, but it didn't work out. I became homeless and just lay around because I had no self-worth and no self-esteem. My mother wasn't involved in my care because I never did go back home to live with her. I had some more children, and my brother took them in. I took no responsibility. I couldn't do nothing for my children.

I was out there homeless on the streets, selling, shooting up, sleeping in abandoned cars, and all that stuff. I had a mental illness, and I was trying to medicate myself with all those different kinds of dope. From there I started into the adult prison system. The judge gave me a twelve-year sentence the first time. I was out only a short while before I went back in. When I came out many years later, it was with a "gold seal,"

where the state of California says, "We're through with you."

In prison, I was officially diagnosed with depression. They put me on Thorazine, and every kind of "zine" you can think of, because they didn't know what they was doing. They just tried to keep you quiet and they made you work hard. That was what it was like in prison for me. Did I get therapy in there? You got to be kidding! I just learned about therapy recently.

When I got out of prison, my life was hell. I did the same things all over again. I tried to medicate myself with heroin, morphine, and cocaine. When it got really bad, I had to make money to buy drugs, so I started stealing and stuff like that to maintain my habit.

I began living in housing for the mentally ill called a board-and-care facility. It was almost like being in jail. You were told when to get up in the morning and when to go to bed at night. You were under lock and key. If it was raining, you had to spend the day outdoors except during mealtimes. The doctor who came to see me there diagnosed me with schizophrenia. I kept running away from the board-and-care. I've got barbed-wire cuts on my legs to prove it.

I was introduced to Oasis House, a mental health program run by black people. They understood me. I started working there cleaning toilets. The staff there taught me how to handle money and how to cook. I had forgot everything because I was a street person. I had spent years being homeless; pushing shopping carts, selling empty bottles, eating out of garbage cans, stuff like that. The folks at the program nurtured me back.

When I was doing the program at Oasis House, it would take me two hours to ride the bus to my doctor's office. I wouldn't be in there five minutes before my doctor would write the prescription. He never even would look up at me. I would have to turn right around, and I'd have missed the bus back home. I'd have to wait at the bus stop an hour or more for another bus because I didn't have the funds to travel in taxis. It posed a hardship to me until I switched over to a doctor closer to my home.

What turned my life around was love, which I wasn't getting from my own family. People at Oasis House began to believe in me. They told me that I was worth something, and they began to tap the talents inside of me. For instance, I didn't know I could write poetry or that I was an artist. I didn't know any of this. But now I do. People believing in me made me start believing in myself. I began to believe that I was somebody, and that I was the most precious thing on this earth. No matter what anybody else says, I'm the greatest! And that's where I'm at today.

When I was sixty-three years old, I started working for a mental health association in Los Angeles in a program called Project Return: The Next Step. It was run by clients as a self-help program, and I was hired as its first administrator. I didn't know nothing about nothing, but they took me anyway. I believe the only reason they took me on was because I'm black and I knew how to stand and say, "Enough is enough." I was the backbone of the program. It was hard, hard work, and I didn't know how to ask for help. Everything I accomplished came through blood, sweat, and tears.

I began working for the Los Angeles County Department of Mental Health in Continuing Care, and I still work there. My job is helping mentally ill people who are going through some of the same things I went through. I visit lots of people and offer them services. I take them to get their benefits and walk them through the social service system. People in the system nowadays don't have to go through as much as I did, because there are some decent programs to help them.

I go see clients at the "Twin Towers," which is what the jail in Los Angeles is known as. This jail is often called, "the mental health capital of the world." It's a jail system full of almost nothing but mental health people. They ain't got no place to put the real criminals. Many of them are there just for jaywalking!"

The prison system is what I call the revolving door for the mentally ill. My work is to try to get people who are mentally ill out of jail, because most of them need psychiatric treatment. It's going to take a lot of work to change the sys-

tem. We've got a director now who's structuring all kinds of programs, but we got these old senators who don't like to change. There are always these stumbling blocks because they keep throwing stuff in the way. I hope someday that we can empty the "Twin Towers."

As part of my job, I see clients at board-and-cares, group homes, and hospitals. I also see clients who are getting ready to transition into independent living. If I can, I mentor them just like I was mentored at Oasis House. I teach them how to manage their money, how to buy groceries, and how to take public transportation.

I used to run from the sheriff and the police. They was mean to me when I was in jail, ooh whoooo! Now when they need something from the Board of Corrections, the sheriff calls on me. Ain't that funny how you can turn around and become the only person who can help them?

I sit on so many important mental health boards, even state boards, because I'm honest and I tells them how I feel. People say, "If you don't want Pearl to tell you how she feels, don't put her on this committee. Don't put her on this board."

I travel all over now, speaking about mental illness and the prison system. I've gotten lots of awards. I've been all over the world telling my story. When I speak, sometimes my story is so strong, the people in the audience don't need to ask questions. In fact, most people can identify with what I'm saying.

A few weeks ago, I gave a talk at the World Assembly for Mental Health in Vancouver, Canada. When they first invited me to come, they called me "Dr. Johnson," but I'm not no doctor. I wanted to tell them that, but my grandson said, "Well, Grandma, you've got enough credit and awards to be a doctor." When I gave my talk there, I gathered everyone in the room into a circle so if someone needed to cry, there'd be a shoulder to cry on.

At the World Assembly, there were no clients other than me on the stage. There were lots of politicians, lawyers, and doctors trying to find ways to get us mental patients committed against our will. There is another solution: You don't

Involuntary commitment don't help nobody. I was committed all the time, and it didn't help me. Let me ask to go to the hospital if I need it. Don't just come along and pick me up and take me there. Provide mental health services for me and I won't have to go through that!

— PEARL

have to put people on the back wards of the hospitals. There's a solution, even if it ain't nothing more than love.

Involuntary commitment don't help nobody. I was committed all the time, and it didn't help me. Let me ask to go to the hospital if I need it. Don't just come along and pick me up and take me there. Provide mental health services for me and I won't have to go through that! They are trying to pass a bill in California to stop involuntary commitment, but it ain't been going anywhere for two years. I work with legislators trying to get them to change the laws.

I'd like to see a lot of the people who are still on skid row get out. A lot of them are businessmen who used to have good jobs and homes and cars and babies. Their companies close, and they exhaust their bank accounts and stuff. They start living out of their cars until the banks repossess their cars. Then they lives in a cardboard box with their children. I'd like to see the mental health system take a look at these situations, and not so readily put these folks in jail. It's a trauma to have the rug pulled out from under you. I'd like to see the system help them and be kind to them, and give them treatment if they are mentally ill, and not just use them for money profit. And that's what a lot of the system is. Everybody got a job, but ain't nobody trying to help nobody.

I still got my doctor, and I still got my Haldol and other meds. I thought I was secure, but I just got a thirty-day notice to move because the landlord wants to raise the rent up to $459. Here I'm making $525 every two weeks. How can you survive on that?

If I come home late at the airport after one of my trips, I'm scared to go home alone. Even when I get off after my four hours of work each day at the jail at 11:30 A.M., I go home to my apartment and I don't come out again till the next morning. You can all call it depression or whatever, but I ain't hardly crazy.

Theodora's my baby, my firstborn. All the rest of my children have died. My granddaughter Audrey is Theodora's daughter. Both of them are mentally ill and have been in jail. Audrey just got out of prison last month.

I haven't settled in with the church, but Theodora has. Now that Clinton, no, what's that boy's name? Bush. Now that Bush has signed the bill for faith-based charity, that's Theodora's thing all wrapped up in a neat package. She prays. She reads her Bible. She has a couple of friends and they do a prayer service every morning. I know that's Theodora's gift. I prophesize on her. My gift is being a warrior. I'm a fighter. I'm going to tell you how it is. Either accept me or lock me out.

With all the wrinkles and everything, I still think I'm fine! One day last week this boy drives by me and turns his car around and yells, "Hey, Pearl, you want a ride?" I was trying to see who is this who got the nerve to turn around and come after me like that. Turns out it was one of the guys from where I work. I said to myself, "Pearl, baby, you still got it, girl!"

THEODORA

My mother, Pearl, didn't raise me up herself, because she was in jail when I was a kid. My auntie and then my uncle and his wife raised me. My auntie would take me to see my mother in the prisons. I went to see her quite often.

I've been in and out of jail myself for prostitution. The prison staff calls folks like me who are mentally ill "Dings." They say, "There goes that 'ding' again." In 1975, I was facing fifteen years in prison for drugs. I got blessed and the judge sentenced me instead to one year in a residential drug rehab program. I chose to stay there for a second year because I needed more help learning how to cope with everyday life. I got out in 1977, and I've been out ever since. I lived for quite a while on skid row and I learned a lot being down there. I met a lot of people and I saw for myself that the jailhouses are becoming shelters for those who are mentally ill.

I've been in a few different mental hospitals. I was in a public hospital for about a week in the seventies and they put me on Thorazine. Around two years ago, I was in a private hospital through my job insurance. I can't remember my diagnosis. I just know that I don't like being around a lot of people. I prefer to stay in my room watching television by myself. I've always been a loner except for spending time with my two brothers. I've always been protective of them, but they're gone now. They died. It used to be the three of us against the world. I was an angry kid, but I don't like talking about it.

I still isolate myself. I stay in my room unless my friends coax me to go out with them. Even when I do go out, I am still in my own world. I don't have to be giddy and happy. I try to maintain myself by just being in my own world. It's safer that way. Even when I go to work, it's safer not to say nothing or tell anybody anything, because they can use it against you.

When I was growing up, my uncles and aunts were up in age and they didn't understand the situation as far as me and my brothers were concerned. One of my aunts was very negative and she downed us. She told us we weren't nothing and that we were always going to be nothing. It was like I had to fight to try to show her that I was going to be something. I finally gave up and said, "Forget it." I was just going to be what they told me I was going to be. Nothing.

I have medication for my mental illness, but I still can't sleep at night. It's been a long time since I've been able to sleep and not feel guilty of anything. I'm always feeling guilty of something. I've been through a lot. Some people I've confided in say that I should be very bitter. I was messed with the first time, when I was only two or three years old, by a man who was painting my house. He was stirring paint, and I was kneeling down near him. I had a diaper on and he put his hands in my diaper. I remember that as if it was yesterday. I was also molested by one of my uncles and my "play-uncles" when I was a kid, but I never told anyone about this because I was afraid that my brothers and I would get separated if I did. When I finally talked about it in a mental health program, I was already a grown woman. I had to be beat up or get drunk or be on drugs to have sex because I was so against anybody touching me. I got pregnant with each one of my four kids when I was high on alcohol or drugs.

Pearl, Audrey, and Theodora

I've had knives held to my throat and guns put to my head. I've had to jump out of cars. A man once picked me up hitchhiking. He made me get down on the front seat of the car and he had a gun to me. I was praying and asking the Lord, "Is this where I'm going to die?" Then he drove me way up in the hills and pulled out a knife and told me to strip. He made me walk down Mulholland Drive in Beverly Hills naked. I was walking down the street and some white folks helped

One of my aunts was very negative and she downed us. She told us we weren't nothing and that we were always going to be nothing. It was like I had to fight to try to show her that I was going to be something. I finally gave up and said, "Forget it." I was just going to be what they told me I was going to be. Nothing.
— THEODORA

When I was able to work, I had to hide my mental health history so my employers wouldn't know that I have a mental problem. When they find out stuff like that, they are quick to let you go because they don't want any problems at their facilities.

— THEODORA

me and took me down into Hollywood. I had to hitchhike home from there.

There are all these mental health programs now, but all most of them care about is how many heads they can get into their programs. Just statistics is all you are to them. Some folks need more than going to a group therapy session or to a counselor who just sits there and looks at them, saying, "Uh hunnnh, yeah, okay." When the session is over, they're still in the same state of mind as they were when they got there. They need a doctor or someone who can identify with them and give them answers. Even when you go to some of these mental health doctors, they only have ten or fifteen minutes to deal with you and then they're sending you on your way, and you still haven't got what you needed. The people that need the help aren't really getting what they need.

If you mess up in some of these programs, you're banned for life. That's another thing that's really off, especially at the residences for the mentally ill downtown. You're banned for the least little thing, not necessarily because you're on drugs or alcohol. If you defend yourself with the management or talk to the manager wrong, he will have a meeting with the higher-ups and have you banned out of his facility for the rest of your life. There's no more coming back. You're out of it. How do I know this? I experienced it. One time, I got into a confrontation with a manager. He let me sleep in the place that night, but the next day he told me I was out of his program for the rest of my life. He told me to move out that same day. This isn't hearsay; it's what I experienced.

When I was doing better, I went to work as a legal clerk. I worked in the California Superior Court for seven years doing criminal cases. I did the depositions in Sacramento, and when I came to Los Angeles, I worked in the victim witness assistance program—first for the D.A., and then at the public defenders office. People said to me, "Now you're on the other side of the table." Me, a person who came from being in jail, was working in the courts! I've been fortunate getting good jobs, because I didn't even graduate from high school. I didn't go past tenth grade.

I worked until I had hand surgery for my carpal tunnel a year ago. I also had a semi-breakdown, so I'm still off work. I'm on disability. I'm going to have to learn how to live on eight hundred dollars a month from where I was making pretty good money before. I got to hurry up and find something that's going to help me, because if you don't meet a certain criteria for housing, you lose. If you don't meet a certain criteria for food, you lose. You try and get light and gas, you lose. They always have something to stop you from trying to make it. They put you in a place, but they don't want to help you. All they want to do is keep you in that place until you give up and you end up sleeping in a cardboard box just to be able to eat. That's what happens in the system and in my life.

When I was able to work, I had to hide my mental health history so my employers wouldn't know that I have a mental problem. When they find out stuff like that, they are quick to let you go because they don't want any problems at their facilities.

When I worked in the court system, one time I had a problem arise. I practically had a nervous breakdown, and I lost my job. So here I was, trying to work every day and be there and give my all, and they still find something to let you go on. It's rough.

I get help from a couple of friends I've had since I was fourteen. My friends have hung in there with me over all the years and they keep me kind of halfway sane. They became real close to me because they had a situation, too. Their mother was an alcoholic, but I didn't know that back when we were kids. We've talked about it as grown-ups, and I've said, "No wonder we've stayed close friends over the years." When I got into trouble, one of my friends came to visit me in jail. Although she has never lived the type of life I lived, she still came to see me. After my hand was operated on, she came to my apartment to make sure I was eating. She brought me cases of water and juices. If I needed her now, she'd be right here.

My daughter, Audrey, just got out of jail. I help her in all kinds of ways. When she was in jail and she had problems, she would call me and say she needs money. I'd rush and send the money to her, and then she'd say to me, "Ain't you got nothing but one hundred dollars?" That hurt. I'm helping her now by having her stay here with me. But there ain't no, "Thank you, Mama." Nothing. I've done everything I could possibly do for each of my kids, but I'm still the bad guy.

I'm fifty-three years old now, and I always have to keep my mouth closed. Everyone else can make their comments and say what they want to say and it's okay, but as soon as I open my mouth and say anything, I'm totally wrong. It's been like that since I've been a little kid. It still goes on today. I don't think it will ever change. I been getting the short end of the stick ever since I can remember. It's hard, so I stay in my room. I don't want to be bothered. All I want to do is to keep to myself. If I die in there, well, just let me die by myself.

I carry a lot of guilt. If I drop a piece of paper on the ground, it bothers me if I don't pick that paper up. I carry that type of guilt every day. It haunts me, and that's why I can't sleep. Little things like that haunt me, and then when I discuss them with my friends, they say, "You didn't do nothing wrong." I need to get reassured. I've been wrong so long, I never know when I'm doing right unless somebody tells me, "Theodora, what you did was right. That was a good thing you did." And I'll say, "Oh, okay." Then I feel a little better. But when I'm told by my family, "No, you're wrong. You should keep your mouth shut. Don't say nothing. Let them other folks talk," it bothers me because I can't defend myself. That's why I need counseling, so I can weigh out my rights and my wrongs.

I've been needing deep-down therapy ever since I was a kid, but I've never gotten it. At the mental health center, you only talk to your counselor in a group. I think I need more of a psychiatrist, more of that kind of one-on-one treatment instead of just going to a group thing. I need to be able to talk without breaking down in tears. I've had to hide things that I went through. I tried to kill myself many times, but no one knows that. In my situation, help isn't available, because I don't have the money. I'm in limbo.

AUDREY

I was seeing a doctor back when I was a little girl in elementary school. The doctor told me that I'm bipolar-schizophrenic.

I wound up going to prison way back when. I was always in the streets running, doing drugs and stuff. Just doing my own thing. I got incarcerated in 1996. I got out in 1998 and I wasn't out a good week before I did something stupid and went back in. So I consider myself ain't never really being out till April 2001.

They don't do nothing to help you in jail. They put you to the side and the doctors will see you when they can. My mother and my grandmother called the mental health people at the jail so often that they finally seen me. The counselor told me, "Your mother just called and da da da da . . ." I told the counselor, "Well, I wouldn't have to call home and complain if you guys would do what you are supposed to do." Then I said, "I'm in a state of depression right now. My roommate done told you guys that, but you ain't doing nothing about it. What does it take to get help from you? If I killed myself, then you guys would be like, 'Oh, we should have listened to Audrey.'" After I told the counselor that, the staff took all my clothes and put me in a padded cell all by myself with just a sheet. Well, not even a sheet, but a little cloth thing because you can't have blankets, sheets, or clothes or nothing. If you're suicidal, you've got to be naked.

When I was suicidal, the doctors took me off my meds. They told me, "You don't need the medication. You just need to grow up." I thought, "What kind of place is this?" It's crazy. The whole time that I was in jail, nobody there did nothing to help me. I think that's why I was so crazy in there. I didn't give a care. I was fighting everybody. I went through a lot of days of depression up there in prison.

There were a whole lot of other women in jail with mental illness, too. The officers would sit and laugh and crack jokes about us, saying, "Look at them. They're crazy!" They didn't listen to us about our mental problems or even about our physical problems. If someone was lying in their bed and

They don't do nothing to help you in jail. They put you to the side and the doctors will see you when they can. My mother and my grandmother called the mental health people at the jail so often that they finally seen me.
—AUDREY

When I was suicidal, the doctors took me off my meds. They told me, "You don't need the medication. You just need to grow up." I thought, "What kind of place is this?" It's crazy. The whole time that I was in jail, nobody there did nothing to help me. I think that's why I was so crazy in there. I didn't give a care.
—AUDREY

Once upon a time I had dreams and hopes. In a sense I still do, but I don't know if I'll be able to live up to them.

— AUDREY

complaining to the guards about their heart, the guards used to get an attitude and tell them, "It's nothing but indigestion." Next thing you know, that person be dead as a doorknob. Straight dead. Anything go wrong with me, I was afraid they'd let me die and then call my family a month later. They don't do nothing to help you.

I had a special name for the white folks in jail. Instead of saying, "Honky," I'd call them "Keeblers." It was just a word I would use if one of them would piss me off. I wouldn't let them know I was talking about them, but other black people would know that I was referring to white people. I've met lots of respectable, nice, and kind white people since I got out of jail. They say, "Hi, Audrey, can I help you with something?" Whew, this is new to me.

My grandmother Pearl's motto is, "Don't throw away the vision just because the plan fails." When I was in jail, she wrote me a lot of letters. In every letter she sent me, she wrote her motto. She knows that I've had a whole lot of visions, but my plans have always failed and I'd get in trouble. But just like Grandma says, "Don't throw the vision away if the plan fails." If someone else told me that, I wouldn't believe it. But if she says it, I'm going to believe it.

My grandmother sent me a list of all of her awards and I let everyone at jail read it, even the police, my psychiatrist, and my psychologist. My grandma is my girl! She's there for me, and when I'm in my times of trouble and problems, she talks to me. My grandmother has achieved a whole lot. She's come a long way. I keep any article in the paper that pertains to her, because she's the one! She's on the top of the world. I don't keep anything about nobody else because they're not important to me. I ain't proud of anyone else.

Wherever I go in the mental health system, everyone knows my grandmother. I say, "You guys might know my grandmother, Pearl Johnson," and they all do. They say she goes to meetings and that she's on lots of important committees. She's topnotch. She helps everybody who's messed up.

I listen to the church a little bit, but nobody can help me but me. I can't help anyone else, not right now. My grandmother helps a lot of people. She did jail time and was an addict, and she turned out to be a totally different person. My grandmother did a complete turnaround. She's changed. She's speaking in public. She gives me hope.

Once upon a time I had dreams and hopes. In a sense I still do, but I don't know if I'll be able to live up to them. My grandma always tells me, "You can do it no matter how old you are." My dream has always been to have a daycare center or be a foster parent, because I love children. I love them to death. I can hang with them all day. I'm like a kid myself.

I don't have any kids of my own, because I've always done what I wanted to do. I'm just cool. I'm just me. I'm just the one. I don't need any added luggage on me. I'm cool like I am. Whoever don't like it, oh well.

The way the world is going now, sometimes I'd rather be in jail than out here. Too much stress out here. Period. You get booted out of jail and you have nowhere to go, what you going to do? You're going to result back into your old ways. If I go back to jail again, I go up for life because I'm a "three-striker." Three strikes and you're out. I will never come out again.

I don't want to do life in prison. That's all that I focus on because there sure are a lot of things I would like to do. I be antsy, itchy to do them, but I know where it's going to lead me. Before I get ready to make a move, I say to myself, "Damn, if I do that, I'm going to get a life sentence." One part of me says, "Do it. You'll get away with it." Then another part of me says, "No, there's your life sentence." So I'm listening to this voice right now and staying out of jail.

My psychiatrist has been helping me forever. He ain't stopped. The mental health people work with me. I can call on all of them whenever I want to talk to them. They have this little new thing they got going, this hotline thing. You can call them and there's always somebody there on-call. Even if my case manager isn't there, somebody else will talk to me until they find her, and once they find her, she comes over or she calls me back.

My little sister, Tracey, likes to check on me every day. She calls me up and says, "How you feeling? You doing all right today, Audrey? I know you just getting out of jail and I want to make sure you all right. I know you been going through some problems and I just want to make sure everything is fine for you. Is there anything I need to do? Take you anywhere? Do anything for you? I don't want you to get in no trouble." I'm like, "I'm fine, Tracey. I'm fine." Another sister calls me all the time, and I talk to my brother once or twice a month. He don't call me like my sisters do. My sisters like to get me on the phone and talk and talk and talk. I'll be like, "I'm tired." Then my sisters will say, "Unh-unh. Nope. You're getting antsy, so we're keeping you on this phone. It's getting late and you have no business going out." They want to keep me safe in the house. They don't want me to get in trouble again.

Since I been out of jail, I ask nobody for nothing. I'm not going to ask for help, because you get it thrown back at you. I just asked for something recently, and I ain't heard the last of it. I been having my own means of support, doing whatever it is I do to get by. And no, I'm not comfortable and yes, I'm unhappy, but I got to live like this for a minute. Eventually I'll move out of my mother's place and be on my own. I might still be miserable, but that's me.

Fred, Penny, Joe, and Claire

THE FRESE FAMILY

<u>HUDSON, OHIO</u>

FRED FRESE / PENNY FRESE / JOE FRESE / CLAIRE FRESE

FRED

I WAS DIAGNOSED WITH PARANOID SCHIZOPHRENIA when I was only twenty-five years old. For the next ten years I was in and out of various mental hospitals. I was told many times that I was insane, and I was given little hope that I could ever lead a dignified or reasonably normal life.

Today, I am the Director of Psychology at Western Reserve Psychiatric Hospital, a state hospital in Ohio. Ironically, I used to be a patient in the Ohio State mental health system. Traditionally, it has been taught that you don't recover from schizophrenia, that it is a degenerative brain disorder. I was told over thirty years ago that the symptoms of schizophrenia only get worse, not better. The thing is, people do recover, but because there is such a stigma about mental illness, people who get better often are reluctant to acknowledge that they have ever been sick.

My first breakdown occurred when I was an officer in the Marine Corps, responsible for the security of atomic weapons at a naval air station in Florida. It was a stressful job, and I felt under considerable pressure. After nine months on assign-ment there, I began to believe that enemies of our country had hypnotized certain officers and that they were planning to use their power to threaten our national security. Having "uncovered" this threat, it occurred to me that the best person to share this information with would be the psychiatrist at the hospital on the base. When I went to see him, he seemed very interested in what I had to say. After listening to me carefully, however, he informed me that I would be staying in the hospital. I was escorted through a ward and into a padded room with no furniture. The door was locked behind me, and I was left all alone. I knew, of course, what had happened. The psychiatrist was under the control of the enemies! I was sure that I would be shot and killed.

Within a week or so, I was transferred to Bethesda Naval Hospital in Washington, D.C. Upon arriving at Bethesda, I was taken to a large "secure section" in the officer's psy-chiatric ward. Before long I met with another navy psychi-atrist. In the course of talking with him, I mentioned that, among my other duties, I had been the mail officer for our unit. He became very interested in the use of the term "mail." He explained to me that my use of the term "mail," which

I fly a lot, and in the past, my fellow travelers would often ask me, "What do you do?" I would say, "Well, I give talks." They'd ask me what my talks were about, and I would say, "Schizophrenia." That would end the conversation right there. Zip! Just a few years ago, people didn't know what to say. Now, it's different. People are much more willing to talk about mental illness.

— Fred

nia. I am an advocate for people with this illness, and I have written many articles about my experience with it. I've also appeared on several national radio and TV shows. When I'm interviewed, it never ceases to amaze me the number of times the interviewers themselves have grown up with schizophrenia somewhere in their families.

I fly a lot, and in the past, my fellow travelers would often ask me, "What do you do?" I would say, "Well, I give talks." They'd ask me what my talks were about, and I would say, "Schizophrenia." That would end the conversation right there. Zip! Just a few years ago, people didn't know what to say. Now, it's different. People are much more willing to talk about mental illness.

On one trip, a passenger followed me off the plane all the way to baggage claim. He kept going on and on. Apparently, he had never talked to anyone about the fact that his mother has schizophrenia. When he realized that I was listening to him, he poured his heart out to me.

I still have to take antipsychotic medication, and I try to avoid stressful situations. Without these drugs, I would be back on a locked ward. With the help of my family and coworkers, I'm now able to know when my thoughts and behaviors are becoming abnormal. You really need someone else to tell you that you're beginning to get a little "schizzy." Several times a year, I have to stay home from work, increase my medication, and do what I call "cruising the cosmos," when I just sit and watch images that are like daydreams. I stay up late and weave intricate ideational relationships, often involving numbers and colors. After a few days of singing, dancing, and eating raw acorns, I return to a fairly normal life once again.

Knowing that there is a strong genetic component to mental illness, I was not totally surprised when our daughter, Claire, began having emotional difficulties and went on medication. Although I had gone public about my own mental illness, Penny and I were hesitant about whether or not to be open about Claire's illness. She has severe depression and was among the first in her age group to take psychotropic medication.

One psychiatrist told me that he thought Penny and I should keep quiet about our daughter's illness. He said it would be a "Faustian bargain" to do otherwise. If we went public about Claire, she might regret this when she got older. The choice was not easy for us to make—whether we would go on hiding in the shadows, or whether we, as a family, would just stand up and say, "Hey, we're not ashamed of this." Clearly, that's the choice we made.

PENNY

When Fred and I were graduate students together, we developed a friendship and saw each other daily. Friends would caution me and say, "Watch out for Fred, he's divorced." I thought, "Well, who cares?" I wasn't interested in a romantic relationship at all. After all, I was a nun living in a convent!

I began to notice that Fred was real slippery when it came to any sort of personal stuff. He would change the subject if I asked him any personal questions, and he certainly never told me about his divorce. I began to wonder why he didn't talk about it with me, since we didn't have a romantic relationship. One day I said to him, "You never talk much about yourself." Fred agreed, and replied, "I'll talk about myself, but not today. Tomorrow." So we met the next day, and he said, "Let's go for a walk in the woods." I was feeling smug, because I was certain that he was going to reveal that he was divorced. I had my response to him all ready. I was going to say, "What possible difference could your divorce make in our relationship?"

After Fred and I had walked for about an hour, I could tell he was very uncomfortable. I finally said, "Look, why don't we just talk now?" We sat at a picnic table and, instead of talking about his divorce, he started talking about being in the Marine Corps and guarding atomic weapons, and then he talked about having a breakdown. When I heard the word "schizophrenia," I had trouble breathing. I got very light-headed, and my chest got real tight. I thought, "Oh, my God! I have just walked an hour into the woods with a man who is telling me he is insane!" Both of us were very shaky when we walked back to the car. Fred had made this big revelation, and I didn't know what to think. We didn't talk all the way home.

My sister was studying nursing, and she was doing her psychiatric residency at the time. I immediately got her on the phone and asked her, "What should I do? Fred just told me he has schizophrenia!" She replied, "Well, is he sick now?" I said, "No, I don't think so, but of course you never know about these things." She said, "Well, then don't treat him as if he were sick." So my friendship with Fred continued.

As time went on, I decided that I needed to end my friendship with Fred. It had become inappropriate for me as a nun to have this close a relationship, since it was becoming clear to me that Fred and I were falling in love. I talked about this with a wonderful nun I knew. I told her, "I've developed a friendship with this man and I can't just give it up, because there's a complication. He will think that I don't want to be friends with him because he has schizophrenia. I have to find a way to end it in a kind way." She said, "You know that you must give it up." And I said, "Yes, I know that, but I want to be very careful how I do this."

When I told Fred that I had to end my relationship with him, he answered, "Okay. Well, let's just moderate it." I said, "I can't do that! We can't moderate it. We have to give it up." After talking about this for a long time, we agreed to end it completely. When we said good-bye to each other, I thought, "Good. Now I'll be at peace." But I was a wreck! Just a wreck! I was doing the right thing, but I wasn't at peace at all. And that's when it occurred to me that maybe I wasn't meant to give Fred up. Life without him was unthinkable. So things went from there, and here we are, still enjoying our marriage of twenty-four years.

All four of our children have varying degrees of depression and they have all been on antidepressants. Our daughter, Claire, has had the toughest time of it. She was only eleven when she was diagnosed. She always had troubling symptoms.

From a very early age, she would go through long periods of crying. She also couldn't make quick turnarounds or transitions. For example, I would come home and say, "Okay, everybody get in the car. We're going out for ice cream." All the kids would run for the car except Claire, who would just stand there screaming.

Claire was very contrary, but Fred and I just thought that she was a difficult child. Her preschool teacher even changed jobs after she had Claire in her class! She said, "Claire is one of the most unusual children I've ever had." From an early age, Claire was incredibly hard to handle, and she had a scream that could shatter glass. In the beginning, I didn't pay too much attention to Claire when she acted up, because I had learned that it didn't pay. A little complaint could become a huge problem.

In the sixth grade, Claire became a basketcase. She had been having trouble in school because she was the ideal kid to pick on. The other kids could always get a response from her, so she became increasingly isolated. She would come home from school crying every day and would scream and hit her siblings. She worried that nobody liked her, and I worried along with her.

Claire was so nervous about going to school in the morning that she would start in on her younger sister, Bridget, and then both of them would be in tears before they left the house. She was totally out of control, and when her tantrum was over, I would think, "Something is terribly wrong here. No child should leave for school like this every day."

One day, I found Claire in her room with tears streaming down her face. "I'm thinking of killing myself," she said. "Do I have to kill myself before anybody will pay attention to me?" And I was thinking, "Oh, no! No! This will go away. I don't want to deal with this."

I went to Claire's school to talk to her teachers. I said, "I don't know what's going on here. Claire can't seem to keep her life together. We have mental illness in our family, and she's at risk for a breakdown." Her teachers were punishing her at school, saying that she was irresponsible. They

When I heard the word "schizophrenia," I had trouble breathing. I got very light-headed, and my chest got real tight. I thought, "Oh, my God! I have just walked an hour into the woods with a man who is telling me he is insane!"

—PENNY

At one point in middle school, I had a breakdown in math class. I cleared out the entire room! My medication had just been upped, and I was really, really high. I was way up there, having a good time singing and dancing all over the place! Then I started pacing in the back of the room, holding my head in my hands and saying, "I don't know where I am. I don't know where I am!" The teacher hadn't come in yet, and my friends were getting kind of weirded out. One of them approached me really gently, took my hand, and said, "Come on, Claire. Come on." I was like, "I can't! I can't." He said, "It's okay. Come with me. Just go slow." I wasn't really functioning. I was shaking, and I couldn't move.

My friend took me up to the front of the room, because by then the teacher had arrived. She didn't even notice the state I was in. She was doing paperwork and stuff, and she didn't realize that everyone was looking at me with petrified expressions on their faces. My friend told the teacher, "I think Claire needs help." Then I started screaming. The teacher said, "Everyone go to the lunchroom!" She calmed me down and took me to the nurse's office right away. I called my mom, and she asked me, "Are you okay?" And I was like, "I'm okay." The next day, the kids in my class said things like, "Claire, that was so cool. Can you do that again? We really want to get out of class again!"

I don't like having depression. It makes me tired and cranky, and I can't be the person I want to be. There are times when I wish I didn't have it. Then again, I see how sad my dad is when the rest of the family is having ice cream and he can't because he has diabetes. I wish he didn't have diabetes. When my mom has a hard time walking when she gets up in the morning. I wish she didn't have arthritis. When I say something stupid in front of a cute guy, I wish I didn't have such a big mouth. I wish nothing bad ever happened to me or to my family members, but everyone has their cross to bear. I'm just lucky that my family is able to cope with mental illness as well as they do.

When I applied to college, I didn't see a reason to hide my mental illness. I had to apply to get a single dorm room on the basis of my depression, which I got with no contest.

Now I have a reputation on campus for being very open about my mental illness. I've never encountered any sort of negative reaction at all. None of my boyfriends have ever shied away when they hear that I have depression. By the time I know someone well enough to date them, they already know me well enough to know what I'm like.

My dad was always open with all of us kids about his schizophrenia. He told us about it, but we weren't supposed to talk about it to other people that much. I don't remember his behavior being scary or even awkward for me. Dad would have episodes where he would pace and hum and dance and talk to himself. I remember that once he tried to eat acorns. When he had these episodes, he stayed home and played kickball with us. That's what his illness meant to me when I was very young: Dad would be at home playing with us!

When Dad had psychotic episodes, I would say to my friends, "My dad's sick, so you can't come in the house." If they did come over while Dad was behaving strangely, I told them what to expect. Usually, I acted as if it was no big deal, and my friends would follow my lead. Sometimes I was afraid that Dad's behavior might scare them, even though it never scared me. I always thought it was kind of cute and funny, but I could see how someone could get very confused if they didn't understand what was going on. My family has never embarrassed me. Never!

JOE

Claire and I support each other just like any other siblings. We have a normal brother and sister relationship and we have a mutual concern for each other when we are having problems. In the past, it wasn't cool to hang out with my little sister, but we got along okay. When she would go into a rage or something, I would go into my room and not really worry about it. I would just wait for Mom to go in and fix her!

With my dad, things were a little bit more awkward. When he had a psychotic episode, I wasn't quite sure what to do. Should I join in the fun, or should I act concerned? Most of the time, I joined in the fun and marched around the house with him. We never had friends over during these times; we just told them that our dad was sick. That was pretty much the extent of it. Ninety-nine percent of the time we were just like any other family.

I was pretty darn cool when I was a little kid. In fact, I was the happiest kid in the world! I had lots of friends and I was fun to be around. I was a little ham, and I would ham it up whenever attention was focused on me.

Things started turning sour for me when I was in middle school. I became very worried that I wasn't going to be popular. I was extremely self-conscious and totally obsessed with how I came across socially. I thought I might do something bad, or say something stupid or uncool, or just look weird. I know that lots of kids can be like that in middle school, but I was like that to the extreme. It became crippling. I began to calculate every movement of my body, and I became obsessed with where my hands should be. I came off looking jerky and stiff in my motions because I literally didn't want to make any wrong moves.

I lost all of my friends because I gradually stopped talking to them. Before I knew it, I wasn't cool anymore. I was the biggest nerd in school, which is what I had tried so hard to avoid! I began to get very depressed.

I went to a new school in my freshman year of high school. I didn't know anyone there, and I was away from the few friends who had stuck by me during middle school. Everybody else made friends and stuff, but I was so paranoid that I didn't even bother to try.

On the first day of school, I went to lunch and sat by myself. Because of the lunch schedule, there were only two other kids in the lunchroom. They were sitting separately and I was like, "Okay, I'll sit separately, too." These two kids started talking to each other, but not to me. I thought, "This is going to be a long year! I can tell already." They began to hang out together at lunch, and I would sit by myself every day. I could hear them talking about me. It was a very embarrassing situation. After several months, they said, "Hey, why don't you come over and sit with us?" They were the first kids I had spoken to at school all year!

I had to go to gym class every day and I'm not at all physically adept. My posture was awful, and my hands were always hanging stiffly by my side. I just didn't know what to do with them. I told my mom that I didn't want to go to gym class because the kids made fun of me. The school made special arrangements for me so I didn't have to go anymore. Then I became even more removed from my peers, because gym class was where you could talk to each other. But if I had gone to gym, the kids would have said to me, "Hey, loser."

I was pretty much out of it at this point. I didn't have too much going on in my life at all. I would come home from school and either go to sleep or just lie in bed. I wasn't doing much of anything. Unlike Claire, I never screamed at anybody. I didn't do anything like that. I simply removed myself from most interactions with my family. I think that's why it took longer for my parents to realize that I was so depressed.

By my sophomore year, I was suicidal. I never thought I would actually kill myself, but I did think about dying most of the time. I would go to sleep every day after school, and while I was falling asleep, I would fantasize about my death.

By Christmas of that year, I went on medication and I responded very well to it right off the bat. Within a month or so, I was completely changed! I tried out for plays and made friends with lots of the kids in the theater group. In my senior year, I ran for student government and I won.

When I went to college, I wasn't great about taking my medication every day. I never actually thought, "Okay, I'm tired of it," because I knew that things could get bad without it and that I needed to be on it. When I didn't take my medication regularly, I had bad depressive episodes. I've gotten into the habit of taking my antidepressant daily. It's been a miracle for me.

I've never had any qualms about telling anyone about my mental illness, and I still don't. I think of it as a disease like diabetes or any hereditary illness. I'm not ashamed of it. It's not my fault and it's not my parents' fault. I'm fine as long as I'm on my medication. I have nothing to hide.

> *I've never had any qualms about telling anyone about my mental illness, and I still don't. I think of it as a disease like diabetes or any hereditary illness. I'm not ashamed of it. It's not my fault and it's not my parents' fault. I'm fine as long as I'm on my medication. I have nothing to hide.*
>
> —JOE

Maria and Cesar

THE MARQUEZ / HERNANDEZ FAMILY

BALDWIN PARK, CALIFORNIA

MARIA MARQUEZ / CESAR HUMBERTO HERNANDEZ

MARIA

THE FIRST TIME MY FAMILY WAS NOTIFIED of my brother Cesar's mental illness was on May 29, 1991. I still remember that date.

Cesar got in trouble with the law because he had a substance abuse problem with marijuana. He was sent to Tehachapi State Prison, in California. We called the prison to find out how we could visit him and, according to the jail personnel, Cesar had to send us visiting forms. We wrote to him and told him we needed him to mail us the forms. He wrote back saying he didn't want us to visit him. He refused to call or write us after that.

We received a letter from Atascadero State Hospital, which explained that Cesar had been taken from the jail and admitted to the psychiatric hospital for evaluation, care, and treatment. They told us that he had many symptoms, including depression, paranoia, hearing voices, and fighting with other inmates. Cesar was diagnosed with paranoid schizophrenia.

The news of Cesar's diagnosis affected our brother José the hardest. He was working at a state hospital as a psychiatric technician and he knew a lot about mental illness. Cesar's illness really hurt José because he couldn't accept that this had happened to his younger brother. When my father found out that Cesar was sick, he thought that Cesar was under a "woman spell." My father never acknowledged that his son had a mental illness, and so he was never able to help him.

The first time my mother and I visited Cesar in the hospital, he looked very ugly. It seemed that his face and body were swollen. He was also fat. It was depressing to see him, and our mother cried. He did not want to see us very long the first time we visited him.

After our first visit to the hospital, we went back at least once a month to see Cesar. As time progressed, he looked better and enjoyed our company. Our family would spend

Maria

the entire day with him. We also mailed him food, drinks, chips, Cornnuts, and just about anything he requested. He would make collect phone calls to our grandmother and to us every time he felt like talking. He sent Christmas gifts to the cousins in El Paso and mailed Christmas cards to everyone in our family.

While Cesar was in Atascadero, he was doing well. After he recovered, they told him he was going to be transferred to another jail, called the California Men's Colony. After he moved there, Cesar called us less, and we worried about him.

At that time, the Los Angeles riots had broken out and we thought the jail had locked up all the prisoners so that a riot would not break out in there, too. However, after the riots were over, we still did not hear from Cesar.

On May 26, 1992, Cesar was released. We had called the staff and asked them to let Cesar know that the family was going to pick him up. However, by the time our mother and I arrived, Cesar was already at the Greyhound bus depot. We drove there, but when we walked in, we couldn't see Cesar. He had gone for food and when he came back, he did not react happy in seeing us. He did not even want me to look at him. Our mother hugged him, but he wanted his space. We got his box of belongings and drove Cesar home.

On our drive back home, we stopped at a gas station to use the rest room. Cesar went into the men's room and he did not come out for a long time. My mother's girlfriend was with us and she said she could hear someone hitting the wall. We were not aware of it, but Cesar was going through a crisis. He was hearing voices and feeling things. When he got back in the car, he was quiet and needed the window to be rolled down. I can recall Cesar making a fist and then closing his hand as if he had something in it. In the long run, we determined that Cesar was catching things that he thought he saw and was trying to throw them outside the car. When we got home, he did not sleep that entire night, and our mother stood up watching him. He went outside for a walk, and our mother followed him. Our mother was scared.

The next day I called the California Men's Colony and asked how could Cesar be released in the condition he was in. The social worker said a psychiatrist had evaluated Cesar before he was discharged. I went to Cesar's parole officer and explained the problem to her. I informed her that Cesar could not report to her, because there was something wrong with him. The parole officer said that she would come to the house. When she did come, Cesar was in the bathroom with the shower water running as if he was going to take a shower. We opened the lock on the door with a nickel, and she

THE MARQUEZ/HERNANDEZ FAMILY 103

took Cesar to see a psychiatrist. This doctor asked Cesar some questions, but he didn't answer them correctly. The parole officer called us and said that Cesar was arrested.

We did not understand why Cesar was arrested, since he had not committed any crime. We called the jail and informed them that he needed special treatment. A few days later he was transferred to a state prison. My mother and I went to get an application so that we could visit him there. They said it would take about thirty days for the processing.

Cesar was taken to the prison hospital. According to the staff that worked there, my brother did not want to eat and was staying by himself. We requested to see him, but apparently our applications got lost. We pressured the parole officer, and they arranged for our family members to see Cesar. Our mother, our grandmother, and José went. They told me that Cesar was handcuffed behind his back, and that he would not face them. Cesar raised his head once to look at our grandmother, and then he lowered it. We were told that in order for Cesar to be released he needed to go to a parole hearing in thirty days.

Before Cesar's parole hearing, my mother and I consulted an attorney to see if he could help. The day of the hearing was on July 1, 1992, at 1:30 P.M., in downtown Los Angeles. That day my entire family went to the hearing: mother, grandmother, father, brother, and sister. Cesar was released on the terms that his brother José would be responsible for him. Cesar was given to us by a social worker from the jail. We went home happy. We thought it was all okay.

My mother and I went for counseling. The lady spoke English and Spanish. She directed us to a mental health clinic that had a Spanish-speaking support group, which met every Wednesday night. The lady guided us in the right direction.

Cesar was not doing very well at the time. He continued to act strange. On the night of July 14, 1992, Cesar went out for a walk and never came home to sleep. The next day, the Baldwin Park Police Department brought him home. He was nude. They said they had found him walking down Main Street naked and a lady had given him a towel. José and Grandmother were at home and they went outside to get Cesar back inside the house. He did not want to come in. He was just standing outside the police officer's car. José then explained to the police that Cesar was mentally ill. Since Cesar refused to go inside the house, the police officer took Cesar to a mental health center. Before they drove off with him, Cesar was given some clothing to wear, but he still didn't want to put anything on.

I went to my local Catholic parish to ask for help. The priest told me that if I thought my brother was on drugs, I should throw Cesar out into the street. The priest also told me that people who are mentally ill or on drugs act the same. I went home more confused than ever.

Cesar has been in and out of hospitals for a long time. At the present time, he is doing well after being hospitalized for three years. He was discharged in January 2001. He has enrolled in a community college and wants to be a physical education teacher. He lives in a sober community and shares an apartment with six men. Cesar continues to say that he does not have a mental illness; however, he takes his medication every day.

I went to my local Catholic parish to ask for help. The priest told me that if I thought my brother was on drugs, I should throw Cesar out into the street. The priest also told me that people who are mentally ill or on drugs act the same. I went home more confused than ever.
—MARIA

Alexandra, Armené, and Abraháni

THE MARGOSIAN FAMILY

LEVERETT, MASSACHUSETTS

ARMENÉ MARGOSIAN / ABRAHÁNI MARGOSIAN
ALEXANDRA MARGOSIAN

ARMENÉ

WHEN I WAS A YOUNG CHILD, there was a huge boulder three stories below my bedroom window. I always felt that this boulder was meant to be there so that I could kill myself by falling on it.

I felt inadequate and sad when I was as young as seven. I knew something was wrong, but I didn't know what it was. I only felt safe when I would read or spend time in the library. I remember thinking, "One day, it's going to be different for me. I'm not always going to feel this way."

My family was dysfunctional. For instance, my brother always did unusual things with me. Sometimes he would dare me to do things that were extremely dangerous and could even be fatal. He once made me run down the street with a garbage bag over my head. My mother didn't have normal responses to incidents like this. She didn't get upset or protect me from him. In fact, when I was a little girl, my mother sexually abused me. She told me that my vagina was dirty and she used to scrub me so hard that I couldn't urinate for hours and hours. She had a rule that I wasn't allowed to go

to the bathroom at school, so for twelve years, I never even saw what a girl's restroom looked like.

When I was a bit older, my brother sexually molested me and told me that our parents would kill both of us if I told them about it. Around the same time, my father used to tell me how ugly I was and that no man would ever want me. I would try so hard to be thin that I wouldn't eat anything at all for weeks at a time. My parents didn't seem to care.

I was in all honors classes at school. I was under a lot of pressure from my parents to always get straight A's. If I got one problem wrong on a test, my father would tell me how stupid I was for making a mistake. I never felt that I was good enough.

My first serious breakdown occurred when I was fifteen years old. I was so depressed that I dropped out of school and basically slept for three months. My parents would say, "We're sick and tired of coming home and seeing you lying around the house. You have to get a job." My father finally found me a job at a restaurant, but it took me over two hours to get there by public transportation. I worked sixty hours

Those of us who are poor and mentally ill can get treated pretty shabbily by the mental health system.
—ARMENÉ

Alexandra

or more a week and I was also responsible for cooking meals at home and cleaning the house.

My father beat my brother, my mother, and me for years. Once I accidentally broke a twenty-cent teacup that he had bought in Paris. He beat me so brutally that later that night I attempted suicide for the first time. My father grabbed me just as I was going out the window. He made me sleep in his bed that night so that he could "keep an eye on me." I needed therapeutic intervention, but since my family didn't believe in therapy, I didn't get any help.

I saved enough money from working that I was able to afford to go to a Catholic high school several hours from home. Although I was only sixteen, I rented a room that was off-campus and supported myself by working on weekends. I was so lonely that I asked my aunt, who lived in a neighboring town, if I could live with her. She allowed me to stay with her for only one week. Eventually, I moved back home.

When I went to college, I eloped with the first boyfriend I had. Fourteen months into our marriage, I asked him to leave because he was beating me. He moved out, but six months later he began to stalk me. I had to get a restraining order against him, which he violated several times. He went to jail three times, and each time my father and brother would bail him out.

After my divorce, I got involved with another man who was also abusive. I married him three years later. He attempted to kill me when our daughter, Alex, was two years old and I was pregnant with our son, Abraháni. When my son was six months old, I finally went into a battered women's shelter. The shelter staff was neither supportive nor helpful. At one point, the children and I had pneumonia, and they would not even help me get to the hospital. I had to do everything on my own. I asked for therapy, but they said they didn't provide therapy for women in the shelter.

After two months in the shelter, I was accepted into a transitional living program for battered women and their kids. It was just temporary housing without any real program in place. It was awful. Four months later I received a rent subsidy and I moved again. This was my third move in nine months with two children under three years old.

Everything was falling out from underneath me. I was overwhelmed, and I started to feel very bad about myself. I was all alone with two young children and I had no one to turn to for support. Although I have had depression most of my life, this time it was far more profound. I decided to go to the local mental health clinic, where I requested therapy for both my daughter and myself. Alex was only three years old, but she had observed the beatings I had sustained by her father. I felt we had been through so much that I wanted to make sure she was okay emotionally. The staff at the mental health center told me that Alex didn't need therapy. As for me, they said that I had accomplished so much during the past nine months, why would I need any therapy? They couldn't understand why I was so depressed, and I couldn't really explain it. Those of us who are poor and mentally ill can get treated pretty shabbily by the mental health system.

I wanted to make everything the best for my kids, but the life I was leading was not what I had intended for them. I started to feel that the world would be a better place for my kids if I wasn't around. I thought to myself, "I'm the problem here. If I were out of the picture, my children would have a great life." I felt hopeless. I couldn't keep up with all the things that I had to do to survive. I began to feel suicidal because I didn't think that my life was ever going to get better.

I finally got permission from the clinic staff to see a therapist there. After seeing him for a few weeks, I wasn't feeling any better. One day, I told my therapist that I was afraid to leave his office because I wanted to attempt suicide. He didn't believe me! He said, "Well, you've survived so far. You'll survive another week." When I left the session, I bought over-the-counter sleeping pills and then went home. I cooked dinner, bathed the children, and read them a bedtime story. After they were asleep, I took out some photographs of them and thought, "These are the most perfect and beautiful children. Anybody would want to take them in after I'm gone." I wrote them a long letter saying good-bye, and I took the pills.

I ended up in the ICU. From there, I admitted myself into the psychiatric unit. While I was there, I kept asking the doctors for antidepressants. They said I didn't need them, and that I had my intellect to fall back on! They thought that my depression was only situational.

Abraháni and Alexandra

I was referred to a different therapist after I was discharged from the hospital. She wasn't helpful, either. She would just sit there and say, "Umm-hmmm." I would leave my therapy sessions feeling just as bad as when I went in.

When the Department of Social Services discovered that I had tried to kill myself, they appeared at my door unexpectedly on New Year's Eve. I was home with my children. They asked us a few questions, and a few weeks later I received a letter from them stating that they were keeping my case open. They wanted the children to be in contact with their biological father, who didn't know where we were living. DSS

Some people say, "Why don't you just get it together?" For those of us who have a psychological disability, we are, in a sense, trapped in an invisible wheelchair. If people could actually "see" our disability, I'm sure they wouldn't say half the things they say.
—ARMENÉ

Abraháni

asked the court to order weekend visitation for Alex and Abraháni with their father, and they kept threatening that they were going to take the children away from me. They liked the children's father. They said he behaved like a gentleman with them.

In the meantime, I ended up back in the hospital because I thought I was going to hurt myself again. I assumed that I'd get the help I needed there. I didn't know exactly what that would be, but I thought, "If they could just give me some medication, I'll be okay." My doctors said, "You don't need any." I was hospitalized for two weeks that time.

A few months later, I found a psychiatrist at a different mental health center. She realized that I needed medication to stabilize my condition. In fact, she couldn't believe what I had gone through. She knew that I was a good mother and that I needed some help to get better. The medication she put me on helped to save my life.

DSS dropped their case against me because they could not prove neglect or any kind of abuse toward the children. I spent the next five years, however, battling the court system in a custody and visitation case against the children's father. I went through four court investigations, two trials, and three different judges, trying to prove that visitation with their father would endanger my children. The psychiatric evaluations ordered by the courts revealed that although I had depression, I was a very caring and empathetic person. The children's father was discovered to be very violent. I was finally victorious, and the children's visits with him were ended.

People fear mental illness. I've even lost friends because they thought that my condition might be contagious. People rarely think of a psychologically disabled person as someone who can be a loving and caring mother. Some people say, "Why don't you just get it together?" For those of us who have a psychological disability, we are, in a sense, trapped in an invisible wheelchair. If people could actually "see" our disability, I'm sure they wouldn't say half the things they say.

I feel that I've survived an incredible amount. I find it miraculous that I can be kind and loving to others. In fact, to raise awareness about the struggles of battered women, I've created a "purple heart pin." With any profits I make from selling them, I want to provide financial aid to battered women, and to welfare mothers and their children.

Given everything that we've been through together, I'm amazed that my children are thriving. Although I'm on state assistance and we live in poverty, I've managed to have the children attend an excellent private school. In the end, it was my children who saved my life. They are my true heroes. They've taught me what is really important in life.

My daughter was in a reading group last summer with some of her friends. One of the books she read was about children who are different from their peers. In the story, the kids discover that they are valued for their differences. When Alex and her friends talked about this book, she spoke right up and said, "This story reminds me of my mother. She has a psychological disability. People can be like my mommy and still be a nice person. She's wonderful just the way she is." Even though I'm open with my children about my disability, I've never shared anything about my mental illness with their friends. I was so proud that Alex didn't feel ashamed of me. She didn't feel there was anything wrong with me or that my illness was a bad thing to talk about.

Sometimes my children say things like, "Mommy, I don't see why you have to go to therapy. You don't need therapy! You're fine the way you are." And I always say, "I'm fine *because* I go to therapy!"

My kids know that they are strong people. They say, "We can do anything!" Sometimes when I feel that I'm not doing enough for them, they say, "But Mommy, you're doing everything! You always figure everything out. You are a huge success!" Once when Abraháni was only six, he actually said, "We have full confidence in you."

My kids are such an inspiration to me. Every time I look in their eyes and I see them gleaming, I think, "This is what I live for." Just that look in their eyes!

> *Sometimes my children say things like, "Mommy, I don't see why you have to go to therapy. You don't need therapy! You're fine the way you are." And I always say, "I'm fine because I go to therapy!"*
> —ARMENÉ

Jane and Tex

THE MOSER FAMILY

HOLYOKE, MASSACHUSETTS

JANE MOSER / REV. R. LEROY "TEX" MOSER

JANE

MY HUSBAND, TEX, AND I HAVE FOUR SONS, all of whom are grown. When we tell the story of our oldest son, David, we say that the real tragedy is that his story is not unique. David, who is now forty-eight, has schizo-affective disorder. He has been sick ever since he was seventeen.

As a child, David never acted out. He didn't fight or rebel in any way. He was very attached to his family, was active in church activities, and received all kinds of academic honors. His behavior was exemplary, and his life seemed to be going in all the right directions.

When David went to college, his pattern became a bit rocky. He excelled in the courses he was interested in, but he didn't bother to go to many of his other classes. He just wouldn't show up for them. This was so unlike him that Tex and I thought it was very strange. David also wasn't returning his library books, and we would get huge bills from the college for his overdue books. There were all these subtle signs that there might be something wrong with David. We worried about our son, but because he wasn't living at home, Tex

and I couldn't figure out exactly what was going on with him. We wondered if we weren't just overreacting. At one point, we tried to persuade David to get some help. He thought we were both a little odd for suggesting this, because he didn't think there was anything wrong with him at all.

David continued to have a rocky time of it after he left college. He lived nearby and worked in a publishing company doing research. He also opened an art gallery. He had such unlimited energy! But then he lost his job, and the gallery fell apart financially.

When David moved to Michigan, Tex and I began to get bizarre letters from him. These letters were beautifully written, but filled with strange ideas. David would mention people who were beaming messages down to him, and tell us how he had just exorcised his dog. It was all very odd. For the first time, I acknowledged to myself that he might be psychotic.

The young woman David was living with in Michigan began to call us because she felt threatened by him, but she couldn't really pin down exactly why. Tex and I became even more concerned. We'd talk to David on the phone, and he would try to convince us that the problems were with his

As parents, we had to make the decision to go to court so that our son would receive treatment. If David had been diagnosed with a life-threatening medical condition and was resisting treatment or surgery for it, we would have done the same thing. The psychiatrist warned us that we might become the enemy in David's eyes. He was right. We hoped that if David was required to take medication, he would get better and understand why we had taken this action. Unfortunately, this didn't happen.

—JANE

girlfriend, not with him. He could sound pretty credible. When his girlfriend decided to leave him, her father was so nervous about David that he took a security guard with him to pick up her things. There was actually a confrontation between the guard and David.

Things got so bad with David that he was evicted from his apartment and ended up living in his car. We persuaded him to come back home and live with us. We tried to get him to go see a therapist, but he refused. Tex and I and our three younger sons decided to see a psychiatrist to get some guidance. He was very helpful. He told us that bad parenting hadn't caused David's behavior, and that David might be mentally ill.

David began to threaten us. When his behavior was considered dangerous by the legal system, he was hospitalized, and initially diagnosed with bipolar disorder. This was our first real understanding of what was wrong with our son and it felt like a light breaking through. The psychiatrist said to us something I'll never forget: "I've got good news and bad news for you. The bad news is that David has a very serious mental illness. The good news is that we can treat it."

David wouldn't accept help of any kind, so the hospital instructed us to get a court order for treatment for him. We did so, and treatment was ordered. The lawyer assigned to our son immediately fought to protect David's rights. Both David and his lawyer threatened to sue the hospital, so the hospital released him without treatment. Of course, this simply confirmed David's belief that there was nothing wrong with him. He told us, "You see, there's nothing wrong with me. You sent me to a hospital and they let me go!" That was when David began to turn against us.

As parents, we had to make the decision to go to court so that our son would receive treatment. If David had been diagnosed with a life-threatening medical condition and was resisting treatment or surgery for it, we would have done the same thing. The psychiatrist warned us that we might become

the enemy in David's eyes. He was right. We hoped that if David was required to take medication, he would get better and understand why we had taken this action. Unfortunately, this didn't happen.

After he left the hospital, David lived on the streets and in the woods outside of town. He came to our house several times in the middle of the night and yelled and screamed off-the-wall things. If his brothers were there, they would try to reason with him, but nothing worked. The neighbors would call the police out of sheer frustration. We finally got a restraining order to keep him at least one hundred feet from our home because the police told us that it was the best thing for us to do. There were times when the police would take David to the state hospital, but he would be out again in a matter of hours! It was a revolving door kind of thing. We were all incredibly frustrated and frightened.

One night, David broke into our house while Tex and I were asleep. He beat us badly and almost killed me. We had a large house, and the neighbors couldn't hear us calling for help. Fortunately, our son Stephen and his wife were living with us at the time on the third floor of the house. When they heard us screaming, they were terrified and called the police. Stephen finally subdued his brother. After the assault, the court sent David to a state prison hospital for evaluation. The medical staff there wanted him hospitalized, but a court-appointed psychologist, who had only met with David for twenty minutes, found him competent to stand trial on several felony counts. David had to go to Superior Court and stand trial. It was out of our hands.

Our son wouldn't allow his lawyers to enter a "not guilty" plea on his behalf. They realized that David was mentally ill, but he refused to accept this. He fired one lawyer after another. When he eventually stood trial in Superior Court, Tex and I had to testify against our own son. We didn't have any other choice. A lot of people didn't understand that we were powerless over much of what was happening. David was sentenced to jail and stayed there for five years.

Tex and I tried to have David evaluated while he was in jail so that he could receive some treatment, even if it was against his will. We were unsuccessful. When David came up for parole, he refused to participate in the proceedings because he considered himself a political prisoner. The Massachusetts Department of Mental Health got involved in his case and managed to arrange for David to be involuntarily committed to a state hospital for an evaluation after he was released from jail. David was found to be mentally ill and a danger to others. The Department of Mental Health attempted to get a court order to keep him in the hospital for at least six months. Once again, lawyers were assigned to his case, but David just kept firing them. His commitment hearings would get postponed, so for months he didn't receive any treatment. When the judge heard the case after months of delay, it turned out that he had never presided at a commitment hearing before. This was his first!

The judge ordered David to be brought into the courtroom with his hands and feet shackled. There was an armed guard watching him at all times. The court proceeding felt surrealistic to me; it was like being in *Alice in Wonderland*. David was allowed to act as his own lawyer. He claimed that Tex wasn't his father, so the judge kept referring to my husband as the "alleged father." I can't describe how awful it was. The judge would allow no medical or police records into evidence. It was as if we were in a first-degree murder situation instead of what was simply a civil hearing to determine whether the court could mandate treatment for our son.

The judge asked David, "What is it that you want, Mr. Moser? Tell me what you would like to see happen." David replied, "I can't say it out loud, but there's a conspiracy against me. I have to go to the FBI and report it. That's what I want to do." Believe it or not, the judge released him. David was free to go. He simply disappeared. For five long years we had no idea where David was, or if he was dead or alive. The Homeless and Missing Persons Network searched for him

Jane and Tex with a photo of David

to no avail. Then something truly extraordinary happened.

A man from Virginia called our son Paul, who teaches at Oberlin College in Ohio. This man had befriended someone who called himself Mogli and lived in a pup tent in a national forest nearby. Mogli had disappeared, and this man was trying to find out who Mogli really was and where he might have gone. Since Mogli was very secretive, the man had only one clue to his identity. At one point, Mogli had let slip that

Mental illnesses are brain disorders. If you accept that basic fact, then our laws should reflect that understanding. They don't. What this country does is tell a person whose decision-making parts of their brain are damaged and dysfunctional that they can make their own rational decision about whether or not to get treatment. This is simply not right.

—*JANE*

he had a brother who taught at Oberlin. Unbeknownst to Mogli, Paul had written and produced a play about his missing brother. A professor at Oberlin who had received the initial phone call about Mogli had seen the play and made the connection that Mogli and David might be one and the same person.

This kind gentleman promised us that he would find our son, and he did. David was in jail. Without provocation, he had seriously assaulted another man who had befriended him. In his delusional state of mind, David believed that the man had been stalking him.

History repeated itself. David was evaluated and diagnosed with paranoid schizophrenia, but he was still found competent to stand trial! There were two trials. Our son Peter went down for the first one. David would not even speak to his brother. He refused to allow a plea of mental illness and he fired his lawyer. Although the district attorney and the defense lawyers and the judge were very kind and thoroughly understood that David was mentally ill, they had to comply with the law. The trial resulted in a hung jury.

Tex and I went down for the second trial, but David would not speak to us, either. During the proceedings he was allowed to defend himself. David's strange behavior and speech betrayed his paranoia, but the judge remained patient. This time, the jury found him guilty, and our son was sentenced to two years in prison.

In prison, David again refused treatment. As the time came close to his release date, the mental health staff there worked diligently to arrange for a civil commitment hearing. At that hearing, the judge mandated treatment for David in a state hospital in Virginia. This was the first time that he had ever received medication. Very slow but steady progress was reported to us.

After six months and an extension of the commitment, David was transferred to another state hospital. After a few more months, he was released. The court ordered mandatory outpatient treatment for him, and a community-based

mental health team helped him find housing and work and provided his medication. Unfortunately, David still refused to be in contact with his family or friends.

Tex and I are so grateful for the caring people who persisted again and again to bend the interpretation of their laws whenever possible to serve David's best interests. But the fact remains, Tex and I are angry. We are angry on behalf of our son and the thousands like him who have suffered needlessly for years when court-mandated treatment could have relieved the terrible symptoms of their mental illnesses.

People use the words "mental illness." What exactly is "mental?" Put your finger on mental. Pick it up and hand it to me. Mental is a function of an organ called the brain. This is so hard to get across to people. Mental illnesses are brain disorders. If you accept that basic fact, then our laws should reflect that understanding. They don't. What this country does is tell a person whose decision-making parts of their brain are damaged and dysfunctional that they can make their own rational decision about whether or not to get treatment. This is simply not right.

When our own son assaulted us, there was so much media attention that we had no choice but to speak out. We said to ourselves, "Okay, so this has happened. Let's try to make it

When our own son assaulted us, there was so much media attention that we had no choice but to speak out. We said to ourselves, "Okay, so this has happened. Let's try to make it understandable to the public." As a result, a lot of people have contacted us and have literally whispered, "This has happened in our family, too." Not only did they feel the stigma of mental illness, but they also felt tremendous shame around the issue of violence.

—*JANE*

understandable to the public." As a result, a lot of people have contacted us and have literally whispered, "This has happened in our family, too." Not only did they feel the stigma of mental illness, but they also felt tremendous shame around the issue of violence.

It's difficult to get people to speak out publicly about mental illness. It's even more difficult to encourage them to acknowledge that there has been violence in the family because of it. In our family, we hadn't been used to violence. It isn't our family style. It's not easy to rush out and tell your friends that your son is threatening your life or throwing things at you. A friend of mine has referred to this as "the closet within the closet."

The most poignant thing for me is that when mental illness strikes, the person you know is no longer there. They become someone else. And yet they *are* there. This loss brings a grief that never ends. With a death, there's closure, but with mental illness, there isn't. David will never again be the handsome, exuberant, talented, loving young man that he once was. Nor will our family ever be the same again. We have been on a never-ending roller coaster of emotions until we have become weary of it. Despite the fear and uncertainty, however, tentative hope and love go on.

Tex and I have chosen to channel our emotions positively by working to change the laws so that someday brain disorders will be treated as medical conditions deserving of prompt medical attention. People who suffer should not be relegated to legal and judicial systems, where they are viewed as perpetrators. We hope and pray that someday no family will need to tell a painful story like ours.

> *The most poignant thing for me is that when mental illness strikes, the person you know is no longer there. They become someone else. And yet they are there. This loss brings a grief that never ends. With a death, there's closure, but with mental illness, there isn't.*
>
> —JANE

TEX

When my son David was a senior in high school, his behavior became quite erratic. He got into drugs and he ended up breaking into a drugstore with a friend. When the police arrived, he was sitting on the floor eating an ice-cream cone. After this incident, he had a very strange affect for quite some time. In retrospect, we believe that this was David's first psychotic episode.

Jane and I didn't really know anything about mental illness back then, even though I was a professional clergyman. We didn't understand mental illness as a biological disease at all.

David was accepted at Yale and Wesleyan, but when these colleges were informed by his high school about the break-in, he was rejected at both places. He did get accepted at the University of Rochester, but he dropped out after his second year there. At that point, he had pretty much withdrawn from the college scene anyway.

David was very open with us at the time and even confided in us that he had almost killed a man in a fight. He was very worried about this and didn't quite understand what had happened. This incident was associated with his drinking, and Jane and I debated whether or not he was an alcoholic. We decided he wasn't. We now think that he might have had another psychotic episode.

David moved to Michigan, where he got involved with a fundamentalist Christian group. He carried a Bible around with him and had a very strange holy demeanor. My mother died around this time, and David showed up at her funeral in a terribly unkempt state. He was dressed in dark clothes, and all of his exuberance was gone. This was a very frightening experience. It was crushing to see him that way, and Jane and I were sure that something was terribly wrong. David moved back home, and I put him to work cleaning up our backyard so he would have something to do. He didn't leave our house or contact any of his old friends. He carried a machete with him at all times.

> *David used his formidable intellect as a barrier against getting help. It was as if his intelligence was subservient to his being sick. He built a fence around his illness, and there was no way he was going to get help on his own. This is one of the agonies that so many families have to live with.*
>
> —TEX

One of the casualties of a sick person's psyche is often the loss of capacity to manage one's own life. Here is someone who is shot to pieces by his illness, and then the law says to him, "You need to make the decision as to whether or not you want to be treated." It all becomes quite nutty.

— TEX

David used his formidable intellect as a barrier against getting help. It was as if his intelligence was subservient to his being sick. He built a fence around his illness, and there was no way he was going to get help on his own. This is one of the agonies that so many families have to live with.

When David began to threaten us, a psychiatrist signed something called a "pink paper," which allowed the court to involuntarily commit David to a hospital for ten days. This came right after the Rogers Order was passed in Massachusetts. This order states that even if you are committed to a mental hospital, your family or guardian has to go back into court to get permission to have you involuntarily treated with medication if you refuse to take it. We think this is a travesty. Even though the court gave very specific instructions and permission for the hospital to treat David, the hospital refused to give him medication against his will. We wish that David had gone to a state hospital instead of a private one. I don't think they would have been so squeamish about treating him.

The Rogers Order is still in effect in our state. A good friend of mine, who used to be a Clerk of Courts, once told me, "You have to almost catch the person with a bloody knife in their hands to get them committed for treatment." Jane and I continue to struggle with the legal system. We want to make sure that people who are mentally ill will be helped by early intervention if they can't help themselves.

One of the casualties of a sick person's psyche is often the loss of capacity to manage one's own life. Here is someone who is shot to pieces by his illness, and then the law says to him, "You need to make the decision as to whether or not you want to be treated." It all becomes quite nutty.

After his first hospitalization, David didn't come back home to live with us. He mellowed out a bit, but then his unruly behavior escalated once again. He got into more and more difficulties with the police, and he fought in bars and on the street. One terrible night, David broke into our home and assaulted my wife and me. We would have lost our lives that night if it hadn't been for our son Stephen.

After forty days of evaluation in a state prison hospital, David was declared competent to stand trial by a court psychologist. This was unbelievable to us. After the trial, he was sentenced to jail. Months later, I met someone who had been on David's jury. He told me that the jury knew for sure that David was mentally ill, but if they had found him "not guilty" because of mental illness, they were afraid that he might just walk free. The jury found him guilty because they wanted him in jail in order to protect our family from any further danger. They didn't want him to go to a state hospital where they assumed that David would end up right back on the street. This, of course, is not true, but nevertheless it's a popular perception. Usually people are committed to a mental institution for a longer period of time than if they were sent to jail for the same crime.

Almost any other disease leaves the psyche intact, but mental illness can destroy a person's identity. This reality is the hardest to come to grips with for family members. One of the miraculous things about some of today's medications is that they can recover a lot of who the person was before he or she got sick. What gets me so frustrated is that the law says if you treat a person involuntarily, you're taking away their liberty. Baloney! You're giving it back to them!

It's important for the public to understand that, if treated, mentally ill people are no more violent than the general population. If they are untreated, they are several times more violent. Many people have come up to me and said, "There but for the grace of God goes my son." It just so happens that their kid never got into trouble with the law, but they so easily could have.

The stigma against the mentally ill has to be fought on the basis of truth, which means bringing it out into the open so we can come to a better understanding of what mental illness is. Even within the mental health community, people try to separate the "bad" mentally ill from the "good" mentally ill. And really, they are all part of the same family.

It can be all-consuming to cope with a mentally ill person. We know families that are torn apart by the strain of dealing with mental illness, and the incidence of divorce is very high. We hear stories all the time about siblings who move as far away as possible from their families in order to escape the situation at home. We're fortunate in that our family is pretty much together in terms of how we understand what has happened to David.

It amazes me that many families still play the "guilt" game and the "self-blame" game. "You did this. You did that. It was your fault. Maybe you didn't treat him right." This Freudian-type attitude is so ingrained in our society. It just hangs on.

When you've been to hell and back, what else can life do to you? Curiously enough, it gives you a certain freedom. At least, I think that's been true for us.

What gets me so frustrated is that the law says if you treat a person involuntarily, you're taking away their liberty. Baloney! You're giving it back to them!

— TEX

Betty, Elizabeth, Great Grandmother "Mema," David, LeeAnn, Mary Catherine, and Melissa

THE WILSON/FRANCIS FAMILY

COVINGTON, TENNESSEE

BETTY FRANCIS / ELIZABETH WILSON / "MEMA" HOWARD
DAVID FRANCIS / CHRISTIE LeeAnn FRANCIS
MARY CATHERINE JONES / MELISSA WILSON

MELISSA

THERE'S A LOT OF MENTAL ILLNESS IN MY FAMILY. I have major depression, and my daughter, LeeAnn, has schizo-affective disorder. My father was also mentally ill. He committed suicide when I was just a little child.

Depression is like a thick, huge dark cloud slowly coming down on you. It's as if the whole world is that cloud, and you know it's moving in on you, but you can't prevent it. And when it gets there, it squishes you. At one point, my depression was so bad that I couldn't function. I couldn't even hang up my clothes. One day my mother found me sitting on the floor of my closet hoping that no one would open the door. Soon after that, I was hospitalized for a few weeks. After going on medication, I felt much better.

I'm withdrawn by nature. I don't care if nobody comes to my house. I like to stay home, and I don't even go to church. I didn't used to be that way, but I am now. I don't like to be with people too often, although I do need a few friends. Every morning I go outside and listen to the birds singing. Then I go to work. I keep Grandmother Mema company and drive her wherever she wants to go, because she doesn't drive anymore. This makes me feel good and it gives me something to do.

Mental illness should never be hidden. Once it becomes part of your life, you have to deal with it whether you want to or not. I never hid mine from anyone. If you hide your illness, it makes your life even harder. When I got sick, I told lots of people what I was going through.

Most people don't know enough about people who are mentally ill. They think that they are just lazy, and they don't give them much credit for anything. If you have a heart attack, it's fine for you to go home and stay in bed, but if you have a mental illness, you're supposed to get right up and go back to work.

When my older daughter, LeeAnn, was fourteen, she became real depressed, too. It took her father and me a while to figure this out, because she usually hid her problems real

Most people don't know enough about people who are mentally ill. They think that they are just lazy, and they don't give them much credit for anything. If you have a heart attack, it's fine for you to go home and stay in bed, but if you have a mental illness, you're supposed to get right up and go back to work.
—MELISSA

119

LeeAnn, Elizabeth, and Melissa

LeeAnn had a problem with hearing voices. She said she could hear the neighbors saying bad things about her. She also had trouble sleeping. She could only fall asleep if the fan was turned on high to drown out the voices she heard. I think this was a wonderful solution to help herself get to sleep.

There was a time when LeeAnn was suicidal. Once I caught her putting her fingernails in an electrical wall socket. She tried to fall on a fork one day. I was determined that she wasn't going to kill herself, no matter what I had to do—even if I had to lock her in her room. My goal was simply to keep her alive. When LeeAnn got really bad, I would put her back into the hospital in a locked unit. It was the only safe place for her.

LeeAnn once took an overdose of her medication. When I counted all the pills left in the bottle and realized that she had taken enough of them to cause a seizure, I called an ambulance. The ambulance wouldn't come because she hadn't had the seizure yet! I got mad and told them, "You all just don't understand. She has already overdosed. She's going to have a seizure soon." I was angry with LeeAnn, too, and I said to her, "You get over there and sit on the couch and don't move. You're going to have a seizure." I couldn't drive her to the hospital myself because I was scared that she might have the seizure in my car. Eventually, she did have one. When her body quit jerking, she didn't move. I thought she had died from a heart attack. I put a pillow underneath her head because I didn't know what else to do. I called the ambulance again, and this time they finally came to get her.

When LeeAnn started in a day treatment program, there were days when she didn't want to go. I would say to her, "If you're not going to get up and go, I'll call your daddy and he'll come over and make you go." I had to ask my ex-husband, David, for help some days because I couldn't get our daughter into the car myself. There were other days when I had to physically pull LeeAnn by the arm out of her bed and get her dressed. There was even a time when I had to bathe her and wash her hair, which embarrassed LeeAnn. Gradually,

well. If ever there was an actress, she sure was one! She wouldn't tell us much, but we knew something was wrong.

When she was fifteen, LeeAnn had a psychotic episode. She talked about being in a black hole and she thought that someone had put a voodoo curse on her. She truly believed that she was dead. We took her to a hospital and visited her every day for months. In the beginning, she thought the people there were trying to kill her. When she was discharged, she could barely write her own name. I didn't think she could go back to her high school studies ever again. Since then, LeeAnn has been in and out of the hospital six times.

she started doing much better on her hygiene. LeeAnn still takes her baths in the dark because she thinks that people can see her in the mirror. She certainly copes with her illness in unique ways.

LeeAnn has finally been put on a medication that has saved her. She is still disabled, but she rents her own trailer now and she drives a car. She keeps her clothing at the trailer, but she sleeps at her dad's house next door. LeeAnn sleeps until lunchtime every day because the medication makes her drowsy. In the afternoon she visits her grandmother and me. She still doesn't have any friends, but LeeAnn is blessed by having lots of loving family members around her.

LEEANN

I was going out with a guy, but my best friend took him and stole him from me. I got really depressed because I liked him a lot. I wanted to kill myself.

One day, I had a hallucination that I had been run over by a Mack truck. In the hallucination, I was riding down the road in a car with my friends and I saw a huge truck pull in front of us and we hit it. I actually believed that this had really happened. I was paranoid and thought, "Oh my God, I'm dead. Why isn't my mother crying? I'm dead." I kept trying to talk to everyone in my family, but I didn't know if they could see me or not. I just sat there bawling. I went to my grandmother's house and told her that I didn't know if I was dead or alive. I didn't know what was real and what wasn't.

When I first got put in the hospital, I was diagnosed with schizophrenia. Two of my friends came and brought me a "Get

> *When I had to leave school, I lost all of my friends. They went on with their lives without me because I was in and out of hospitals so many times. They didn't understand. I hope I'll make some new friends someday.*
>
> *— LEEANN*

Well" balloon, but they didn't actually come into my room to see me. I don't see them anymore.

When I had to leave school, I lost all of my friends. They went on with their lives without me because I was in and out of hospitals so many times. They didn't understand. I hope I'll make some new friends someday.

BETTY

It took me a long time to accept the fact that my granddaughter, LeeAnn, has a mental illness. I couldn't even tell some of my family members. I wasn't ashamed, but it was so horrible for her. She would eat and throw up and she eventually got down to just skin and bones. We'd be driving down the road and she would think people were following her. I would have to hold her hand because she was so frightened. She also used to have terrible anxiety attacks. No matter how much the family hurt for LeeAnn, it was nothing compared to what she went through. LeeAnn has got cousins her own age, and I want them to do more for her. I've read them the riot act.

I wish people knew more about mental illness. There are so many kids who are sick, and the schools need to be more educated about mental illness. I wish the schoolteachers could pick up on these children and maybe help save them from their misery.

It's really hard to imagine that there can be a light at the end of the tunnel, because sometimes you just don't believe it.

MARY CATHERINE

I have a different kind of mental illness from what my niece LeeAnn and my ex-sister-in-law Melissa have. I have obsessive-compulsive disorder and panic disorder. I've had obsessions ever since the sixth grade, when I had counting

> *I wish people knew more about mental illness. There are so many kids who are sick, and the schools need to be more educated about mental illness. I wish the schoolteachers could pick up on these children and maybe help save them from their misery.*
>
> *— BETTY*

LeeAnn and Elizabeth

family and friends would think I was nuts.

When I tell people about my obsessive-compulsive disorder, some of them say, "I'm kind of like that, too, but I can stop." I can't. Everyone has some compulsions and obsessions, but not to the point where they take over your life.

A few years ago, I began to have an overwhelming feeling of anxiety that would just spread over me. I would get up and go to the school where I was a teacher, but I felt absolutely terrible. I didn't think I would make it through the day. It was an oppressive feeling that I wouldn't wish on anyone. I thought that maybe I was having a heart attack. One day I just passed out cold! I was taken to a hospital, where they did lots of tests. The doctors thought I might have a heart problem or an ulcer. It turned out to be panic attacks. It was the month of May, and I couldn't even finish out the school year.

I went on medication and I felt much better. I felt so good, in fact, that by the time the next school year started, I had stopped taking my medicine. That turned out to be a big mistake. I was in a store one day and I thought I was going to pass out. I realized that something wasn't right. I had a sick feeling like I was going to throw up, and the thought of suicide entered my head. I said to myself, "Oh, gosh, I've never had thoughts about suicide before." It scared the living daylights out of me. I kept saying to myself, "Be calm. These thoughts and feelings will go away." They would go away, but then they would come back. I saw a psychiatrist, who put me on a combination of several different medications, and I was able to go right back to work.

I wasn't ashamed to tell people at school that I was seeing a psychiatrist. They wanted to know what was wrong with

When I tell people about my obsessive-compulsive disorder, some of them say, "I'm kind of like that, too, but I can stop." I can't. Everyone has some compulsions and obsessions, but not to the point where they take over your life.
— MARY CATHERINE

compulsions and rituals. I would do certain things over and over again. I would think that something bad would happen if I didn't touch something three or four times. Even though I would tell myself that this was utterly ridiculous, it didn't make any difference. I would still have to do my rituals to stop the anxious feelings. I could control them to a point, so I was able to keep them pretty well hidden. I was afraid that my me, and I told them. They were all very encouraging, and some of them said, "Oh my Lord, I think I need to go see a psychiatrist, too."

"MEMA" HOWARD

It was terrible when my great-granddaughter, LeeAnn, got sick. Our church said prayers for her. We all did a lot of praying. I give God a lot of credit for how good she's doing now. We're just so proud of her.

I've been alone for twelve years, and LeeAnn visits me often. She's able to do my driving and my shopping for me now that she's so much better. We're doing fine together. The only way you can tell that she's sick is that she sleeps all the time. I'm afraid LeeAnn has that sleeping sickness. Sometimes I can't get her up for anything.

I've had a hard road. I had five children, and three of them died when they were babies. Only two of them survived into adulthood. One of my sons married Melissa's mom. He became mentally ill and he got so bad that we couldn't even go see him. He withdrew from everybody. We had him in the hospital and he had the lobotomy surgery. We spent twenty thousand dollars on him. We had done everything we had

been told to do, but one day he just walked out of church, got into his car, went to the river, and drove in. We followed him to the river, but we were too late to stop him. If we had gotten there sooner, maybe we could have saved him. He was only twenty-six years old.

DAVID

Melissa and I got divorced before our daughter, LeeAnn, got sick. In the beginning, I thought LeeAnn had bulimia or anorexia. It was like a bad dream. It seemed so cruel and unfair to basically watch her start to die.

I am not ashamed that my daughter has a mental illness, but I don't talk about it much. I've told a few close friends at work, but that's it. In the beginning I was in denial, but I'm past that now.

ELIZABETH

LeeAnn is my half sister. I was scared when LeeAnn first got sick. I cried and thought she was going to die. I feel happy that LeeAnn is so much better.

I wasn't ashamed to tell people at school that I was seeing a psychiatrist. They wanted to know what was wrong with me, and I told them. They were all very encouraging, and some of them said, "Oh my Lord, I think I need to go see a psychiatrist, too."
—MARY CATHERINE

Jonathan, Jennifer, and Jeremy

I kept telling my psychiatrist, "Well, if I could just go sit on the railroad tracks, a train will run over me and everything will be fine." He said, "No, Jennifer, it won't be fine. I'm not going to let you sit on the railroad tracks."
—JENNIFER

at night, I would just go straight to bed. I wasn't fixing supper for my kids or even talking to them much. I think I stayed with their dad as long as I did because he took care of them at night.

I was familiar with all the different kinds of psychiatric medications because of my job at the clinic. I finally went to my family doctor and told him that I thought I needed to be on an antidepressant. When I described my symptoms, he diagnosed me with major depression and started me on medication. I had basically diagnosed myself, so I kind of went into treatment backwards.

I did okay for a while, but I became depressed again about a year ago. I was going through my divorce and recovering from a hysterectomy at the time. I kept telling my psychiatrist, "Well, if I could just go sit on the railroad tracks, a train will run over me and everything will be fine." He said, "No, Jennifer, it won't be fine. I'm not going to let you sit on the railroad tracks." He didn't think he could trust me, so I wound up in a psychiatric hospital for the first time. My mom took the kids so I didn't have to worry about what was going on with them. I stayed in the psych unit for four weeks.

I pick and choose the people I tell about my diagnosis. I've got a couple of friends who understand. One of them is a psychiatrist who finished his residency this past summer. He listens to me, and we talk through a lot of stuff. Sometimes I tell my clients about my depression if I'm trying to talk them into going into the hospital for treatment. It seems to give them a sense that, "Well, if Jennifer's functioning, then maybe there's hope for me."

I've done some research into my Native American Apache heritage. It seems that their attitude toward mental illness has always been one of acceptance. I want to track down the trib-

I've done some research into my Native American Apache heritage. It seems that their attitude toward mental illness has always been one of acceptance.
—JENNIFER

managed to get through graduate school in social work. If I had gone through school sober and on antidepressants, I would have learned so much more.

I met my ex-husband in a bar one August, and we got married in November of the same year. It was one of those whirlwind-type things. If I had been sober, I wonder if I would have married him. I don't think so. I question some of the decisions I've made, and I know I would have done far better if my depression had been diagnosed and treated much earlier in my life.

After graduating, I got a job as a social worker at a mental health center. My boss didn't like me, and she did a real good job of making me miserable. The stress level was way too high, and I began to have crying spells at the office. When I got home al elders who can tell me more about my ancestors, because there's so much depression in my background. Now that I'm not so depressed and I can think again, I'm trying to find my roots. This is one of my quests.

JONATHAN

When Mom was depressed, I spent most of my nights in my room not paying much attention to her.

The day my mom was hospitalized, I was at school. A guidance counselor called me into his office and told me that I would be going to my grandmother's house instead of going home that afternoon. I'm like, "Hey?" So when I went over to my Gram's place, I said, "What happened to my mom?" Gram said, "She had a nervous breakdown." There's really no such thing. A nervous breakdown would be if your nervous system shut down. You'd be kind of dead!

The first time I knew Mom was on an antidepressant was during an ice storm that hit a couple of years ago. I was playing with my LEGOs and a tree came through the roof into the living room. Boom! I was sitting there and I saw it happen. It smashed my mom's irreplaceable Mardi Gras mask, which had been painted by one of our relatives. I went into a fit, yelling, "Oh, my God! A tree just fell through our roof!"

Mom was standing in the kitchen saying, "Thank the Lord we're okay! Thank the Lord!" And I'm like, "What the hell is she talking about? My mom has lost her mind!" We were still living with my dad at the time, and he said that if it weren't for her medication, Mom wouldn't have been as mellow as she was that day.

The only person outside of my family who I've told about my mother's depression is my ex-girlfriend. I told her that my mom was in the hospital because she had a nervous breakdown and that I hoped she would get better. It was hard to explain all this to the other kids at school. Try explaining depression to a bunch of lawyers' kids! They think they're better than you are. Anyhow, it's not really anybody's business.

Before I was diagnosed with my own depression, I spent all my time in my room. It was how I'd get away from my problems and just be alone. I could always turn on my music and tune out. When I get depressed, I disappear. Period. I'm just gone. I don't care about anything. Sometimes I'm suicidal. I get through each school day by putting on a happy face and pretending there's nothing wrong. I'm like a clown who wears a mask and disappears behind a curtain. No one can see me.

Depression is like being trapped in a deep, dark hole where you feel like you've got to run, but you can't. Life is uncertain. Eat dessert first.

> *When I get depressed, I disappear. Period. I'm just gone. I don't care about anything. Sometimes I'm suicidal. I get through each school day by putting on a happy face and pretending there's nothing wrong. I'm like a clown who wears a mask and disappears behind a curtain. No one can see me.*
> —JONATHAN

> *Depression is like being trapped in a deep, dark hole where you feel like you've got to run, but you can't. Life is uncertain. Eat dessert first.*
> —JONATHAN

Marco, Maria, Luz Maria, and Julio

THE JAURA/CHAN FAMILY

LOS ANGELES, CALIFORNIA

MARCO CHAN / MARIA T. BONYADI / LUZ MARIA JAURA
JULIO CHAN

MARCO

I HAD THE ALL-AMERICAN FAMILY UNTIL FIVE YEARS AGO. I was married and had two children, a boy and a girl. I had a good job as a salesman in wholesale produce, and I was making good money. I was hardworking, responsible, and very successful. I had a nice car and a nice house. I wasn't in need of anything. Every once in a while, I might get a little blue here and there, but never to the point where I needed medication or therapy or anything like that. I thought that I was invincible, like Superman. My life was good.

When I was thirty-four, I had a divorce with my wife. The divorce didn't come from me; it came from her. What really took me apart was when I went into the court system, I felt like a victim. I felt like I was raped, crucified, and taken advantage of. I couldn't do anything about it. I just gave up on life. I didn't see any reason to go on, and I quit wanting to live. Depression kicked in, and I've been fighting it ever since.

When I first had the troubles, I became nonfunctional. The changes in me were very noticeable. I couldn't eat cor-rectly. It would take me an hour to eat a bowl of cereal. I was moving very slowly, and my speech was slurred. To have a normal conversation with someone took me ten or fifteen times longer than usual. I couldn't drive. My brain was in slow motion. I was almost zombie-like.

I knew something was wrong and, right away, I sought out psychiatric help. If you've got a big cut on your arm or something, you know you've got to go to the doctor and fix it. I was diagnosed with acute and severe major depression. I went into therapy and was immediately put on medication.

I would sometimes get the feeling that my friends and family thought that I was faking it. They didn't really know what to make of me; they just didn't understand. My employers didn't understand, either. I couldn't make it to work on time, and there were days when I would even miss work. Lots of people said to me, "Well, you look fine and you seem fine. Why aren't you functioning? Just get over it! Get on with your life." It was hard for me to explain to them that it wasn't quite that easy.

My emotions were out of control to the point where I even became suicidal. One of the biggest problems for me

Lots of people said to me, "Well, you look fine and you seem fine. Why aren't you functioning? Just get over it! Get on with your life." It was hard for me to explain to them that it wasn't quite that easy.

—MARCO

129

My brothers and sisters were there for me. I don't know how well they understood to what degree this disease had taken over my life, but they all wanted me to get better. They were willing to do just about everything and anything that they could to help me. I felt a lot of comfort and a lot of love from my family, and I still do.

—MARCO

was that I would wake up in the morning with no desire to get out of bed. I had no ambition. I was even off work for a while. When I went back to my job, I struggled. I was much better, but I still had difficult times when the depression would hit me hard and take over my whole being, my feelings, and my emotions. I had a lot of anxiety and stress. My mind was scrambling.

I had an interview with a psychologist who asked me a lot of in-depth questions, including some about suicide. I was very truthful in my answers, and I told her that at one point I had wanted to kill myself. She must have thought, "This man is going to go out and kill himself!" She took it upon herself to call the police and let them know that I was possibly a danger to myself. The police took me to the county hospital.

When I was in the hospital, I could have said, "My life is coming to an end and I'm just going to die here." But I didn't do that. Instead, I did as much as possible to help myself. I also did everything I could to show the doctors that I was okay. Yes, I was suffering from depression, but I knew I didn't need to be in that hospital. Some patients there were totally out of control. They were hitting themselves against the wall or walking around in circles. I wanted to get out of there! When a doctor finally came to interview me, he said, "You know what? You do have some problems, but there's no reason why you should be in the hospital." So I went back home to live with my mom.

My mom understood quite a bit about what was going on with me, because she has schizophrenia. She had experienced a lot of what I was going through, so she was able to help me better understand what was happening. Mom gave me a lot of support. I lived with her for almost three years.

My family members were also supportive. My brothers and sisters were there for me. I don't know how well they understood to what degree this disease had taken over my life, but they all wanted me to get better. They were willing to do just about everything and anything that they could to help me. I felt a lot of comfort and a lot of love from my family, and I still do.

There are times when people have thought that I'm a lunatic or that I'm crazy. For example, I once went out of the country for business. When I came back, I was going through customs and for some reason I was sent to a side room. Maybe I looked kind of weird or dangerous, but for whatever reason, I was chosen to be searched. They wanted me to open my luggage. When I opened it, they saw a package that was all wrapped up. One of the officers said to me, "What do you have in there?" I said, "It's a present for my mom." She asked me to open it. I was a little nervous and anxious by then, and I told her, "You know, I just want to go home. I want to get this over with." And the lady said, "Open it." I said, "No. You open it." We got into a power struggle because I refused to cooperate.

When the customs officers asked me a question, I wouldn't answer them. They put me in another room, and some security guards came. They were treating me the way they would treat a criminal, because they thought I had drugs or contraband or something. The head of security wanted to ask me some questions, but I wouldn't talk to him either. I sat down on the floor, put my head between my legs, and completely shut down. By this point, I had gone into a crisis mode. The customs people didn't know what was happening to me.

The friend that I was traveling with tried to explain to the airport officials that I was suffering from depression, that I was on medication, and that there was nothing to be feared. The security people called the paramedics who came and put me in a wheelchair. The paramedics said, "There's nothing wrong with this guy. He's just going through a crisis." The security people finally opened up the present I had for my mom and saw that it was nothing but a picture. Everybody, even the head of security, was apologizing to me. By the time everything was said and done, they felt so bad for what had happened.

I have always sought out the best mental health care that I could find, and I feel that I was fortunate to get very good services. I didn't go through the county or state for any of my mental health services. I have a lot of reservations about the public mental health system. I think that they try to do the best they can, but their facilities are overwhelmed with patients. I don't think they fully understand or care about their patients. They look upon people who have mental illness as people they don't want to deal with. It's as if they are saying, "These patients aren't bleeding; they're not dying. Just put them over there, and we'll do the best we can."

I only go through private sources for my mental health care. I have to pay for my doctors out of my own pocket, and my experiences with these private doctors have been very good. They've helped me, and I believe in them. I've had times when the anxiety and the fear set in, and I need to see and talk to them. When I do, I can sense their care and understanding.

I've started a new life. In the beginning of my relationship with my new wife, I didn't really say anything to her about my depression. It started off just like any other normal relationship. As we got more serious, I would tell her that I had to take medication for a certain condition or that I had to go see the doctors for therapy. I wouldn't exactly say that I was mentally ill. As we got closer, I pretty much told her everything about why I was taking the pills and about why I was seeing the doctors. She was very surprised, because for the most part, when I'm not depressed, I'm a very productive person. I'm very responsible, and very aggressive in wanting to do the best I can.

I talk about myself to other family members and friends as little as possible. For example, I haven't worked for the past three months because I went into another crisis. I don't say nothing to nobody. If anybody should ask me, "Why aren't you working?" I'll say, "I'm on vacation," or "I'm on a sabbatical." I'm a very private person.

My depression still continues to be a problem for me. I think my mental condition has actually worsened. I don't want to have the depression. I don't want to feel the way I feel. I'm always looking for answers and for help. I go to my psychiatrist; I go to my therapist; I go to support groups; I take

Marco and Luz Maria

my medication. I don't want to vegetate in a room somewhere and let my life go to waste.

I don't know what lies in the future for me, but I hope that someday soon I can return back to my normal self.

MARIA

My brother, Marco, pretty much got sick overnight. He was a "normal" person and then, from one day to the next, his life got turned around. I wasn't as much a part of his life as our brother, Julio, was at that time. Marco leaned toward people he had closer relationships with, but he did feel my support. Marco's psychologist called us siblings up and said, "I

When someone is mentally ill, you have to deal with it. If you hide it, what are you going to tell people at work when you have to leave to take care of problems at home? If people know the truth, they become more understanding.

—MARIA

think Marco needs to see and feel the support of his family." It was necessary for the family to participate in therapy with him, and we did.

Marco is a very private person. He chose who he wanted to confide in, and I respected that. If he felt like sharing things with me, then I was there for him. I think I was afraid to talk to Marco when he first got sick. I understood his illness, but I didn't know how to relate to him. I was afraid I might say something in the wrong way and set him off. Because Marco was not functioning with a "normal" mind, I was scared he might take whatever I said the wrong way. I understood that my brother was having a problem, and anything that we needed to do for him, we did. Our family always told Marco that we loved him, and he felt our love.

My mother, Luz Maria, also has a mental illness. She was hospitalized for the first time a month after her mother's funeral. Marco called me at work, saying, "Maria, Mom's lost it. You've got to come home." We tried to get Mom to go to the doctor on her own, but she wouldn't go, so I called the police. When the police came, they called the ambulance and tried to get my mother to go to the doctor, too, but she wouldn't go with them, either. Then the sergeant assessed the situation and said that Mom was gradually getting worse and that she needed help right away. The only way to get help for my mother was to have her arrested.

My siblings and I saw our mother deteriorate in a matter of two or three hours. She was carrying on, getting worse and worse. So we decided, yes, let's have her arrested because she needs the help. The only way to get her in the police car was to have her handcuffed. We were all crying because it hurt us to have to do this to our mother.

When people first asked me what was wrong with my mother, I felt a little bit embarrassed. But as time went on, I heard myself saying, "My mother has a mental illness problem." By the time Marco got sick, I could say, "This is what's wrong with my brother, and this is what we're doing to help him."

I became more open when I realized that Mom had a problem that wasn't going to go away. I now know that her illness is here to stay and we have to help her. Over the years, she has had three hospitalizations. Mom is a U.S. citizen; she's a human being with rights, but she's ill and she can't always make decisions on her own. So who is going to make these decisions for her, even down to feeding her and taking care of her personal necessities? The last time she got sick, we had to bathe her, clean her, wash her, feed her, and dress her. It got that bad! Now my mom can feel her depression coming on, and she knows what to do to try and avoid it.

When someone is mentally ill, you have to deal with it. If you hide it, what are you going to tell people at work when you have to leave to take care of problems at home? If people know the truth, they become more understanding.

JULIO

My sister, Maria, says that Marco got sick pretty quickly, but I think his illness was happening all along. For me, his divorce is the thing that really spiked it up. It was like there was always a fire going on in Marco, but the divorce was the big fuel that tore into him.

I think a lot of stuff had been accumulating for Marco. Everyone in our family was taken by surprise by Marco's illness, but I wasn't too surprised. When you start to add up all the incidents that had happened over the years, then maybe there was a sign. When you put it all together, I think Marco's illness was slowly developing. It just blew up one day.

Marco and I worked together for almost two years, so we hung out and talked a lot. When he started having his crisis, he began living with our mother, but I was the one who was really a strong arm for him. I was not afraid to confront him or talk about anything with him.

Marco is our older brother and he has always been a leader in our family. He was a very good leader. Even if someone is losing it, they still want to show that they're capable of being a leader. Nobody really wants to say, "You know what I think? I can't be the leader of this family anymore." I think that's what happened to Marco. He was worried that we were going to get mad at him if he stepped aside.

How did my brother get this illness? How did my mother get hers? The only answer that I keep getting is that, just like cancer and heart disease, mental illness can run in a family. That's what I'm starting to understand. I think mental illness originates more from our mother's side of the family, because she was the one who started getting ill first. Our father didn't help, because he was a bad father. I think all of my brothers and sisters and I have some kind of mental illness, some more so than others.

My wife and I and our newborn baby were living with my mother when Mom's mental problems started. When my wife and I chose to move to our own place, it affected Mom. Mom began telling me that our father was back in town to kill her! At that point I believed her story, because he had been abusive to her before their divorce. Little did I know then that she had schizophrenia.

My siblings blame me for moving out, but I think my mother's illness was caused by a combination of a lot of things. When my mother fell apart, we had to call the police. We didn't call them thinking she'd get arrested. We called the police for assistance. Mom was handcuffed because that was the only way to get her to go to the hospital. Even though she's probably convinced that it all went the wrong way, it was the right way because we eventually got her some help.

From the police station, my mother was taken to a hospital. A patient there asked her, "Why are you here?" My mother said, "Well, I think it's because I killed my mother."

How did my brother get this illness? How did my mother get hers? The only answer that I keep getting is that, just like cancer and heart disease, mental illness can run in a family. That's what I'm starting to understand.

—*JULIO*

Julio

From day one, I was never embarrassed to tell anybody about my family. I figured it's better for everybody to know. This way, I found out that I wasn't the only one who had a family with problems. Everybody else did, too. Some had smaller problems; some had bigger ones. Some of this, some of that.

—*JULIO*

Mom actually believed that she had killed her own mother! My mother was transferred to a locked facility, where she got well enough to come back home.

From day one, I was never embarrassed to tell anybody about my family. I figured it's better for everybody to know. This way, I found out that I wasn't the only one who had a family with problems. Everybody else did, too. Some had smaller problems; some had bigger ones. Some of this, some of that.

I remember the paramedics coming, and then the police came, too. The voices in my head were getting louder. The policemen put handcuffs on me because I was not cooperating. They were only following procedures.

— LUZ MARIA

LUZ MARIA

(translated by Maria Bonyadi and Maria Marquez)

I had my first crisis after the death of my mother in 1989. A month after her funeral, I woke up feeling weird and strange. I sat down on a couch, still in my pajamas. I started hearing voices inside my head that were yelling and telling me horrible things. I began to scream.

I don't know who came into the room to help me, but I didn't want to move from that couch. I remember that my daughter, Maria, took me to the bedroom to help me get dressed, but I refused. The dress she wanted me to wear was the one that was bought for my mother before her death. It was given to me after she passed away, and I hated it very much. After I got dressed, I sat back down on the couch again.

I remember the paramedics coming, and then the police came, too. The voices in my head were getting louder. The policemen put handcuffs on me because I was not cooperating. They were only following procedures.

I was taken to the police station, where I had a lot of hallucinations. I saw God and the Devil. The police locked me up while they were waiting for a psychiatrist to arrive. I was very scared. I remember very clearly all that went on around me that day. I remember seeing my children's faces and that they were all crying.

The psychiatrist who saw me at the jail told me that all this was happening to me because of my mother's death. He also told me that I had to go to a hospital for a few days. I spent one night in a state hospital and then a week in another hospital. During my stay there, I told a patient that I was in the hospital because I had killed my mother. Of course, this wasn't true.

While I was at the hospital, I was diagnosed with manic-depressive illness and schizophrenia and was put on medication. I participated in a lot of activities and groups, and I even won a trophy for dancing. My children visited me often, and I was given a one-day pass to go home to visit with them.

When I got out of the hospital, I went back to see the doctor who had been treating me for depression before my crisis. I had already gone to group and individual therapy to deal with the abuse my children and I had received from my ex-husband. This doctor changed and adjusted my medications, and I slowly began to get better and return to my everyday life.

During the Gulf War, I had a relapse. I was going to school and taking computer classes. When I typed, the computer screen would tell me, "Look at the news! Look at the news!" I immediately recognized the signs of psychosis and went to see my doctor. I also began suffering from paranoia. I felt like I was being persecuted by my ex-husband and by some other family members. I believed that people were trying to hurt me.

I got better for a while, but I started getting ill again in 1992. On special occasions or on days that would remind me of my mother, such as her birthday, Mother's Day, and the anniversary of her death, I would get very depressed. As these days would approach, I would start to have a relapse and get sick.

In Mexico, many people try to hide mental illness if it's in their family. They deny it, and sometimes they even put people away. They say, "Let's not talk about it." In my own family, I had two cousins on my father's side who suffered from mental illness. There were probably more, but these two are the ones who lived near me.

One of my cousins was a singer. She had an emotional crisis at a very young age and was never able to go back to singing. She would often get lost and be missing for many months. Then she would come back around. She was hospitalized several times, but she was always able to escape. She lived like this for about forty years until ten years ago when she was never heard from again. We don't know what actually happened to her.

My other cousin suffered from problems similar to my own. She was diagnosed with bipolar disorder. I became aware of her illness when I would go visit her and see bottles of medications in her bathroom. They were the same ones that I was taking. She wouldn't take her medications unless she was very ill. I would tell her to take her pills, but she refused. Maybe she was ashamed and could not accept her condition. Perhaps the lack of care and attention was the reason she passed away.

I used to go to a support group at the clinic, but that ended a few months ago. I don't know if they will bring this group back, but many of us benefit from help like this. My son, Marco, says that this is an example of how the county mental health system does not care for us. They do not understand how important it is for me and many others to get this kind of support. Marco says that without these groups, you can get lost in your own world.

Patti, Lynette, and Jeremy

THE MARGULIES / THOMPSON FAMILY

MADISON, WISCONSIN

PATTI THOMPSON / LYNETTE MARGULIES
JEREMY LEE MARGULIES

LYNETTE

I DIDN'T KNOW ANYTHING ABOUT DEPRESSION until I was hit with it in a big, big way.

I had my first major depressive episode in 1989, but at the time, I didn't know what depression was. I didn't know anybody else who had it, so I had no idea what was wrong with me. I thought I was the only person in the universe who felt the way I did.

If I had known more about depression from the beginning, I might not have suffered as long and as hard as I did. Now my mission is to get the word out and let people know that having depression is not a taboo. After all, it seems like half the population is on antidepressants! In fact, I've written a musical that I star in about my experience with depression, called *Soul Journey*.

My illness began after a long-term committed relationship ended abruptly. My partner and I owned a house together, and we were raising her kid. I was very involved in my community and I was also a singer in a very popular band. Boom! All of a sudden, it was all gone. After my partner told me that she wanted to live separately, I went emotionally downhill in three days. I was in total blackness and despair. Good-bye. Good night. I didn't know what was happening to me. I had never been so depressed before. Breaking up with someone is a common life situation, but I wasn't living in reality. Imagine what it's like to have no control of your brain. It's scary. Something in my brain was broken. But mental illness isn't like a broken leg. You can't just put on a cast and fix it.

The week after my relationship ended, I moved from Wisconsin to my parents' home in Florida. I needed to be taken care of and I needed unconditional love. I thought, "Okay, whatever is happening to me will certainly go away in a week or two." But it didn't. I went through torment for almost a year. At first, I couldn't eat and I couldn't sleep.

> *I wasn't living in reality. Imagine what it's like to have no control of your brain. It's scary. Something in my brain was broken. But mental illness isn't like a broken leg. You can't just put on a cast and fix it.*
> —LYNETTE

My parents are the reason I'm alive today. They were supportive, they loved me unconditionally, and they stuck with me even though they didn't really understand what was happening. They knew there was something terribly wrong with me, and, at the time, they felt helpless. What did they see when they looked at me? They saw a person who used to be full of life but was now dead inside. They saw me crying and begging for help for hours on end. It must be devastating for parents to witness this kind of despair in their child.

— *LYNETTE*

I lost about fifty pounds in two months, and I probably only slept about forty hours in that entire time. The only thing I could manage to do was take a shower in the morning. I think what actually got me into the bathroom was looking in the mirror at my body. I would see myself and think, "That's not me." I was on an emotional roller coaster, and I was suicidal for over a year. I should have been in a psychiatric hospital, but when I left town to go live with my parents, I lost my job and, with it, my health insurance.

I didn't get adequate help at first. I went to see a therapist who did me a terrible disservice. You would think that a mental health professional would have had the sense to put me on medication. Instead, she would say things like, "Well, you're not going to let your 'ex' have power over you, are you?" Meanwhile I was spending most of my time curled up in a fetal position, sobbing. I couldn't function at all, and I suffered deeply. Three hellish months later, I finally saw a therapist who put me on medication.

I was hesitant about taking drugs, because I didn't know anything about antidepressants. They weren't even a part of my vocabulary back then. I didn't want to take any medication because I thought it might alter my mind. Well, my mind was already severely altered. I was not with it enough to know what I needed! I didn't know that my depression was far more than just grief for my lost relationship. I didn't know I had an illness. I certainly didn't know that I couldn't get over it by myself. I didn't know any of these things.

In the beginning, I thought, "I'm going to feel this way forever." Thanks to my medications, the therapist I was seeing, and my parents, I gradually began to get better. In fact, my parents are the reason I'm alive today. They were supportive, they loved me unconditionally, and they stuck with me even though they didn't really understand what was happening. They knew there was something terribly wrong with me, and, at the time, they felt helpless. What did they see when they looked at me? They saw a person who used to be full of life but was now dead inside. They saw me crying and begging for help for hours on end.

It must be devastating for parents to witness this kind of despair in their child.

There is mental illness in my family. I have a nephew who is manic-depressive, and my uncle's wife hasn't been able to really function well for thirty years. So mental illness is not something my parents are unfamiliar with. My parents and I didn't keep my depression a secret. They had a huge community of friends, and I met them all. I wasn't ashamed that I was sick, and I was very verbal about what was going on with me at the time.

I met my current partner, Patti, three years ago at a women's pancake breakfast, and we've been together ever since. She always wanted to have a baby, and about five months ago she gave birth to our son, Jeremy.

I made a big mistake a year ago. I went off my medication because I wasn't sure if it was working. Three months after Jeremy was born, I got really depressed for the first time in ten years. I never realized how all-consuming taking care of a baby could be, and I didn't anticipate such a massive change in my life. When Patti went back to work, I was the at-home mom. I started to lose it, and everything snowballed really fast after that. I was also sleep-deprived, and that's always been a big trigger for me emotionally.

In three days, boom! I went back down into the depths of pain. Jeremy was not responsible for my depression; he was not the culprit, my illness was. This time I knew what was happening to me. I said to myself, "This will pass, but I'm in deep shit right now." My therapist recommended that I go to a friend's house because I was so uncomfortable at home. When the therapist asked if I was suicidal, I answered, "Well, I think I am." Twelve hours later I was on my way to a psychiatric hospital.

I got admitted to the psych unit through the E.R., where I was triaged with other patients who were waiting to be seen. I was sitting on the floor crying and I couldn't even talk. I was finally taken into another room, where I had to tell my story at least four times before I was sent upstairs to the unit. I remember seeing crazy people in the hallways. It was just so intense. My brain wasn't functioning right. I felt as if I were on the verge of being dead.

A nurse, bless her heart, said, "Let's forget taking Lynette's blood pressure. Let's give her some anti-anxiety medication right away." Before the meds kicked in, I was out of it for two days. I'd see friends later on and ask, "Did you know I was in the hospital?" and they'd say, "Well, yeah! I was there visiting you." Or, "Oh, yeah! I talked to you on the phone." It was like having an alcoholic blackout.

I was in the hospital for eight days. I don't think I had any therapy during that time. It was pretty clear that I knew my story; I knew what was happening and why it was happening. It was just a question of waiting until the medication kicked in.

For the last month or so, it's been completely uphill for me. Lately I've been feeling one hundred percent myself. When I was depressed, I couldn't deal with Jeremy because I was so sick. I couldn't do anything for myself, and I wondered, "How the hell am I going to take care of this baby?" I felt very guilty about this, and Patti had a hard time with it, too. Now that I'm okay, I think Jeremy is fabulous. I love him. Being a mom is totally joyous. I've got a lot of love to give, and Jeremy is the object of my total affection.

PATTI

Since I've been with Lynette, I've become more open about my own depression. Because of my relationship with her, I've been able to find words for my feelings, and I can better identify what happens to me when I get depressed. I can say to Lynette, "I have some depression today" and, because of her, I can actually describe what I'm feeling. In the past it was just a long silent struggle for me.

When I look back at my own life, I think that I've had depression for most of it. I remember being a freshman in high school and writing a suicide note in class. I hoped the nun who was circulating through the classroom would real-

Patti, Lynette, and Jeremy

ize that I wasn't doing my homework and would come over and ask, "What are you working on?" I wanted her to see my note and read it. She never did, and I remember feeling terrible that my little scenario hadn't worked out the way I wanted it to.

I began having serious thoughts of suicide after a long-term relationship I was in ended back in 1993. This was the first really huge blow that I had ever had. I started dating again, and eventually I began to come out of my depression.

About two years later, I started thinking about suicide again. I was with a new lover at the time, and we had to give our dog away because we were living in an apartment that didn't allow animals. When my girlfriend left to drive the dog to her parents' house in Nebraska, I was home alone the entire time. I remember being wide-awake at three o'clock

I come from a family where you shut up and buck up. Until I met Lynette, that's how I handled my depression. My mom has a lot of issues about what other people think; she is really into how you present yourself to the world. To say that you were gay or that you were on antidepressants or were suicidal, or that you were getting a "C" in school were things you just didn't talk about in my family.

— PATTI

in the morning, plotting how to kill myself. There was no real reason why I needed to do that. My job was good, and our relationship was good, but I still felt terrible. I wanted to call a suicide hotline, but I thought there was probably somebody out there who was a lot more suicidal than I was and that I shouldn't take up the hotline's time!

That summer I had suicidal thoughts every hour, and then every five minutes. I would be sitting and having a conversation in my head. "I'm going to be dead tomorrow and aren't you going to be sad? Ha! Ha! Ha!" I was always scanning the environment for a particular place where I could kill myself. "Oh! There's a balcony here. I could probably jump off." I work on a busy street, and every time I crossed it, I would have this constant thought: "Okay, I'm going to let a bus hit me now." It was crazy thinking.

My partner completely freaked out when I told her I was suicidal. One day, I came back home, and all of her stuff was gone and so was she. Then I realized, "Okay, great, I live alone now, so I can kill myself." Part of the reason why I hadn't killed myself sooner was because I didn't want a roommate or a partner to come home and find my dead body.

I sat in my house one night with the lights out, and imagined a gun in my mouth. In my heart, I didn't really want to do it. Deep down, that's when I realized I was really sick and had to get some help. I was heading into a serious meltdown.

In desperation, I called my HMO and tried to get an emergency appointment with a therapist. I had never seen a therapist before, ever. They offered me an appointment a month and a half later! I was still on total meltdown the next day and I called again to see if I could come in right away. They said, "Okay, instead of the nineteenth, why don't you come in on the sixteenth?" I screamed over the phone, "Why can't you see me now?" They finally said, "Okay! Come right in." So I did. The therapist I met with said, "Why don't you go home and sleep and you'll get better. Relationships are hard when you lose them."

I finally called my nurse practitioner and told her, "I'm thinking about suicide every single second of the day; it's a

constant thought, and it's been going on for months. I really need help." She saw me early the next morning and gave me a prescription for an antidepressant. I remember getting this medication and thinking, "I must be crazy." I didn't want to have to take a pill in order to get through the loss of a relationship. That night I went to an Al-Anon meeting to find some support. In front of about thirty strangers, I said, "I was just prescribed an antidepressant and I'm really suicidal and I'm afraid to take it because I don't want to be labeled as crazy." It turned out that just about everybody else in the room was on antidepressants, too, so I thought, "Oh, all right!" That's when I started taking medication.

I come from a family where you shut up and buck up. Until I met Lynette, that's how I handled my depression. My mom has a lot of issues about what other people think; she is really into how you present yourself to the world. To say that you were gay, or that you were on antidepressants, or that you were suicidal, or that you were getting a "C" in school were all things you just didn't talk about in my family.

There is depression in my family. My dad has depression, and I think my brother does, too. My sister has also struggled with depression and she has had bouts of suicidal thoughts for the last four years. She's seeing a therapist and is doing much better. She's even earned her master's degree in social work.

When I got pregnant, I went off my medication. That was a bad mistake. It wreaked havoc on me and on my relationship with Lynette for the entire nine months of my pregnancy. Not only was I physically sick all the time, I was also really depressed. I was very disappointed when I found out that we were going to have a boy. I had always dreamed of having a girl who was a tomboy. Lynette really understood how I was feeling, and she hung in there with me the whole time. She is very intuitive, and she recognizes when I'm getting depressed even if I myself don't see it coming on. She'll say, "You just worked a fifty-hour week, and you got slammed at work for something, so no wonder you're a little bit down."

I always wanted to have a baby and, when I was single, I searched for a partner who would want to have one with me. Having a baby was my number one priority. Lynette also wanted to have a baby, and I held her to it. When she got so depressed shortly after Jeremy was born, I felt guilty because I thought that somehow I had caused her depression. It wasn't that she didn't want to have a baby. It was just that there was so much stress in our relationship after Jeremy was born.

It's only been a month since Lynette has been out of the hospital, and I'm still working through it. It was a very scary time for me, and I'm still a little nervous because she's been on a bit of an emotional roller coaster recently. I've kind of lost faith that Lynette's going to be able to hold it together, that we're going to be able to do this family thing, and that she's going to be able to be there for Jeremy. I worry that she may not be able to withstand the stress of our life with a new baby in it.

When Lynette was hospitalized so soon after Jeremy was born, I was a tiny bit resentful. I'd just gone back to work and I was working forty or fifty hours a week trying to catch up after my maternity leave. With Lynette in the hospital, all of a sudden I was a single mom. When she got out, we both struggled to figure out our mutual roles in our rela-tionship. I wanted to help her and yet I needed to keep my distance so that I didn't get myself lost in her depression.

In the throes of coping with Lynette's depression, I found myself pulling away from her and becoming very protective of our son. Lynette was rejecting him. When she was sick, she thought that Jeremy was the culprit for what was going on with her. I had to get in between the two of them and defend our son.

I encouraged our friends to help Lynette in her time of crisis. Some friends came over one night to take Lynette out for the evening. Jeremy was sleeping, so I showed them pictures of him. Lynette started screaming and yelling at us to get the pictures out of the room because she couldn't stand to see them. That was really scary for me.

Lynette and I have been in therapy for a long time, and we talk about the whole circle of guilt that we both get caught up in. For instance, sleep deprivation is a trigger for Lynette's depression. I go out of my way to try to make sure she gets all the sleep that she needs. But in the meantime, I'm sacri-ficing myself by staying up all night with Jeremy. Then I get crabby, and Lynette feels guilty because she knows I have to get up and go to work in the morning. We just keep going around and around. We're still trying to figure everything out.

Dorothy and Mike

THE McLENDON FAMILY

FRANKLIN, TENNESSEE

DOROTHY McLENDON / MIKE McLENDON

MIKE

WHEN I WAS A CHILD, I LIVED IN AN IMAGINARY WORLD because I couldn't cope with the real one.

By the time I was six or seven, I had developed symptoms of obsessive-compulsive disorder. By the time I was ten, I was doing things repetitively like straightening towels over and over again. If I didn't do things "just right," I had a tremendous amount of anxiety.

My home environment was stressful because my mom was a single parent and we struggled financially. I didn't feel anchored there. My mom wasn't secure emotionally and she also did certain things repetitively. I can remember her cleaning things over and over again, which probably reinforced my own bizarre behavior.

In junior high, my behaviors became more and more extreme. I would sit in complete silence in the middle of the floor. I needed to be alone and I didn't want anyone near me. I thought people could get at me in a supernatural way, so I would just sit there and hold my breath.

By the time I was fifteen, I could no longer conceal my behaviors. One symptom I had was checking, and the other was more internal. I had repetitive thoughts that kept coming and wouldn't stop. If I was reading a book and I didn't read each sentence over and over again, I thought that something bad would happen.

Kids at school began to make fun of me. I would carry a little satchel around and they called me "the professor." I thought all the other kids were my enemy, and I couldn't relate to my peers at all. I also avoided contact with adults. It made me anxious to think of other folks coming into my world. I was afraid they would disrupt the harmony and sense of balance I was trying so hard to maintain.

I got thrown out of school in the middle of ninth grade because I just couldn't hack it. When you write something down twenty or thirty times and then erase it over and over again, obviously you're not going to make an "A." My teachers didn't understand what was going on, and the kids were just brutal. I had always done well in school, and it hurt to get thrown out. It bothered me a lot.

I was very confused and frightened by my behaviors because I knew they weren't normal. I understood reality and I knew that other kids my age didn't have these kinds of problems. I should have been out riding my bike and having a good time. Instead, I was under a tremendous amount of stress. I felt like a crockpot that had been left on the stove too long. I constantly struggled to keep my sense of self.

—MIKE

I was very confused and frightened by my behaviors because I knew they weren't normal. I understood reality and I knew that other kids my age didn't have these kinds of problems. I should have been out riding my bike and having a good time. Instead, I was under a tremendous amount of stress. I felt like a crockpot that had been left on the stove too long. I constantly struggled to keep my sense of self.

I went into a state hospital because my mother didn't have a lot of money. A psychologist there came up with many different diagnoses to describe what was wrong with me. At one point, a television camera recorded my twitches, my inability to wash my own hair, and the constant struggle I had taking care of myself. If you looked at me then, you could see that I was a very disturbed child. It helped to talk about my problems with professionals who didn't judge me or call me crazy.

I got out of the hospital and eventually I plowed my way through high school. I tried to figure out ways to battle my symptoms on my own. I exercised and worked hard. I had the ability to go faster, but my illness kept pulling me back, which made me go slower. I would say, "Mom, this is holding me back."

I knew something wasn't right during college. It was pure agony to live in that world, and I hated it. There were times when I wanted to put a gun to my head. I hated myself because I couldn't control what was going on with me. My strange behaviors and obsessive thoughts were still with me, and it took sheer willpower to suppress them, at least to some degree.

I really didn't know what was going on. I said to myself, "Well, I have a choice. I can either languish the rest of my life feeling sorry for myself, or I can battle my way through it." I decided to battle through it, and I had just enough steam to perform well academically. I have a personality that is aggressive by nature, and I handled a lot of my problems on my own. I fought my way through my difficulties like a steam engine.

My social life stank. People picked up on weird things about me. I had never learned to socialize well as a child, and this still affected me in college. I didn't date much, and when I did, I tended to get overly involved with the opposite sex. I made a conscious choice not to tell anyone about my problems, because I was afraid of how I would be perceived.

I didn't get appropriate therapy until I was well into my late twenties. I wasn't formally diagnosed with OCD until three years ago. My disease had been tearing me apart for so long, and my therapist was the first person who could identify it and explain my behaviors. He really cared about me, and I was so relieved. I didn't feel like a freak anymore. Finally, I knew that there was nothing to be ashamed of.

Medication has helped me tremendously. It kicked in, and wow! Recently I've started working again, and I'm able to do accounting and auditing easily. Now I can drink a beer with the guys, socialize, do karaoke, and go to parties. I enjoy the ladies an awful lot. I'm dating and having fun. But even today, my world is small.

The kind of woman I want to be with should be understanding of my illness and love me for who I am. Certain people are shallow and judge others from the outside. That kind of person wouldn't accept me, so meeting the right person is very important to me. I want to share my life in partnership with someone who will help me meet my goals, whether professional or political, or whatever. I will raise my kids as a stable father who plays ball with them, pays attention to them, and loves them. I want my children to have a secure life and a secure upbringing. I can make that

I'm not particularly optimistic about the good graces of humanity. There are good and bad people out there, and if someone chooses to use my illness against me, that's their problem. I don't feel that I have to reveal all that much about my illness to other people. It's part of my life, and something I have to deal with on my own.

—MIKE

conscious choice; it all comes down to choice. Some things are overpowering when you have OCD, but there are things you can choose to control.

I'm not particularly optimistic about the good graces of humanity. There are good and bad people out there, and if someone chooses to use my illness against me, that's their problem. I don't feel that I have to reveal all that much about my illness to other people. It's part of my life, and something I have to deal with on my own.

God has sent a lot of people my way who have helped me enormously. I've had good role models in my church who have supported me, and the biggest thing I've learned is compassion for others. If I come across people who want or need help, I'll give it to them.

I still have obsessive thoughts, but I can control them better than ever before. I can block them out by thinking about something else, or by talking to a friend. I recognize my behaviors now for what they are—they're petty, they waste time, and they take away from my life.

The key to OCD is to fight it. OCD feeds on itself, and the more attention you pay to it, the worse it gets. Some people may not have as much willpower as I do, but I think it's possible to change your life, to turn things around for yourself, and to get help if things aren't right. It's not good to languish in your own problems. That's the worst thing you can do.

DOROTHY

When Mike was younger, he would walk up the street toward our house and just stop dead in his tracks. He would pace back and forth, and I'd say, "Mike, the neighbors are watching." But he'd repeat this behavior over and over again anyway. I couldn't get through to him at all.

Mike's entertainment was being by himself. He was always alone. He thought that everyone was out to get him, even me. I used to worry about him, wondering what I

Dorothy and Mike

People think that having a mental illness is a shameful thing, and they don't respect you if you have one. I don't think they should look down on it, or say, "I don't have anyone in my family like that." People should be more tolerant.

— DOROTHY

had done wrong. I blamed myself for his problems, but I don't do that anymore.

The church gave Mike a lot of support when he was older, and support is what you really need when you have a mental illness. You need someone to understand you. I think that being religious has helped anchor Mike. His medications and his doctor have helped a lot, too, and this is wonderful. Mike has done remarkably well. He's become a different person. The world's too big to give up on, and my son never did that.

People think that having a mental illness is a shameful thing, and they don't respect you if you have one. I don't think they should look down on it, or say, "I don't have anyone in my family like that." People should be more tolerant.

Carol, Celeste, Antoine (Carol's great-grandson), and Wilma

THE CHAPMAN / SIRMONS FAMILY

PITTSBURGH, PENNSYLVANIA

CAROL CHAPMAN / CELESTE CHAPMAN / WILMA SIRMONS

CAROL

My daughter, Celeste, was a mental patient for seven years. I'd think Celeste would be okay, and then she'd call me crying, "Ma, come and get me. I'm having a bad day." I went through this several times when Celeste would go on and off her medicine. One day I went out to her house and she had her baby girl sitting out in the car all alone. And it was snowing! God was with us that day.

I had to raise Celeste's daughter all those years because Celeste wouldn't stay on her medicine. I used to say to her, "Look, if the medicine don't work for you right, tell your therapist what it's doing to you and he'll help you. Just don't get off of it. That's the worst thing you can do."

I'd bring Celeste over to my house to try to watch her, but I couldn't keep doing that because she was so manic and out of it. I finally had to commit her to a mental hospital because I was afraid she might harm herself. And given the state she was in, she would have.

When Celeste was in the hospital, she'd be mad at me and at everyone else. A lot of people told me, "I wouldn't go see her if I were you," and I'd say, "Well, she's my child. If I don't go, don't nobody go." I had sense enough to know that the way Celeste was acting was the sickness and not her. I knew my daughter! She wouldn't act that way unless something was wrong with her. So I kept going to visit her and I didn't pay her no attention when she'd get mad at me. I had to keep checking on how they was treating her and what they would be doing with her. You have to check on your people because if you don't, they just throw the mentally ill in the corner somewhere and let them sit there.

Celeste called me up from the hospital one time. She was crying because she didn't have no cigarettes. I always tried to keep her as happy as I could while she was in the hospi-

> *When Celeste was in the hospital, she'd be mad at me and at everyone else. A lot of people told me, "I wouldn't go see her if I were you," and I'd say, "Well, she's my child. If I don't go, don't nobody go." You have to check on your people because if you don't, they just throw the mentally ill in the corner somewhere and let them sit there.*
>
> —CAROL

tal, so I hopped on a bus to go out there, even though it was a long trip. I got stranded that day at the hospital because the bus stopped running. I had to call my girlfriend to come and get me.

A doctor at the hospital told me that Celeste was schizophrenic, but it turns out he was wrong. For a long time, they didn't diagnose her right. Finally, the insurance money ran out for the private hospital, and we had to put Celeste in a state hospital. I didn't want her to go there, but I had to sign her in. I thought, "I can't do nothing else. I'm just going to pray and put it in the hands of God."

Going to the state hospital turned out to be the best thing that ever happened to Celeste, because the doctor there diagnosed her right. He was concerned about her. He called me and said, "I don't think that Celeste has schizophrenia. I think she has manic-depression." I said, "I tried to tell the doctors that she was depressed, but they wouldn't listen to me." He said, "I think you're right. I want to try this new medicine on her. Can I?" I said, "Yes! I think me and you are thinking along the same terms." This doctor helped Celeste to get it together. She stayed in that hospital for about three months and she's been on the right road ever since. That was fourteen years ago.

When I would get upset, I liked to go out to the store and look at furniture and then I'd be all right. I did good, but I guess it was my spirit with God that helped me. They didn't have programs back then to help folks like us, and I went through this all by myself. I went through a lot. That mental illness sure is something!

I've been a caregiver all my life. I took care of my husband for twenty-six years because he was a stroke victim. I'm taking care of Antoine, my great-grandson, and another grandkid, too. They both live with me. I also raised my oldest daughter's children from infancy. They're all grown up now and they help me out because I'm a widow. They're good company for me, and I'd sure be lonesome without them, having been around children all of my life. But I'm not raising no more kids! I've told all my children that.

Celeste is doing great. For the past two summers, I had surgery on my ankles and I couldn't do anything for myself. Celeste took care of me. She brought me breakfast in bed for two summers in a row. Every night I'd call her and ask her if she'd come over to wash my back and she'd say, "Yeah, Mom, I'm coming." I took care of Celeste all those years when she was sick, and then when I got sick, she treated me like a queen! It came back. It always comes back.

CELESTE

I was sick for the first seven years of my daughter's life. It all started right after my baby girl, Rahshedia, was born. I ended up in a hospital and I missed her first birthday.

The stress of trying to work and raise a child as a single mother was just too much for me. Rahshedia had her days and nights mixed up, and I was exhausted. I'd get up early every morning, take her to my parents or to daycare, smoke a joint, go to work, pick up the baby, and come home and try and cook dinner and get her to bed. It was hell. At the end of the day, it was like, "I deserve a drink. I need a drink." I'd go straight to the bar and stay there all night long till I closed the bar. Then I'd go to the nightclubs. I was drinking and drugging every day. My mother had to raise my child because I was never around.

I had lived with Rahshedia's father for about five years. When I got pregnant, I thought he was going to marry me. When he left, it broke my heart. I had to come back to my family unwedded with an unborn child. It took everything I had to pull myself up and just walk with this pregnancy. At the time, I worked with a lot of women in a safety appliance factory. Everybody but me was married, and I didn't know anyone else who was having a baby out of wedlock. I knew things like that happened, but I didn't expect it to happen to me. It was a big pill to swallow.

I got into a very depressed state and I got rebellious, too. I was mad at the world. One morning, I called the people at work and accused them of tapping my office phone with a tape recorder. They told me they were going to fire me if I didn't come in. I said, "Oh well, I feel better now, and I'm coming right in." When I got to work, I went into the ladies' room and took a kitty nap on the couch. Someone woke me up, and I just snapped. I woke up swinging and fighting. My coworkers couldn't settle me down, and so they had to take me to the nearest hospital. I ended up in a mental ward, and I've been sick for twenty-two years.

My therapist at the hospital was white. I thought, "How would you know my feelings or what I'm going through? I can't talk to you, because I'm feeling this 'black thing.'" I felt like I couldn't explain myself to him.

I went through hell with my hospitalizations. I didn't want to take the medicine the doctors gave me. Even though I had popped pills in the drug scene, I had no acceptance of the pills that could save my life. I'd go two or three days without taking my meds and I'd say to myself, "Celeste, you don't need this stuff. It's making you weak." I'd throw the meds away and pick up the booze and the drugs again. When I didn't take my medicine, I had no comprehension. Sometimes I'd be so far off; I had to have shock treatments to bring me back.

My problem was with this bipolar thing. I just couldn't accept the fact that I had a mental illness, and I didn't want to be labeled as mentally ill. It wasn't until I started taking my medication fourteen years ago that I was able to comprehend the things that had happened to me. At Alcoholics Anonymous I got into recovery from my addictions. I met this woman there named Dot, and she helped save my life.

Dot was a beautiful person. I would call her in the middle of the night crying and complaining and she always listened and had words of wisdom for me. "Pray," she said, "let's pray!" Dot would pray with me right then and there on the phone. "Skig, honey" she would say, calling me by my nickname, "the reason why you can't get this program is because you won't take your medication." I said, "Oh, yeah?" But I

really wanted to work with this woman, and so I started taking my meds every day. I got my life back.

I went to AA meetings every day to learn how to undo all the unmanageability in my life, and there was a lot of it. I really had to work on acceptance of my medication. Today, I take it with my vitamins, and it's just like another vitamin to me. It's good for my body because I can go out and drive a school bus and work in the real world again and be whole.

I can't say enough that if you take your medication, work with your therapist, and stop all the lying and cheating and hiding, the door to recovery will open up for you. To get to the other side, you have to give yourself a chance to work things through. I was in one-on-one therapy for seventeen years, and now I go every six weeks to talk about my meds or about any problems I'm having. I don't even feel mentally ill anymore.

As soon as I got myself together, my mother took me back to church and reintroduced me to God. Now I have a God of my own understanding. He helped me, through meditation and prayer, to get stronger and walk my walk. God has been my instrument, which is why I give my life to him. Every morning before I go out the door, I give time to God. I read my Bible and my meditation books from AA and other groups I'm in. I get down on my knees and I ask Him to help me.

I feel like I was a victim who has recovered. Not "recovering." I have *recovered*. I did turn around. God turned all of this around. I thought I'd never ever be happy again, but look, I'm getting ready to get married and I have a job. My fiancé owns a transportation business and I drive one of his school vans for him. I'm up with the sun and the birds. I spend about forty-five minutes in prayer and meditation before I go out into the real world. My life is working out real good!

My daughter is twenty-one years old now and she lives with me. We're thick as thieves! Rahshedia calls me up like I'm one of her girlfriends. "Ma," she says, "I just called to see how you're doing." I'll say, "I ain't doing nothing, you know?" And we talk. I know that she loves me, and that's the best thing. Where I was putting love into men and other things, God gave me a child to truly love me.

My therapist at the hospital was white. I thought, "How would you know my feelings or what I'm going through? I can't talk to you, because I'm feeling this 'black thing.'" I felt like I couldn't explain myself to him.

—CELESTE

At first I thought I had something to hide, but if you start hiding things, you'll never get to the root of your problems. If I can step up and say, "Yes, I suffer with a mental illness, but I've been helped through medication and therapy to deal with the real world," maybe it will help some folks. If there's anyone I can help by sharing my story, I would be real happy. I have nothing to hide.

—CELESTE

At first I thought I had something to hide, but if you start hiding things, you'll never get to the root of your problems. If I can step up and say, "Yes, I suffer with a mental illness, but I've been helped through medication and therapy to deal with the real world," maybe it will help some folks. If there's anyone I can help by sharing my story, I would be real happy. People should know to take their medicine, give it a chance, get into therapy, talk about everything, and get it out! That's what really helped me. I have nothing to hide.

WILMA

Celeste is my cousin, and we've been very close ever since we were kids. When she got sick, she would call me or I'd call her and talk her through some real hard times. There were days that she would call me and say, "I don't think I'll make it." I'd ask her to tell me what was going on. She'd say, "I'm thinking this... I'm thinking that..." I just walked her through her troubles.

When Celeste first got sick, there weren't any support systems for families. The family wasn't important to the mental health professionals; it didn't count. Back then, doctors just institutionalized people. They'd keep them in the hospital, and families had no say-so.

As African Americans, we have been the last ones to know anything about any mental health services out there. We're the last to know because most institutions are all white—the therapists and the doctors. They have preconceived ideas of how they're going to treat us and what they think of us before they even get to know us. Sometimes that interferes with getting effective services. It can stop a true client-therapist relationship from developing. When our white counterparts go in for mental health services, they're already connected culturally because of their skin color. We African Americans have to fight a little harder and become more educated. Educated consumers are the most powerful consumers, black or white.

We know racism exists in the mental health system. There's a lack of concern for people of color. It's like the professionals see a black patient and say, "Oh, here's another one coming in. We'll treat them with whatever medication their insurance plan can pay for."

In actuality, it shouldn't have taken so long for Celeste to be diagnosed correctly. She had all the typical bipolar symptoms. She was telling the professionals what she was feeling, but who was paying attention? I'm not saying that this only happens to African Americans, but we certainly have a hard time in this system.

We want African-American doctors and we know they're out there. I'm not saying that a black therapist will be better than a white therapist for me, but I may feel a little more comfortable going into a clinic knowing that there's somebody there who looks like me. We all come with preconceived ideas about each other. Sometimes we play them out; sometimes we don't. But for the most part, the bulk of the power is in white hands.

In order to help our people, I started a support group called Minority Families of the Mentally Ill, where we can all come together and be informed. In our programs, we teach our mental health consumers that they have the right to speak up and say what they don't like about the system. For example, Carol has the right to sit in on a therapy session with Celeste if Celeste wants her to be there, but lots of doctors

As African Americans, we have been the last ones to know anything about any mental health services out there. We're the last to know because most institutions are all white—the therapists and the doctors. They have preconceived ideas of how they're going to treat us and what they think of us before they even get to know us.

—WILMA

and therapists don't like that. Furthermore, Celeste has the right to say, "I want my mother in here with me."

Mental health consumers and their family members often worry about repercussions if they ask too many questions of mental health professionals. People need to learn how to demand information from their doctors. If they're given a medication, they should ask about its potential side effects. For instance, they need to know if their medication will inter- fere with other meds and with their sexual relationships. Will they be able to live a normal life?

I'm an optimistic person, and I'd like to think that things are getting better and that they're going to get even better in the future. When family members like Celeste and her mother and myself come out and share our stories and let people know that we are here and that we do exist, we have a voice. We are speaking up. We want things to change.

> *Mental health consumers and their family members often worry about repercussions if they ask too many questions of mental health professionals. People need to learn how to demand information from their doctors. If they're given a medication, they should ask about its potential side effects.*
>
> *— WILMA*

Paige, Jacqueline, Tracey, and Cara

THE BAPTISTE FAMILY

NEWTONVILLE AND BROCKTON, MASSACHUSETTS
AND GAINESVILLE, FLORIDA

PAIGE LAFRENIERE / JACQUELINE BAPTISTE / TRACEY BAPTISTE
CARA BAPTISTE / CHRISTOPHER O'LEARY

JACKIE

ALL THREE OF MY DAUGHTERS, TRACEY, CARA, AND PAIGE, have suffered from mental illness. My husband, Bob, had been diagnosed with multiple sclerosis before the girls got sick, so we already had a lot of problems in our family. It was just one thing after another. I felt like my whole world was falling apart.

I was devastated when Tracey first got sick. She was only thirteen. A therapist told me there was a good chance that Tracey would have to be institutionalized because she was so ill. Consequently, she became my main focus, and the rest of my family was pushed into the background. My husband felt as though she was taking my attention away from him. It was a constant tug-of-war between Bob and Tracey, and I was caught in the middle. It's so painful to remember this period in my life that I can hardly talk about it.

Tracey's illness got progressively worse. Going out at night was terrible for her, so she always stayed home. Even if I could persuade her to go out during the day, she would never go out after sunset. Tracey wouldn't even step out the door. This went on for years. For years!

Tracey had a lot of boyfriends, but they didn't know there was anything wrong with her except that she'd always make an excuse to avoid dating at night. Eventually, a boy named John became her steady boyfriend, and he found out what was wrong. John and I schemed together. We decided that he would ask Tracey out just to sit in his car, and then he would drive her around the block. He did this, and when she got home, she was in a terrible state.

Bob and I only discussed Tracey's illness with a few close friends. We didn't even explain to her teachers what she was going through. I didn't think they would understand that kids could have psychological problems.

Later on, Cara also started having severe panic attacks. She's been through one therapist after another and has been on all kinds of medications. Some have helped her, and some haven't. It was hard watching both of my daughters struggle through adolescence. Paige had a much milder case of agoraphobia, which didn't develop until she was an adult.

153

For the remainder of college and into my young adulthood, my agoraphobia was under control, but I never felt completely free of it. In my mid-twenties, I decided to return to therapy because I was afraid my anxieties could come back one day. During the next couple of years, I continued the type of personal exploration I had begun with my therapist, but I now had a more mature sense of myself.

I began to do bodywork with a woman who practiced shiatsu massage. The intensity of that physical opening up, along with our spiritual discussions, pushed me to a deeper level of healing. This process also precipitated my worst fear: a relapse into agoraphobia. For a period of six months, I only left the house when I had to. I tried to hide my symptoms from my five-year-old son because I didn't want him to know his mother was unstable. I'd get anxious if Christopher went outside and didn't come back inside when I called him. I simply couldn't go out of the house and get him.

It's nearly impossible to adequately describe the complexity of my ultimate recovery. This last relapse seemed, for me, a necessary final step. I had to let myself experience the terror again to truly learn that it had no power over me. I still occasionally experience symptoms, especially when I'm extremely tired or stressed, symptoms that in the past would have escalated into an anxiety attack. I now know how to handle those sensations.

When Christopher was an adolescent and had reached a certain level of maturity, I shared my personal history with him. Fortunately, none of my early experiences have adversely affected him. He recently graduated from high school and is taking a year off before college to live, work, and study art in Florence, Italy. Christopher is unusually easygoing, flexible, and adventurous.

Ironically, agoraphobia has emboldened me. Perhaps because my life was once so severely restricted, I now strive to transcend limits and fully experience life. People who know me now have a difficult time imagining that I was once so disabled. I rarely think about that part of my life anymore. It's not that I'm avoiding it—it just feels over. I no longer fear that my illness will come back.

Tracey and Cara

severely agoraphobic again. The stress of leaving my family and friends after so recently achieving a sense of equilibrium was overwhelming. I never divulged my history of mental illness to my professors or to the school, because I was afraid they'd ask me to leave. This was before the Americans with Disabilities Act, which would have protected my right to receive an education.

That year, I went on medication for the first time and took both tranquilizers and antidepressants. I continued going to the university, and then, feeling more in balance, I went off all meds about a year later. A few months after that, I became pregnant with my son, Christopher. Although I was only twenty, in some ways, having a child stabilized me. I was now responsible for someone else's life.

CARA

When I was a little girl, I saw what was happening to Tracey, and I developed a lot of fears myself. I even became afraid of Tracey! When she would have a bad panic attack, my mother would shove me out the front door while yelling, "Go over to Nana's! Go over to Nana's!" I remember thinking, "Whatever is wrong with my sister is going to happen to me if I wear her clothes, if I touch her, or if I'm near her."

By the age of six, my symptoms were coming on strong, but I didn't know what was happening to me. I have memories of feeling anxious all the time. I had a lot of phobias and a lot of nightmares throughout my childhood. From a very young age, I was also depressed. As early as seven or eight, I was basically a ball of confusion.

I had my first full-blown panic attack when I was in the eighth grade. It happened unexpectedly when I was in a movie theater. I was just sitting there watching the movie with a friend, and all of a sudden, I started to feel like I was choking. I couldn't breathe. In a panic, I ran out of the theater. I felt like everything was closing in on me. I didn't feel real. By the time I was an adolescent, I was agoraphobic, just like Tracey.

When I got sick, I had a totally different experience at school than Tracey did when she was sick. The kids were horrible to me, absolutely horrible. They began to torment me. Girls would follow me home from school and push me down. One girl had food in her mouth mixed with soda. Her friends held me down, and she spit it into my hair. Another time, I was attacked by a bunch of boys that I had been friends with for years. One day they said, "We're taking a shortcut to someone's house, through the woods. Come with us." And then they almost raped me. One of them helped me escape, and I ran home.

Things got even worse. The kids at school spread rumors about me, saying that I went with everyone and things like that. Some of them said that my friend and I were lesbians, and they called us "dykes." It got to the point where I couldn't drive anywhere; I couldn't even go to a store. It was as if the entire town tromped on me.

The most difficult time for me was just before I turned twenty-one. I had phobias about everything, and my symptoms were out of control. I became totally incapacitated. I didn't eat, and I got down to sixty-five pounds. I couldn't get out of bed, because it was the only place I felt safe. The doctor said I was having a "breakdown," and he also diagnosed me with Tourette's Syndrome. I went on medication and started to feel better.

Tourette's Syndrome is a neurological disorder; it is not a mental illness. Most doctors believe you're born with it. Basically, you have a lot of uncomfortable sensations in your body. The only way I can explain it is that I often feel like I have to twitch. It's like when you're trying to hold in a sneeze and then, all of a sudden, there's a catharsis when you actually do sneeze.

My tics move to different parts of my body for a few months at a time, and then they move somewhere else. For the past year, my symptoms have included coughing, making noises with my throat, and sniffing through my nose. I've never felt comfortable in my body. It may seem that I am, but I'm not. When I was a child, I used to feel like I was possessed. With Tourette's, there are lots of psychological things that go on in addition to all the physical tics. For instance, I have intrusive thoughts that just pop into my head.

I get a lot of dirty looks when I'm out in public. The other day a salesclerk looked at me and shook her head, like she thought I was on drugs or something. People definitely treat you differently when you have Tourette's, but I'm pretty used to it.

Although my Tourette's is quite obvious, I haven't told too many people that I also have an anxiety disorder. Of course, my current boyfriend knows, and I recently told one of my friends. Other people I know must wonder why I'm so afraid. They say, "Why can't you drive over to my house?" Or, "Why can't we ever make plans?" I find that my friends don't call me as much as they used to. They probably figure, "Well, Cara can't really do this or that. So why bother with her?" I've been socially isolated in the past year because my panic attacks and depression have returned full force.

I had my first full-blown panic attack when I was in the eighth grade. It happened unexpectedly when I was in a movie theater. I was just sitting there watching the movie with a friend, and all of a sudden, I started to feel like I was choking. I couldn't breathe. In a panic, I ran out of the theater. I felt like everything was closing in on me.

—CARA

I'm usually a pretty outgoing person, so I feel that I'm missing out on a lot.

My boyfriend doesn't say much when I'm in the middle of a panic attack, but he tries to help by rubbing my back. He tells me, "You're going to get over this." He is usually supportive, but there are times when he'll say, "Cara, I don't get it. You had a panic attack a few hours ago. You got through it. And now you're getting all panicky again! Why is that happening? I just don't understand."

Both of my sisters have problems with me. They don't understand why I don't have it all together yet, but I've had some really traumatic things happen to me. I had Tourette's, then I had agoraphobia, then I had panic attacks, and then I had clinical depression. I have even been diagnosed with bipolar disorder! I've had so many strange behaviors in my life; it's no wonder that my sisters never understood me. I sometimes feel like I'm the black sheep of the family. This makes me sad because I really want to be close to them.

I've tried talking to both of my sisters, but I don't know how open they are about wanting to understand me. I don't often let them know how much their emotional distance hurts me. When I bring this up, their response is usually, "Well, Cara, you did this," or, "Oh, Cara, you did that…" It's as if they've labeled me, "That's Cara, and she has her problems." My sisters have never even asked me, "What is it like to have Tourette's Syndrome?" Or, "How does it feel to be bipolar?" They've never discussed any of this with me. Never!

I had a tubal ligation because of my Tourette's, so I can't have children. There is a very high likelihood that my child could develop Tourette's as well, and I didn't want to put a child through that. But I love my nieces and nephews. They're such great kids. I know I'm a good auntie.

I recently got a little pug named Lucy. She's wonderful. Research shows that animals, especially dogs, have a calming effect on people with anxiety disorders. Pets are a diversion. You don't focus on your anxiety when you have a dog to care for. Sometimes I'll feel a panicky feeling coming on and I'll hug Lucy. Just the smell of her and her little kisses calm me down.

My mother is also an important support to me. In fact, I'm overly dependent on her. She lives in Florida, but she comes up to stay with me for a few months every year. A short time ago, my mother was due to arrive for her annual visit. Right before she came, I had one of my first panic attacks in a long time. My boyfriend said, "You're finally starting to be independent. You're working; you're doing other stuff; and now that your mother is coming, you feel like you're going to fall back into that dependent role with her." He's right. I do rely on her way too much for my own good.

Mom is a lifeline for me. I know I have to work on this whole dependency thing, but I get addicted to her when she comes to visit. My therapist has told me that many people with agoraphobia and panic disorder have problems separating from their mothers. When my mom goes home after a visit, I fall into a depression. I don't want it to always be that way.

Deep down I know I can have a fulfilling life, and I hope that someday soon, things will be easier for me.

PAIGE

I became agoraphobic as an adult. Although I didn't have it anywhere near as bad as my sisters did, I still felt like it was something I had to fight off. I was also having panic attacks, but I never talked about them with my family. My attacks only lasted a matter of months, and once they stopped, I haven't had any at all.

I had a brief bout with depression three years ago because I was under a lot of stress at the time. When my sisters get depressed, they start to think they don't want to be on the planet anymore. I never felt like that. My depression was very different from theirs. I just didn't want to get up in the morning and face another day. I went to the doctor and took antidepressants for a year or so. I have stress and worries now, but it's just the regular kind of stuff that everybody has to cope with.

It was hard for me when my sisters got sick. The year Tracey didn't come out of her room, my mother focused her attention completely on her. Cara fell by the wayside, as did my dad, and then me. Later on, when Cara got so sick, my mother did the same thing. Everything got focused on Cara. It's always been difficult for me to deal with this.

I used to get angry when Mom would do things for Tracey or Cara instead of teaching them how to manage for themselves. After I moved out, I went over to Mom's house for dinner one night. Cara was fifteen, and Mom was cutting her steak! I was, like, "Why are you doing that?" I suppose it was easier for Mom to just do it.

When I was younger, I gravitated toward my grandmother, Nana. She and I were very close, and our relationship was my saving grace. She was always there for me. Nana was an amazingly solid person, and we all needed that kind of solidity when we were young. She helped us all survive. Thank goodness she lived right next door. The path between our houses was well-worn. It felt like a lifeline to me.

I don't harbor any resentment or hurt about how my family handled things. Mom and Dad did the best they could. I'm sure that when my kids grow up, I'll be hearing from them about the mistakes I've made.

CHRISTOPHER

My mom, Tracey, kept her anxiety from me when I was growing up so it wouldn't affect me. I don't think I have any kind of anxiety disorders or anything like that. I'm kind of the opposite of anxious.

I really didn't notice my mom's illness at all. I never had any memories of times when I thought, "Uh-oh, my mom's mental illness is acting up again." I do remember her staying in the house a lot of the time—actually almost all the time—but I still didn't connect that with her being mentally ill until she told me that she had agoraphobia.

My mom told me that she used to try to hide her illness from me, and I guess she did a pretty good job. I didn't know anything at all about her illness until she told me when I was in high school. I can't even remember exactly when she told me about it. Maybe that's because it didn't hit me really hard or make me concerned, since she seemed over it.

Christopher

If I had to give advice to other kids dealing with the mental illness of a family member or a friend, I guess I'd say that it's not the person's fault, so you can't get mad at them. Mental illness is a different world with different rules, so one can't always expect to understand it. Just try to help. That's all you can do.
— *CHRISTOPHER*

Ever since my mom told me about her illness, it's never been a big issue for me. It wasn't until she was interviewed for *Nothing to Hide* that she actually told me the whole story about everything she went through when she was sick. I've told friends about my mom, and they were fine with it, but I haven't told anyone the details. I've just said that my mom used to be agoraphobic.

It doesn't hurt me to hear words like "psycho" or "crazy," because I don't think of my mom as crazy. In fact, it's hard to picture her as ever being crazy. I don't even think I associate the word "crazy" with mental illness when I hear it being used. It means something more like "wild and crazy kids." In my head, "psycho" is different from "crazy." It's used more to refer to someone who's actually psychotic, and I don't hear it used very much.

If I had to give advice to other kids dealing with the mental illness of a family member or a friend, I guess I'd say that it's not the person's fault, so you can't get mad at them. Mental illness is a different world with different rules, so one can't always expect to understand it. Just try to help. That's all you can do.

Standing: Betty Lou, Rachel, and John *Seated:* Muriel and Ruth

160

THE SHEPARD FAMILY

WESTFIELD, MASSACHUSETTS

BETTY LOU SHEPARD / RACHEL SHEPARD / JOHN SHEPARD
MURIEL G. SHEPARD / RUTH E. SNOW

BETTY LOU

ONE THING I REALLY REGRET IS NOT KEEPING A JOURNAL over the years. So much has happened to our family that it's hard to keep track of it all.

Both my husband, John, and my daughter, Rachel, are mentally ill. John has been hospitalized four times, always on locked units. Rachel has been in and out of hospitals ten times. Ten times!

John and I first noticed there was something wrong with Rachel when she was in the second grade. She couldn't sleep alone in the dark, and she had other symptoms as well. For instance, she burned herself once and didn't react to the pain. She didn't even cry. We brought her to see a therapist, who treated her for several years. When Rachel's symptoms improved, the therapist released her from treatment; however, she told us our daughter might not make it through her adolescence without additional help. She was right.

When Rachel went to high school, her entire world fell apart. She began to hear voices, and she even made a suicide attempt. She had been a straight-"A" student, but she ended up missing so much school that she had to drop out. Surprisingly, she went back the following year and got straight "A's" again, and graduated. I don't know how she did it. Rachel got very sick again in her twenties when she was working at a hospital as a nursing assistant.

John had two hospitalizations for manic depression in the summer of 1974, and two more in the winter of 1989. He was first hospitalized when our children were the ages of eight, ten, and twelve. His mother was baby-sitting for us, and she called me and told me to come home from work, that there was something wrong. John had suddenly walked out of work. We had to call the ambulance to take him to the state hospital. He spent a month there, and after he was released, John tried going back to work. He ended up in the psych ward of the local hospital for two months. After that, he was out of work for another fourteen months.

John's mother, Muriel, has always provided lots of support to our family, and my friends have helped me by taking care of my children when I would visit my husband in the hospital. They all knew that John had manic-depression, but it wasn't something that I discussed with just anyone. Several

I've been lucky. My family has been very understanding, and, fortunately, Betty Lou and I are still together. Many marriages break up when someone in the family has a mental illness. Everyone has their breaking point, and some people can take more than others can.

—JOHN

used to bother me to say to people that I had been in the funny farm, but it bothers other people. I don't say things like that anymore.

I've been lucky. My family has been very understanding, and, fortunately, Betty Lou and I are still together. Many marriages break up when someone in the family has a mental illness. Everyone has their breaking point, and some people can take more than others can.

Because of deinstitutionalization, there are more mentally ill people in jail at any given time than there are in all the psychiatric hospitals put together. People were taken out of the state hospitals and put out on the street before support systems for them were available in their communities. Sixty percent of the people who were released from our local state hospital went off their medications within three months. Many of them ended up in jail or on the streets.

I helped lead a forty-week training session with a local police department. I told them that the mentally ill people they deal with are usually off their medication or refuse to take any. I want the police to know that for every mentally ill person they have to deal with, there are doctors and lawyers and schoolteachers and college presidents and people like me who are mentally ill and are doing very well.

Now I work in several group homes and in a homeless shelter for the mentally ill. I've heard that some mental health agencies have a rule against identifying yourself as a consumer when you're working with other consumers. I figured it would be easier to get close to the residents if they knew that I'd been through what they're going through. But the other day, I was talking with one of the ladies who is new at the group home, and I had the feeling that it wouldn't be too wise to let her know that I'm a consumer. I didn't think she would appreciate being taken care of by another consumer.

I still don't have a whole lot of self-confidence, and I'm still introverted and bashful about approaching people. I know there are lots of people who are better at interacting with other

people than I am. I still worry that I'm going to do something wrong, but all in all, it's been very satisfying to help others.

RACHEL

I was a little girl when Dad first got sick, and I didn't understand what was going on with him. I do remember a time when he was trying to drink a beer and his hands were shaking so much that I asked him, "Dad, what's the matter?" He said, "Oh, don't worry, Rachel, I'll be okay." I was with my grandma, and she called my mom. The last thing I remember was an ambulance coming to get my dad.

I was fifteen when I took an overdose. When I was sixteen, I started hearing voices, but I wasn't open to getting help like my dad and my Aunt Ruth were when they got sick. As a teenager, I self-medicated with alcohol. As time went on, I was always very wary about taking medication. When I worked as a nurse's aide, I learned about the side effects of medication. I wouldn't even take aspirin unless I really had to. I had to get to the point where I hit rock-bottom— yelling at my parents and not handling things very well—before I said, "I've got to go on medication."

I was on a religious kick for a while. I was worried about Mom and Dad, and I kept telling them, "You guys should accept Jesus or you won't go to Heaven." I went on and on about this. I was just distraught. Then I started seeing things out of the corners of my eyes and I heard voices all night long. Mom would say, "Rachel, you've got to go to the hospital." Finally she talked me into it. I was about twenty-six when I was hospitalized for the first time. I've had a total of ten hospitalizations since then, every other year or so.

The first time I was in the hospital, I was really frightened. I had to go to support groups with other patients. If you didn't go, the doctors would keep you in the hospital until you started to participate and they saw some signs of improvement. As an inpatient, you quickly learn that you can either make things worse for yourself or you can help your-self. I learned to do what I had to do.

I lost a lot of my old high school friends because they didn't understand my illness. I was fortunate, though, that I had a boyfriend who was very understanding. When I was a teenager, my Aunt Agnes was also really good to me. She told me, "Anytime you ever need to talk, you can call me up." I always appreciated her offer. I've never forgotten that. I still like calling her up and talking to her.

After my first hospitalization, I worked as a nurse's aide. One night, when one of my patients was failing, I got scared. I called my mom and cried on the phone. After that, I became very ill. I knew then that I wasn't going to be able to han-dle the stress of working.

I always got the feeling at work that once my supervisors knew I had a mental illness, they didn't trust me. They were concerned about whether the patients would be affected. That's understandable, but it felt very strange. I once went out of my way to try to help somebody, and that got me in trouble. The supervisors thought I was being disobedi-ent, but all I was doing was trying to clean up a patient's bed. After this incident, the hospital let me go because they had an excuse to. Sometimes, I wish I could go back to work.

I can usually tell when I'm off-balance. My mind goes in circles, and it takes me a while to relax. It's hard to explain. I can feel an imbalance going on inside my head. To this day, I still get panic attacks. I'll be somewhere and all of a sud-den I don't know where I am. It's like you're there but you feel like you're not there. It's a real panicky feeling, like all your perceptions are off. A few times I've felt like I was going to have a heart attack.

I'm going to graduate from a state college with a bach-elor's degree in sociology this spring! I'm on disability, and that's difficult for me. I feel I should get a real job, but it may take me a little more time. I go to a clubhouse where I have a job in their vocational program. I'm hoping to go out

on my own someday soon. I look at my dad and I see how well he's done at work. That's my goal, too. I want to be able to get a job that I can stick with, to stay out of the hospital, to stay on my meds, and to do what I need to do.

I'm afraid of being asked about medication when I apply for a job. If you tell an employer, "Yes, I'm on medication, and yes, I'm mentally ill," you're not going to get that job. I'm more open about my illness now. I would rather not have to lie.

RUTH

I'm John's sister, and Rachel is my niece. I was diagnosed with manic-depression around 1982. I was nearly fifty, but I knew something was wrong for a long time before that. I've only had one hospitalization, and that was many years ago. I put myself in the hospital, and my husband got me out. I was a patient for only a week. I've been on medication for almost twenty years.

You try to find something funny in things. You put on your happy face before you get where you're going. Or you try to. It helps.

MURIEL

I'm over one hundred years old now. John and Ruth are my children, and Rachel is my granddaughter. I've been saying, "Live one day at a time" for over ninety years. I learned this when I was still living on the family farm.

As the oldest girl in my family, I was the mother's helper who looked after the younger kids. It would be hot and I'd go and sit down under the tree and I'd say to myself, "Oh, will my mother please not ask me to do anything for ten min-utes." That's how I learned to live one day at a time.

staff said, "This issue has to be addressed." They referred me to a psychiatrist, who diagnosed me with clinical depression.

I felt like I was finally being taken care of. The school had stepped in and said, "All right, this is what we're going to do, and this is what you have to do." It was out of my hands, and I was relieved because I didn't have to manage everything on my own anymore. Once my school got involved, I felt like I could let myself go and just be me. School became a safety net that was there to catch me.

I only told two other people besides my mom and my therapist about my situation. One was a girl who had gone to my school the year before, and the other was one of my teachers. They were both incredibly good listeners and very supportive. They didn't try to "fix" me. They simply let me be me and say what I wanted to say. You can be irrational when you're depressed, and they understood that.

After I was diagnosed, I was put on medication. I began to feel much better and was able to finish my high school education. When I graduated, I assumed that I would get well because I was away from the social and academic pressures of school. I guess I still wasn't willing to admit that my depression wasn't circumstantial. I didn't want to believe that there was something wrong with me. I preferred to blame my environment for causing my problems. Being strong-willed and stubborn, I decided to go off my medication.

My first term at college was miserable, and I had my worst bout of depression yet. Besides the emotional strain, I wasn't able to eat or sleep at all, and I had a lot of physical pain as well. I felt like I had a huge lump in my chest that I couldn't get rid of. It was almost impossible to swallow, and there was nothing I could do about it. When I was studying, I was so tense that I felt like screaming or kicking something really hard. I felt as if my muscles were going to jump out of my skin.

I went to all of my classes, but I could only concentrate on one course at a time. Each week, I prioritized my four courses and picked one that would get my full attention. All the rest, I let slide. Given the circumstances, I did pretty well

academically. I don't know why, but there was something about working against the odds that inspired me to do the best I could.

During my daily routine of academics and athletics, I had to fit in about two hours of total dysfunction. I would sit in the library and study for a while and then I would cry. I would call my mom and bawl over the phone, or go for a walk and cry.

I was socially isolated during my freshman year. I had two roommates, but I never told them what was happening to me. I would never break down in front of them. I was always in a nook by myself in the library where I could quietly fall apart. I'd call my mom from a phone in the basement. I think my roommates may have suspected that something was wrong, but they never brought it up.

I felt comforted when I called my mom, but it was a double-edged sword. She provided a huge amount of support, but because I knew I had her support, I would let myself fall apart even more. If I was sitting in the library about to cry, and I knew that my mother wasn't available to speak to me, I would try harder to keep myself together. If, on the other hand, I knew that I could reach her, I would let myself go. My crying episodes would stop after a certain amount of time, so it was just a matter of weathering them when they happened. Even though they would get worse when I talked to my mom, she would always weather them with me.

At first, I was so ashamed of my tears that I would try not to cry, or would only let myself cry for half an hour or so. If I did cry, I would reprimand myself the entire time, thinking, "This is terrible. You are so weak." I felt guilty whenever I called my mom, because she would get so upset when she heard me sounding so miserable. But she had told me that she wanted me to call her whenever I needed to. She wanted to know how I was doing. This was comforting and eased some of the guilt I felt. It showed me the extent of her love. She was willing to suffer in order to help me.

One time when I was having a good day, I called my mom to show her that I was actually happy for once. That afternoon,

I lost it again and I just didn't have the heart to call her back. I wanted to give her a day off. Instead, I called one of my old friends to weather the episode with me, but it was clear that she really didn't get it. Normally, if you call someone and you're crying, they'll say, "What's wrong?" And if you can't really explain what's wrong, then you sort of look around for something else to say to them, like, "Oh, well, I have a test tomorrow and I'm nervous about it." Then they might say, "Okay, how are you going to study for this test?" And they'll try to strategize and make it all better, but depression is not a rational thing. Most people don't understand it, which is why I don't tell too many of my friends about my illness.

My mom is someone who does get it. She has never said to me, "Why are you doing this?" She has always said, "Okay, well, this is what we're going to do about it. I'm going to call the physician and we're going to get you back on medication, and dah-dah-dah-dah." She would also talk to me about my cats and other stuff that would make me smile. I'm lucky to have someone who truly understands. It's been just the two of us—me and Mom—for a while now.

NANCY

When my daughter, Cathy, was in junior high, she would lie in bed in the morning and I could hear her sobbing. I would ask her, "What's wrong?" and she would answer, "I don't know. I don't know. I'm just so sad."

I feel a lot of guilt about this time in Cathy's life because I thought she was simply struggling with teenage hormones. I knew my daughter wasn't happy, but I assumed this was just a normal part of being an adolescent. She was in a real state of flux and was very unsettled. Cathy had to hide her abilities because other kids at school put her down for her academic prowess. In retrospect, this was the beginning of some real problems for her.

There's no history of depression in my immediate family, so I didn't recognize Cathy's unhappiness for what it actually was. I wish I had understood what was happening at the

time, because I could have possibly saved her from years of misery. That's water over the dam now.

When Cathy went away to boarding school, she was absolutely miserable. I knew she was depressed, but I thought she was simply having adjustment problems. She didn't have any support system there or anyone to talk to at first. She once called me at two o'clock in the morning, sobbing. She had been staring at her desk for two hours, trying to study. She kept saying to me, "I can't do it. I can't do it." She was hysterical. But she never once said to me, "Mom, come get me. I want to come home." Instead, she would say, "When is this misery going to stop? I want to get on with the business of being at school." Even though my daughter knew she was in the right place, her emotions were not letting her proceed with her life at the school. She wanted to feel better and she was incredibly frustrated that she couldn't make this happen of her own volition.

I remember the time Cathy was in an important diving competition. She cried the whole time! She would do her dive and then would go sit at her coach's feet and just sob. She did this in between each one of her eleven dives. I was sitting in the audience observing her, but I was unable to go to her. It was horrible.

When Cathy was finally diagnosed with major depression, I was relieved that there was a reason for her emotional distress. Once she realized that her depression was not something that she was responsible for, and once she understood that she had a chemical imbalance in her brain, everything began to improve. When Cathy was able to say, "This illness is not caused by something that I did wrong, and it's not my fault," she felt a certain freedom.

It took Cathy a while to come to grips with the realization that her illness is something she will have to cope with for the rest of her life. The summer before she went to college, she went off her medication. Things got bad again during her freshman year. I would get these long phone calls in the middle of the night when she would just sob and sob. I couldn't curl up, relax, or go back to sleep after our conversations. It was a very painful time for me.

When my daughter, Cathy, was in junior high, she would lie in bed in the morning and I could hear her sobbing. I would ask her, "What's wrong?" and she would answer, "I don't know. I don't know. I'm just so sad."
—NANCY

There's no history of depression in my immediate family, so I didn't recognize Cathy's unhappiness for what it actually was. I wish I had understood what was happening at the time, because I could have possibly saved her from years of misery. That's water over the dam now.
—NANCY

I told Cathy that she had to go back on her meds. She was resistant at first, but I urged her to call her counselor. She did, but the counselor was unable to get her an appointment with a doctor for three weeks. I said, "That's unacceptable." Cathy needed to see a doctor immediately because it takes weeks to get meds into your system. She needed to start her meds yesterday! So I said, "Cathy, do you mind if I call some people?" She agreed, so I called her boarding school's health center and, ten minutes later, her former doctor was on the phone with me. I told him what the situation was, and he said, "Tell her to go to the pharmacy in the center of town in half an hour and the prescription will be there for her." Sometimes you need angels like that in your life.

When I knew Cathy was in crisis, I stayed home most of the time because I wanted to be available to her if she called. Luckily, I wasn't under the pressure of juggling a work schedule when Cathy got sick. I had a lot of freedom that way. If I knew she was in trouble, I'd hang out at home and not go out nearly as often. That was my choice. It was what I wanted to do. I never felt, "Oh, God, it's not fair that I have to be so available to my daughter." Never! I've always assured her, "I'm going to be here for you. Just call me if you need me." She was always my top priority.

Cathy's father and I are divorced, but we've always had a very positive relationship. He was sympathetic and would ask me, "What can I do to help?" But he didn't really understand what was happening to his daughter. Luckily, I have some wonderful women friends who have been invaluable to me. They get it.

Another important source of support for Cathy was her cats, and they still are. This may sound ridiculous, but they have always been a security blanket for her. When she was younger and the cats were close to her size and weight, she would carry them around. When she would get upset, she would grab a cat and cry into its neck. Even now, during her school vacations, she's drawn back home because that's where her animals are. Cathy needs to spend a certain amount of time with them.

I take my cues strictly from my daughter. I ask her, "What can I do that would be the most helpful for you?" Whenever I've said, "I'm going to call so-and-so for advice," I've always added, "Do you feel okay about that?" Even when Cathy was in crisis, I never took the initiative and did anything without asking her first. This approach has allowed me to take action on her behalf, but it's also allowed her to make decisions for herself.

Cathy was always a perfectionist, but being on an antidepressant has given her the ability to be more evenly balanced. For instance, when she was in high school, she would never take an evening off from studying. Now, if there's a musical group she wants to see, she'll tell me, "Mom, I'm going to a concert tonight."

Since Cathy has gotten so much better, my life has also changed for the better. I have fewer worries now that I know she has a handle on her illness. I have much more freedom because I know she's okay. If she does get into trouble, she has a better idea of what she needs to do. She won't be as blindsided as she was early on, when neither of us had a clue what was happening.

Standing: Lillian, Chelsea, Martin, and Chanel *Seated:* Beatrice G., Beatrice K., Teal, and Darcie

THE KAHN FAMILY

LAWRENCE, MASSACHUSETTS

LILLIAN DELLA PENNA / CHELSEA KAHN / MARTIN KAHN
CHANEL KAHN / BEATRICE GRIFFITHS / BEATRICE KAHN
TEAL KAHN / DARCIE KAHN

BEATRICE

WE HAD THIS PERFECT LITTLE FAMILY, OR SO I THOUGHT. But then, all of a sudden, everything changed.

When my daughter, Darcie, was only five, she came running in one day from the yard asking me, "Mom, do I have blood on my hands?" I said, "No, honey. Why? Did you fall?" Five minutes later, she was back again with the same question, "Mom, do I have blood on my hands? Please, Mom, you have to tell me." I said, "Darcie, look at your hands. Do you see blood?" But she kept repeating, "Mommy, you have to tell me. You have to tell me." This went on all day.

When Darcie developed other unusual behaviors, I called her pediatrician and he gave me a psychiatrist's phone number. I went upstairs and dialed the number, but the minute his secretary answered, I hung up. I was so afraid. A psychiatrist? Was my kid nuts? Literally, that's what I was thinking. I called back and made an appointment, but later that day, I cancelled it. I said to myself, "I can't do this. What's this going to fill my daughter's head with?"

Over the next few years, four different doctors told me that Darcie was fine and that she was just going through a phase. Although I knew in my heart that something was wrong, I wanted to believe them. They all said she was very smart and that we simply needed to stimulate her mind with extracurricular activities. I would have liked to give it a whirl, but Martin and I could only afford to do so much. We had three other children, and we couldn't afford to give Darcie lessons or special experiences. It wouldn't have been fair to her sisters.

When Darcie was in the third grade, I finally called our insurance company and said, "Look, I've gone to everybody on your list and they're all telling me there's nothing wrong with my daughter. I want to speak to somebody in charge and tell him about my daughter's behavior and then have him tell me there's nothing wrong with her. I've found a doctor who is solely a child psychiatrist and I want to take Darcie to see him and I want your company to pay for it." After I described Darcie's behaviors in detail, the insurance company agreed that I could bring her to see the specialist.

Chelsea, Chanel, Teal, and Darcie

iors. Hopefully, the medication will work." I told him, "Every book I've read recommends behavioral therapy for OCD, and I want Darcie to have that." After three visits, he finally said okay, but he signed me up with a therapist in his office who knew nothing about behavioral therapy!

I told this therapist that I wanted to sit in on a lesson with Darcie so I could learn how to help my daughter. I went in and listened to them talking about an imaginary story. The next visit, the therapist asked me to stay in the waiting room. I told him, "You're not treating her illness. I want you to treat her illness." He said, "Well, Mrs. Kahn, you know more about OCD than I do." I said, "See you later."

I found another doctor who specialized in pediatric OCD. It's a world of difference having someone who knows how to treat this illness. Darcie has been seeing him for several years now, and she's learned behavioral therapy. With this kind of therapy, you expose the client to their biggest fears and make them stay in an uncomfortable situation as long as they can without pushing too far. For example, Darcie is afraid that her hair will get stuck in a light switch and cause a fire. Her OCD is telling her to check to make sure that one of her hairs isn't stuck in the switch. If she walks past a light switch and flinches, I coach her and send her back to do it again.

Darcie's younger sister, Chelsea, has been unbelievably helpful to her. Darcie had a habit of picking at her skin, and we would all try to get her to stop. The two girls slept in the same room, and Chelsea would tell her, "Darcie, you can't do that. Hold my hands so you won't pick." Chelsea has always been a stable influence on Darcie.

We were once out in a crowd, and Darcie was getting real tense and aggravated. She was crying, "I can't stand this crowd." I took her into a public restroom, where I tried to calm her down. A few minutes later, I heard a little knock on the door. It was Chelsea. She came in and just stood there making funny sounds. Chelsea would almost literally stand on her head to distract her sister and get her to laugh. This time, she got me laughing and Darcie, too. It broke the tense moment!

Four years after we had begun searching for an answer, this doctor diagnosed Darcie with obsessive-compulsive disorder. She was only nine. It was devastating news to hear, but part of me was relieved to know what was wrong. I immediately started to read a book called *The Boy Who Couldn't Stop Washing,* and I could see Darcie in every page. I would get up in the middle of the night and sob into a pillow in the living room. I thought, "This can't be happening to our family."

I began reading everything about OCD that I could get my hands on, and I quickly learned a lot about the variety of symptoms that people with OCD can have. When I saw Darcie's doctor, I told him, "She's touching every object in stores. She's still tapping. What do I do?" He said, "I don't know. I know how to identify the illness and how to treat it with medication, but I don't know how to treat the behav-

Darcie used to get real uptight three or four times a day at school. Whenever she went to see the school nurse, she would knock on Chelsea's classroom door. Chelsea's teacher would send her out, and the two sisters would hug in the hallway. Chelsea would say, "It's okay, Darcie. It's okay." Darcie would go on her way, but first she had to hug her little sister for support.

In fifth grade, Darcie's teacher treated her miserably. The behavioral therapist wrote a letter to the teacher, saying, "In order for Darcie to do her schoolwork and have everything flow well so she's not a disruption in class, please give her five passes and leave them on your desk each day. Each time she needs to leave the classroom, she won't need to ask your permission. She can just go up, get one of her passes, and go into the bathroom for five minutes and five minutes only. Darcie will not abuse that privilege." Even that was too much to ask of this teacher!

I went in to speak with Darcie's teacher, and she told me, "I see Darcie in the playground, and she's running around and having a good time. There's nothing wrong with your kid." I said, "Of course she's out there having fun, because there's no pressure on her. There's nobody sneezing or coughing or touching her. There's no test being given. Anybody can be fine out on the playground." I had to take some control and fight back because it's terrible to watch your child suffer. Eventually, Darcie had to leave school. We had her tutored at home the rest of that year.

We often need to reassure Darcie. When she is symptomatic, we tell her, "This is your OCD. Your mind is sending you false signals." I make Darcie repeat this three times. By telling herself that her mind is playing tricks on her, she begins to relax a little.

When my youngest child, Teal, was born, she came out stiff as a board. She was a great little baby, but we have pictures of her looking rigid. My sister, Lil, was in the delivery room, and she kept saying, "Uh-oh, another one with OCD." I went into a very bad depression after Teal's birth, and I was put on an antidepressant. It took me six months to get back to normal.

When Teal was three years old, I took her to visit a girl-friend in Virginia. Away from the commotion of our family, I noticed that Teal was a little insecure. My friend said, "Bea, why does she keep asking you if you love her? I mean, a hundred times?" I kept trying to deny it, but the minute Teal refused to wear her shoes and socks, I knew. It was like being hit in the face. When she turned five, her OCD came out in full force.

In some respects, it was a little easier hearing the news of Teal's diagnosis than it was the first time around with Darcie. At least I was familiar with this illness. I knew what to say and what not to say. I knew how to handle it and I knew which medications worked. I already had a good doctor. That part was easy, but having another sick child in the house was hard. Every now and then, if Darcie and Teal are both not doing well, I cry and let it all out. Then I'm okay. You can't always keep everything together. I still sometimes have to say to myself, "I can do this. I can do this."

Teal would stay in her nightgown all day long if we didn't go out. She doesn't like to wear shoes and socks, just like Darcie. They give her an uncomfortable feeling. If Teal complains that her shoes or socks are hurting her, we make up a little dance. We stamp our feet up and down and say, "It doesn't hurt. It doesn't hurt."

Over the years, I've had a lot of support from my entire family. When I would get overwhelmed, my oldest daughter, Chanel, saw me cry an awful lot. She would say, "C'mon, Ma, I'm going to watch the kids." Then she would take them out for lunch or would do something special for me. When Teal was real sick, my sister, Lil, was always there, always calling me on the phone, asking, "Are you okay?" She's been incredible, too. It's not Darcie's illness or Teal's illness. It's the family's illness. Everybody in our family pinch-hits for each other.

After our family was in an article on the front page of the local Sunday paper, a young man called me and said, "I was diagnosed with OCD two years ago, and nobody in my family knows. I don't want them to know." A couple of weeks

We often need to reassure Darcie. When she is symptomatic, we tell her, "This is your OCD. Your mind is sending you false signals." I make Darcie repeat this three times. By telling herself that her mind is playing tricks on her, she begins to relax a little.
— BEATRICE K.

It's not Darcie's illness or Teal's illness. It's the family's illness. Everybody in our family pinch-hits for each other.
— BEATRICE K.

At first, I was embarrassed about my illness. On TV, if someone goes to see a psychiatrist, other folks say to them, "Oh, you're a mental patient." Although sometimes it's funny on TV, it makes people feel ashamed to say, "I have to go to see a psychiatrist."

— DARCIE

DARCIE

The first time I went to a psychiatrist, my parents told me that he wanted to put me on medication. I was only nine years old. I thought, "I'm not crazy. I'm not going on this stuff." I cried because I didn't want to take pills. I didn't understand what was going on.

The little things that everyone takes for granted are things I just can't do. I know that people often stare at me. I'm not oblivious to what goes on. At first, I was embarrassed about my illness. On TV, if someone goes to see a psychiatrist, other folks say to them, "Oh, you're a mental patient." Although sometimes it's funny on TV, it makes people feel ashamed to say, "I have to go to see a psychiatrist."

At school, a couple of the boys used to tease and bother me. They were just plain rude. I try to block out specific things they said, but I do remember coming home from school crying all the time. Some of my teachers understood what was going on with me. My fourth-grade teacher had worked with people who were mentally ill, so she was very caring and helped me a lot. But my fifth-grade teacher was real mean to me about it. She'd get disgusted with me. I'd go to the bathroom sometimes just to get away from her for a few minutes and try to get myself under control. All I needed was to get away. But then she'd roll her eyes at me, and that made it even worse.

I'm still not ready to talk to my friends at school about my illness. I did do a report on OCD and one on depression, and my classmates asked me a lot of questions. They know what I'm dealing with, but I don't want to discuss my personal life with them. I tend to deal with it myself and keep things inside.

When you have OCD, you get very good at hiding it. When the lights were off at night and my parents were downstairs, that was my time to pick my skin. But then my sister, Chelsea, would tell me, "Don't pick." She still does that.

One of the medications I took made me gain a lot of weight and gave me insomnia. I couldn't go to sleep until after midnight, and I'd sleep until three in the afternoon. I watched all the old shows on TV. That was kind of fun.

I really don't know how to describe OCD, because each person has different symptoms. It's hard for everyone who has it. It's hard and it's scary. It's definitely a lot of work, and it's not something fun to have. It's not something you'd pretend to have. No one would want to live like this!

I can't stop doing my rituals, because I just have to do them. I used to be afraid, for example, that my hair would go into a light switch and would catch on fire. When I walked by a light switch, I had to go back and check to see if my hair was in it. Even though I know my thoughts are not real, I can't stop worrying.

When my symptoms first started, I saw that the rest of my family wasn't like me. They didn't do the same things I did. I felt like I was different from the other kids. I was the odd one out.

I was invited to be on *The Oprah Winfrey Show* to talk about having OCD. It was hard to be on national TV because so many people were watching me, but it made me feel good about myself because I knew that some people would be helped. It was also good for me to meet other people on the show who have OCD. It made me realize there's nothing to be ashamed of. I have OCD and I'm still a normal person. I still do things that are fun, and I'm not odd or weird because I have it. No one is perfect.

At least twenty times a day, someone in my family says, "We're a team." And we are.

I really don't know how to describe OCD, because each person has different symptoms. It's hard for everyone who has it. It's hard and it's scary. It's definitely a lot of work, and it's not something fun to have. It's not something you'd pretend to have. No one would want to live like this!

— DARCIE

TEAL

I was afraid my mom didn't love me, and I said, "Mom, do you love me? Do you love me? Do you love me?" I asked her a hundred times. Even if she said, "Yes," I had to ask her again and again.

My shoes and socks would always hurt me, so Mom told me to go around and stomp my feet.

CHANEL

It's hard to remember when Darcie first got sick. I do remember watching my mom cry a lot. I felt sorry for her. She was so upset because there was something wrong with her baby. I didn't understand because I was pretty young, and I just thought Darcie's behavior was funny. We didn't know what was wrong with her. It took a long time to get the right diagnosis.

CHELSEA

Darcie and I were always very close and we still are. It was hard when she got sick. She kept getting stuck doing things. She couldn't stop. She just had to do them. Sometimes it was kind of heartbreaking. I would try to coach her and make her laugh even though she would yell at me.

Sometimes I kind of feel left out because my sisters get all this attention, but then I tell Mom how I'm feeling. I feel better because I know that Darcie and Teal don't do these things just to get attention. They need the attention because of their OCD.

BEATRICE

As their grandmother, my heart was broken when Darcie and Teal got sick. Now my granddaughters are doing well on their medication. It's still a sad situation, but it's unbelievable how much love there is in this family, and that helps a lot. Maybe some families don't have that love.

support or when he wanted to see us. I got tired of that stuff. One time he asked me, "What do you want from me?" I said, "What I want is a father, not a drinking buddy who comes to see me once a month." I wanted a dad to throw a football around with and to go with to a ballgame. Stuff like that. A normal childhood. It never happened, so I depended on other people to be like a father to me. I was seventeen years old before a neighbor taught me how to fish!

As I got older, my dad had kids with another woman, and I didn't want to see him no more. One day my half brother called me and told me that my father had died. I didn't shed a tear for my dad. I didn't do nothing. I just said, "Okay, fine." My half brother got mad at me, and he didn't show me no sympathy and no compassion. When he told me where the funeral would be, he asked me, "Are you going to show up?" I said, "Hell, yeah, because I want to make sure Dad's dead."

I began to get involved with a lot of things that I shouldn't have, like gangs, drugs, and all of that. My mom and I drifted apart, but a year before she died, she and I became real close again. Most people in my family didn't understand our relationship. All they understood was how mean I had been to my mom and how much stress I had given her over the years. Only Mom and I really knew the closeness we had shared together during her last year. Right before she died, she told me, "You're going to go through a lot of problems because lots of people are going to think that you put me in my grave." I told her, "When you leave, no one is going to want to take me in." And it was true. No one did.

I depended a lot on my mother. When she died in February 1985, everything turned. I was just out of high school, and I didn't really know how to survive without her. Her death was a big blow to me. Folks in my family took in my sister real quick, but they said, "What are we going to do with Juan?" I said, "Hey, I need help here, too." I was left on my own and I did what I had to do to get by.

I got depressed and I ran away. I didn't see my sister for maybe three or four years. I was just out wandering and liv-

ing on the streets, sleeping on park benches, in churches, in parking lots, and anywhere I knew I would be safe. There were times that it got real cold and rainy. There were a lot of police stations downtown near skid row, and they gave out vouchers for a local hotel. The police knew me well. I was no troublemaker or nothing, so sometimes they'd even let me sleep in one of the empty jail cells. That way, I could stay out of the rain and have breakfast in the morning.

Somehow I managed to go to school, even though I was homeless. I got financial aid from the school by using the addresses of friends in my neighborhood. I had always loved to cook, so I took a culinary class. When I finished the course, I found a job, but I was still living from place to place.

I reconnected with my sister one Christmas. I was working at a Christmas tree lot, and I just happened to look up and there she was, staring right at me out of her car window. It was like we knew each other, but we weren't really sure at first. When you're young, a lot can change in four years. She recognized me and got out of her car. She said she was my sister, but I asked her to pull out an ID because I didn't believe her at first. It turned out to be true! I was still living on the streets then, and my sister took me to her house to stay with her for a bit. We both got jobs working in the same place. I worked the swing shift and she worked the day shift, so I could help her take care of her two kids.

Although things in my life seemed to be going a little better for me, my violence continued to get me in trouble. When I got my first job with the state, I worked in a program where you go out in emergencies, like flash floods, to help people out. I beat up one of my coworkers for saying something rude to me, leaving him with a broken nose, a fractured arm, and three missing teeth. I knew something was wrong with me, but nobody would tell me what was causing me to be so violent. With my friends who know me real well, I'm as gentle as a lamb. But piss me off and I'm a raging bull that's going to come after you.

I had a seizure at work one day and ended up in the hospital. After they did a CT scan, the doctors thought that I had a brain tumor. It turns out I had hydrocephalus, which is fluid backing up in my brain. The specialist who was in charge of the neurosurgery department said to me, "Juan, I could save your life by putting a shunt in your head, but you'll probably have seizures for the rest of your life. If you don't want me to save your life now, you'll die within the next six months." He explained that my brain was already at the point of blowing up. After a week of pain and agony, I decided to have the surgery.

When I first found out about having hydrocephalus, I was really depressed. They had me see one of the psychiatrists in the hospital, and he told me, "You have bipolar disorder." I said, "You're telling me that on top of all that I'm going through, I also have to deal with having a mental illness?" But then he told me about what bipolar disorder was, and I felt at ease with the diagnosis. I knew that my behavior was kind of weird. I'd feel real depressed one day, and then the next day or so, I would be real manicky and sometimes violent. Once I understood what was wrong with me, I said, "Okay, what do I do now?" The doctor gave me some meds and told me to go to a mental health clinic.

I didn't show up at the mental health clinic for four years because I thought, "Oh well, I don't need to do this or that." I was still living with my sister at the time. She noticed that I was mixing my meds with alcohol and stuff. There were times when I took too much medication on purpose, and I would get up in the middle of the night and crash. My sister had this glass table and I don't know exactly what happened, but she said that I fell on the table. The next morning, there were bruises all over my body.

I became suicidal. Even after thirteen suicide attempts, I still wanted to die. I didn't know what my purpose in life was. As far as having a profession in cooking, I couldn't get a job in a restaurant because no one was going to hire somebody who had seizures. I felt like the work I loved had been taken away from me. I thought, "There's got to be something that I was put on this earth for, or else let me take myself out."

Juan

Four years after my diagnosis, I finally went to a mental health clinic, where I met a social worker named Susan. She became my case manager. To this day, I think of her as a saint. When I first talked to Susan, I said, "I don't want to be here; you guys ain't going to be able to help me do the things that I want to do. I can't go back to work because my insurance won't cover me on account of the seizures, but I want to cook; that's what I was trained for, and that's what I want to do." Susan said real bluntly, "Juan, you could do that; we can teach you that here." I said, "I don't want to be taught. I want to cook and teach others how to cook." She said, "You can do that here, too." I could always turn to Susan for encouragement. If I felt like I couldn't do something, she was there to say, "Yes, you can do it. Tell me what you need and we can get it for you."

With Susan's help, we got all the equipment I needed to open up a kitchen in the clinic. I started training other mental health clients how to cook basic meals. Some of the clients didn't even know how to boil water! I was in charge and that made me feel like I had some stability in my life. And some of the people who worked under me were able to get jobs and function in society.

Even though things were working out for me at the clinic, I was still getting violent. There was one client there who was taunting me and raising hell about stuff. One day, I grabbed him by the throat and I wouldn't let him go. All the staff came, but nobody could get me off him because I'm too big. By the time they finally pulled me away from the guy, he was blue in the face. They had to give him CPR.

After that episode, a lot of the staff didn't want to work with me, but Susan wasn't scared of me, and we continued working together. Then there was another incident at the clinic when another client grabbed me by the shirt and hit me upside the head. I said, "Okay, you want to fight?" I was cooking that day in the kitchen, so I grabbed a knife and chased him into the next room. Susan is about four foot nine, a real short little Jewish woman, and she got in the middle between my knife and this guy. I yelled at her, "Don't move or I'll stab you." She goes, "You want to stab me?" I stopped just before I was going to insert the knife into her. I looked at her and said, "You should thank my mom. She always told me never to strike a woman, whether they piss you off or not. So you're lucky my mom's words stayed in my head."

There are certain staff members in the clinic who know how to deal with me. When I blow up, I don't want four or five staff surrounding me. I'm not an animal. I'm just pissed off. So now, if I blow up, there are certain people who say, "I know how to calm Juan down. I know how to talk to him." And they do know how. It's a mutual respect. You respect me, and I'll respect you.

I haven't attacked anybody in maybe a good four or five years now. That's a miracle! It's a long time for me because I have an urge to fight. Now it's more like if you piss me off, I say, "Okay, fine." I might cuss under my breath or something, but I've learned to control my temper.

I've found out that I'm very good with people who have mental illness, because I understand their pain and what they're going through. Over time, I've come to realize that there is something I was put here on earth to do. I'm meant to help people, whether it's to be a listening ear or a shoulder to cry on. I want to help my fellow man.

I believe there should be a voice out there for those who can't speak for themselves. For that reason, I got trained to speak on panels sponsored by my clinic. I like being out there for the consumers who don't have a voice. However, during the training, I didn't like it when I was told, "This is how you should do it." I stood up and said, "No, I don't want to use a fact sheet. I want to speak from my own experience and tell people how I feel." So far it's been going okay and I've gotten a lot of good feedback. I don't get paid for speaking, but the clinic always helps me out. If I need airline tickets and money to get to a mental health conference, it's there. They say to me, "Juan, you let us know what you need and we'll push for it." As long as I'm doing okay and people respect me, then I guess I'm doing the right thing. I enjoy the fact that people believe in me.

I love the challenge of speaking at these conferences. Sometimes I've been asked by one of my supervisors, "Juan, are you going to buy a suit to wear when you speak on this panel?" I say, "Look, when I was a little kid, my mom always had me in suits and ties. I've grown up now, and I hate them. I can't stand them. I don't know why, but I'm just not the suit-and-tie kind of guy. Anyway, the people who come hear me speak don't come to see how I'm dressed; they come to hear my message."

I've read all the latest data from Dr. Satcher, the Surgeon General of the United States, about mental illness. It's clear that programs for minorities are needed nationwide. Last year, I was invited with some other people to go to an anti-stigma conference in Washington, D.C., to help come up with ideas of how to better serve the Latino community. It's difficult for Latinos in the mental health system because they follow a lot of basic traditions. When it comes to mental illness, many of them don't believe in going to the doctor. They just throw whoever is sick into a little room and say, "Stay there and we'll feed you a bone every once in a while and check up on you."

To get professional help has been uncommon for Latinos, so our goal at the conference was to come up with some ways to change this. We want to let the Latino community know that we're there for them, and that they can come to our clinics without the fear of having the immigration people come. We want all Latinos to know that even if they don't have citizenship papers or they don't have any money, they can still come to get help.

A lot of Latinos fear that if they come into these mental health places, they're going to be stripped of their dignity and their beliefs. As Latinos, we do our own thing. We were raised differently from Anglos. For instance, let's say an Anglo grandmother comes in for some medication, and the doctor gives her a prescription for a pill to take three times a day; she's probably going to take the meds. But let's say a Latino grandmother comes in. Even if she believes in her doctor, she probably won't take the medicine. If the doctor doesn't spend the time finding out why she won't take it, then we're defeating the purpose. I know a lot of Latino grandmothers who are second- or third-generation immigrants who won't take their medication. On the other hand, a friend of mine has a grandmother who believes in the Virgin Mary. She keeps all of her medicines right in front of the statue of the Virgin Mary, and she believes that if she takes her pills right there, Mary will protect her.

If we can get the professionals to understand that, with Latinos, they're dealing with a different culture, we'll be much better off. Doctors have to sit down and try to find out what their clients believe in and what their culture is like. A lot of

Latino people think that if someone in their family is stricken with mental illness, somewhere down the line, one of their relatives did something bad and God is punishing them by making this person sick.

At my clinic, we try to let Latinos know that we understand their beliefs, but that we can also help them lead a better life. We say, "We don't want you to change your lifestyle or stop praying or doing what it is that you do. We just want you to know that there is help out there for you. We understand where you're coming from, because we're Latinos, too."

Both Asians and Latinos seem to have the same kind of stigma around mental illness in the family. They're ashamed of it. When one of their family members is sick, the rest of them feel that this person is worth nothing. Sometimes family members encourage the mentally ill person to commit suicide because they have brought shame to their family and the only way to undo that is to get rid of the person causing the shame. It's hard for me to even picture this.

The media has a lot to do with creating stigma. When John Hinckley shot President Reagan, the police found out that he was a mental patient. The media made it sound like everybody with a mental illness is going to go out there and shoot people. The media doesn't fully understand that there are good people out there who have steady jobs, have a home, have a partner, and who are also mentally ill. They can't conceive that people with mental illness can have healthy relationships or normal everyday conversations.

There was a time when a mental health group was trying to put up some new housing for the mentally ill in a neighborhood, but the neighbors didn't want it there. I went to a meeting and said, "Hey, we have the same feelings you do. We pay taxes and we have families. We want to do the same things you do." Then the neighbors said, "Yeah, but we don't want your kind here." They made it sound like we were going to be out there in their neighborhood and cause a ruckus and hurt or kill somebody. Like I said, that attitude comes from the newspapers and TV. People have this negative view of the

I've found out that I'm very good with people who have mental illness, because I understand their pain and what they're going through. Over time, I've come to realize that there is something I was put here on earth to do. I'm meant to help people, whether it's to be a listening ear or a shoulder to cry on. I want to help my fellow man.
—*JUAN*

Stephanie and Kerry

THE GILMORE FAMILY

RALEIGH, NORTH CAROLINA

S TEPHANIE G ILMORE / K ERRY G ILMORE

STEPHANIE

I WAS IN AND OUT OF PSYCHIATRIC HOSPITALS fourteen times before I finally stabilized. For years, I was either too delusional or too psychotic to even know who I was.

When I was in college, I knew there was something wrong with me. I was doing research with a grad student who was screening people for depression. I told him that I'd been taking an abnormal psychology class where the teacher had profiled a person who had manic-depression. I asked him point-blank, "Do you think I'm manic-depressive?" He said, "No, not at all. That's crazy!" This was before I got very sick, but I was already on my way down.

I gradually crept into a full-blown psychosis. When my parents came to visit me in my apartment, I was able to hide the worst of my misery from them. However, they quickly realized that something wasn't right with me. We decided that I would leave college and return with them to their home in South Carolina. My mom helped me clean up my apartment and get everything packed, but she had no idea that I was sinking so far so fast. I didn't realize it, either.

Before my parents and I could leave town, I wound up in a psychiatric hospital in seclusion, strapped down to a bed. A nurse tried to feed me milk and I spit it out on her sweater. I went through a series of inpatient hospitalizations from the time I was nineteen until I was twenty-eight. I'm thirty-two now.

During my first hospitalization, I was diagnosed with bipolar disorder. It was hard to control in spite of all the medications I tried. Some of them would do a little bit of good, but sometimes I used to throw my pills away. Many manic-depressives do this. They feel good; they want that high; and they don't think they are sick. In fact, at times my psychosis felt wonderful. Can you imagine thinking that Sting is singing just for you? I'd ask him to sing to me, and I'd actually hear him say, "Sure." So I'd put his CD on, and he'd sing all his songs right to me. Why would I want to come out of that state of mind?

When I wasn't in a hospital, my mom would come into my room at eight o'clock each morning and give me my medications. There were times when she was really scared of me because I would throw things at her. I seemed to get worse and worse as time went by. I walked around the city talking

189

You probably have seen people walking around talking to themselves. You might think they're completely out of it and crazy, and you might laugh or joke about them. You might even be scared of them. Perhaps deep down you know this could happen to you someday. These people are human beings. Period. The mentally ill have souls just like every other human being.

— STEPHANIE

to my voices, and I went through times when I believed that my brother and my dad were both gay. I even thought Dad wanted me to commit suicide. I remember telling him that I was going to try to ruin his career by accusing him of sexually abusing me. At one point I was so paranoid that I kept a knife by my bed and put my desk up against my door every night so no one could get into my bedroom. These delusions felt so real. After all the hospitalizations and medication and therapy, I had reached ground zero.

I lost a lot of my friends because of my illness, and even my own brother couldn't stand me. I would say inappropriate things and not even realize it. I can't imagine the impact my behavior had on my family. I can't imagine how they coped with me living at home in a full-blown psychotic state.

I tried going back to school several times, but I could never stick with it. When I came out of my psychosis, I decided to try once again. I ended up taking a class, sticking with it, and getting a "C+." It wasn't an "A," but I did okay. When I signed up for two more classes, I was determined not to get any more "C's." I got an "A" in one and a "B" in another. It was huge for me. Huge! My dad died in 1996, but he lived long enough to see me become successful. This was a blessing.

I'm not a churchgoer, but I feel very spiritual. I pray first thing every morning, and I write my own prayers. I just pray for faith in God. I say, "Give me strength." I think that God and my medication together have both played huge roles in making me well. But number one, I had an incredibly good childhood; and number two, my parents loved me no matter what. They never gave up on me and were always supportive. They were completely and totally immersed in helping me recover.

I stay on top of my medications and I'm completely involved in the process of getting well. If I'm having a stressful day, I'll adjust my dosage myself. My doctor supports me in this. It's empowering to take control over my illness and not let it control me.

I believe that you get back from life what you put into it. I'm learning to shut up, stop complaining about my prob-

lems, and instead, use that negative energy to do something about them in a positive way. It's up to me to make my life the way I want it to be. It's my responsibility. I never realized this before I got sick, but after getting better it became clear that I was in control of my life. I am in control more and more every day. My self-esteem has improved, and I no longer feel that I need to identify myself solely as being bipolar. I'm Stephanie first.

I feel like I got a second chance, and I want to give back to the mental health community. I've been on the board of the County Alliance for the Mentally Ill for the past two years. I want to be an advocate for those mentally ill people who don't have the ability to speak for themselves. I've been there myself, and now I want to help. I consider the mentally ill *my* people.

My mom also suffers from a mental illness. She has very serious depression, and she's more depressed than I have ever been. I try to help her in every way I can. I talk to her each day, we go out to eat often, and we go to the movies together. It's very hard for people to accept that my mother is ill. Our family members and close friends don't want to believe that this beautiful, intelligent, vital woman is depressed all the time.

You probably have seen people walking around talking to themselves. You might think they're completely out of it and crazy, and you might laugh or joke about them. You might even be scared of them. Perhaps deep down you know this could happen to you someday. These people are human beings. Period. The mentally ill have souls just like every other human being.

KERRY

When Stephanie first got sick, we'd be driving along and all of a sudden she would say, "I'm going to get out of the car," or, "I'm going to attack you." My husband, Tom, and I became her enemies, which can often happen with bipolar illness.

When Stephanie was in the hospital, Tom and I could sleep at night knowing that she was safe. When she was home, as soon as we had one problem licked, we had another one on our hands. Mental illness is a trial for the whole family.

When Stephanie was sick, she and her dad would get into bad fights, which would set her wheels going even more. I would ask Tom to avoid controversy, but he'd say, "If Stephanie asks me a question, I'm going to tell her the answer." It was very scary because he had a temper. It got so he wouldn't say anything, because he was absolutely freaked out by her behavior. Stephanie was like a tornado ready to erupt at any time.

Tom was diagnosed with melanoma when Stephanie was at her worst, so it was a crazy time at home. I was afraid he would leave us because things were so unpleasant. I went through months of worrying that I might have to give up my husband because he and Stephanie were constantly at war with each other. I was frightened and physically worn out from having to separate the two people I loved the most. I didn't know what was going to happen. As Stephanie got better, so did Tom, and their relationship improved.

Tom and I were very protective of our daughter. When Stephanie was able to go back to work, we advised her not to say anything during job interviews about her mental illness. She could reveal her history after she got hired and had proved herself. She said, "No, I have to tell the truth." So Tom and I sat there and thought, "Oh gosh, Stephanie will never get a job." But she was honest and she got a job at a small, independent bookstore. She's done great there. If there's too much stress, Stephanie doesn't work full-time. Her employer understands completely.

Getting a job did a world of good for our daughter. If you knew Stephanie ten years ago when she was so sick, and again right now, you'd be amazed. Many of my friends say, "I don't believe the change in her!" Her illness masked the wonderful person she is.

I've been dealing with major depression since I was in my thirties. For many years I didn't even know what was going on with me. When my children were young and I had to do all those things that you have to do for your family, I felt like a slug. I got involved in the PTA, but I was always dragging. My husband kept saying, "Let's do this or that..." Or, he would ask me, "What do you think, Kerry?" And I'd answer, "I don't care," because I didn't. When I'm feeling depressed, nothing goes on in my head. Absolutely nothing.

When the kids were younger and off at school, I was so depressed, I would stand in the corner of my room and cry. This became a way of life for me. When the kids came home at the end of the day, I would do what was needed to be done and nothing more. When my husband came home from work, I'd disappear, read a book, or whatever. I wanted to be alone. If I could have hidden in a closet, I would have.

Chemically, depression just takes away all your oomph! It's all gone. When I'm depressed, it's hard to make conversation with anyone. I don't have my motors going. It's a feeling of nothing. It's just not caring about your family, about important things, or about anything that might usually feel joyful. Everything is on dead stop. You're always thinking, "This will be over in a minute, and then I can bury myself in a book." All you feel is pain, so you try to dull it any way you can.

Over the years, I've been on every possible combination of drugs. Sometimes they've worked, and sometimes they haven't. I'm usually a very hopeful person, but I have very little hope left. I will continue to try everything I can to get better, because my family motivates me to go on. But if it were just up to me, I'd say, "Forget it. I've had enough."

I live with depression every day. Electroshock treatments might be my last resort. My doctor wants me to try them, and I have faith in him. They frighten me, but I've done a whole lot of research, so I have fewer qualms about them now.

When I feel bad, I don't even want to be around my friends. They are lovely ladies and, when my sense of humor is working, they are delightful people. But they don't know about my depression, which is just as well. I can be around Stephanie because she accepts me for who I am. I don't want to be with anyone else, because I'm just going to sit and be empty. I'd rather be empty alone. I just look out the window and the world goes by. It breaks my heart.

Chemically, depression just takes away all your oomph! It's all gone. When I'm depressed, it's hard to make conversation with anyone. I don't have my motors going. It's a feeling of nothing. It's just not caring about your family, about important things, or about anything that might usually feel joyful. Everything is on dead stop.

— KERRY

I can be around Stephanie because she accepts me for who I am. I don't want to be with anyone else, because I'm just going to sit and be empty. I'd rather be empty alone. I just look out the window and the world goes by. It breaks my heart.

— KERRY

Back row: Lisa Anne, Adam, and Robert *Front row:* Ronnie, Brian, Annalise, and Thomas

THE DARLINGTON FAMILY

SOUTHWICK, MASSACHUSETTS

LISA ANNE DARLINGTON / ADAM BROWN / ROBERT EAK
RONNIE DARLINGTON / BRIAN BROWN / ANNALISE EAK
THOMAS DARLINGTON

TOMMY

WHEN MY SON, KEITH, WAS DIAGNOSED with paranoid schizophrenia, it hit my wife, Ronnie, and me very hard. We didn't even know exactly what it meant. Six months later, our son was dead. Everything happened so fast. We never had time to adjust to his illness, and Keith didn't have the time to adjust to it, either.

Ronnie and I didn't know how severely sick Keith had been until after his death. We should have recognized the early warning signs of mental illness years ago, but unfortunately, you often learn about these kinds of things after the fact. If only you could stop somebody before they make a decision to commit suicide. My son never had an opportunity to become the person he wanted to be.

The hardest thing Ronnie and I ever had to do was write Keith a letter and tell him he had to leave our home unless he began to participate fully in his own care. He was almost twenty-two years old and he was still living up in his bedroom. When Keith moved out of our house and got his own place, he went into a crisis. That's how we were able to get him to go to the hospital.

When our son was hospitalized, he was put on many different medications in an effort to find the right one. He suffered from their side effects. His hands would tremble, and he would drool. Although Keith seemed to be pretty well stabilized when he left the hospital, he still took his own life. He never even had enough time to get on the right medication.

Keith never wanted to be a burden to anybody. He told us many times, "Don't worry about me, Mom and Dad. I'm okay." When he was discharged from the hospital, the staff recommended that he become independent as quickly as he could and provide for himself. They wanted him to go back to his own apartment and support himself without our help. If we had to do it all over again, we wouldn't do it the same way. We wouldn't have listened to the professionals. We wouldn't have had Keith go back out on his own so soon, because now we know that he just wasn't capable of living independently.

> When my son, Keith, was diagnosed with paranoid schizophrenia, it hit my wife, Ronnie, and me very hard. We didn't even know exactly what it meant. Six months later, our son was dead. Everything happened so fast. We never had time to adjust to his illness, and Keith didn't have the time to adjust to it, either.
>
> — TOMMY

193

After Keith moved back into his apartment, he was worried about how he would pay for his food. We assured him he would qualify for food stamps, and just a few days before he killed himself, he finally got his first food stamp allotment. It was only twenty-nine dollars for the entire month! This was all the government was going to give him. Keith said, "Dad, this can't be right. Twenty-nine dollars is all I get?"

I felt so bad about the food stamps, because I had assumed Keith was going to get enough to live on. I honestly thought the government was going to provide for him. This was the proverbial straw that destroyed his life. Keith was rational enough and smart enough to figure out that twenty-nine dollars was not going to do anything for him. It was not going to buy him enough food to live on.

We understand now that the most critical time for people who are suicidal is when they are thinking clearly. They see their lives stretching out before them and they think, "What kind of a future do I really have?" They make a non-delusional assessment of what their future holds. I think that's what Keith was struggling with. He was thinking clearly at the time of his suicide. He just didn't like his options.

RONNIE

My son, Keith, committed suicide when he was twenty-two. My husband, Tommy, and I have often been asked, "Who do you blame for Keith's death?" I usually answer that the only person I can really blame is Keith. He made a terrible choice. I think he just got tired of struggling with his illness.

After our first child, Lisa, was born, her dad and I thought we would never be able to have another baby. I had three miscarriages, and when I became pregnant with Keith, I assumed I would miscarry again. But I carried him full-term, and Tommy and I always say that Keith was our second miracle after Lisa.

Keith was a joyous, happy child. He looked at things in such a lovely way. When he was in high school, he felt that all the flags in the world should be taken down, because they divide countries and, therefore, they divide people. This was so like him. Keith was such a gentle soul.

When Keith was about fourteen, we saw a change in him. He got very sullen and quiet and didn't seem happy. We assumed this was because his best friend had leukemia and was at death's door. His friend recovered, but Keith didn't. He was in a very deep depression. We took him to a doctor, who confirmed that he was suffering from "teenage depression." Naively, we never considered that he might be mentally ill. We thought that when he passed through his teenage years, his depression would go away.

Keith was very talented musically. When he was seventeen, he started to play the guitar and write music. He also took piano lessons. When he asked us to buy him a piano, there was no way we were going to do that. After his second or third lesson, Keith's piano teacher called us and said, "You've got to come over and see your son play the piano. You should buy him one." Tommy and I thought she probably owned stock in a piano company, but we went to hear Keith play. As we stood behind him, he put his hands on the keys and he just was gone, lost in the keyboard. He played absolutely beautifully, and on that same day we bought him an electric piano. Soon after that, however, we started to see a disturbing pattern in our son's behavior. Keith never stuck with anything; his interests only lasted for short periods of time. He didn't even continue his piano playing. Keith began to withdraw, and he got quieter and quieter.

When Keith was seventeen, he decided he wanted to drop out of high school. I was driving him to school one day when he told me, "You can leave me at school, but I'm going to walk right back out the door after you leave. I don't fit in there."

After he dropped out of school, Keith wanted to go to Ohio with some of his older friends. Tommy and I did a tremendous amount of soul-searching, and we laid as many obstacles in his path as we could. We told him, "You have to save enough money to pay for your transportation to get there and pay for two months' rent for an apartment." To our dismay, he sold his guitars, his valuable books, and his records. In two weeks, Keith had everything together and he left for Ohio.

Keith was in Ohio for less than a year. When we spoke to him on the phone, and later on when we went to visit him, we realized that he wasn't well. He seemed fearful of so many things. Soon, Keith came back home to live with us because he felt much safer there.

Keith wasn't able to consistently hold a job. The people he worked for at McDonald's all liked him, but he felt like he never did a good enough job. Keith's last job was in the pressroom at a local newspaper. From what I was told, he apparently would often have conversations with himself.

Keith became even quieter and more withdrawn. This was what frightened Tommy and me the most. I even said to Keith one day, "You're becoming a part of the wall, a part of the woodwork. You're just fading away from us." Tommy and I were in the car with him one day and I said, "Keith, it's like you're going down a black hole and we're holding you by your shirt and your shirt's coming off!" And he replied, "Well, you should just let me go." He said this calmly, as if it were just a simple fact. Tommy and I didn't know how to respond, because, again, the words "mental illness" never entered our minds.

Keith became increasingly frightened of so many things. He was afraid of his food; afraid that somebody would come through the television set and get him; afraid that somebody was in his closet or under his bed. He even said to me a few times, "You've really got to watch out for them." And I'd say, "Well, hon, who's 'them' you want me to watch out for?" And he'd say, "Well, you know, people are watching you. They know everything about you. You and Daddy just don't know it." Once, Keith told me that if he were in the animal world, he would be on a lower echelon, and therefore he shouldn't even be here. That really frightened us.

Every night, Tommy and I would go to the foot of the stairs and say, "Hey, Keith, dinner's ready. Are you coming down for dinner?" We'd hear his soft voice, "No, I don't think

so. Not now." And he just wouldn't come down. He also became very paranoid about his food; he felt that most foods would give him cancer. On the other hand, he would sometimes fix us big meals. He would go into the kitchen and use every pot and pan to make culinary inventions for us. His meals were great, but Keith would never eat any of them.

During this time, Keith began to do all kinds of artwork. He was a gifted artist even though he'd never taken any art lessons. He started to sketch on his own. He was a realist, so when he sketched a flower, it looked so real that you could almost smell its fragrance. Yet, Keith never appreciated the beauty and talent of his work. Both Tommy and I would say to him, "You know, Keith, you don't have to get a job. You can just work on your art or take more piano lessons. Whatever you want to do is okay with us. We'll back you up." But Keith never thought he was good enough to do anything right. He would often say to me, "You and Dad always say I'm a miracle, but some miracles shouldn't be born." A chill would go down my spine whenever I heard him say that.

Keith was a big reader. He would read everything from books on Zen Buddhism to comic books and everything else in between. He would have intellectual discussions with us, and Tommy and I would say, "Whoa! This is over our heads!" We couldn't comprehend most of the books he was reading.

There were many nights when Tommy and I would just hold on to each other and not say a word because we were so afraid for our son. Keith was our child, and as parents, we are supposed to make our children better. We couldn't do that. I was naive enough to believe that my love for Keith could heal him. Tommy and I thought that love heals everything, but it really doesn't. It gets you through things, but it can't make anybody better.

Keith's depression was hard for everyone in the family, but I think Tommy and I were the only ones who could understand what he was going through. Actually, we didn't really understand it at all. I'm not sure anyone can understand mental illness unless they experience it themselves. We even went into counseling together because we felt we had to go some-

There were many nights when Tommy and I would just hold on to each other and not say a word because we were so afraid for our son. Keith was our child, and as parents, we are supposed to make our children better. We couldn't do that. I was naive enough to believe that my love for Keith could heal him. Tommy and I thought that love heals everything, but it really doesn't. It gets you through things, but it can't make anybody better.

— RONNIE

I work now as an advocate for people who have mental illness. Most of them seem to have such gentle souls, and this world needs individuals like that. These people who are so sick get up every day in spite of their disabilities. They are the true heroes. The rest of us just schlep along and do the best we can to help them.

LISA ANNE

There are three different "Keiths" in my mind: the Keith I knew before I got married and left home, the Keith who was in the hospital where he was diagnosed with schizophrenia, and the Keith who is no longer here.

When my brother was alive, I used to think of him as a person who was just somewhat different and eccentric. I told myself, "Well, Keith is a musician. Musicians are a different kind of artsy people." When he was moody and not talkative, I just thought, "My brother is an artist." I had always heard about people who play the guitar and don't talk for days while they're writing their music. They don't pay attention to anything else.

It's hard to understand mental illness unless you know someone who experiences it. You think of the mentally ill as "those people," like the ones who talk to themselves on the street corner in the rain. You think, "Oh, those poor people!" You don't ever think of someone like Keith, who could carry on a conversation, move into his own apartment, and act just like anybody else, as a person who could take his own life. I don't think anybody realized just how sick he was.

I was married when Keith was a teenager, and I moved out-of-state. I never saw all the gradual changes that my parents saw in him. When I talked to him on the phone, he sounded fine. I don't know if my parents decided not to tell me what was really going on because they didn't know themselves, or whether they just didn't want to get too in-depth with me about Keith since I was living so far away. I guess it might have been easier for me to deal with his death had I

actually seen him go downhill. When I came back home, he was clearly very sick.

I would like to tell other siblings who might be in my situation not to be mad at anyone. But being angry is something that you've inevitably got to go through. I can't imagine another situation that would make you feel angrier than when a person you love has taken their own life. For siblings dealing with a brother or sister who has a mental illness, I say just hang on and enjoy being with the person who is mentally ill, no matter what their capacity. Stay with that person, try to involve yourself as much as you can, and keep an open mind. It might not be the same person that you were used to. It may not be the same brother that you grew up with, or the same sister, but deep down inside, the same person is in there somewhere.

My sons, Adam and Brian, are more compassionate toward people who have mental illness because they knew my brother. They are accepting and responsive to anyone who is different. Teenagers might be more apt to tease kids who are different, but my boys are not afraid to show their feelings and be a little bit nicer and kinder toward anyone who is suffering.

ADAM

I was shocked when I heard that Uncle Keith had killed himself. I was like, "He can't be dead. I just saw him two weeks ago. We were playing guitar together up in my room. He just can't be dead."

I'll never forget the day he died. I went to school the next morning as if it were just a normal day. My friends noticed how sad I was, and they asked me what was wrong. I said, "My uncle was mentally ill and he just killed himself." They were all like, "Oh, well, gee, that's too bad." They didn't know what to say to me.

With Keith, it was sort of like looking into a mirror, because both of us really loved to play music and we always

It's hard to understand mental illness unless you know someone who experiences it. You just think of the mentally ill as "those people," like the ones who talk to themselves on the street corner in the rain. You think, "Oh, those poor people!" You don't ever think of someone like Keith, who could carry on a conversation, move into his own apartment, and act just like anybody else, as a person who could take his own life.
— LISA ANNE

loved to draw together. And we both read constantly. We were so alike, it was strange!

The only possession I have that reminds me of Keith is his wallet. He gave it to me not too long before he died. I was walking home from school one day, planning to go to a store and buy something. I pulled out my wallet, and one of my friends said, "Well, where did you get that crappy wallet?" And I said, "This is my uncle's wallet! He killed himself. This is the only thing I have to remind me of him. So will you shut up about it?" And he goes, "Oh, well, sorry."

I'd like to tell other kids that just because someone has a mental illness, it doesn't mean that they are mentally retarded. Having a mental illness can mean that you can't store as much information in your brain. I mean, there's a million things that could be mental illness. Nobody should judge people who have it.

I'm not really sure what all the technical terms about mental illness mean, like schizophrenia and stuff like that. But if someone asked me why my uncle killed himself, I would say that he decided that he just couldn't handle what was going on. Or maybe I'd say that he wanted to make things easier for people who couldn't handle what was going on with him. Keith tried to be thoughtful and make it so that no one had to worry about him.

No matter what, if you know someone who is mentally ill, don't ever give up hope. There's always some hope. Just try to be with that person and teach them about the wonderful things that can come out of life. Tell them about the good things they can do and how many people they can help.

A friend of mine and I have a lot in common. Both of us like to write, and we both like the *Star Wars* series. His father hung himself. A girl walked up to my friend one day and said, "Why don't you just kill yourself like your father did? You'd do us all a favor!" He threatened to beat her up, so he was put into a mental institution. He called me up recently and said, "Well, I don't know what's going on, because everything's been going against me. Nothing seems to be working in my favor." I told him, "Well, what you've got to do is try and work to accomplish something and make things go good for you. If you just sit back and watch everything go by and let things go bad, then you're going to fail. But if you try your hardest to do whatever you can to make everything get better, then it's going to get better." He always says to me, "Adam, I can trust you with whatever I have to say. I know you're going to give me positive input." I've never really thought about it, but he is one of my best friends.

BRIAN

I don't remember much about the time when Uncle Keith went into the hospital. I was too young then. Keith was like another big brother to me. He was the one that got Adam and me into playing the guitar and stuff.

There's a grown-up who always walks by our school who I think has a mental illness. I always make sure to tell the other kids not to make fun of him.

I don't really know what schizophrenia is. I do know that it makes it kind of harder for people to do things and stuff. And I didn't think it affected Keith very much, because he was doing things perfectly fine and everything.

I would like to tell other kids that it's not their fault if they have a mental illness, and that it's not a big deal if they do. If they are mentally ill, it doesn't mean that they're any less of a person. Anybody can get a mental illness. Anybody.

Karen, Molly, and Bill

THE CISCO / AVERY / PAUL FAMILY

WAUWATOSA, WISCONSIN AND MADISON, WISCONSIN

KAREN AVERY / MOLLY CISCO / BILL PAUL

MOLLY

WHEN I WAS A LITTLE GIRL, I KNEW THERE WERE THINGS that I experienced that other people didn't. I had a sense of not wanting to be alive, of wanting my life to be over.

I can remember lying in a snowdrift one night when I was six, looking up at the stars and wishing that my life would stop, that everything would just stop. I also remember hiding in a closet and wishing I would die. I didn't think about doing anything to actually hurt myself when I was that young, but I kept hoping that my life would end.

I got upset when I started to do very poorly in school. My father told me that I wasn't allowed to act sad or cry in our house. None of us kids, not even our mom, were allowed to show our emotions at home. When my mother's mother died, my father got mad at her for crying. I can distinctly remember seeing Mom in the bathroom with her head in the linen closet and her face buried in towels, so nobody would hear her cry.

Humor was usually okay with my father, but when I began to fail at school, he punished me by not allowing me to laugh in our house anymore. Not only was I prohibited from expressing anger or sadness, but I wasn't even permitted to be openly happy! In order to survive in my family, I learned to hide my feelings.

I made my first suicide attempt when I was twelve by overdosing on pills. I called a friend to say good-bye, which I now think was my way of asking for help. Her mother contacted my parents. My father asked me to come downstairs and when I did, he hit me. Then I was locked in the bathroom until my parents took me to the hospital to get my stomach pumped.

I overheard my parents talking with the doctor in the hospital. He told them that I needed to get help. My father said,

My life has calmed down now, and I feel at peace for the first time. I take my medication religiously, see my therapist often, and surround myself with people who accept me.

All of me! I know who and what is important to me. I know that what I can't get from my biological family, I can get from Bill and Karen. They mean the world to me. They are my true family.

—MOLLY

didates have to say about mental illness because he has a sister who is mentally ill. He's always talking about "mental health issues." Mental health issues? That phrase just cracks me up. I mean, if you have a spinal cord injury, does that mean you have spinal cord issues? The last time I visited him in Iowa, he arranged a tour of a mental health institution because he thought I would like to see it. Actually, I was sort of worried that the hospital might keep me there!

I was originally diagnosed as having clinical depression, but last year the doctors told me that I have bipolar disorder. I can go through both mania and depression in the same day, which puts me at a higher risk for suicide. This new diagnosis was difficult for me because I had to take additional meds. I thought at first that this meant that I was getting worse, but the new medications have stabilized me. Now I'm a lot less likely to have suicidal thoughts. Until I took these new drugs, I would read the obituaries all the time because I was preoccupied with death. I'd be driving down the road wishing I'd have an accident and die. A lot of that kind of thinking has finally stopped.

My current partner doesn't want to talk about my mental illness with me at all. "Don't ask, don't tell," is his policy. It's not like he tells me not to talk about it; it's just that there's a disinterest on his part. If I had the flu, he'd be very supportive, but mental illness is something he can't fix. He won't even acknowledge that I see a therapist. He will remind me to take my medication, but that's about it. There's no discussion with him about what it feels like to be bipolar. In that way, my partner is very similar to my parents. This has made my recovery harder, and I think it makes Karen and Bill even more important to me.

In spite of this, my partner is part of my recovery because he has provided me with a very stable life. I've needed that desperately because I couldn't take care of myself when we were first together. I've never been good about paying bills, and my phone would get turned off on a pretty regular basis. As I've improved, I've become more responsible for myself.

My life has calmed down now, and I feel at peace for the first time. I take my medication religiously, see my therapist often, and surround myself with people who accept me. All of me! I know who and what is important to me. I know that what I can't get from my biological family, I can get from Bill and Karen. They mean the world to me. They are my true family.

BILL

I first met Molly back in 1983, when I was a social worker employed as a case manager on the Developmental Disabilities unit in a hospital. Molly was working in a sheltered workshop as one of the managers. I got to know her professionally, and we just sort of clicked. She can be pretty snippy and rude in a charming, delightful way. Molly has a terrific sense of humor, and I think I do, too, so we had a pretty good repartee right from the get-go. It's never stopped!

I get a lot from Molly. When I have problems, I talk to her just like she talks to me. She helps me get a different perspective on things. We have a mutual understanding that life is hard, whether she's telling me things that are troubling her or vice versa. A lot of the time we don't have the answers and all we say to each other is, "Christ, life is hard. I don't get it!" This is a big part of how we support each other. We commiserate about just how tough it is to be a human being.

There are probably a couple of things that make my relationship with Molly work so well. I'm a gay man, so no sexual stuff goes on between us. I've been involved with the same partner for twenty years, and he has also been diagnosed with bipolar disorder. When I became friends with Molly, she knew that I understood her illness and that I cared about and loved someone else who had the same thing.

The only time I find my friendship with Molly frighteningly burdensome is when she calls up and says, "I'm going to move to your city. Can I come and stay with you and bring my three basset hounds?" I get a little freaked out about that! Otherwise, I love talking to her. I definitely worry about her if I haven't heard from her.

Molly and I rarely see each other. We actually make jokes about this. We're phone friends and we talk at least once a week, but we never go to the movies anymore because I hardly go out. We used to make plans and then one of us would wind up canceling. We got to the point where I would say, "Let's go to Paris for the week," because we both knew that we weren't really going to go.

KAREN

I met Molly through work. I didn't like her at first. She seemed kind of wild, which was sort of scary for me. However, I loved her sense of humor. We connected because we were dealing with a common issue. Molly and I both have a mental illness.

My diagnosis is obsessive-compulsive disorder. I never really faced the fact that I had OCD before I met Molly. I was kind of teetering and going back and forth between therapy and medication and all of that, but I was actually very resistant to the diagnosis. I had previously been diagnosed with post-traumatic stress disorder, but I saw that more as a reaction to something I couldn't control. I thought that being diagnosed with OCD meant that there was something wrong with me. I didn't understand it at first.

Molly and I are alike in many ways, and in other ways we are totally opposite. Totally! I used to think she was extremely impulsive. Over time, I came to see that she had a very thoughtful way of approaching me. She understood things about me that I didn't realize she understood. Molly respected my need to go through my process at whatever level or speed felt right to me. I'm still working on intimacy issues, and my relationship with her is the most emotionally intimate I've ever been in my life, including my relationship with my own husband.

Karen, Molly, and Bill

I didn't move into Molly's life; she invaded mine! When we met, she had just found out that she was bipolar and was quite upset about the diagnosis. I was at a point where I was beginning to acknowledge and accept my illness. So we were preaching to each other about accepting what we had, blah blah blah.

I'm not a person who is real open about my life. I don't cover things over with humor like Molly does, and I don't reveal personal stuff to other people. It's not so much that I want to keep secrets, but rather that I value my privacy.

Teri

TERI BURCH FAMILY

SONOMA, CALIFORNIA

TERI BURCH

TERI

I'VE BEEN LOOKING FOR SOMEONE TO "MOTHER" ME for most of my life. I've been looking for someone to take care of me and to do the things for me that I needed as a child, but never got.

I come from a middle-class African-American family, and I believe that my parents tried to do the things for me that they thought were important. My mother would take me to plays at the Pasadena Playhouse and stuff like that, but it seemed like the moment I got a little bit older, a lot of the good stuff she did for me just stopped.

I didn't get the proper nurturing that a child should get. My mother even refused to hug me. She was emotionally abusive, which did a lot of damage to my self-esteem. I didn't do well in school because there were always problems at home. My parents fought all the time, and my home life was chaotic. My mother was constantly out of control. She was a very good schoolteacher, but not so good a parent.

Mental illness runs in my family. Both sides of my family are crazy, I swear. Just take my word. My Aunt Dorey on my father's side needed help because she was so mixed up.

She kept decompensating and getting worse. I also have an aunt on my mother's side who's been missing since 1966. Back in that era, there weren't enough proper medications to help her, and being African-American was another strike against her. Aunt Joyce was a very tall, dark lady. I don't know why, but I remember her legs for some reason. My grandmother didn't know what to do with her or how to get the proper therapy for her. If Aunt Joyce had gotten the right medication, maybe she would have been okay. She would walk from town to town and get involved with men. What happened to her was that my father threw her out of our house. He had become afraid of her because she carried weapons. When I was growing up, all I heard about was the craziness going on with Aunt Joyce. It frightened me, but the thing that really scared me as I got older was that I began doing the same things she did. I was becoming so terrified of people that I began to carry weapons, too.

When I was twelve I began to have nightmares every night. I was a big Kennedy fan, and I read a lot about his assassination. There was always something on TV about it that I would watch. I would dream that I was riding in the motorcade with the president when he got killed. I would watch

Whenever I went into the hospital, my mother was always there to make sure the nurses were doing the right thing. Mom had a concern of them overmedicating me. Thank God, she did things like that. Some people have nobody to watch out for them in the system.

— TERI

his head get blown off and I'd wake up screaming. I would think, "My God, am I going to turn into a killer?"

I've been scared all of my life. I was a very sickly child, which didn't help my social skills. I didn't have any friends. I was just plain afraid of people. I was very quiet at school, never saying a word. I just kind of sunk in and became numb with no facial expression or emotion. I hardly ever laughed. I stood out because I was so different. When you have problems, kids pick up on it. They saw that I wasn't any good at academics or sports. I had nothing that they could see to respect.

I was walking down the street once and a bunch of girls started throwing rocks at me. They began to tease me about my African features, and what really hurt me was that they were black children. I became afraid of my own people! My mother had some derogatory thinking about our people, too. She had horrible things to say to me, just horrible things to tell a child. It was this constant confusion with me. It's a wonder I didn't shoot my brains out.

When I was in the sixth grade, my teacher called my mother. She said, "Look, Mrs. Burch, I see some very serious problems going on with your daughter." Because my mother was not the type of African American to have a stereotypical attitude against therapy, she took me to a clinic in Pasadena, where I met with a black female psychologist. I looked at her and was scared to death. For one thing, she was kind of hard. I think she really was trying to reach out to me, but I was too far gone.

This psychologist would take me out to McDonald's and I would panic. My heart would race, and I wanted to run. She kept trying to work with me, but I thought, "I can't deal with this. I want out. Get me away from this woman." She said to me, "Teri, I'm giving you my advice. If you don't get help now, you're going to go down the tubes."

I didn't listen to my psychologist and I quit therapy. Later on, I went to a child guidance center and backed away from that, too. My mother never insisted upon it or anything. I just got the hell on out of there because I was afraid of these people telling me to "draw this, and draw that." I

was scared to death. By the time I was a teenager, I had all of this anger inside of me. I had nothing inside of me that I respected.

One of the worst years of my life was when I was seventeen. I ran out of my classes at high school because I was so frightened of people. My classmates teased me. They didn't understand me because I had problems with my sexual identity. I'm not saying that I'm gay, but there was some confusion there. They used to call me asexual, homosexual, everything in the book. I did have four girlfriends who stuck by me, and I'm sure glad of that.

I graduated high school by the skin of my teeth. After graduation, I went to a community college. Because I no longer had the closeness of my four high school friends anymore, I was walking through junior college with nobody. Nobody. I went downhill emotionally. My mother saw me lying in a fetal position one day, and the next thing I knew she took me to a psychiatric ward down in Los Angeles. She said, "Look, girl, if you don't get yourself together, you're going to end up like this." That place scared the shit out of me. The people in there were very, very sick. I think my mother was trying in her own way to stop something, but she basically scared me out of my mind.

When I was twenty-one, I went to live in a board-and-care apartment because the professors at my college could see that I really needed help. Even though my mother was still abusive to me, it was scary for me to leave home. That's when I began my journey of being an African American in the mental health world.

I went to a clinic where I was diagnosed with major depression and anxiety. A psychiatrist there began medicating me with all different types of drugs. I was medicated to the point where I was a zombie. People began to become aware of me because of all of my problems. I know people talk. Gossip is gossip. I became known as the "weird" person, not just in the neighborhood, but with my family as well. I'm talking about my mom and dad. My cousins all backed away from me, too, which really hurt.

I developed agoraphobia. I would go out of the apartment at first, but as I got older, I only went out at night so nobody could see me. I had one friend left who was still trying to deal with me, but all my other girlfriends turned away from me. I was too needy, always trying to grab on to somebody to be like a mother to me.

I began to hear voices. I didn't know what was happening to me, and I wondered, "Am I losing my mind?" I thought somebody had put a chip in my brain. I began going in and out of hospitals like a revolving door. I don't know whether this was paranoia or not, but I felt like some of the hospital staff thought, "What is Teri doing here again?" I sensed their resentment toward me.

In one situation, I felt mistreated by my therapist. She did something that really crushed me. I did a lot of research and put together an original tape of soul music from the early 1930s, and I gave it to her. Two months went by, and she said nothing. Finally I said, "Doctor, did you listen to the tape I gave you?" It turns out that she left it in her car on a hot day and it got burned up. I was only trying to get her to be there for me and I kept feeling her rejection. I think it was partly my fault because I kind of burned her out.

I was so needy that sometimes I tried to get my therapist to care about me in ways that were negative. Not that I would be outrageous or anything like that. It was all the phone calls that I made to her in this hysterical voice, wanting her to be my mommy, which made her feel uncomfortable with me. My parents went to talk to her, and all she said to them was, "You know, Teri has some emotional problems." That's really all she said! She didn't say anything else.

I decompensated very bad about five years ago. I was gravely disabled and homeless. I began walking through the city of Pasadena at 2:00 A.M., hearing voices twenty-four hours a day. One voice I heard was my psychiatrist's. In my mind she became my mother and was controlling me. That's serious when you get controlling voices. It's hard for me to talk about this, but I was at my day treatment center one day when a voice told me, "If you don't pull your pants down right now,

you're going to get killed." So I did, in front of a whole group of people! I still don't understand why I wasn't hospitalized right then and there.

I'd always taken good care of myself, because my mother raised me to be neat and clean. She would tell me, "Look, Teri, I don't care how you feel, just keep yourself up." When I got so sick, I started sleeping in a parking lot. I was filthy, and my hair was a mess. I don't know who finally put me in the hospital, but it was the worst hospital I've ever been in. There were so many African Americans in that place. Most hospitals I've been in, I'm one of very few African Americans. I wondered, "What's going on here? Are these people being shipped in on a boat from Africa?"

I was constantly hearing voices telling me what to do. It was horrible. I was trying very hard at that time, saying to myself, "Teri, look, you have got to pull yourself together." I began to bathe and clean myself up, even though it was incredibly hard for me to do. The voices got to the point of my wanting to kill myself. When I got out of this hospital, I remember lying down on the street and hoping a car would run me over so I could stop hearing the voices in my head.

Whenever I went into the hospital, my mother was always there to make sure the nurses were doing the right thing. Mom had a concern of them overmedicating me. Thank God she did things like that. Some people have nobody to watch out for them in the system. It's a wonder I didn't end my life, although I did try. I tried to hang myself in my board-and-care once, but my roommate was there to stop me.

Although my mother helped me when I was hospitalized, she was mostly not supportive to me. She just was not there for me. But one day she came by my apartment to visit, and for some reason I reached out and hugged her. She hugged me like she had never hugged me before in the whole mother-and-daughter relationship we've had. That was the last hug I really got from her.

I know that it was very difficult for my father to see me ill. He didn't understand, and he may have been thinking, "Oh, my God! Teri is crazy." He never called me that, but

I notice that they tend to put board-and-care apartments in the poorest parts of town because when they put one of them in a wealthy area, people fight the city. I've experienced that firsthand. One of my board-and-cares was in a well-to-do area, and the folks there tried to shut the place down. They just didn't want mentally ill people living around them.
— TERI

A lot of black people I've been around, when they think of therapy they automatically think "crazy." I don't think it's just the black community; I think other races may have this belief, too. But I've been around my people and I know they say this stuff.

— TERI

he was frightened. I know he was. Deep down I know my father loved me. I never had any type of physical abuse from him. He was the one who would hug me. If he hadn't done that, I think I probably would have been even sicker.

Over the years, I've lived in several different board-and-care apartments. I lived in one where I was the very first person to move in there, and I was also one of very few African Americans in the neighborhood. Now this is what the problem was. A lot of Caucasian men started moving into the board-and-care. They were mentally ill too, but they all accepted me. However, the neighbors began to spread rumors about me because I was friends with these young white guys. I became known as the prostitute of the neighborhood because I was black and walking with white guys. It got to the point where I became really, really paranoid. I was afraid of people, and now something had happened to reinforce what I felt!

I notice that they tend to put board-and-care apartments in the poorest parts of town because when they put one of them in a wealthy area, people fight the city. I've experienced that firsthand. One of my board-and-cares was in a well-to-do area, and the folks there tried to shut the place down. They just didn't want mentally ill people living around them.

I've had to deal with a lot of bigots throughout the years. I lived in one board-and-care that had an intercom system. When the staff announced dinner over the intercom, you came downstairs. Well, this Caucasian young man got on the intercom one day and began to use the "N" word, screaming it all through the apartment building. This made me so mad that I called the NAACP. Now, it may be the silliest thing, but the person I talked to there said, "Look, there's nothing we can really do because this man is mentally ill."

Over the years, I've learned not to react explosively to bigots, because when I do, I get put in restraints. I've realized that my only weapon is to educate bigots. I've sat down with some of the worst racists you've ever seen in your life and said, "Look, an African American created the stoplight that you see right down the street. An African American cre-

ated the air conditioner. An African American created peanut butter." And on and on. My people created so many things, not just for the United States but for the world.

I'm doing a lot better now. The apartment building I've lived in for six years is run by a program that gives the mentally ill a chance to be independent. I do my own cooking and shopping. When my boyfriend and I were living together, we did the cleaning together, just like a couple. We ran a household, just like a couple. I began to buy things. I fixed the place up with couches and stuff.

I keep my place tidy because it's therapeutic for me. When the landlord walks into my apartment, she says, "Good God, I can't believe this place." Me and the other people in this apartment building are all mentally ill, either with schizophrenia, or bipolar, or schizo-affective illness. The other residents don't always keep things up like I do, but somehow they manage. I may have been brought up in Pasadena and gone to school there and been physically taken care of by my parents, but I "grew up" here. I will always treasure this apartment because I pay my own rent and I have my own checking account. I've come a long way.

I'm most proud of the fact that I didn't commit suicide. I'm also proud that I've never, ever used street drugs. I have never tried marijuana or cocaine even though it was out there. I've said, "Hell, no!"

I've grown to see what my talents are. Last year, I began teaching a self-esteem class at the place where I receive treatment. I've also received many awards over the past few years. For Black History Month, I wrote two presentations, one in 2000 and one in 2001. The first one was on the history of soul music. I was showing dances and doing a James Brown thing, and I captivated everybody in the audience. I'm proud of all I've accomplished.

I want to be the Harriet Tubman who brings not just my people, but all people, to the side of good mental health. I want to help other mentally ill people get to a point where they can live as comfortably as possible. I still have the Bible where I wrote, "Lord, if you can get me together mentally and physically, I want to be able to meet a goal that I think you're going to like. I want to be able to reach people so I can really make a difference."

I think my people are going to have to learn to speak up more. A lot of black people I've been around, when they think of therapy they automatically think "crazy." I don't think it's just the black community; I think other races may have this belief, too. But I've been around my people and I know they say this stuff. They're not comfortable in revealing things about themselves. The black community really has to change something within their thinking.

When you say a person is nothing but a schizophrenic, it's an insult. It's almost like saying a cuss word. I think it's horrible thinking, really. It's like saying, "All black people eat watermelon." All mentally ill people don't go out and murder people. Most mentally ill people are not violent. Most people who have schizophrenia are isolative. They are into their own world.

Did the mental health system fail me? I think in some ways, yes, it did. The professionals should have set more boundaries and limits with me, but it's really up to us consumers to correct our own problems. We need some assistance, of course, but it's really up to us as people with mental illness to get up and fight. And that's what I've begun to do. All the things that I've been through, even though they were painful, have shaped me to become a person I respect.

I'm going back to school to become a dual diagnosis counselor. I don't know what it's like to get high on drugs or alcohol, but I do know what it's like to be mentally ill and I do know that I truly care about people. That's the bottom line. I've been told that I have a gift with people. I know how to address them. When it's needed, I have a very soothing voice. I know how to comfort them.

I started going to church again last week. This was a big step for me because I've spent a lot of my life hiding from people. For some reason, I walked out of my apartment last Sunday and went to a local church I found in my phone book. The first time I went to this church, I got up and spoke. I'm getting used to public speaking. I get scared, but everybody gets scared. I just have to work on myself to calm down

Teri

enough to get my thinking where it's slow enough for me to verbalize whatever I want to say. So I spoke up and said, "Well, you know what? The reason why I'm here today is because I need another direction in my life." Everybody turned around to see who was this woman speaking.

I've decided not to have children because I'm afraid they might be mentally ill like me. I don't want any child of mine going into an institution. I plan to live a good life. I want to laugh. I'd like to step out and have fun at this point in my life. And that's something that I never could have said before.

I'm trying to do something different in my life. Whenever I used to walk down the street, people would say, "Oh, my God, why does she look so angry?" I'm slowly trying to change that. Now I walk down the street, and I'm saying, "Good morning, ma'am." If I'm in a store and I'm assisted, I'll say, "Thank you, sir."

If you don't respect yourself, you get stepped on. I did get stepped on a lot. Now I'm learning to respect myself. People only respect you when you respect yourself. That's just the way life is.

Josh, Jessica, Cal, and Mary

THE ROWLAND FAMILY

NORTH ADAMS, MASSACHUSETTS

JOSH ROWLAND / JESSICA ROWLAND / CAL ROWLAND
MARY ROWLAND

MARY

WHEN MY SON, JOSH, WAS A TODDLER, HE WAS EASILY FRUSTRATED. He couldn't even handle playing with blocks. If his blocks didn't set up right, he would pick them up and throw them around his room.

By the time Josh was three, he was destructive of his own property. He was so hard to control that my husband, Cal, and I thought something was wrong with him. Compared to our daughter, Jessica, he was so much more aggressive. Our friends kept telling us, "Josh is a boy. What do you expect? Boys are just more aggressive than girls." Even Josh's doctor agreed. First we were told it was the "terrible twos," and then it was the "aggressive threes." We got one fruitless explanation after another for his behavior.

By the time he was four, Josh was highly anxious about going to preschool. It would take me two hours to get him dressed, and then I had to physically put him on the school bus. When Josh was five, he would assault other kids and he was destructive to himself. It was horrendous. The first time Cal and I went to see a mental health professional, he told us that Josh had separation anxiety because I had gone back to work after five years of being an at-home mom. He told me, "Stop worrying, Mary. Just give Josh an extra hug every day and he'll be just fine." This same therapist, by the way, kicked Josh out of his office because he wasn't behaving properly!

When Josh was seven, he had a full-blown psychotic episode which lasted over five hours. He destroyed everything within sight, and we couldn't control him. Cal and I didn't know what to do. We didn't know how to access emergency services, and we didn't even know that such a thing as a crisis team existed. So we dealt with our son as best as we could. When Josh finally collapsed with exhaustion, I picked up the phone and called a pastor in our community who also had a child with problems. I was crying hysterically. I must have sounded like a madwoman on the phone, because the pastor and his wife met me at the church within twenty minutes. This was the first time I had ever connected with anyone who could cry with me and who could say, "I know how you feel," and actually did.

Cal and I went round and round searching for answers from one professional after another. We tried all kinds of

215

It was so emotional to be told that your kid is sick, but it was probably one of the best days of my life. Most people wouldn't understand this, but because we finally had some answers, we could begin to see a path for working things out. Josh was hospitalized a few days later so he could be stabilized.

—MARY

techniques and every behavior modification program in the book to help our son. Nothing worked. After seeing our family for months, a child psychologist said to me, "Mary, I can't do anything for you. You've done everything you can. This isn't about changing behavior. This is about having a problem. Your son has bipolar disorder." This was the first time that Cal and I understood that we weren't the worst parents in the world. We finally knew that we hadn't messed up royally and that we didn't have a rotten child.

I had repeated the story about Josh to so many professionals by that time that I had written a six-page report about his behavioral history. I gave it to the psychologist to look over, and then Cal and I told her even more about Josh's life. After about half an hour of listening to us, she said, "Stop blaming yourselves. You didn't do this to Josh. You've got a kid who has a mental illness. It's not your fault. It's not the end of the world. There's no cure, but there is treatment."

It was so emotional to be told that your kid is sick, but it was probably one of the best days of my life. Most people wouldn't understand this, but because we finally had some answers, we could begin to see a path for working things out. Josh was hospitalized a few days later so he could be stabilized.

Josh had literally never told me that he loved me until after his first hospitalization. He hadn't been able to get in touch with his emotional side enough to be able to express love. I'll never forget the day about two weeks after he came home from the hospital. I was doing the dishes, and he came up behind me and said, "Hey Mom, I love you." I can't even describe how that felt. After that, he could say it occasionally, and now he says it a lot. He has begun to share hugs. More and more now, I even get a happy little peck on the cheek.

Our family used to have a super close friendship with our next-door neighbors, but after Josh's hospitalization, they went clean into the woodwork. It was the strangest thing I'd ever experienced in my life. Up until that time, we had the kind of relationship where we'd play cards together by the hour and have picnics together in our backyards. Our kids played together constantly. If Josh had a major episode where he

would put a dent in their front door or something like that, I'd simply get a phone call saying, "Mary, he did it again!" Cal would go over and fix whatever Josh had damaged. For some reason, Josh's difficult behavior never put a strain on our friendship until he was diagnosed with a mental illness. At that point, they began to avoid us.

I finally called my neighbor and said, "Come on over and let's chitchat over coffee. We haven't talked in a while." She did, and I put my feelings right out on the table. I said, "What's going on? I don't understand the sudden change in our friendship." All she said was, "Well, we've just been real busy." It took me another six months before I finally figured out that they didn't want to be friends with our family anymore. Now, we just speak to them from a distance. This was very sad for me. People can be so ignorant about mental illness.

On the other hand, my mother has made a huge change in her attitude. This was a woman who used to talk about "crazy" people and make every ignorant statement about them that could possibly be made. Now when someone says something negative about the mentally ill, my mother steps right up to bat and says, "Just wait a minute. Let me explain to you what mental illness really is." My mother has been transformed, and she has become incredibly supportive of Josh and our family. I also have two brothers who live nearby, but we keep a kind of distance. We talk, but we don't talk about Josh being sick. I choose not to make a major issue out of it. I don't drill knowledge about mental illness down anybody's throat if they aren't ready for it.

Our daughter has always been good at expressing how she feels. When Josh was at his worst, Jessica kept telling us, "Stop shutting me out! I need to be involved. Don't send me to my room whenever he acts out. How come I get punished every time Josh has a problem?" I could sympathize with her, but I needed to protect her until things with Josh got back under control. Jessica suffered from "unavoidable neglect." That's my terminology for what siblings of the mentally ill have to deal with.

When Josh came home from his first hospitalization, we tried everything we could to help him. I gave up my full-time career in public relations because my life seemed so overwhelming. I felt like I needed to stay home and put the pieces of our lives back together. This put a pretty large hole in my personal plans and in my wallet, too, but I was convinced that it was the right thing to do. However, it finally got to the point where Josh became my only life. I'd be with him all day long, and by the time Cal came home from work, I was so fried that I just wanted to get out of the house and go for a walk. Cal would ask me to fill him in on what had been happening that day with Josh and I'd give him a thirty-second version of it as I walked out the door. There were also times when I would call Cal at work and say, "I can't do this anymore. I've had Josh in restraints for forty-five minutes, and he has unplugged every phone in the house and threatened to jump out the window." That was my life.

Seeing other little boys about Josh's age playing in the neighborhood made me feel resentful. It was just so unfair that my little guy didn't have that carefree, spontaneous life he was supposed to have at his age.

We had a horrible time getting special education services for Josh, because he was able to keep himself together pretty well in his school setting. He would contain his emotions all day and then he'd come home on a crazy, chaotic, noisy school bus and just explode the moment he came into the house. Even if Josh looked good to the school personnel, he rarely got past our front door before he would start up with oppositional behavior and aggressiveness.

In spite of Josh's difficulties, the school turned us down for special education services over and over again. When we met with the school administrators, it didn't matter to them that Josh had a diagnosis; it didn't even matter that he had been hospitalized. I was told, "Yes, your son has a major mental illness, but it isn't affecting his progress in school."

I remember the principal saying to me quite condescendingly, "Well, Mary, if you hadn't told us about your son, we never would have known he had any problems at all." So

Jessica and Josh

I flipped open Josh's journal in which he had written all kinds of suicidal and homicidal notes while he was sitting quietly in class not bugging anyone. I said to her, "Doesn't this indicate to you that there's something wrong with him?" Even so, Josh still got turned down for special services. I gave up.

A year later, I said to myself, "They're not going to wear me down any further. I'm going back into the battle." But just when we got to the point where we started to win the fight with the school, Josh was hospitalized again. Everyone involved in his case, including Cal and I, felt that Josh needed to go into residential care. Our community just couldn't give our son what he needed at the time. And without enough community support, neither could we.

Life was especially diffi-cult for me before Josh was diagnosed with bipolar disorder. I tried so hard to be a good dad, but it was tough to understand what was happening with my son. He was like Jekyll and Hyde, and that's kind of what our relationship felt like to me.

— CAL

Taking our son to a residential treatment program was perhaps the hardest thing I've ever had to do. I knew it was the right thing for him and for the entire family, but that didn't make me feel any better about it. For the next couple of months, I found myself walking through my days feeling empty inside. It felt so painful, almost as if I had lost my son forever.

I truly didn't know what would happen next. Josh did so well in the highly structured settings of the hospital and the residential program, I wondered if he was a child who would never be able to function in the outside world. We drove an hour and a half to see him two to three times a week, and for a long time I would cry all the way home.

Josh has made tremendous progress in his residential treatment program. After three months there, he started to come home for visits. It was wonderful having him home again, but it took several months of visits before it didn't feel as if he were simply a guest in our house. Our family has healed and reconnected in a positive way.

Josh will be coming home soon to attend a local school. My frustration is that it shouldn't have gotten to this point. Kids should be taken care of on a preventive basis in their own community. A child should go into residential care only after everything that can humanly be done is tried. Our community mental health system did all that was possible, but our school system sure didn't. Josh wasn't recognized as a child in need of special education services until he was on his way out of the area and into a program a long way from home. I'm left wondering what might have been different for Josh if the school had just attended to his needs earlier. Residential care doesn't necessarily indicate a failure of the system, but in our case, it did.

If people could see Josh now, they'd see he is the warmest, most compassionate, caring little person in the entire world. He is thinking about going to college now, and this is a kid who wasn't even thinking about going to high school a couple of years ago. It's really neat that he has started looking to the future in a very positive way. Young people need to have dreams.

CAL

Life was especially difficult for me before Josh was diagnosed with bipolar disorder. I tried so hard to be a good dad, but it was tough to understand what was happening with my son. He was like Jekyll and Hyde, and that's kind of what our relationship felt like to me.

I was so proud when Josh wanted to play T-ball. It was a true father-son kind of thing. But his anxiety got in the way because he didn't have the same natural athletic talent some of the other boys had. He would always fall apart after each game.

I'm an avid bowler. When it was time to sign up for the local junior bowling league, Josh said he wanted to join. I was so pleased because he said he wanted to be just like me. Hearing something like that really makes a father feel good. Unfortunately, Josh had the expectation that he was going to be able to bowl as well as I could. When he realized he couldn't, his frustration got the best of him. He became so frustrated, he wouldn't bowl at all. He'd kick things, and he'd go into a rage. Sometimes it got so bad, we would have to leave the bowling alley.

I tried to help Mary with Josh, but I was at work during the day. She was the one at home with him, and by the time I'd get home, she'd be so tired and at her wits' end that we seldom had any time for just the two of us. Nearly all of our conversations revolved around what Josh's day had been like.

Once Josh was diagnosed, as tough as it was to hear that he had a mental illness, I finally felt like I had some control. There was something we could do and there was an explanation for what was going on with him.

I didn't talk about Josh at work except to my boss and his wife. I knew their son had some problems, although not anything like what Josh has gone through. Over the years, my boss has been very supportive. He still is. He would tell me to take time off or to leave early whenever it was necessary. He still touches base with me about Josh and asks how he is doing.

It hasn't been easy, but having answers and a direction to go in has made all the difference in the world. We are coming back together as a family. It may be a little different from other families, but we have managed to survive all this together.

JESSICA

I was in sixth grade when Josh first went into the hospital. I was only eleven at the time, and I didn't really know what was going on. It was as if everything in my life just stopped. I got frustrated with Josh because I thought this was all his fault.

When Josh came home from the hospital, it was kind of weird. In my own little world inside my head, I just wanted things to go back to how they were before my brother got sick, even though I knew this couldn't happen.

It was a tough time for me, and I was really upset. Whenever Josh had an episode or was acting out, my parents would send me to my room. I felt like I was being punished. I didn't understand why they were shielding me from what was happening with my brother.

In those days it was as if we had two families. Mom and I were one family, and Josh and Dad were the other. Josh couldn't sit through a dance recital of mine or any of my chorus concerts, so Mom would come to watch me while Josh and Dad would stay at home. But it's different now: Josh is at a point where he can sit through my extracurricular events. If I'm in a dance recital, he can watch it. When Josh comes home on a visit, there really isn't much of a separation anymore. We are just a normal family now, and we all do things together.

Josh's illness was hard on me. I lost a couple of very good friends because they were afraid of my brother. This didn't make any sense to me. Before Josh was diagnosed, they were, like, "Okay, he's just acting like a jerk. I can deal with that." After Josh was diagnosed, they would say, "Oh my God, Jessica's brother is a maniac. He's a crazy lunatic! I can't hang out with her anymore or go to her house."

Luckily, I made other good friends because of Josh's situation. The pastor of our church has a child who also has a mental illness. This kid's younger sister became one of my best friends. She helped me through everything because she knew exactly what I was going through.

I think there's a stigma against the mentally ill because people are scared of them. A lot of things happened in the past, and most people don't realize that things have changed. People with mental illness are treated more normally now; they're not locked up forever and ever. I help my friends understand mental illness by including Josh when they are around. I never say, "Josh is coming home this weekend, so you can't come over."

Josh's illness can be treated and helped with medications and with therapy. Mental illness doesn't end a person's life, and it's actually a very common thing to have. When my outreach worker told me that lots of famous people like Beethoven and Charles Dickens have had bipolar disorder, it made me feel much less isolated from the normal world.

JOSH

Being bipolar means that I can get hyper real fast and aggressive, too, and then I can become really depressed. Or I can be all of those things at the same time.

I go to a special school and I live there, too. I have treatment and I go to programs. I take a lot of meds, and they make me feel better.

To earn points at my school I have to stay focused and do what my goals say I should do. It's getting easier to meet my goals. I don't have a lot of friends at home, but I have some at the school where I live. If I have a problem, I talk to staff, not to my friends.

At my residential center, they took me to a fancy restaurant once. I had a Shirley Temple. I played in a golf tournament at a country club and had a fancy dinner there. I've also been on the news on television talking about my illness.

When I grow up, I want to go to college.

> *I lost a couple of very good friends because they were afraid of my brother. This didn't make any sense to me. Before Josh was diagnosed, they were, like, "Okay, he's just acting like a jerk. I can deal with that." After Josh was diagnosed, they would say, "Oh my God, Jessica's brother is a maniac. He's a crazy lunatic! I can't hang out with her anymore or go to her house."*
>
> —*JESSICA*

Standing: Dean and Marilou *Seated:* Jake and Cassandra

THE WONG/KOENIG FAMILY

LOS ANGELES, CALIFORNIA

DEAN WONG / MARILOU WONG KOENIG
JAKE KOENIG / CASSANDRA KOENIG

DEAN

I'M MARILOU'S OLDER BROTHER, and she and I have always been good friends. In the 1980s, I was living in California, and Marilou was still in the Philippines. My relatives over there told me she was having difficulties, but I assumed her problems were just the result of growing up in our dysfunctional family.

Marilou was diagnosed with schizophrenia. When I heard she was very sick, I offered to help take care of her. She never got along with any of our other brothers, our mother wasn't all that helpful at the time, and our father had already passed away. Marilou agreed to come to the United States and live with me, and I became her primary support.

My sister arrived in Los Angeles with very few possessions. I said, "Okay, I'll buy you a whole new wardrobe so there'll be no excuse for not getting a job just because you don't own a dress." She worked for about eighteen months, but then she had a major relapse.

When Marilou first came to live with me, religion was of no importance to me. I was born and raised a Catholic, but I hadn't practiced for many years. However, I did believe in the Miracle of Lourdes. I decided to send Marilou to Lourdes to be immersed in the water just in case a miracle might happen. I think it helped her a lot, even though good results didn't come immediately. After she returned from France, her demeanor was much more confident. This was a hint to me that maybe there was somebody upstairs.

When Marilou lived with me, I wouldn't let any of our relatives visit us unless they accepted the fact that I'm gay and that Marilou has a mental illness. I would tell them, "I'm gay, and Marilou might be pacing the floors all night. If you don't like it, we don't want you here!" That was the rule of my house.

Our mother is seventy-eight now. She moved to San Francisco from the Philippines and is very independent. In Asian families, the mother is always right. "Mother" is a title you hold, like "Queen." My mother is very success-oriented,

Marilou has changed the lives of everyone in our family. She has given us a wonderful gift. Her schizophrenia has humbled all of us and has helped everyone in our family become more generous, caring, and sensitive. When I was making my own adjustment to being gay, I thought about Marilou dealing with her mental illness. For both of us, it's just the way things are. Sometimes she tells me, "Dean, I'm cured of schizophrenia." And I'll joke with her and say, "Oh, yeah, and I'm straight!"

—*DEAN*

and she used to be extremely frustrated by the fact that her daughter was sick. She's more understanding now. Actually, Marilou has changed the lives of everyone in our family. She has given us a wonderful gift. Her schizophrenia humbled all of us and it has helped everyone in our family become more generous, caring, and sensitive.

When I was making my own adjustment to being gay, I thought about Marilou dealing with her mental illness. For both of us, it's just the way things are. Sometimes she tells me, "Dean, I'm cured of schizophrenia." And I'll joke with her and say, "Oh, yeah, and I'm straight!"

For the past few years, Marilou's husband, Jake, has been her primary support. Jake is mentally ill, too. He's a good provider and a kind man. Marilou and Jake are well-educated about their mental conditions, and they've learned how to go on in spite of their symptoms. They know all about medications and their side effects. They watch out for each other. When their symptoms are flaring up, both of them know what to do to help each other, and they seek help from professionals immediately.

When Marilou and Jake both tried to hurt themselves in l996, they were hospitalized. In the long run, this turned out to be a positive event in their lives. After they recovered, they became much more aware of their symptoms and of ways to prevent future relapses. They also became even more devoted to each other.

Marilou is now able to take part-time jobs once in a while, and Jake helps out with maintenance work in the apartment building where they live. They are off welfare and they're struggling, but they are both fully functional. It's amazing what the two of them have achieved over the years.

I'm involved with mental health advocacy. I pattern my work after AIDS advocates who believe there should be no stigma and no discrimination, and that everybody should have the opportunity to get healthy. When I was first helping my sister, a lot of people were helping me. Eventually, these friends pushed me to become a board member of a family support organization. Now I'm president of the Asian Pacific Alliance for the Mentally Ill. Our membership has almost thirty families! I'm helping others, and this makes me feel good.

Jake once told me, "A lot of people can't live full lives unless they find somebody to love." In the groups I lead for families of the mentally ill, I emphasize this point. With love, things will fall into place.

MARILOU

I had been hearing voices and having hallucinations since I was twelve, but I didn't know I had an illness. When I told my mother about my voices, she said, "Just listen to them." So I listened to them until they would go away. And they would go away.

Even though I wasn't well, I graduated from college in the Philippines. The first two years of school were very hard, but I stuck with it. My friends said that I could relax after my third year. When I did relax, my grades went down, but I still managed to graduate. My musical interests kept me busy having fun and helped me get through school.

I went into a mental hospital in the Philippines in 1984, where I was diagnosed with schizophrenia. I followed the hospital's rules and tried to make myself happy. When I came over to the United States to be with my brother, Dean, I didn't take my medicine for six months, so I relapsed. I had a full-time job then, but I couldn't go back to work anymore. I'm on medication now. I'm afraid to skip taking it because I don't want to have another relapse.

When I arrived in America, I only had two pairs of pants, two shirts, an old coat, my toothbrush and toothpaste, and a little makeup. Dean bought me my entire wardrobe, and he taught me how to interview for a job. We gave each other a lot of comfort, and together we were able to get through each day.

Dean has helped me a lot. He has always been very open with me, and I became open with him as well. I had been taught early on that if you can't say anything that is helpful, don't say it! So I was very silent most of my life. With Dean's support, I gradually learned how to put my feelings into words.

I still hear voices. They bothered me a few months ago, but I usually don't mind them. They don't make me as afraid anymore. My depression still comes and goes. I believe I have to go through life day by day, so that's what I do.

Sometimes I feel like I'm at a dead end. I think I will never get out of the depression, because I'm just lost. I can't improve my piano playing or hold a full-time job anymore. I've always thought I should be a professional who makes no mistakes and who is able to solve every problem that comes up at work. Unfortunately when a problem crops up at work that I can't fix, I quit. That's how it is for me.

Most of the time I call Dean or some of his friends if I'm feeling depressed. Or I turn to Jake and tell him, "I'm sad, darling." Jake is always able to pinpoint the problem and say just the right thing.

I've learned to talk to God every minute of the day. My actions should be a prayer. I believe there is a soul, so I feed my soul by going to the Catholic Church. It gives me a routine to follow, and I find a lot of enlightenment there. Church is like a traffic light for me. It gives me the signals of when to stop, when to be careful, and when to go.

JAKE

I used to be afraid of the idea of mental illness. I thought that the label "mentally ill" was only used for people who were mentally retarded or who were totally out of control. I didn't know there were different stages and kinds of mental illness.

I've had symptoms of depression and manic states since elementary school. My diagnosis is bipolar disorder or manic-depression. My illness runs through my bloodline. My father battles with depression, and he lives in a chaotic state of mind. He's always refused to go for treatment.

Standing: Jake, Cassandra, and Cassandra's friend *Seated:* Marilou and Dean

When I got out of school and started working, I had a bad attitude. My first wife saw the orneriness and meanness in me. Luckily, her mother was a psychologist, and she recommended that I seek professional help. Before then, I didn't know I could get help from anyone but my parents. I realized I was fighting something inside of me and that there was definitely something wrong with me. I went into therapy in 1990 and started to take medication. It helped me, but I still couldn't hold a job without having problems.

At the time, my memory wasn't working as well as it used to, and my concentration was poor. The doctors recommended that I stop working, stay home, and have a non-stressful style of life. They said, "Don't try to battle your illness. Just take the medication and try to relax." So that's what I did, and since then, I've felt a lot better.

Marilou and I met and began dating when we were neighbors in an apartment building for mentally ill people. We have different illnesses and we were each going to different treatment centers, but we were interested in each other. Our relationship has worked out perfectly for us, and both of our doctors consider us very stable. We're not totally healthy or free of our illnesses, but we can live on our own without the constant involvement of doctors, staff, or social workers. We're pretty much in control of our own lives.

Until I met Marilou and got a happy and stable home life, I struggled with depression. It's just about all gone now. I feel healthy most of the time, almost as if I'd never had an illness at all. I have a better quality of life than I ever had, even as a child. Once every few weeks I get a little bit stressed out and I'll have problems with concentration, but, all in all, everything has become more manageable. Since Marilou and I got married, we've been much less depressed. I think our marriage helps our mental health more than the medication does.

Psychologists and doctors should urge their patients to strive for relationships. It's important to respect your illness, but at the same time it feels better to be part of a normal family. I'm coping with my illness far better, now that I'm handling all kinds of responsibilities. I'm taking care of a

> *Psychologists and doctors should urge their patients to strive for relationships. It's important to respect your illness, but at the same time it feels better to be part of a normal family. I'm coping with my illness far better now that I'm handling all kinds of responsibilities. I'm taking care of a home and a family and a daughter and an automobile and paying the bills.*
>
> —*Jake*

home and a family and a daughter and an automobile and paying the bills.

My daughter, Cassie, lives with my sister and her husband because they can provide medical insurance for her, which I can't. They also are able to give her a home life with her cousins. Cassie spends most of her weekends with Marilou and me. When she visits us, she brings her friends over to go swimming in the pool at our apartment complex. I also go to most of Cassie's softball games.

I've explained to Cassie that I go to a doctor in order to control my depression. When she asked me to define "depression," I defined it as best I could. I told her my illness is under control because the doctors have given me the right medication. I explained to her that part of the reason I was mean to her when she was very young—and she remembers this—was because I wasn't on medication and I was struggling with my illness. Cassie understands that I take medication that helps me, and she's really happy that I'm happy. It's been a good year for us.

There are many people who don't understand mental illness at all. Some folks think the world is controlled by a good cold beer or by a shot of whiskey. They believe drinking alcohol will stop the chemical imbalance in the brain that controls depression! Most people know that's not true. I sure know that.

Everybody should be fair and generous. They shouldn't steal, lie, or cheat, and they should work hard. These are my principles. I think spirituality is an individual thing. I meditate a lot. I know there's somebody up there, a higher being, watching out for everybody. Believing in God and believing in myself has helped my depression.

I like being a believer. I look forward to going to church every Sunday and I like knowing that my movements and my actions are actually being watched and judged. Until I became a believer, I didn't expect things could get better for me. Spirituality gives me a positive attitude to apply to my life. It has helped me through a lot, and it will help me through most anything I can possibly come up against in the future. It's my strength.

CASSANDRA

I know my father, with his bipolar depression, loves me. I wish I could live with him permanently, and I miss him. I live with my aunt and spend weekends with my dad and my stepmother, Marilou. When I receive directions from him that I'm not in agreement with, we talk it out. Sometimes he goes my way, and most of the time I go his way. I don't resent him for this because I know he loves me.

My dad knows what activities I enjoy most, and we do them together. He welcomes my friends to come along with us, too. He picks me up from my aunt's house, and he drives me and my friends around to have a fun time. When I was a bit younger, Dad and I liked to go feed the ducks. It was fun. Now we go bowling. Dad's better than I am at bowling. He taught me how to play. I like to bring my friends to visit when I stay with him and Marilou.

When I miss my dad during the week, I call him up and he's always willing to spend time with me on the phone. It sometimes seems that his bipolar depression is not present when he's with me. I love him very much.

George, George Jr., Faye, and Hunter

226

THE SHANNON FAMILY

BEAUFORT, NORTH CAROLINA

GEORGE SHANNON / GEORGE SHANNON JR.
FAYE SHANNON / HUNTER SHANNON

FAYE

ON THE DAY MY HUSBAND AND I MOVED INTO OUR BEAUTIFUL, brand-new home, I remember thinking I had everything I'd ever dreamed of. At thirty-eight, I was happily married to my college boyfriend, we had two healthy sons, and I loved my work as a clinical social worker in a hospital. In retrospect, this period in my life was just the calm before the storm.

There were problems on the horizon. My father had suffered a stroke and was slowly dying. My mother, who was an invalid, needed to go into a nursing home since my dad could no longer take care of her. I was most troubled, however, by the discovery that my husband's pacemaker had a defective part that could crack and kill him instantly. During the month we had to wait before it could be removed, I couldn't sleep more than four hours a night. I would lie awake just watching him breathe. With so much stress in my life, I started to fall apart emotionally.

I began to have psychotic thoughts. I became convinced that my conversations were being taped, and that my office was bugged. These ideas just came into my head. Ordinarily, I would have said to myself, "This is ridiculous," but my thoughts seemed so real. It felt like that part in the movie *E.T.* when the little boy first meets the alien and is afraid to tell anyone about it because he's sure nobody will believe him. It was exactly like that for me.

One day, I told a coworker that we were all under surveillance at the office. She immediately informed my supervisor, who called my husband to tell him that I wasn't acting like myself. When George came to pick me up at work, I insisted there was nothing wrong with me, and that it was simply a misunderstanding.

I didn't hear voices or anything, but I thought I was communicating with something that was tapping coded messages into my ears. It was crazy stuff. I talked too fast, laughed too much, and said inappropriate things. I even told a few doctors at work to stop cheating on their wives!

I'm usually the most conservative, rule-following, least troublemaking person anyone could ever meet, but one day I was walking down the hallway at work and I had this thought

228 NOTHING TO HIDE

> *I would sometimes lie on the floor of my apartment, catatonic, with all my clothes piled up around me. When a neighbor came in and found me like this, she offered to get me some supper, but I couldn't even get up to eat. I was that depressed, that sick.*
>
> *— FAYE*

that pulling the fire alarm would be a neat thing to do. Fortunately, I didn't set it off, but I almost did. I could have done anything. I felt like I could go into the operating room at the hospital where I worked and do surgery on patients. Luckily, I didn't attempt to do that, either!

I began to have even more delusions. At one point, I thought George was going to poison the children and me, and I also believed that the FBI wanted me to work on a top-secret project. George was so worried about me that one day, when I was about to take a bath, he said, "Leave that door unlocked. How do I know you're not going to drown yourself in there?" He pleaded with me to see a doctor, but I insisted that I was fine and had everything under control.

I became convinced my husband was planning to sabotage my grandiose plans to work for the FBI. I hired a lawyer and filed for divorce. A few weeks later, I moved into a small apartment near our house. Even though I was still trying to care for the boys, I wasn't capable of it. I asked George to keep them.

I told my sons that I loved them very much but that I had to leave them with their daddy for a while. Even though I was so sick and totally psychotic, I still had sound maternal instincts. I was trying to protect my babies because I knew they would be safer with George. Giving our kids to him was the most painful thing I've ever done. When I'd go visit them, they'd cry when I left to go back to my apartment. It just broke my heart. This was the loneliest time of my life. I felt absolutely worthless and hopeless.

A few weeks after moving into my apartment, my dad died. I went to his funeral in Michigan and gave the eulogy even though I was completely psychotic at the time. I thought I was being taped, and I was convinced that the funeral director was in love with me. In our family, I've always been seen as someone in control of my life. My relatives didn't know what to make of my unusual behavior. They assumed it was caused by the stress of losing my father.

When I returned home, I started giving away my furniture and clothing to strangers. I would knock at people's doors and leave stuff for them. I gave away a nice fur coat and my beautiful lace wedding dress and I sold my wedding ring for dirt. One night I packed up my sets of dishware and silverware and left them on a doorstep in a poor section of town. I even threw away precious family photographs! By then, George had hired detectives to follow me because he suspected I was having an affair. Even though he believed I would never do something like that, he needed a reason to explain my behavior. He was in denial about the reality of my illness.

I would sometimes lie on the floor of my apartment, catatonic, with all my clothes piled up around me. When a neighbor came in and found me like this, she offered to get me some supper, but I couldn't even get up to eat. I was that depressed, that sick.

I alienated every relationship I had. George and I were fighting all the time. My friends and family had given up on me because I was so obnoxious. I wasn't even able to be a good mother. My sister has schizophrenia, and I began to worry, "Oh, my God. Am I going to end up like her? Will everybody think horrible thoughts about me, too?" I felt like some kind of a leper.

I had a lot of experience working with psychiatric patients. As I got sicker, I finally recognized that I was exhibiting the classic symptoms of bipolar disorder. I started asking my friends at work, "Do you think I have pressured speech? Do you think I'm manic?" I was doing things like going out in my car at night and speeding at one hundred miles an hour. It's amazing that I survived.

My bosses probably saved my life by insisting that I take a medical leave of absence. In front of all my friends and colleagues, they told me, "Faye, go home now or else Security is going to come and get you."

I went to my doctor and asked him for a specific medication that I knew was being used to treat bipolar disorder. I all but wrote my own prescription! The doctor confirmed my diagnosis and agreed to give me the medication. I knew I was sick, but I didn't realize how sick I was.

When I took my first dose of medication, I slept eight hours straight for the first time in almost four months. It was my first miracle! Then I was also given an antidepressant, which helped stop my compulsive worrying. I felt sane again. Once I could think clearly, I was able to straighten out my life. I salvaged my marriage and tried to be the best mom I could be. It was difficult, but I went back to work and faced all the people who had seen me behaving so erratically.

I'm a social worker, and I think I'm more helpful now to folks than before I got sick. I realize that patients are afraid and I try to comfort them, to reassure them, and to pamper them. Not that I used to be cold, but I've learned from my own experience to be even more compassionate than I was before.

I decided to share my experience so I could show people that there is hope for a happy life despite having a mental illness. My story was featured in *Good Housekeeping* magazine, and I've written a book entitled *Manic by Midnight*. I've also been on television and in the newspaper. The subject of mental illness doesn't intimidate me.

Even the most hopeless of situations can be turned around with medication and therapy. If I could straighten out the mess bipolar illness made of my life, anyone can.

George, George Jr., Faye, and Hunter

GEORGE

When Faye first got sick, it took me about three months to figure out what was going on with her. I was in denial at first because I wouldn't allow myself to believe that something bad was happening to me or to my family. It was too horrible. I just waited for it to go away. When some of our friends heard how Faye was acting, they would say, "Why, that evil woman. How dare she do that to her family!" I guess they were in as much shock as I was.

In a span of two hours, Faye would get so depressed that she would literally be flat on the floor. Two hours later, she'd be dancing around the house, all bubbly. Talk about bipolar!

Then she'd go take a bath and start talking to herself or to somebody imaginary. If I'd say something to Faye that she thought was humorous, she would become hysterical. She couldn't stop laughing even if it wasn't all that funny.

You can overlook the first ten or so strange things, but eventually you have to face that something is wrong. One day, Faye's boss called me and said, "You need to come over here right away and take your wife home." When I got there, Faye was in total denial that anything was wrong with her, in spite of the fact that she had been going around to her

When I look at my wife now, I don't think of her as mentally ill. I just think of her as Faye. However, my friends and the community at large may not quite grasp this perception of my wife. There's that label, "crazy." Once it's applied to you, it's very hard to shake.

— GEORGE

colleagues saying things like, "They're listening to us through the light plugs." I thought maybe Faye was trying to fake being sick so she wouldn't have to work anymore. But this didn't make any sense to me, because she liked her job. It dawned on me right then and there that she had a serious problem.

I told Faye's boss that I'd come back in half an hour and take her home with me. I went and sat in my car in the parking lot to give myself time to think. I remember saying to myself, "Faye is psychotic. No, she can't be. Yes, she is, George. Faye is psychotic." At first, I wasn't so much worried about Faye as I was about myself. I thought, "This can't be happening to me. This is going to ruin my life!" Finally, I went back inside to get Faye, and she agreed to leave with me. She drove her own car home, and I followed her. Looking back on it, I never should have allowed her to drive because she was really wacked out.

When we got home, things seemed to be pretty normal, but only for a couple of hours. Later that evening, she said, "George, I want a divorce." Up until then our marriage had been pretty good. There wasn't any reason to get divorced. When I realized Faye was serious, I felt lost. We became more and more distant even though we were living under the same roof. We stayed together for about two weeks, and then Faye got her own apartment. We lived apart for five months.

Within two or three days after Faye started taking her medication, it was as if someone had taken a VCR tracking device and tuned her brain in. She was back to normal. I guess we're lucky because it's not that way for everyone with mental illness.

When I look at my wife now, I don't think of her as mentally ill. I just think of her as Faye. However, my friends and the community at large may not quite grasp this perception of my wife. There's that label, "crazy." Once it's applied to you, it's very hard to shake.

Faye and I are worried about the possibility that our children might develop mental illness because it's on both sides of our family. But even if our boys do develop problems twenty years or so from now, chances are that treatment for mental illness will be much more advanced than it is now.

Mental illness can be a dangerous thing, and it's not something to play with. You have to get past the shock and denial, and as soon as you understand you've got a problem, don't try to treat it with over-the-counter remedies. Go get yourself a psychiatrist! The sooner you get on medication, the sooner you'll get back your equilibrium.

The stigma against mental illness is definitely out there, and Faye and I have run up against it several times. I think one of the reasons why so many people have such a hard time with mental illness is that they worry it could happen to them or to someone they love. By acting like it can never happen to them, or by ridiculing people who are mentally ill, they probably hope that this protects them in some way. It doesn't. Mental illness can happen to anyone. If it does, you need to cope with it and not put your head in the sand. You need to deal with it and make the best of it. You don't need to be afraid of it. It's not a death sentence.

I'm surprised our marriage survived Faye's illness, but I think it's made us stronger in a strange kind of way. I love Faye more now than I ever have.

Madelyne and Jamie

THE COX FAMILY

SHREVEPORT, LOUISIANA

Madelyne Cox / Jamie Cox

JAMIE

I REMEMBER CRYING MYSELF TO SLEEP AT NIGHT when I was in elementary school. It wasn't like I lived in a home where there were horrible things going on. There was no abuse. In fact, I had a very stable home life. But still, I'd cry myself to sleep every night. I just didn't feel good about myself. I think my parents were clueless that children could be depressed.

When I had difficulty falling asleep, I'd look at the clock and think I had to remember the specific time forever into history. I'd say to myself, "Okay. The clock says it's exactly nine twenty-seven P.M. I've got to remember this exact time forever and ever." Who knows why I thought that? It was an overwhelming compulsion. I didn't tell my parents, but even if I could have verbalized this, my parents wouldn't have thought anything about it. They wouldn't have even called in a doctor. I believe I could have benefited from some intervention way back then.

It wasn't until I was an adult that I was diagnosed with both OCD and depression. I went on medication, but things continued to get worse. When I was thirty-one, a number of painful losses occurred in my life. My dad died suddenly. We were very close, and his death was a huge loss for me. The next year, I left my husband and moved into an apartment with my daughter, Madelyne. The following year I lost my job. Then the man I was seeing split up with me. I absolutely adored him, and we had talked seriously about getting married—the whole nine yards! I really thought this was it, but one day he just dropped out of sight. When I finally found him, he told me, "What if you were to get sick and have to be hospitalized? Where would I be if that happened? It really wouldn't be good for me." When he said that, I thought, "Well, that isn't going to happen." Clearly, it bothered him that I had to take medication. I think he was afraid that I might have to be institutionalized someday. The loss of this relationship was especially hard on me, so I ended up going to a very sweet therapist. He helped me, but he developed brain cancer and died.

All of these losses were life-changing events for me. I finally got to the point where I was crying every day at work. I also had two frightening episodes at work, which I now know were panic attacks. I got real weak, sweaty, nauseated, and

At first, Madelyne said that maybe mental illness was kind of like having a new religion. I made it really clear to her that you don't decide whether to have a mental illness. Once she realized religion is something you choose to believe in, she understood that having a mental illness is not at all like "having" a religion.

—JAMIE

all that stuff. The nurse took my pulse, and my heart rate was over two hundred! I finally agreed to go to the E.R., and from there I was sent to the psychiatric ward.

It never bothered me if people knew I was depressed. It wasn't embarrassing or shameful. But when I was hospitalized, it upset me because I was a social worker in the same hospital. Everybody talks, and I could imagine my colleagues saying, "Did you know that Ms. Cox, the social worker, is in the psych ward?" I don't think I understood at that point that psychiatric units are not just for the worst of the worst. I didn't realize that people like me who are depressed but not psychotic are sometimes hospitalized for short periods of time. So when I was admitted into the psychiatric unit, I kept it a big secret.

Even though my parents and my sister were supportive and helped me during my hospitalization, it was real embarrassing to them. It still is. My illness is especially embarrassing for my mother. I don't really know why. Every now and then, I've kidded her and said, "Oh, Mother, watch out. My OCD is coming out!" I used to think it was funny, but I learned that this made her real mad, so I stopped teasing her.

My mother grew up in a time when people who had a mental illness were considered "crazy." There wasn't medication and all that stuff they have now to help people, so you kept those things quiet. And my family still does. We don't talk about family problems. Our family doesn't have any problems! We smile when we're out and we pretend everything's lovely and perfect. We don't let anybody know that anything is wrong unless we have to. It's just the way it is.

One day I got really riled up about something. I don't normally scream or anything, but I was very angry. My mother said, "Jamie, you are sick! You are just sick!" I knew she meant the mental illness thing. And my sister said, "Obviously, you haven't been taking your medication." They were both very catty. They couldn't have said anything more hurtful to me. I don't mean to sound like we're divided people—we're not. In fact, I've long since forgiven them, because I know they didn't realize how absolutely to the bone their comments went.

But even though they helped me when I was in the hospital, I don't want to discuss my illness with them. I feel too vulnerable to their way of thinking.

I didn't want my daughter, Madelyne, to know that I had been in a psychiatric hospital, because I was afraid it would be hurtful and scary for her. I certainly didn't want some of her family members on her father's side to know. After all, it was such a big deal for my own family.

I'm kind of a loner, which is fine with me. I'm real content having one close friend I can trust. I've always been that way. I'm still at a point where I come home after work and don't go anywhere. I'm not comfortable going to places where I don't know people. It's not a phobic thing. It seems to be a personality thing. If I have to give a talk in front of people, it doesn't bother me. But relating one-on-one with someone is kind of scary for me.

I'm still a social worker in a hospital. My supervisor at work told some of the hospital bigwigs that her staff included a person with depression, which was a reference to me, as well as three other folks who had also been hospitalized with other types of mental illness. My supervisor let me know that the administrators said, "You need to get rid of those people. They're going to be trouble." Even though my supervisor told me this jokingly, those of us who have been with this hospital long enough knew it wasn't a joke.

Just yesterday, I finally told my daughter about my mental illness for the first time. I asked Madelyne if she knew the meaning of "mental illness." She said, "What's that?" We looked it up in a dictionary, but mental illness wasn't even listed. There were several other words with "mental" in them, like mental retardation, but not mental illness. So I explained to her the best I could about brain chemicals. Madelyne is old enough to have studied at least some of that basic stuff in science class at school. I said, "All people's brain chemicals aren't the same; they don't fire the same way." I also told her there were many different kinds of mental illness. We talked about people who have auditory and visual hallucinations, but the main kind of mental illness we talked about was depression. I also explained that medication helps many folks get better, including me.

At first, Madelyne said that maybe mental illness was kind of like having a new religion. I made it really clear to her that you don't decide whether to have a mental illness. Once she realized religion is something you choose to believe in, she understood that having a mental illness is not at all like "having" a religion.

I'm glad I've told Madelyne about my illness. The primary reason I wanted her to know is because she could develop depression at some point in her life, too. If she does, I want her to know that her mom has it and she's still able to work, and it's okay. When things got really bad, her mom went to a hospital, and that was okay, too.

I'm also glad that my daughter understands that mental illness is not the same as mental retardation. I wouldn't want her to think that mentally retarded people are mentally ill any more than I would want her to think that mentally ill people are retarded.

I told Madelyne that I don't mind if she tells her friends about me, but I explained there might be kids who will make fun of her or of me because of my illness. There will always be kids who will say, "Your mom is crazy," or "You're going to be crazy, too." I hate for my daughter to have to experience the bad part, but she will have to learn that some people just don't understand.

People who are not well-educated don't necessarily bother me when they make negative comments about mental illness, maybe because they simply haven't had the opportunity to learn anything different. Mental health professionals and other well-educated people ought to know better! I want everyone to know that folks who have any kind of mental illness, even if it is as difficult to treat as schizophrenia can be, are not crazy. They just have a different chemical makeup than other people. Anyone can become mentally ill.

Mental health is one big continuum. Many people might be right in the center, where their mental health is pretty good. And some people will be just a little farther off the center. It's not like, here are the mentally ill people and here are the healthy people and here are the others. Sometimes I'm just as mentally healthy as my next-door neighbor. Even the very sickest people have their good days. The majority of people out there wouldn't even know that some of the people they meet are mentally ill. Many folks with mental illness act just as normal as anyone else can. Basically, we're all the same.

MADELYNE

My mom talked to me the other day about both mental illness and mental retardation. Someone who is mentally retarded might not be able to read or comprehend as well as other people, but someone with a mental illness could still have a high I.Q. My mom told me how you don't choose to have either of them. It just happens, even though you don't want it to.

Joyce and Greg

THE LINDSAY FAMILY

PITTSBURGH, PENNSYLVANIA

JOYCE LINDSAY / GREG LINDSAY

JOYCE

WHEN I WAS GROWING UP IN NORTH CAROLINA, all I was ever told about mental illness was that it was "lockup time." Mental illness was something that was kept in the closet.

My husband, William, and I have two sons. Greg was my sister's biological child, and she couldn't raise him. We adopted Greg right after he was born and raised him with our son as brothers.

When Greg finished high school, he was nineteen and didn't have a job. Sometimes you have to remind young people these days that it's time for them to look for work. Greg couldn't seem to find any employment, so my husband and I sent him up to New York City, where we thought he might have a better chance. Greg joined the navy instead! His older brother had already been in the service, so it was pretty easy for Greg to follow in his footsteps. Greg took his basic training in California and was stationed in Virginia. For two and a half years, we never heard a word from him.

Out of the blue, the navy notified us that Greg was sick with paranoid schizophrenia and was in the Norfolk State Hospital. I didn't understand this at all! It was my first real introduction to mental illness.

I kept in contact with the navy by phone, and they also sent me information about Greg's disease. They even put me in touch with a support group called Sharing and Caring at a psychiatric center near my home. I attended a meeting, and it was unbelievable. I was listening and learning, but not fully understanding. I still hadn't seen Greg, so I had no idea what everyone was really talking about. I continued to go to the meetings every week anyway. They were held only a block and a half from my work, and I told my boss just how important it was for me to take the time to attend them. Each time I went, the more I heard about what mental illness can do. I was shocked!

One night, someone from the navy called and said that Greg had been discharged. He had gone to the airport, missed his flight home, and ended up in a hotel, where he had gotten sick again. Greg was put in a state institution, so I had no way of getting him home.

I asked for help at my support group, but they were no help at all. Finally, I got a friend to drive my husband and me to where Greg was hospitalized, so we could bring him

237

I hate the word "confidentiality." I once went to talk to one of Greg's doctors to learn more about his case and get some information about the dates of his hospitalization. I had Greg's signed permission, but the doctor refused to talk to me. If a family member goes to the psychiatrist with the patient's permission, the information they want should be released.

—JOYCE

home. When we arrived at the hospital, I had my first experience being behind locked doors. It was very frightening. As soon as the doors were unlocked to let us in, the other patients ran right up to me. They scared me. When I saw Greg from a distance, he looked fine to me, but as I got closer, he didn't look the way he used to look at all.

When we got Greg home, he was in terrible shape. He couldn't sit and he couldn't stand. His legs would shake, and his hands would shake. He refused to sit at the table with us. He couldn't even hold his fork. He was totally different from the son we used to know. It was awful to see him that way. I'm not a crier, but I would go in my room and sit on my bed and just rock and rock and rock. I asked my husband, "What's happening?" The situation was so new to me that I still was not clicking. I just didn't get it.

As time went on, Greg had one hospitalization after another. He would come home from the Veterans Hospital, and we could almost set our watch by him. In a week's time, he would be back in again.

I didn't like the VA hospital. Greg would go there, get his medications, and go home, but no one ever monitored him on his meds. The doctors told me Greg was a young man and that he should go out and do what young men do! That wasn't helpful advice at all. I had to find out for myself about the drugs they had him on. I soon figured out that the medication they had Greg on wasn't doing anything for him. As long as his drugs weren't working, it meant more and more hospitalizations for my son.

I hate the word "confidentiality." I once went to talk to one of Greg's doctors to learn more about his case and get some information about the dates of his hospitalization. I had Greg's signed permission, but the doctor refused to talk to me. If a family member goes to the psychiatrist with the patient's permission, the information they want should be released.

When he was home, Greg liked exercising every day. He did push-ups just like he had done in the service. He also liked jogging and walking. One day, he went out for a walk and didn't come back for two days. Didn't call or nothing.

When we found him, he was in jail! I didn't like that, because I thought the authorities should have notified my husband and me right away. What had happened was that a young lady was walking near Greg when he heard a voice telling him that a car was going to hit her. In order to "save her life," he put his hands on this lady and moved her aside. She filed charges against him. Before Greg got sick, he had never been in trouble in his entire life. I had taught my sons right from wrong. But after Greg got sick, I didn't know right from wrong myself!

After he got out of jail, I said, "Greg, it's time to go back to the hospital." He didn't want to go back to the VA hospital, but he agreed to go to a private psychiatric unit. The staff there decided that Greg needed long-term treatment, so he wound up back at the VA hospital after all. During his stay there, he went into another patient's room, and the lady claimed that he touched her. She also pressed charges against him.

Greg refused help from the VA, and since he wasn't capable of standing trial, he was sent to the state hospital with the charges still pending. It was a big mess. He was jailed for several weeks, and the prison authorities didn't want to give him his medication. They refused to take the responsibility of giving him the weekly blood test that was necessary with this medication.

The worst experience of Greg's life was being in jail. He didn't like it at all. When he was in there, Greg didn't know what the outside world was anymore. Finally, he was given his meds in prison and he made a U-turn. He started to get better.

Greg was given seven years' probation by the judges because they wanted to make an example of him. This didn't make any sense to me because the woman had already dropped the charges against Greg. I should have sued, but at that point, I didn't even know what day of the week it was.

Greg was released from jail at nine o'clock at night, with no medication and no money for bus fare. If this is the way the legal system operates, it sure needs some work. Greg had to walk all the way home. The doorbell rang, and my husband opened the front door. There was Greg! I got home from work at eleven o'clock that night and there was my son. I said, "What happened?" We took him right up to the psychiatric hospital and got him his medication. We sure were glad to see him.

There was no place for Greg to go after jail other than back home. There was supervised living and other housing for the mentally ill, but no one wanted someone with a criminal record, whether it was due to their mental illness or not. I thought that was unfair. When I first told the people at my support group that Greg was back living at home, they told me that I shouldn't keep him there. This got me scared. I thought, "Why can't I have my child living at home with me?" Looking back, I'm glad I decided to bring him home. I went with Greg every step he took.

I was trying to maintain a home, go to work, and deal with Greg and all these hospitals, all at the same time. Anybody who says, "I can't do this for my family member because I work," is lying! I've been there and I've done it all. It wasn't easy, though. Sometimes I would go to work sick as a dog. I would be so tired that I was dragging my feet.

Soon after Greg came home from jail, we were driving past People's Oakland, a local drop-in center for folks who are mentally ill. I said, "Greg, do you want to go in?" He said, "No," and that was it. He didn't want to do nothing after he came home from jail. He would just look out the window, but he wouldn't go outside.

Greg goes to People's Oakland now. He goes with their groups to ballgames and even on vacations. The whole caboose. Last week was their Thanksgiving dinner, and Greg got a little trophy for playing softball. He hasn't gotten into any kind of trouble since he started going there in 1998.

Greg's doing fantastic now. No drugs, no alcohol. You couldn't ask for a better son than him. The last time he was in a mental hospital was in 1992. Now that's saying something for him! That's really saying something. Greg gets up; he does his laundry; he does his room; he takes his medication; and he's doing what he should do. Greg's favorite words these days are, "I'm all right."

I've tried to get Greg's brother to join the sibling support group at People's Oakland, but he won't go. He's afraid that Greg's illness will rub off on him. My husband doesn't usually go, either, because he says, "Everybody talks at once. I can't hear." I tell him, "You're nothing but a big baby!" He only goes if there's a crisis with Greg. But I'm a believer in preventive medicine. Catch it before it happens. I'm that type of person.

In the meantime, I've been working and running to meetings and conferences because you can't know enough. I had a very close ally who worked in the mental health system and she told me that in order to learn about mental illness, you have to attend meetings, seminars, and conferences. You can't learn nothing staying at home.

Greg has an aunt who calls me "the meeting lady." She'll say, "Joyce, what are you doing today?" And I'll say, "Oh, I'm going to a meeting." She says, "You're the meeting-est woman I've ever seen. The thing about you is you keep abreast of what's going on."

My husband is getting old. He's ninety-one now, and he says, "Joyce, you can't keep running to all these meetings!" Fathers don't understand like mothers do. I say, "I can't learn nothing looking at you! This is for Greg!" Even now, I still learn something new every day by talking to different people about mental illness. It's an ongoing task, that's all.

GREG

I've been doing pretty good in the last couple of years because I take the medicine regular. I never miss it. I used to get sleepy. Upset stomach sometimes. But nowadays, I feel pretty good. I used to shake all the time, but I don't anymore. People should take their medicine regularly and their illness will go away. I feel better since I started taking it.

I go to People's Oakland every day. I like the field trips we take. We went to a lake in Ohio last year and on a boat trip. I get along with people pretty good. I don't have no problems with them. Everything's going pretty good for me. I'm all right.

I was trying to maintain a home, go to work, and deal with Greg and all these hospitals, all at the same time. Anybody who says, "I can't do this for my family member because I work," is lying! I've been there and I've done it all. It wasn't easy, though. Sometimes I would go to work sick as a dog. I would be so tired that I was dragging my feet.

—JOYCE

Standing: Jenny and Ann *Seated:* Jane

THE CUMMINGS FAMILY

VISTA, CALIFORNIA

Jennifer Badgerow / Ann Cummings / Jane Cummings

ANN

THERE IS A HISTORY OF MENTAL ILLNESS IN MY FAMILY, which begins with my grandfather. He had manic-depression and he committed suicide by jumping out of a fourteen-story building in the 1930s.

My father had manic-depression, too. He was a colonel in the Marine Corps, and his illness hit him during his thirtieth year in the military. He was forced to resign because he couldn't do his job properly. My father's brother, a priest, developed schizophrenia and was institutionalized back in the 1950s. My mother's half sister also suffered from schizophrenia.

I developed depression when I was seventeen, but I didn't know I was suffering from a mental illness. I was a cheerleader and I remember going to a football game and saying to my boyfriend, "I can't understand why I feel so sad. It's hard to go out on the field and pretend to be happy."

I couldn't stay focused during my senior year of high school. I was working toward a 4.0 average because I wanted to go to a good college, but it became extremely difficult to

hang on. Somehow, I was able to get through that year with an "A" average, and I was offered four scholarships to different colleges. I went to an Ivy League college, but I struggled emotionally and academically.

I was able to finish up my freshman year in college, but the week before I went back to school for my sophomore year, my father had the first of many manic-depressive episodes and attempted suicide. This left me shaken, scared, and even more depressed. I tried to keep up with my studies, but I was simply not able to continue. I had no idea what was going on with me, no idea that I was also suffering from a mental illness.

I knew I had to take time off from school to try to cope with my father's illness and its affect on our family. I also needed time to deal with my own mental and emotional struggles. I was filled with intense anguish when I realized that I couldn't keep up with my academic demands. I had to drop out of college and give up all my scholarships and grants.

I clung to a normal life to the best of my ability, and two years later I went back to college. My father's worsening illness and my own undiagnosed depression affected my con-

When I think about the millions of dollars that were spent on President Clinton's affair with Monica Lewinsky, I wonder why I couldn't get decent psychiatric help for my son. It could have saved his life. He was a good, kind, intelligent, wonderful human being. His life was worth saving.

—ANN

centration, my memory, my ability to problem-solve, and my ability to handle stress. I was unable to complete the semester, so I decided to drop out of college once again.

I finally gave up on school altogether. I got married and had two children, Jenny and Brent. After the birth of my son in 1984, I started having severe problems with depression again. That year, my father made his tenth attempt at suicide, and this time he succeeded. Soon after that, I was diagnosed with major depression and started on numerous drug trials. My emotional pain continued to worsen because the medications never completely stabilized me. I went on one medication, which initially made me feel like a new person, but I had to go off of it because I began to have severe side effects.

When Brent was seven, he was also diagnosed with depression and was treated successfully with antidepressants. My ex-husband wasn't working at the time, so we no longer were able to pay for medical insurance. I couldn't continue to get the kind of high-quality psychiatric help that Brent needed, because I just couldn't afford it. It took heaven and earth to find a good psychiatrist who would accept state health insurance.

When Brent was thirteen, we finally found a psychiatrist who worked with poor people. It soon became obvious to me that she didn't give a damn about any of the children she was treating. I thought, "How can his woman be the head of this program when she has absolutely no empathy for what these kids are going through?" She told me, "Brent's not depressed. He doesn't need to be on antidepressants anymore." She took him off all his medication even though he had attempted suicide the year before she saw him in treatment. How much more evidence did she need that Brent was depressed?

Three weeks after he stopped taking his medication, my son committed suicide. He hung himself in the backyard of my mom's house. I have a lot of anger and resentment about this. When I think about the millions of dollars that were spent on President Clinton's affair with Monica Lewinsky, I wonder why I couldn't get decent psychiatric help for my son. It could have saved his life. He was a good, kind, intelligent, wonderful human being. His life was worth saving.

Before Brent died, I had gone off my medications because none of them were working. After he died, I was hospitalized immediately, and then entered various treatment facilities to help me with my depression and grief. In 1995, I was in a residential treatment facility that encouraged its clients to return to school. I signed up for classes that fall, but the week they started was the one-year anniversary of my son's death. I was hospitalized again for six weeks and had sixteen electroshock sessions to treat my severe depression. I not only forgot who I was, but also where I was, where I lived, my enrollment at school, and even the fact that my son had died. As my memory slowly returned, I had to relive his death all over again. I was not fully functional or cognizant at that time.

Depression is an oppressive darkness and gloom. No happiness. No spark for life. It is sitting in a corner unable to move. It literally felt as if a physical weight prevented me from being able to do ordinary, everyday things, like brushing my teeth or organizing my medications. The simplest aspects of living that most people take for granted, like deciding what shirt to wear, became impossible for me. I wasn't capable of cleaning my house, taking a shower, or taking care of myself at all. I had absolutely no concentration. I had difficulty speaking and talking. I couldn't formulate sentences. I stuttered. I isolated myself, stayed in my room for days at a time, and didn't go out or talk to anyone. I was angry a lot of the time.

I felt very much alone, very guilty, and very ashamed of my mental illness. I blamed my illness for the death of my son because he didn't receive the protection, love, and support that he needed at the most critical time in his life. This guilt is still difficult to bear.

I've found that most doctors who specialize in the field of mental illness have very little empathy or understanding. They are afraid of mental illness, which surprises me, because I assumed they were educated about it in medical school. I thought that learning to care about their patients was a requirement, but most of them say, "Hands off, I don't want to deal with it."

I spent many years on a quest to find a good doctor for myself. When I met my current psychiatrist, he told me, "This problem is not bigger than I am. I am bigger than this problem, and I can cope with this. I can get you better." He said it with such confidence and strength that I thought to myself, "At last I've found someone who can help me live with my illness."

At my psychiatrist's suggestion, I joined an intensive partial hospitalization program for four hours a day. My family members felt less responsible for me because they knew that professionals were overseeing the physical, emotional, and mental aspects of my life. My family was relieved not to have to play so many different roles in my life, which they'd never really been trained to handle in the first place.

A turning point in my recovery came when I turned over the decision-making about my illness to professionals. I finally acknowledged that, not unlike an alcoholic, I wasn't in control of my illness and that I needed to give other people control over my treatment in order to get better. When I met my current psychiatrist, I began to do this, but I didn't do it all at once. It was a gradual process of letting go. I slowly learned to let the clinic staff help make decisions for me. It was very difficult to accept their input at first, but I soon saw that their advice helped me pull my life back together again.

It took me a year to stabilize. I am currently on fourteen different medications and in intensive therapy. My psychiatrist has supported my intention to return to school, provided I only take six units a semester. I can't go back to school unless I get some financial aid, and so far, I haven't received any. I've just written a letter to the financial aid office explaining my mental health history in the hope that they will reconsider my request for help.

Since I've become stable, I am a more loving, calm, and logical person. I'm not as reactionary as I used to be. In the past, I would overreact to certain situations in our family. It was a hardship for my children because I would respond so inappropriately. At the time, I was angry, irritable, and

Jane, Jenny, and Ann

not functioning most of the time. But, thank God, I kept looking for help.

I have to protect my stability, and my family helps me do that by reducing my stress, by not letting me take on too much, and by keeping my life balanced physically, mentally, emotionally, and spiritually. My mother and my daughter, and even my sister, who lives in another city, all assist me in maintaining that balance. I constantly turn to them and say, "I'm considering this. Please help me with this decision."

JENNY

When I was in third grade, I had to get up and dress myself and make my lunch and get on the school bus all by myself because my mom was in bed all the time. I never really saw her awake. I didn't know then that it wasn't normal to live this way. I thought all the other kids did the same things I did.

During my mom's last hospitalization, my grandma got kind of afraid because Mom would call us both up and say weird things. She just wasn't making any sense. She didn't know who she was or where she was. I wanted my mom to stay in the hospital, but my grandma decided to take her out.

When Grandma and I were driving her home from the hospital, Mom asked us where we were taking her. We answered, "We're taking you to your house." And she said, "What house?" She had completely forgotten that she had a home. Now that we can laugh about it, we call our home "Whathouse."

When Mom was discharged from the hospital, they forgot to give her any of her medications to take home. I guess they messed up or something. Mom lay in bed and told me that her heart was beating real fast. I said, "Why don't you take your blood pressure medication?" She was like, "What medication?" I had to call 911, and the ambulance came and took her back to the hospital to get her blood pressure medication. After that she stayed with Grandma Jane for a while until she was stable again. Then she came back home to live with me.

After my parents got divorced, my little brother, Brent, and I became best friends instead of fighting all the time. Brent had two sides. One was his theatrical side, which was the side most people saw. Brent could make anybody smile or laugh. He was happy, outgoing, wonderful, and very talented. He sang so well, he would make people cry. Everybody thought he was just amazing. I can't put it into words. It seemed like he was some kind of a gift to the world. But there was another side to Brent.

Nobody outside the family had any idea that Brent was having a hard time. But he was. He didn't get along well with our dad, so whenever they were together, Brent would get really depressed. He also had a lot of problems at school. I kind of had to take care of him. I wanted to face all these problems for him so he could just be a happy person, but Brent had a darkness in him that he didn't know how to get rid of. He was constantly trying to fight it, but he didn't know how to. I miss him so much.

When I try to talk to most people about my family situation, it's like they have all the answers. They tell me how it is, and I try to tell them, "No, that's not how it is. No, that doesn't help." Then they think I'm weird or something and that I'm not playing with a full deck. They think I'm making bad decisions about my family. They just don't understand what it's like to live with someone who has a mental illness. I can talk to my best friend, Julie, because she does understand what it's like. She's been through it herself. Julie knows there's no right or wrong answer. It's just day by day.

When I told another close friend what was going on with my mom, she told me I should move out and leave my mom behind. Where would that get us? I'd have to work twice as hard to pay rent by myself and if I move out of our house, then my mom couldn't afford to live there on her own. Yes, I want to live my own life, but she's my mom. If she needs my help, I want to be there to help her. Most people don't seem to understand that. They don't try to understand; they just see what's going on, and then they get angry about my situation and try to tell me how to fix it. It's easier not to explain it to them. It's easier not to talk about it.

This is my life, so I have to try and make the best of it.

JANE

I'm Annie's mother and Jenny's grandmother. Even before I was married, my husband would go through periods where he would tell me he was depressed. I'd say, "Really? What are you talking about?" His illness was different from Annie's. His was full-fledged intense depression and intense mania. Annie never annoyed me, even at her worst, but her father certainly did. His siblings included a drunk, a manic-depressive, and a paranoid schizophrenic. I thought it had bypassed my husband until he went to Vietnam. When he came home from the war, the man I had known was completely gone.

My husband killed himself. I decided at some point after his suicide that I would live without stress. I thought I would be able to take better care of myself by avoiding all stress. I decided I wouldn't do anything that I didn't like to do. I just wanted to do things that pleased me. When things happened that I couldn't control, I would read a book or do a hobby and relieve my mind from dealing with it. Then Annie comes along and gets sick, and she has to have help. After I decided not to have any stress in my life, I've had to cope with things like Brent's death and Annie's illness. Even Jenny is quite capable of piling on stress by the carload any day of the week.

When she was younger, Annie had a different physical symptom every day. She had pains in every inch of her body. You never knew what the next thing would be. It was a constant struggle dealing with her little physical ailments.

I had no idea how any child who was a cheerleader, getting straight "A's," creative, with a boyfriend at Stanford, who could sit down at the sewing machine and make me an outfit, and was good at everything, could be mentally ill. I just didn't understand it. It wasn't until my husband became acutely ill that I started to read about mental illness.

I wasn't very good at understanding mental disabilities like depression. When my husband got sick, I got an education over the next ten years, but I've never thought that understanding mental illness has done me any good at all. I don't want to hear anybody describe mental illness. Most of the time, they don't know what they're talking about.

The hardest time for me was when the doctors said there was absolutely nothing they could do for Annie. None of the medications had worked, and all that was left to try was electroshock treatments.

When I'd talk to Annie's psychiatrists, I'd often think that they should be locked up themselves. I had a long history with my husband's illness of seeing psychiatrists who belonged on the funny farm, too. I'm not happy about psychiatry, and I seldom pass up any occasion where I can say nasty things about it! Fortunately, Annie's new doctor seems to be a good man.

Annie never had any medication to help this whole mental illness business until her new doctor decided to combine different drugs. Before he got involved in her case, these idiots would put Annie on one medication and then they would switch her to another because it wasn't working. That meant a layoff because she'd have to wait six weeks before she could get started on a new drug.

The most important thing about my daughter is that she always has had a focus, no matter how sick she's been, physically or mentally. In order to get through her mental illness, her focus was centered on finding something that would work for her or finding some doctor who could help her. Annie was trying to do as much as she could to find an answer. Nobody in the family deals with the bureaucracy as well as she does. Now the bureaucracy supports her because she applied to HUD to pay part of her rent. This is how Annie got the house she now lives in with Jenny.

I'm not very good at being a support system for Annie, but I know the things that need to be encouraged in her forward motion. I know how I can help her, and I do what I can when I can. Jenny's been wonderful during emergencies, but the real support Annie gets comes from her own sense of direction and from her doctors. I'm proud she has found a doctor to combine the right medications and arrive at some answers for her.

Annie has gotten well enough so she can handle her own finances. When she's in control of that, you figure she's really doing pretty well. She has even been able to come over to help me. She takes me to the doctor and does my vacuuming. Annie is a great pleasure to me. She is loving and kind and entertaining. She's a great friend. I can count on her. She's a doll.

I had no idea how any child who was a cheerleader, getting straight "A's," creative, with a boyfriend at Stanford, who could sit down at the sewing machine and make me an outfit, and was good at everything, could be mentally ill. I just didn't understand it.
—JANE

Standing: Joseph, Karen, and Louis *Seated:* John and Christina

THE COOLIDGE FAMILY

<u>ORANGE, MASSACHUSETTS</u>

JOSEPH COOLIDGE / KAREN MARIA COOLIDGE
LOUIS COOLIDGE / JOHN COOLIDGE / CHRISTINA COOLIDGE

CHRISTINA

I HATE THE WORD "SCHIZOPHRENIC." I have schizophrenia and I object to being defined by this illness. I don't like it when people say, "Christina's a schizophrenic." It is so degrading. Having a mental illness, particularly schizophrenia, is like hitting the bottom of the barrel. Most people don't understand it.

I started to get depressed when I was a teenager in boarding school. I went to the school counselor and asked to see a psychiatrist. The counselor was into theater, and she said, "No, I think you should go on the stage and act. You're a wonderful actress." I was flattered and thought she must be right. I decided not to seek help.

When I graduated, I still had an empty, listless feeling. I went to a women's college in California, where I continued to feel terrible. I kept telling my friends there, "I'm so depressed." They would say, "We're all depressed, Christina. There aren't any men here!" I certainly didn't get the help that I needed.

After I got my degree, I began to wander around. I couldn't focus on anything. I had hallucinations at the time and I was becoming paranoid. I wasn't really aware of what was happening to me. I thought that I was being drugged and I believed that the CIA was after me.

I finally went to see a therapist who was into trendy primal scream therapy. She didn't like mainstream psychiatry, so again I didn't get the treatment or the medication that I needed. To make matters worse, she came on to me sexually. This really disturbed me, and I stopped seeing her.

When you have a mental illness, complete with hallucinations and paranoia, your judgment about what to do with your life is compromised. I married a man who physically abused me. After a while I left him, but I kept getting into one jam after another. This is not unusual for a person who has a mental illness. I was in total denial that something might be wrong with me, even though I was delusional at the time.

I used to walk around believing that someone was speaking directly to my mind. I thought God was talking to me,

My doctor prescribed medication for me. It took about six months before it kicked in and began to work. One afternoon, the sky was a radiant blue and the light was unusually bright. I remember thinking, "Gosh, this must be the way everybody feels. What a wonderful feeling it is to have my mind clear and not to have all sorts of things rummaging around in my head!"
— CHRISTINA

Standing: Joseph, Karen, and Louis *Seated:* John and Christina

and that I had sinned because I couldn't control my thoughts about the people around me. I lived in a fantasy world in which I imagined people were trying to kill me.

After deteriorating for a number of years, I moved to Arizona to live with my parents, where I saw a psychiatrist. I said to him, "I guess I'm crazy, so I think I need to be in a hospital." The doctor admitted me for a week or so. That's the only time I've ever been hospitalized. The staff wrote things about me in my medical records and they wouldn't share what they wrote with me. One day I took a peek at my records. Someone had written, "Christina doesn't tell the truth." I was outraged! You can say a lot of things about me, but to be called a liar made me furious!

When I was discharged from the hospital, no one really explained what was wrong with me. One day, my mother went to talk to the staff at the local mental health center, and they actually suggested to her that she might need treatment there as well. She said, "It's my daughter who is desperately ill, and you want to treat me?" That was back in the days when they still blamed mothers for causing schizophrenia in their children. Oh, was she ever angry!

My doctor prescribed medication for me. It took about six months before it kicked in and began to work. One afternoon, the sky was a radiant blue and the light was unusually bright. I remember thinking, "Gosh, this must be the way everybody feels. What a wonderful feeling it is to have my mind clear and not to have all sorts of things rummaging around in my head!"

When I first got sick, my family was very upset and angry with me for having an illness. My younger brother, whom I love dearly, told my mother, "I hate Christina. I just hate her." This didn't really hurt my feelings, because I knew this was a reaction to my illness, not to me personally. Later, a counselor told me that it's common for family members to express anger at a loved one who is sick. Once my medication kicked in, my family was wonderful. My sister even said, "Christina, when are you going to go out on a date?" She was ready for my illness to be over!

By 1979, my medication was working pretty well. I was ready to get a job and earn a living, so I went to school to become a librarian. I received my master's degree in library science a few years later. My parents suggested that I move to Boston, where I could be nearer my older brother and his wife. Shortly after I moved there, I landed a job in a law library.

I was referred to a psychiatrist in Boston. When I went to see him, I said, "I have schizophrenia. Can you help me?" He replied, "Oh, you can't have schizophrenia." I said, "Oh yes, I do!" He said, "Well, give me the name of your doctor in Arizona. I want to find out where he went to medical school!" He called my previous doctor, who confirmed that I did indeed have schizophrenia but that I had responded well to medication. This new doctor, who was an internationally known psychiatrist, agreed to treat me. After a while, he put me on a lower dose of medication so I wouldn't experience as many side effects. I continued to do very well.

A couple of years later, I was doing so well that my doctor suggested that I go on a "drug holiday" to see what would happen. I stopped taking all of my medications and, once again, I became extremely paranoid. I thought that the CIA and the KGB were following me. I also thought my mind was receiving special signals through the radio. I was very, very sick.

I met my husband, John, while I was living in Boston. Unbeknownst to him, I was in the midst of a paranoid, hallucinatory episode. Nevertheless, I knew right from the start that I wanted to marry him. I was afraid to tell him about my illness, so I asked my psychiatrist, "Do I have to?" He said, "If John is going to marry you, then yes, you do." I told John that I had schizophrenia and that I was really sick. He took my illness in stride, and we got married the following year. We've been married for fifteen years. He still tells me that when we first met, he was attracted to parts of me other than my mind!

I was stable until a few years ago. My symptoms slowly crept back, even though I was still on medication. I was totally unprepared for this relapse. I couldn't believe my illness had returned. Usually I'm aware of my symptoms, but these were new ones. They included visual hallucinations that I had never had before. My colleagues at work noticed I wasn't doing well, so they called my husband and said, "Christina needs to see her doctor." I had been going to a psychiatrist all along, but perhaps not often enough. My medication was changed, but it took quite a while before I got better.

I always wanted to be what the mentally ill call a "normal person." I wanted a husband and kids, a job, a car, and a house. Now I have them all! In December of 1989, John and I adopted three siblings from Costa Rica. At the time we brought them home, Karen was one, Louis was two, and Joey was four. Each of them has some level of cognitive disability, because of their early years of neglect and malnutrition. Our kids know all about my illness. It's been such a part of our lives I think they've always understood it to a certain degree. It's not much of an issue for them. They've never seemed upset about it.

When our children were little, the cost of daycare was killing us. After much discussion, I asked John, "Why don't you stay home and let me work full time?" And he agreed! He has done a great job being the "Mommy" for all three of the kids. I have been the "Dad," and have gone off to work every day at the local community college.

Mental illness and our society's lack of understanding about it have become two of my causes. I never used to talk about it much, but John has encouraged me to be more open about my experience. I've been on a TV talk show and I speak every year to the nursing and criminal justice students where I work. I've also managed to help change a policy of the National Education Association concerning mental disability.

One of my dreams is to help develop a health curriculum for high school students, which would include a section on mental illness with up-to-date information about the brain, its chemicals and how they function. Over the years, I have read dozens and dozens of books about the brain and its processes. John calls them my "neurological thrillers."

Soon after I met Christina, she told me that she suffered from schizophrenia. I guess it was her way of saying, "Gee, I think this is starting to look like a serious relationship, so I'm going to have to break the news to him."

—*JOHN*

Given the prevalence of mental illness, it stands to reason that somebody in everyone's high school class is going to end up with a biologically based mental illness.

After my retirement, I plan to help and befriend families with mentally ill children. By sharing my story with them, I can be an example of a person who has led a good and happy life in spite of mental illness.

JOHN

I met Christina in 1984, when I was working as a lawyer for a Massachusetts State senator. One day I had to go to the state library, and sitting at the front desk was my future wife. She was one of the librarians. For weeks after that, whenever I went to the library, I couldn't understand why no one other than Christina would help me find the books I needed. It turned out that she had told all her friends not to help me; she wanted to do it herself. We were each in our thirties, so we skipped the whole "dating thing," moved in together and, after a year and a half, we got married.

Soon after I met Christina, she told me that she suffered from schizophrenia. I guess it was her way of saying, "Gee, I think this is starting to look like a serious relationship, so I'm going to have to break the news to him." Her experience in the past had been that guys in her life tended to head south when she told them she had this illness.

Christina didn't come across as a sick person to me. I hadn't noticed any symptoms, so I had no reason to think that anything might be wrong. Her illness came as a complete surprise to me. She hooked me in and then she told me! My reaction was simple: I had said to myself years ago that I was going to marry the first woman I liked who liked me back, and that's exactly what I did.

Actually, it was kind of funny when Christina first told me she had schizophrenia. I think I said, without missing a beat, "Does this mean that we can't sleep together anymore?" After all, a man has got to have his priorities straight! I probably

did a five-second cost-benefit analysis of the situation and the bottom line was that here was a woman in my life who loved me in all the right ways. I was born with multiple birth defects, so I have a pretty extensive medical history. My view was that everybody has to deal with something. Our three kids feel this way, too. Each of them has their own cognitive, emotional, and physical issues to handle. We sometimes say, "The family that medicates together, stays together."

Even though my mother had gone through a depressive episode when I was a kid, I didn't have any more or less understanding about mental illness than your average Joe Schmo layman. I certainly didn't have any unique insight about it, but I think I was very open to Christina's explanations about her schizophrenia. She taught me what it was all about and what was going on with her. I'm pretty well informed at this stage of the game.

Most people with schizophrenia get hammered to one degree or another. Christina has had a better outcome than many of them. There are probably very few people out there with this illness who have a family, kids, a professional degree, and a job. Two things have made a big difference for my wife. Her medication works very well, and she has been in the private mental health care system from the get-go. She was fortunate to receive a tremendous amount of emotional and financial support over the years from her parents. I remember that the first year I did her taxes, Christina's salary was $17,000, and she spent $12,000 of it on doctor's bills and medication. Most people can't close that gap without becoming enmeshed in the state system. She's always had access to good doctors and fine care. Very few people who get sick have that privilege.

If it were up to me, I'd take the whole country's mental health industry apart brick by brick. One of the problems with health insurance is that the companies don't want to pay all kinds of psychiatrists and counselors to help people get over all the upsets in their lives. They don't do a good job making a distinction between someone who has had a messy divorce and wants to see a therapist and someone like Christina, who has an all-day, everyday, lifelong chemical imbalance. This country provides some of the best mental health coverage you can get, and it often doesn't add up to squat.

There was a time back in the early 1990s when I became severely depressed. I had a successful law practice, the kids had just joined the family, and then the New England economy hit rock bottom. My business just dried up and vanished. Pffft! It was gone. I come from a long line of Yankees with big broad shoulders that tend to muscle things up and handle whatever comes their way. I just couldn't do that anymore. I was trying to handle Christina's needs and the emotional needs of our kids and save my law business all at the same time. I became completely overwhelmed.

It got to the point where I felt that my job each day was to get up and be the only one in charge of trying to catch a piano falling out of a fifth-floor window. It was like, "I got it, I got it!" But as much as I tried, it still looked like there was nothing in my life but more pianos coming out of windows. I had this feeling of getting squashed. When I went to a doctor and got on medication, it put a floor under things for me. I realized I didn't necessarily have to be a practicing lawyer. With Christina's encouragement, I left my job. I could just say, "Forget it." This helped both my psyche and the overall health of the family quite a bit.

The kids and I kick Christina out of the house every morning so she can go off and earn a living. I'm the "Mommy" in the family now.

If it were up to me, I'd take the whole country's mental health industry apart brick by brick.
—*JOHN*

You can't stop breathing just because you've got a mental illness. If you're okay enough to be outside of the hospital, you should be okay enough to be seen in public places like restaurants. I know it might not be easy for families to want to take the person who is overmedicated or who just doesn't "look right" out in public, but believe me, we appreciate it. I appreciate just being with everybody.

— DIANA

ill people, at least the ones I've met, aren't that way. My friends aren't like that.

I think I understand my illness better than anyone else does. I know what has happened to me and I know what treatments I've received. I'm in transition now, and I'm getting better because they have all these good medicines out there. I haven't been in a hospital for three years, and I'm trying to make sure things stay that way. I need to keep on growing. I live independently now, and I'm more hopeful than I ever was before, but I can't go any further until I find a job.

You can't stop breathing just because you've got a mental illness. If you're okay enough to be outside of the hospital, you should be okay enough to be seen in public places like restaurants. I know it might not be easy for families to want to take the person who is overmedicated or who just doesn't "look right" out in public, but believe me, we appreciate it. I appreciate just being with everybody. I didn't get taken to our last family get-together to visit my grandma because I couldn't afford the travel costs. That hurt me bad. I probably won't see Grandma again, because she is one hundred years old and she lives so far away.

I've always heard that Asian families think mental problems are shameful and that it means there is bad blood in the family. I've heard of some Asian families who believe mental illness is inherited by every other generation and only by girl children. In some Asian cultures, if you have a mental illness in your family, no one will marry into it even if the person they want to marry isn't the one who is sick.

Stigma starts at home. There was stigma in my family when I was growing up, and there is still stigma in my family right now. I've grown to accept it, and I pray that I can break through the barriers of that stigma with my family members and then with the community.

I was separated from my family during my growing-up years so my sisters and brother could be raised without any problems. I was separated from them for any bad behavior or if my parents thought something would trigger my illness. I was always in the hospital. I was always gone away from my home. I'd return home for maybe nine months and then I'd

be back in the hospital again. I had a hard time figuring out what was going on.

I still feel separated from my family because we're separated by different margins. My siblings are all professional people. Many times I think my family lives in a different world than I do. I live in one world; my family lives in another. I hope my sisters and brother will be closer to me one day. Now they are very pleasant to me, but I find that we don't talk freely. It's just the, "Hi, how are you," sort of things that we say to each other. They've got their answering machines, and often they don't return my phone calls because they're too busy doing things at work and for their children. They're trying to keep up with their world.

I think mental health consumers like me have to be a messenger to their families, to their loved ones, and to their friends. That way, we can all work together as a team. I've always wanted my family to understand mental illness. I once wrote an article about my illness. It wasn't a high achievement in the world, but to me it was very dynamic and special. I gave it to one of my sisters to read and she doodled all over the paper. I felt like she didn't understand a word of it. She didn't like my article. I didn't have the skills to let her know how a mentally ill person feels.

I'm in a stage of my recovery now where I can express myself more fluently, but it's still hard for me to be assertive with my family at times. I've found that friends are the best medicine, and throughout the years, they have helped me the most.

I met Dan at the clubhouse, and we became roommates two years ago. Often people like us can't afford to live by

Stigma starts at home. There was stigma in my family when I was growing up, and there is still stigma in my family right now. I've grown to accept it, and I pray that I can break through the barriers of that stigma with my family members and then with the community.

— DIANA

*My siblings are all professional people. Many times
I think my family lives in a different world than I do.
I live in one world; my family lives in another.*
—DIANA

themselves. They don't know how to get a roommate or what
avenues to take. There is a transitional living specialist at our
clubhouse, and she helped Dan and me get an apartment
together. We're doing okay. We're making it. We kind of out-
grew the clubhouse because we're too busy shopping and getting the things we need for our apartment. We do go to the
clubhouse at Christmas and at different times during the year
just to say hi.

I'm so glad I met Dan. I'm always learning something
from him. We're glad for all the good things that come from
being together. I just got my cosmetology license renewed
and I'm going to get a part-time job. It's been a dream of
mine for a very long time, and I feel good that some of my
dreams are coming true.

GEORGE

When Diana was in seventh grade, a school psychologist
called my wife and me one day. He told us, "Your daughter
climbed up on the roof at school this morning!" This psychologist—a so-called authority—thought there was something wrong with us as parents to make Diana behave the
way she did. We didn't know much about psychology back
then, so we wondered if there was something wrong with
us as parents, too.

As time went on, Diana would have periods of depression when she didn't do anything at all. Some days, she
wouldn't even go to school. She stayed in bed, didn't talk to
anybody, and just looked at the wall. Then she would become
manicky, always wanting to get out of the house and go some-

place. I would have to block the door to keep her in. It wasn't
easy coping. My wife and I were desperate, and we didn't know
what to do. We would say to each other that we'd lost our
daughter. We just lost her.

At times Diana wasn't conducive to reason, and Ruth and
I didn't know what to do with her. Confine her to a mental
hospital? We decided to do just that because we thought she
would be safe in the hospital. When she was in the hospital, we were relieved because we thought she might get some
help, but she really didn't. Diana escaped from the hospital
time and time again, hitchhiking on freeways all over the
country. We were always more worried about her when she
was out of the hospital, because we didn't know what was
going to happen to her.

Ruth and I joined a support group. We grabbed for anything that might help us learn how to keep Diana in a safe place
when she was at her worst. Once when I was at a support group
meeting, I got up and told people we had taken Diana down
to the police station that day and that we had to leave her there
until she could be placed in the hospital. We learned how to
get Diana incarcerated by the sheriff so she wouldn't endanger herself. Now that she is docile and better behaved, we have
slacked off going to these support meetings.

Ruth and I kept Diana's illness under cover as if everything were normal, because we felt the stigma. We didn't want
to divulge information about Diana's mental illness to other
people. Even now our neighbors don't know too much about
our daughter's condition. We keep it quiet.

I think it is more backwards in Asia than here in America.
They don't have all these theories about mental illness. If you
were mentally ill and sleeping all the time, Asians would think
you were just lazy. They might also think you are just plain
old bad and that you might need a good beating or something. If someone has the tendency to talk uncontrollably all
of the time, he'd probably be slapped. Asians think that slap-
ping is a remedy. They're still stuck in the old disciplinary
way of life. In other words, I think that there's no such thing
as being "mentally ill" in Asia.

*It wasn't easy coping. My
wife and I were desperate,
and we didn't know what
to do. We would say to each
other that we'd lost our
daughter. We just lost her.*
—GEORGE

Mentally ill people are just a small segment of our society and we should allow certain people to be like that. There's got to be differences. There are always different groups, and sometimes they don't accept each other. For instance, on a bus, there are people who are going to work, and others who are relaxing, and others who are struggling. We can't have a society with only CEOs.

—Dan

If a child in an Asian family had glaucoma, the parents would talk about it, but if an Asian family had a child who was mentally ill, they probably wouldn't mention it at all.

RUTH

George is Chinese, and I'm Japanese. We got married when the Japanese were at war with the Chinese. We have three other kids besides Diana. The boy has a PhD. One daughter is an administrator at UCLA, and the other teaches fifth grade.

Diana is a very gifted girl. Before she got sick, she used to play the violin beautifully, and academically she was always in the top 10 percent of her class. When she first got sick, she couldn't focus on those areas anymore. That was hard for George and me to accept. At the time, it took a lot of prayers. We're members of the First Baptist Church, and our family has always been very strong in our spiritual life. We had to go inward.

When Diana was younger, we had to travel a long way to visit her when she was in the hospital. It really broke my heart to hospitalize her so far away and only see her on weekends.

I never dreamed I would see the day that Diana would fit in and be part of society again. In the past three years, I've seen a complete change in her, something I thought I'd never see. She has overcome a lot, and I think it's remarkable.

Diana has a deep sense of spiritual strength. She and her friend, Dan, are very spiritual, and they go to church together. They are very loving. I can see the sweetness in my daughter now. Diana writes the nicest thank-you notes. I would like to tell people to never give up hope.

DAN

I have the same problem Diana has. I have bipolar disorder.

I had to find out for myself about mental illness. I had to find out I was different from most people. I learned about mental illness by going to therapy and by associating with other people who were mentally ill. I learned there is a group of people who are a little bit sad and a little bit happy, and they deserve to live, too. They deserve to be happy.

When I was sixteen, I felt different from the rest of my family. They fit together real good. They were in one group, and I was by myself. I did my own thing because I realized that I couldn't fit in with them. Before I was sixteen, we were all real chummy. After I turned sixteen, I became secretive and I didn't want to confide in them anymore. I took all the lumps by myself. I didn't share my problems with anyone else in my family because I thought they weren't interested. I didn't want to get too close to them because I was afraid that they would see the weakness in me.

My family believes that all people should be progressing. According to them, you've got to go to school or to work. If you're not doing something productive, they think there's something wrong with you. They can't see that mentally ill people sometimes burn out and can't do anything productive for a while. They don't realize that mentally ill people are just a small segment of our society and that we should allow certain people to be like that. There's got to be differences. There are always different groups, and sometimes they don't accept each other. For instance, on a bus, there are people who are going to work, and others who are relaxing, and others who are struggling. We can't have a society with only CEOs.

In Orange County, California, where I grew up, most people are so competitive that if you sat on the beach on a weekday, the cops would come over and think you were taking drugs because you'd be the only one there. Everybody else would be at work.

I had to learn to live with my mental illness. I had severe, wild mood swings that made it hard for me to fit in with most people, so I stayed on my own a lot. After I finished school, I supported myself by working in the fields. When you're young, you're strong. You can work fourteen hours a day with a mood disorder and still have the strength to deal with the mental anguish of it. But, as I got older, it started to take a toll on me. Trying to work while coping with a mental illness was like fighting two battles. I couldn't cope anymore. My job performance was getting worse because I was just plain worn out.

I've been accepted by most people around me, but sometimes when I get too manicky, people say, "Oh, Dan, you're too pushy," or something like that. It feels like I have to isolate myself sometimes because when I'm impulsive, I want to go with the way I feel. The environment doesn't allow me to do that because I've got to fit in. I have to accommodate—otherwise, I'll stand out.

I feel better now. I've gotten stronger over the years and I've learned how to build myself up in spite of all the opposition. I've learned there are lots of places where mentally ill people can go to get support. I found groups and made friends with people who are the same as me. Together, we don't have to try so hard to fit into the mainstream.

If you're a little different, people label you or reject you or make fun of you. They talk about you behind your back. In our support group at the clubhouse, we allow each other to be a little different, a little eccentric. I'd rather be with those guys who accept me than in some elite group that's cutting me down. I don't need that.

I had to find out for myself about mental illness. I had to find out I was different from most people. I learned about mental illness by going to therapy and by associating with other people who were mentally ill. I learned there is a group of people who are a little bit sad and a little bit happy, and they deserve to live, too. They deserve to be happy.

—DAN

Pete, Katie, Kevin, and Patrick

THE CURRIER FAMILY

PITTSFIELD, MASSACHUSETTS

PETE CURRIER / KATIE CURRIER / KEVIN CURRIER
PATRICK CURRIER

KATIE

IMAGINE THAT IT'S YOUR TENTH BIRTHDAY. Instead of having a party with your family and friends, you find yourself at two o'clock in the morning in an ambulance on your way to a psychiatric hospital. Imagine that you are acutely ill and very scared.

Your life for the next several months is a round of tests, medications, physicians, and therapists, while most other children your age are enjoying their summer vacation. You have been diagnosed with a major illness that is misunderstood by many people; an illness that causes a great deal of embarrassment and shame. Your family visits you as much as possible in the hospital, but it's difficult for you to understand that your mom and dad can't be there with you every day. You're away from home for ten months. It's hard to imagine this, isn't it? Yet, this is what happened to our son Kevin.

Kevin spiraled out of control when he was a very young child. He was always hyperactive, but he was also sweet and affectionate. When he was six, he had a head injury; he fell and ruptured his eardrum. Not too long afterward, he became aggressive, irritable, and violent. It was like having a whole new Kevin. He decompensated so rapidly that he ended up in a psychiatric hospital a few months later, and since then he has been hospitalized four more times. Kevin has a diagnosis of bipolar disorder, as does our older son, Patrick. Kevin's illness, however, is much more severe than his brother's. The boys, both of whom are on medication, are on different ends of the bipolar spectrum.

Kevin's first hospitalization was his shortest one, only eleven days. The hospital was over an hour away, and we could only visit him for twenty minutes at a time. We weren't even allowed to communicate with his different team members. The people there didn't believe in working with us. In fact, it turned out that Kevin's doctors thought that his acting out behavior was a sign that my husband, Pete, and I had been abusing him. They were suspicious of us! Pete and I were so devastated and shocked that we could barely hold it together. Although we were never formally accused of child abuse, I'll remember this trauma for the rest of my life. We took Kevin out of that hospital against medical advice. The rest of his hospitalizations have been elsewhere, and we've had good experiences. We've been treated with respect and as part of a team. This is so important to us.

Kevin's doctors thought that his acting out behavior was a sign that Pete and I had been abusing him. They were suspicious of us! Pete and I were so devastated and shocked that we could barely hold it together. Although we were never formally accused of child abuse, I'll remember this trauma for the rest of my life.
— *KATIE*

Kevin never got a card or heard from anyone in his school when he was hospitalized. This really stinks, because if he had been in the hospital for anything else, he would have gotten tons of support.

Kevin's bizarre behavior escalated as he got older. When he was ten, he became very acute. He was hypomanic, and out of control both at home and in school. One day he ended up in a tree, pulling his clothes off and singing obscene songs. It took Pete and I three hours to get him out of that tree and into the hospital. When he came home, he was depressed and so suicidal that he made a list of about twenty-five different ways to kill himself with everything from teaspoons to plastic bags! Pete and I had to go through the house and lock everything up. Kevin slept in our room with us. We even had to keep our bedroom door locked so he couldn't get out and harm himself.

We had to readmit Kevin to the hospital. While he was there, we realized we couldn't provide him with the intensive level of care that he needed on a daily basis. We just couldn't keep him safe at home any longer. After he stabilized, Kevin went into an acute residential treatment facility where he lived for almost a year. We only saw him on weekends, although he came home occasionally for short visits.

Patrick liked it when Kevin wasn't living at home. He had us to himself every night, and we played games and did fun things. When Kevin started coming home on weekends, you could see Patrick's resentment building up. He would purposely trigger his brother and then step back and watch the explosion. Patrick still does that sometimes.

Patrick ended up on medication when he hit puberty. Like Kevin, he was always hyperactive, even as an infant. We probably went through three cribs with him! Patrick went on Ritalin when he was young, and then, about a year ago, it stopped working. The dosage was increased, but it didn't help. He also began to have symptoms of obsessive-compulsive disorder; he would count and tap things repetitively. We once stopped at Dunkin' Donuts for coffee, and he started twirling around before he got back into the car. I realized he was counting

the number of times that he turned his body. I hadn't been aware of how much "counting" he had been doing all along, because Patrick hid his symptoms really well, as many kids with OCD do. I didn't even know that he had been acting strangely at school until his teacher called one day to say that he was standing up in class all the time and just blurting things out, along with other bizarre behaviors.

When Patrick asked us if he could try another medication, he was put on a low dose of an antidepressant. He became hypomanic on this medication, so he was switched to the same mood stabilizer that Kevin is on. A week later it kicked in. The old Patrick came back, and he has been doing well ever since. It seems as if both Kevin and Patrick are genetically programmed the same way: They both respond well to the same medication.

Kevin is back living at home with us now and he's doing okay, thanks to the many support systems we have in place for him. A strong parent network in our community has been advocating for change, and the increased services that are now available have enabled Kevin to remain in his own home.

Kevin might not be what you call a "normal" kid, but he is a good kid. He does things that other kids do, like play baseball and fish. Sometimes it's hard for people to remember that he's just a little kid. When he behaves in a bizarre way, the "real" Kevin gets lost. We try to explain to people, "This isn't really Kevin. It's just his disorder. When he's treated properly he will reappear." But usually by that point, people are alienated and confused.

In the beginning, if our friends or family members weren't supportive of us, we kind of pushed them aside in order to avoid their negative influence. We only wanted positive people around us, because our life was already so tough. I have supportive parents who are very involved with our family. They pretty much coparent our kids and are as important to the boys as we are. My father is Kevin's best friend. They talk once or twice a day, and Kevin sleeps over at his grandparents' house every weekend.

Mental illness can happen to anybody, and it can happen overnight. I like the story about a couple who decide to take a trip to Italy. They buy all the right guidebooks and they learn how to speak Italian, and then they get on an airplane and go. When they are about to land, they hear an announcement, "Welcome to Holland." They say, "Hey, wait a minute! We're not supposed to be in Holland. We planned to go to Italy!" The point of the story is that Holland has other things to offer, like tulips and windmills. For Pete and me, with our sons, it's as if we're not in Italy, but we're in Holland. It's different and not what we expected. I wouldn't have chosen to go down this route, but I'm not unhappy that I did.

PETE

Katie does most of the work when it comes to advocating for the boys, and I stay in the background and act as her support mechanism. She's the parent who is in the forefront of things, writing letters and meeting with the people who provide the services for our sons.

When Kevin first got sick, our friends didn't ask us much about him. They didn't say, "Oh, how is Kevin doing?" We heard nothing. In fact, they stopped asking us over to their houses or to go out with them because they thought their kids would catch whatever our kid had. Some of our friends just disappeared. Our entire life, including our social network, has changed because of mental illness. It's like we had an old life back then and a new life now.

I have new friends now. I can open up to them and say, "Hey, this is who I am; this is the hand I was dealt; this is what I'm trying to deal with." They seem to understand that. I've also made a few close friends at work, and they've been very supportive, too. If I need time off, I just ask for it. But no one truly understands what we go through on a day-to-day basis.

Many people don't even understand what bipolar illness is, so you have to explain that Kevin might behave in strange ways. We have new neighbors who just moved in over the winter when our kids were inside a lot. Now that it's spring,

they've asked us if our boys could do some yardwork for them. Patrick would be fine at this, but Kevin wouldn't. I'll have to tell them that Kevin has a problem and give them a "heads up" about him.

Sometimes when you mention mental illness to people, they take two steps backwards. Even some mental health professionals have put us on the defensive, by questioning our parenting skills and our home life. Our parenting skills are normal, but we're dealing with abnormal things on a daily basis. It was a relief for us when Kevin was finally diagnosed. Until then, everyone was looking at Katie and me and wondering what we did to bring this on.

There were definitely times when we felt like we were living in *The Twilight Zone*. We were stuck in the house without any help, and everyone else seemed to be leading a normal life out there. If someone was out walking their dog at night, they might hear me screaming, Patrick in tears, and Katie crying—all because Kevin couldn't fall asleep. If I were an outsider looking in, I might think, "What's going on in that house?" If you see a kid in a wheelchair, you might think, "Hey, that's a tough life. It must be hard on that family." But dealing with mental illness, now that's another story.

Kevin has been taking up most of our time, and it's hard to explain this to his brother, who is only thirteen. Patrick sometimes gets pushed aside because his symptoms aren't as severe as Kevin's are. Kevin's issues come first, and Patrick's issues sort of get shelved. I think there's some animosity between our two sons.

I would spend my last dime fighting for Kevin's right to be successful. There's something wrong with the system when professionals don't realize that this kid of ours has potential. If he had a physical disability, he would get a lot more services, but because he looks like a normal, good-looking kid, he's overlooked. We've had to hire lawyers to keep him in the appropriate classroom, and we are constantly battling on his behalf. There are good people out there who really know how to work well with kids like Kevin, and we need to find more of them. All I can do is just take one day at a time.

When Kevin first got sick, our friends didn't ask us much about him. They didn't say, "Oh, how is Kevin doing?" We heard nothing. In fact, they stopped asking us over to their houses or to go out with them because they thought their kids would catch whatever our kid had. Some of our friends just disappeared. Our entire life, including our social network, has changed because of mental illness. It's like we had an old life back then and a new life now.

—PETE

Standing: Helen *Seated:* Cindy

THE CATES FAMILY

NASHVILLE, TENNESSEE

HELEN CATES / CINDY CATES

CINDY

WHEN DEPRESSION HIT ME IN COLLEGE, I knew instantly that it was far more than just being in a bad mood. It was an experience unlike any I had ever gone through.

When most people are upset about something, they can take their minds off their problems by doing things like go for a walk, soak in a hot bath, or laugh with their friends. My depression wouldn't go away even if someone treated me to ice cream or told me that my hair looked nice or made any of those other gestures that people make when they sense you're depressed. But this feeling was something totally foreign. It was as if something had washed over me, and my brain just wasn't functioning. I felt like I was in a cavern somewhere. I had a bona fide illness, a brain disorder, and I was tormented by it. There were times when I thought I was losing my mind.

People have a hard time understanding that you can be psychologically healthy and still have a mental illness. They automatically think that if you have an emotional disorder, something in your past has triggered it. Either you've had a bad home life or you've been abused or you didn't get enough love from your mother. This isn't necessarily the case. I'm very well adjusted. I had a happy and stable family life, a normal childhood, and lots of friends. My doctor once said, "Psychologically, you're healthy as a horse, but you've got a real bad mental illness."

My mother deals with my illness head-on. She knows how awful it has been for me and she's been extremely supportive. I think the hardest part for my mother is to see my transformation when depression hits me. It's as if I'm not her "little girl" anymore. Instead, I'm a mass of hopelessness walking around in a body that looks like me but really isn't me. Gone are my mischievous personality and my quirky sense of humor. My soul is somewhere else.

I was hospitalized once, and I've been on medication that has kept me stable ever since. My doctor is optimistic that I won't have a relapse. The nature of my depression is that it is very episodic; it comes and goes. When I'm well, I feel totally different and the bad times seem unreal, like a hor-

> *People have a hard time understanding that you can be psychologically healthy and still have a mental illness. They automatically think that if you have an emotional disorder, something in your past has triggered it. Either you've had a bad home life or you've been abused or you didn't get enough love from your mother. This isn't necessarily the case. I'm very well adjusted. I had a happy and stable family life, a normal childhood, and lots of friends.*
>
> *— CINDY*

I think the hardest part for my mother is to see my transformation when depression hits me. It's as if I'm not her "little girl" anymore. Instead, I'm a mass of hopelessness walking around in a body that looks like me but really isn't me. Gone are my mischievous personality and my quirky sense of humor. My soul is somewhere else.

—CINDY

Cindy and Helen

ror movie. If I feel the illness breaking through, my medication is adjusted, and in a day or two, I'm fine again. I had a boyfriend once who said, "If you pray hard enough you will get off these medications." That's not true. I have a lifelong illness and it needs to be managed as such. I will be on meds for the rest of my life. They've saved my life.

Even though many women on antidepressants have healthy children, I'm worried about having kids. I'm also worried about my weight gain. I used to be very thin and I'm not eating any more food than I used to, but I've still gained thirty pounds in the past three years. Unfortunately, this is

a common side effect of some antidepressants, and a lot of women quit their medications because they gain weight. I considered that, but the risk of relapse is not worth it.

My depression is hard for people to grasp if they've never been there. When you drop off the face of the earth for a couple of months, you don't return phone calls, and your whole personality changes, people are curious. My illness was very confusing for my friends and quite difficult for me to explain to them. Sometimes it's even hard for me to understand what's going on. Luckily, my friends have stuck by me.

I don't feel comfortable bringing up my illness with just anyone, because the words "mental illness" create horrific images for so many people. I used to not talk about it much at all. I glossed over it or swept it under the rug, and this wasn't a healthy way to deal with what was going on with me. Now, I'm pretty up front about my diagnosis. I want to talk about my illness, but there are times when other people just don't want to hear about it. When I do talk about my depression, I prefer to use the words "brain disorder" rather than "mental illness," because it's a chemical thing. It's not my fault.

When I started working at a mental health agency, it was the first time I met other people who had experienced the same things that I had. This was very cathartic for me because it was my first opportunity to talk to people who had been there. I had never met anyone before who could tell me, "I've been where you are now, and it's not going to be like this for the rest of your life. You're going to get better."

I'm studying for my master's degree in counseling. When I talk to other students about mental illness, I never disclose that I have a diagnosis. If I discuss depression in class, I don't acknowledge that I have it. I do wonder what the other students would think if they knew, because sometimes I've gotten mad at some of the things they say and laugh about. This one guy wrote a paper about a research project and how he gave a student who had a psychological problem a "zombie pill." He was very flip about it. I felt this was so inappropriate. I wrote to him and said, "How would you feel if your daughter had a problem? Would you be this coy about it?" He realized that he should have been much more sensitive.

Mental illness is not a death sentence. I've been fortunate because I've gotten so much better. That which does not kill me can only make me stronger.

HELEN

When Cindy first got sick, there were times when I just didn't know what to do. The hardest part for me was trying to figure out how to be of help to her. Cindy's doctors didn't bother to communicate with the family or with me. Cindy once asked me if I would go see the psychiatrist with her, and he said he wouldn't treat her with me in the room. It wasn't that I wanted to interfere. I simply had some unanswered questions that were troubling me. I wanted to get answers.

When Cindy was hospitalized, no one explained to me what they were doing to her. I didn't even know if she would ever be well enough to come home again. I made all kinds of inquiries, but they were never answered. The doctor said my questions were ridiculous.

It bothers me when people dwell on their misfortunes. I feel for them, but I try to deal with tough situations and go forward rather than just belabor them. My method of coping is simply to have faith in God and place my trust in Him to care for my daughter as He has promised.

I am neither embarrassed nor ashamed that my daughter has a clinical depression that is categorized as a mental illness. It's an illness like any other illness. It is not a punishment, and it is not caused by anything the patient or family has done. It is treatable. Cindy can and does lead a productive and rewarding life. She has a positive attitude and a happy and outgoing personality. She's educating mental health consumers and advocating for them. I'm so proud of her.

> *I am neither embarrassed nor ashamed that my daughter has a clinical depression that is categorized as a mental illness. It's an illness like any other illness. It is not a punishment, and it is not caused by anything the patient or family has done. It is treatable.*
>
> —*HELEN*

Sandra and Cory

THE BEY FAMILY

PITTSBURGH, PENNSYLVANIA

SANDRA BEY / CORY BEY

SANDRA

PEOPLE WHO HAVE A MENTAL ILLNESS NEED TO BE HEARD. I want to talk about my experience because it's a way of giving back what's been given to me. I also want to help others understand that being mentally ill doesn't mean that you are crazy.

I've been a mental health consumer for twenty-five years. My journey with mental illness started when I was only twenty-six years old, right after I had my fourth child. At first, my family didn't understand what I was going through. They didn't know what I was talking about when I asked them to take me to a mental institution. They thought I was just pretending to be sick. I had to tell them, "I'm not pretending! This is for real."

I finally committed myself to a hospital, where I was first diagnosed as having paranoid schizophrenia and later on as having bipolar disorder. At one point, I became toxic on my medication and I almost died. I was catatonic. That's when my family finally understood that mental illness is a real disease.

I remember seeing my family members crying about me, but I was so psychotic that I didn't really understand why they were upset. People in my family were actually getting into fights over me. One person would say, "Sandra's crazy," and then all the others would get mad at him. I had been in the National Honor Society at school, and my illness just devastated my entire family. Where I had been the strongest member of my family, now I was the weakest.

I had no idea what a mental institution was like until I committed myself to one. I thought it would be like a regular hospital and that I would be safe. I didn't know there would be people walking around acting in bizarre ways. When I arrived and saw the six-inch-thick glass windows with the nurses and doctors safely behind them and everyone else walking around on the loose, I went back into my room, packed my bags, and headed for the elevator. The staff said I couldn't leave. I said, "Well, I'm not staying with these people. They're sick!" This happened on my first day on the ward, but I ended up staying there for thirty days. I began to get better.

AFTERWORD:
UNCLE PHIL'S BRAIN

David Maraniss

The Cummins Family

My mother was newly married and living in New York when she learned that her brother, Philip Dever Cummins, had suffered a mental breakdown. Sixty years later, the moment remained fixed in her memory. She was sitting on a bed in the living room of a cramped apartment, reading a letter from her mother in Ann Arbor. The report from home was warm, understated, and devastating: Irrational behavior. Depression. Hospitalization. All of it took my mother by surprise. A great sadness washed over her, and she began weeping for her brother and how terrible it must have been for him.

There is a story of mental illness in almost every family. My uncle Phil is the central character in ours, the foremost troubled mind emerging from our particular mix of history and genetics. Many relatives were burdened by depression or other disorders before and after him, but Phil carried the heaviest load. He was, in a sense, the exaggeration of us all. The same impulses that others struggled with occasionally, but that could be controlled or concealed enough for them to function in everyday society, overwhelmed him much of his life, starting with that long-ago spring when he was hospitalized at age twenty-two for what

experts today might classify as schizo-affective disorder.

By the time I got to know him, when I was about eleven, Phil was living with my grandparents at their redwood and stone farmhouse on the western edge of Ann Arbor. He had his own hideaway room in the basement down the hall from the white lift-up freezer where my grandmother kept her black walnut cookies. When we visited at Christmas or on summer vacation, the bedrooms filled quickly and I'd be sent down to Phil's room to sleep on a cot. I considered it an honor to be let into his special space. It signified that my uncle approved of me, which meant something, because he didn't approve of much. Some of my strongest childhood memories are of nights spent in that dark subterranean room: Phil on the edge of his bed, flicking the drooping end of his cigarette onto a ridged white saucer, soft yellow light filtering from his shortwave radio, his brow furrowed, a faint smile, and then a series of questions beginning with, "Dave, who has the strongest arm from right to third: Kaline, Clemente, or Colavito?" He might move from there to modern literature, about which I knew nothing. Was he mistaking me for my older sister and brother, the smart ones, or did he sense something that I didn't? I was amazed and secretly heartened by the way he took my answers seriously.

I had only a vague awareness then of the dimensions of Phil's mental history. My family had a strong humanist sensibility that honored every person and preferred poetic underdogs to self-satisfied winners, so this was not a matter of shame. There was nothing to hide in that respect, no embarrassment about having a crazy uncle. But along with the family's sensitivity and prevalent low-grade depression came a powerful respect for privacy and a tendency to avoid acknowledgment of irreversible pain. (My mother is the sort who, if you backed a car up over her foot, would apologize and say it was her fault.) It was from those impulses that Phil's story was left mostly untold.

There were some obvious ways that he differed from other adult males in the family. He never married. He lived with his parents. He did not work regularly and he kept odd hours, often staying in his room during daylight and then shuffling through the house in the middle of the night in his robe and slippers. His brown hair was usually wet and slicked back. He sometimes seemed to be chuckling at a joke understood only by him. When he laughed harder he crinkled his face so violently that it scared me. I heard him now and then criticizing, or even ridiculing, my little grandmother, which simply was not done. His gargly voice had a surprising hint of the south. But almost all that I knew about his history of hospitalization came from a few color slides among the scores of family scenes that my grandfather would show us on his projector. They were of Phil standing near a highway and a country bridge in some faraway place. I was told they were taken when my grandparents visited him during his long stay in North Carolina.

HIGHLAND HOSPITAL. Asheville, North Carolina. An Institution Employing All Rational Methods in the Treatment of Nervous, Habit, and Mental Cases: Especially Emphasizing the Natural Curative Agents— Rest, Climate, Water, Diet, Work, and Play

The old brochure describes such a beautiful place. From the grounds, Phil looked out on a vista of *near-by hills, with their soft green slopes, gradually blending with the more distant, rugged ranges till the skyline is broken by the pearly haze of far-off peaks.* From the tap he drank water of *crystalline clearness, perfect purity, complete softness and cool mountain freshness.* At the cafeteria his body was nourished with *a rational, scientific, wholesome, vitamin-rich, yet dainty, dietary.* From the moment he arrived at Highland Hospital in 1942, he was in the care of *a corps of over a hundred workers* overseen by Duke University professors of neuropsychiatry who believed they could determine the *present disorder and its causative factors* and then provide treatment for *the removal of both cause and effect.* The regimen included frequent examinations and discussions, regular hardball games between two teams of patients and doctors, the Blues and the Golds, light gardening and farming, work in the storehouse, hikes in the hills, horseshoes, table tennis, volleyball, board games, and dances.

Such serene surroundings, such a healthy environment. But for every sign of improvement there came a corresponding spell of withdrawal and despair. When Phil's behavior worsened, doctors tried to jolt him back with insulin shock therapy and electroshock treatments. The positive results in every case proved ephemeral. He remained hospitalized for seventeen years, the prime of his life, during which time the "cause and effect" of his troubles persisted and the only thing removed was part of his brain.

It was only recently, several years after Phil's death, that I began to appreciate the daily struggle of his long stay in Asheville. My awakening came when Aunt Jean, the family genealogist, sent me a box of documents from Phil's life. Inside were letters to Phil from his parents (my grandparents, Andrew and Grace Cummins), and a lesser number of letters from Phil to them or to other family members, as well as voluminous correspondence between my grandparents and various doctors at Highland Hospital. In some ways these papers seem anachronistic, evoking a time long gone from the mental health scene. The transforming world of psychotropic drugs was yet to be discovered. Doctors resorted more often to long-term institutionalization and such things as seizure-inducing shock treatments. The diagnostic vocabulary psychiatrists used then also had an archaic ring, the words less technical, more lyrical. (In their reports on Phil, they often noted that he was "too philosophical in his thinking.") But the story that emerges from the box is timeless nonetheless. There can be nothing outdated about a wounded mind and a family trying desperately to mend it.

Among the scores of letters, one provides the context for the others. It was from Phil to his parents, postmarked April 2, 1945. He was twenty-seven then, and entering his fourth year at the hospital. The previous fall he had sent a fairly upbeat letter home describing his daily routine, but then followed five months of silence. Now came the explanation, the most thorough written account of his despair.

Dear Mother and Dad,

I am sorry to be so tardy in writing you, but it is difficult when one feels that anything one has to say is going to be a burden on the reader. I only hope that things aren't actually as bad or rather as hopeless as they seem to me at present. I know that one should be careful in saying a thing like this. I could go on writing about what is going on here, baseball, work, etc. but that would be just holding back on the things that are uppermost in my mind. For I have been feeling pretty terrible and despondent for a long time now and without any signs of improvement. Dr. Billig [Otto Billig, Highland Hospital's chief psychiatrist] says that he is convinced that I have improved greatly and am still getting better, but to tell you the truth, I feel worse than I did when I came down here and that after four years of so-called hospitalization, I just feel that I am doomed to gradual incapacitation of a more or less general nature, being regarded as something of a subhuman species halfway between a gorilla and a man. For I am pretty much all by myself in the world, have difficulty in making friends and adjusting myself with no ideas practically, nothing to say and getting no enjoyment or satisfaction out of anything I do. I am also tired most of the time, worried, apprehensive, and very unhappy. It's just downright torture, that's all it is.

One shudders to imagine being a parent reading that letter from your son. Not much room for encouragement, but my grandfather, a construction engineer, searched his rational mind for angles of hope. In his next letter to Phil, he argued that the brutally realistic nature of Phil's self-analysis in itself represented an improvement from the bizarre and delusional behavior that had led to his hospitalization in the first place. "To have reached that point has been a wonderful accomplishment," Grandfather wrote. With enough effort and time, he said, a "reasonable amount of happiness would come," although "nobody probably is happy all of the time." Tests showed Phil's I.Q. was an exceptional 150, meaning that he "could accomplish a lot worthwhile for society" as soon as he felt secure and confident. To counter the sense of being alone in the world, he recited a list of his son's old friends and then argued, "After all, one only has a very few real friends." He closed by inviting Phil to visit Ann Arbor. The peas, radishes, and onions were up.

Phil eventually got away from Asheville for three weeks. According to a letter grandfather later wrote to Dr. Billig, the visit to Ann Arbor was soothingly routine, at least on the surface. Phil saw his brothers and sisters, talked about his condition, went to shows, bowled, played table tennis and bridge, watched basketball and hockey games at the University of Michigan, and "voluntarily helped around the house." He also spent "quite a bit of time" reading Thomas Mann's *The Magic Mountain,* in German.

As engaged as he was in Ann Arbor, Phil could not forget his worries. "On the whole his sense of well-being was not good," his father reported. "He complained of headaches and tiredness and evidently thinks a lot about his difficulties." He was indeed a chronic hypochondriac, a trait that later would become all too familiar to many of his younger relatives, including my brother Jim and me and several of our children. During Phil's visit home, he read his father's magazines and took particular note of insurance company ads that would give him "ideas about physical ailments." He would then "magnify the symptoms." He also read an article about mental illness in *Newsweek* that reinforced his feelings of hope-lessness and left him further depressed.

My grandfather suffered from minor depression himself and had reached some conclusions over the years about the best way to counteract it. For the most part he had been suc-cessful, at least to the extent that he rarely showed his inner struggle to his family or society. In letters to his son, one can see him hoping upon hope that what worked for him could help someone he loved who was in a far more debilitating mental state. One night in February 1946, after paying a working visit to a Morton Salt plant in Manistee, Michigan, he took out the desk stationery from the Hotel Chippewa and wrote his son a letter filled with his homegrown psy-chology. It read in part:

I would suggest that you concentrate the mind on something other than yourself. You will feel better and time will go faster. I found that out at the hospital when I was hurting. Effort I believe will make it possible to minimize the pain due to trouble or any other reason. You know Phil if in your letters you did not say you were having trouble one would never know it. I am not saying that as a suggestion that you don't mention it, in fact I want you to feel entirely free to say just what you do feel. I mentioned it only to emphasize how rational, rea-sonable, sympathetic and intelligent your letters are. You know what FDR said during the depression viz "The only thing we have to fear is fear itself" and I believe that applies in your case. The biggest obsta-cle confronting you is the fear you have of the future. Yet your I.Q., your general conduct and ability it seems to me does not warrant that belief. In any case DON'T GIVE UP. Also try to see as many funny things in life as you can . . . I'm making a collection of jokes. Tell me any new ones you have heard. Here is one for you . . .

He then recounted a corny old story involving the pro-ducer Darryl Zanuck and a would-be actor who stuttered. If only a joke collection could have been enough.

The next several months were better for Phil, but he took another turn for the worse in the summer of 1946, a regres-sion documented month by month in reports from the Highland doctors to my grandparents. First came a report that Phil exhibited "a sense of unreality." Next he was show-ing "great concern about other people's influence upon him." By September he was displaying "bizarre behavior" that com-pelled the staff to confine him to the building and resume treatments of subshock doses of insulin. All of this was received with ever deeper sadness and concern by my grand-parents, who refused to give up hope that some treatment could return Phil to a relatively normal life. In the spring of 1947, my grandfather's search for cures led him to explore, for the first time, the possibility of a brain operation. In a letter to Dr. Billig, he asked: "Do you think that this holds any promise in his case and does such a procedure call for a special diagnosis as well as special surgery available only at certain hospitals?"

Literature teems with tales from asylums and mental hos-pitals that are cold or brutal warehouses where patients are mistreated or regarded as the very "subhuman" species that Phil feared he had become. Highland Hospital seems not to fall into that category. As I pored over the letters sent to my grandparents, it struck me from both the frequency and the substance of their reports that these doctors cared about Phil and were doing the best they could, given what their pro-fession understood about mental illness at the time and the limited number of treatments available. Without being overly harsh or fatalistic, they grasped the seriousness of Phil's con-dition and the uncertainty of his recovery. Dr. Billig, in responding to the question about brain surgery, confessed that after treating Phil for more than five years he was "some-what at a loss" about the best course of action. The shock treatments seemed to have lost some effectiveness, he said, but a brain operation, while successful in some cases, usu-ally was recommended for psychoses "of a somewhat different type." He nonetheless told my grandfather that it was worth considering further, and passed along the name of a specialist in Washington.

Two weeks later, another Highland psychiatrist, Dr. Joseph Goldstein, sent a report to Ann Arbor stating that he and others on the staff did not consider Phil a suitable candidate for a lobotomy: "The operation as a rule is hardly to be considered seriously for one who has been making a fairly good hospital adjustment, such as Phil has been doing. It certainly usually is reserved for cases showing much more behavior disturbance. Also, it should be borne in mind that the operation, even with the most favorable response, tends to have certain side-effects, such as impairment in ability to plan, difficulties in initiative, tendencies to impulsiveness, child-like behavior at times, etc., as well as, of course, certain risks and expenses associated with the operation itself."

But as Phil's condition worsened early that summer, the Highland doctors changed course again. What had been deemed no longer effective (electroshock) or unpromising (brain surgery) were back in the mix. They told my grandfather that they had been using a "more intensive" form of shock treatment recently, and then explained, "By intensive, we mean decreasing the time interval between the treatments." There was no change in the total number of treatments or the intensity of each treatment. "It may possibly only have a temporary effect," Dr. Edward A. Tyler wrote, "but would give us some idea as to what we might expect from a pre-frontal lobotomy, if that became necessary at a later date." The alternative, in Tyler's opinion, was to place Phil in the "locked section in the back hall." Not much of a choice.

The cycle of hope and despair continued. Two weeks after my grandfather gave Highland permission to perform intensive electroshock treatments, he received a positive report from Dr. Tyler. There had been a "marked change" in Phil. He was now said to be "very friendly, cooperative, outgoing…again neat and clean" and played "an excellent game of baseball on the 4th of July." The optimistic outlook in this case was even shared by Phil himself, who wrote a buoyant letter to my parents, his sister and brother-in-law. It began:

Dear Mary and Elliott,

How are you people after all these months? I sure would like to see you and the old homeland again before long, at least for a little while. I hope that you are all actually in good health and spirits and are enjoying life.

The folks in A.A. (Ann Arbor) have undoubtedly told you something of what has been going on lately with me. The electric shock treatments which Dr. Tyler gave me are proving very effective in a real way (that is, a way that I can feel & understand).

He was feeling better than at any time since he was a kid, Phil told my parents. In his unforgettable letter of despair two years earlier, he had refused to write about his daily activities in Asheville because they would only mask deeper feelings of hopelessness. Now he was eager to tell relatives what he was doing: how he hit a double over the center fielder's head and made only one error at second base, and shot a bull's-eye in archery from forty yards out and couldn't wait to start pitching horseshoes again, just like he had done in his childhood. He recalled the carefree days in Jackson, Michigan, when he and his brother Bob would play at "the neighborhood courts down the street from Judy's toward E. Sharp Park"—and the time when he pitched twelve straight ringers.

Phil's brighter attitude led to another visit home. A hospital caretaker put him on a Delta Airlines flight to Detroit that landed at eight on the evening of August 11. For the one-week visit, the family was under instructions to "just treat him as though he had been in the hospital for a physical illness and was at home for a short period before his recuperation." He played golf, saw some college friends, and spent two days in Detroit visiting my parents. In a letter back to the doctors, my grandfather reported that Phil "talked freely about the electroshock treatments and seemed to be thinking some of the future"—all good signs.

Then, in November, another unfortunate turn. Phil had relapsed into "fantastic thinking" and was said to be "entirely

Agoraphobia: An anxiety disorder, which refers to a fear of being in places where escape might be difficult. It is also described as a fear of open spaces. People with agoraphobia suffer anxiety about being in places or situations that may be difficult or embarrassing to escape, such as an elevator. In extreme cases, persons with agoraphobia may even be afraid to leave their house.

Anorexia Nervosa: A type of eating disorder characterized by an intense fear of gaining weight or becoming fat, even though the person who has this disorder is underweight. There is a refusal to maintain normal body weight, a severe disturbance in the way in which one's body weight or shape is experienced, and a denial of the seriousness of the current low body weight.

Anxiety: A diffuse or "free-floating" feeling of dread, apprehension, or unexplained discomfort.

Anxiety Disorders: Millions of Americans have anxieties and fears that are overwhelming and persistent, often drastically interfering with daily life. These people suffer from anxiety disorders, a widespread group of psychiatric disorders that can be terrifying and crippling. The conditions classified as anxiety disorders include panic disorder, phobias, obsessive-compulsive disorder, post-traumatic stress disorder, and generalized anxiety disorder.

Attention-Deficit/Hyperactivity Disorder (ADHD): A disorder that is characterized by symptoms of inattention to a degree that is inconsistent with developmental levels. For example, a child or an adult with this disorder often fails to give close attention to details or makes careless mistakes in schoolwork, work, or other activities. They often have difficulty sustaining attention in tasks or play activities, and are easily distracted by extraneous stimuli. It is also characterized by symptoms of hyperactivity—for example, the inability to sit still or to engage in leisure activities quietly. People who have ADHD are often described as being "driven by a motor" and lacking impulse control.

Bipolar Disorder: A periodic, recurrent mood disorder with moods that swing between depression and mania. Also called manic-depressive disorder, it is found in about 1 percent of the general population. People who have this disorder tend to have manic periods when they cannot sleep, are hyperactive, and have grandiose ideas. After a period of mania, a period of depression may follow when life does not seem worth living and suicide is often considered.

Body Dysmorphic Disorder: Severe and intense preoccupation with an imagined defect in appearance, which causes clinically significant distress or impairment in social, occupational, or other important areas of functioning.

Borderline Personality Disorder: A pervasive pattern of instability of interpersonal relationships, self-image, and emotional affect, and marked impulsivity beginning by early adulthood.

Clinical Depression (or Major Depression): An illness expressed by a combination of symptoms, including persistent sadness; feelings of worthlessness and despair. These symptoms can lead to suicide, low energy, diminished sexual interest, lack of concentration, and changes in the ability to work, sleep, eat, and enjoy once-pleasurable activities. Somewhere between 5 to 10 million people in the United States are affected by this illness. The causes of this illness may include genetic, familial, biochemical, physical, social, and psychological factors.

Clinical Depression with Psychotic Features: A condition in which depression is associated with delusional thinking.

Delusions: Fixed, irrational ideas not shared by others, that do not respond to reasoned argument and have no logical basis.

Developmental Disabilities: Developmental disabilities are handicapping disorders present at birth or developing in early childhood. They include mental retardation and pervasive developmental disorders such as autistic disorders. They are not the same as mental illness.

Diagnosis: The classification of a disease by studying its signs and symptoms.

Dissociative Identity Disorder (formerly called Multiple Personality Disorder): The presence of two or more distinct identities or personality states that recurrently take control of the person's behavior.

Dual Diagnosis: Dual diagnosis refers to the co-occurrence of mental health disorders and substance abuse disorders (alcohol and/or drug dependence or abuse). Alcohol and drugs are often used by a person who has a mental illness to "mask" painful symptoms, which they may not recognize or understand.

Electroconvulsive Therapy (also known as electroshock therapy or ECT): ECT is the passage of an electric current through the brain to induce alterations in the brain's electrical activity. This treatment is used primarily for patients who suffer from intractable depression and/or who do not respond to medication.

Flat Affect: Absence of or diminution of emotional tone or outward emotional reaction typically shown under similar circumstances.

Hallucinations: Visual, auditory, or olfactory perceptions that occur without any external stimulus. Sensory messages to the brain from the eyes, ears, nose, skin, and taste buds become confused, and the person may actually hear, see, smell, or feel sensations that are not real. People may have visual hallucinations, such as seeing a door in a wall where no door exists. Colors, shapes, and faces may change before the person's eyes. There may also be hypersensitivity to sounds, tastes, and smells. Sense of touch may also be distorted, and someone may literally "feel" that his or her skin is crawling.

Involuntary Admission: The process of entering a hospital is called admission. Voluntary admission means the patient requests inpatient treatment and is free to leave the hospital whenever he or she wishes. Involuntary admission is when a person who is very ill is admitted to a mental health facility against their will through the use of a court order.

Mania: A mood state with symptoms such as extreme elation, increased energy, rapid speech, and grandiose ideas in which the subject believes himself possessed of great wealth, intellect, importance, or power. People experiencing mania can also exhibit poor judgment and inappropriate behaviors such as disastrous spending sprees, unwise financial decisions, etc.

Mental Health Consumer: The current language used to describe a person who has a mental illness and is a client in the mental health system.

Mental Illness: According to the National Alliance for the Mentally Ill, "Serious mental illnesses are biologically based brain diseases and they are no one's 'fault.' The behaviors of families themselves are not the direct cause of serious mental illness." The National Institute of Mental Health estimates that one out of five families in the United States has a loved one with a mental illness. Far more common than cancer, diabetes, heart disease, and arthritis, mental illness can often be successfully treated, though not cured, with medication. Physiological abnormality and/or biochemical irregularity in the brain can cause substantial disorder of thought, mood, perception, orientation, or memory, which can impair judgment, behavior, capacity to reason, or ability to meet the ordinary demands of life. As with physical illness, there are many different kinds of mental illness."

Mental Retardation: Usually present from birth or early infancy, this condition involves deficits in learning ability and the intellectual process. Mental retardation is not the same as mental illness.

Obsessive-Compulsive Disorder (OCD): A disease affecting more than 4 million Americans. These individuals have persistent repetitive thoughts (obsessions) and have the need to repeat certain actions over and over (compulsions). They are compelled to repeat illogical behavior, such as constant washing of hands, counting windows of buildings or tiles on a wall or floor, and checking and rechecking to see if a particular "chore," such as the locking of a door at night or turning off the stove, was done. These compulsive behaviors or rituals can be extremely time-consuming and can interfere with normal functioning.

Panic Disorder: People suffering from panic disorder, one of the anxiety disorders, experience repeated feelings of intense, sudden terror or impending doom and disruptive physical symptoms that can include: a racing, pounding heartbeat; chest pain (feelings similar to a heart attack); breathlessness; choking sensation; sweating; trembling; and tingling or numbness. Panic attacks can happen several times a week or even within the same day. Panic disorder sufferers often live in fear of having another attack, because they can occur without any warning. In many cases, these attacks come "out of the blue," which is to say they are not directly connected with a specific traumatic event or situation. They typically "peak" within ten minutes of their onset, leaving the individual emotionally drained and frightened. The exact cause of panic disorder is unknown, but it is associated with multiple physiological factors and is responsive to medication. Panic disorder affects more than 6 million Americans and more than twice as many women as men.

Paranoia: Individuals with paranoia often overanalyze situations, are suspicious of others' motives, and perhaps are hypochondriacal. Trivial events are blown out of proportion, and the person generally believes that others are "out to get" him or her or are plotting against them. Some people feel they are being persecuted and are convinced they are being spied on. Paranoia falls within the category of delusional thinking.

Personality Disorders: Personality disorders are habitual patterns of behaving and responding that negatively affect a person's ability to function in everyday activities, especially work, family, and social life. There are biological and psychological components to most personality disorders, and the preferred treatment is psychotherapy, although medication may be needed to treat serious symptoms.

Phobia: A term that is applied to any type of disorder characterized by the presence of irrational or exaggerated fears of objects or situations. Some of the better known phobias are claustrophobia (fear of being enclosed), agoraphobia (fear of open spaces), and hydrophobia (fear of water).

Post-Traumatic Stress Disorder: An anxiety disorder that develops in response to an event that is "outside the range of normal" human experience; it is characterized by intrusive memories of the traumatic incident, emotional withdrawal, and increased arousal levels.

Psychosis: A mental state characterized by significant distortion or disorganization of a person's mental capacity, emotional response, and capacity to recognize reality. A person who is psychotic has a diminished capacity to communicate with and relate to others, to the degree of interfering with his/her capacity to cope with the ordinary demands of everyday life.

Psychotherapy: Treatment in which an individual deals with their problems through verbal "give and take" with a therapist. There are many forms of psychotherapy practiced by social workers, psychologists, psychiatrists, and psychotherapists.

Schizophrenia: A serious illness that often results in psychosis, disorders in the thinking processes, such as delusions and hallucinations, and an extensive withdrawal of the individual's interest from other people in the outside world. People with schizophrenia will often hear voices, which sometimes can be threatening or condemning. Schizophrenia is now thought to be a group of mental disorders rather than a single entity, and onset is generally between the ages of sixteen to twenty-five. It is not the same as multiple or "split" personality.

Side Effects: Side effects of psychiatric medications occur when a reaction to a medication goes beyond or is unrelated to the drug's therapeutic effect. Some side effects are tolerable, but some are so disturbing that the medication must be stopped. Less severe side effects include dry mouth, restlessness, stiffness, and constipation. More severe side effects include blurred vision, body tremors, nervousness, sleeplessness, tardive dyskinesia, suicidal ideation, and blood disorders.

Social Phobia: A persistent irrational fear of situations in which the person may be closely watched and judged by others, such as public speaking, eating, or using public facilities. Social phobias are characterized by fear and avoidance of situations in which a person may be subject to the scrutiny of others.

Thought Disorder: Clear, goal-directed thinking becomes increasingly difficult, as expressed in a diffuseness of speech. Thoughts may be slow to form, may come very fast, or may not come at all. The person may jump from topic to topic, seem confused, or have difficulty making simple decisions. Thinking may be colored by delusions, which are false beliefs that have no logical base.

Tourette's Syndrome: A disorder, which develops in childhood, characterized by multiple motor and verbal tics that may develop into coprolalia (the compulsion to shout obscenities). It is not considered to be a mental illness.

BRING
NOTHING TO HIDE,
the touring photo-text exhibit,
to your community

*Children viewing a
Family Diversity Project's
Exhibit
Madison, WI*

Nothing to Hide: Mental Illness in the Family is not only a book, but it is also a touring photo-text exhibit. It has traveled nationwide since 1999 to high schools, universities, mental health centers, hospitals, medical schools, public libraries, statehouses, corporations, museums, and conferences. You can bring this powerful exhibit to your community as a way of bringing media and public attention to the issues people face when they live with mental illness. By bringing visibility to people coping with mental illness, this exhibit helps fight the stigma associated with psychiatric disorders.

The exhibit consists of twenty museum-quality, framed, ready-to-hang photographs and brief interview text panels. Family Diversity Projects, Inc. distributes multiple copies of *Nothing to Hide*, and their staff will work with you to make this exhibit an educational and enlightening event in your community.

Family Diversity Projects, Inc. (FDP) is a non-profit organization founded by interviewer-editor Peggy Gillespie and photographer Gigi Kaeser. FDP circulates three other photo-text exhibits: *Of Many Colors: Portraits of Multiracial Families*; *Love Makes a Family: Lesbian, Gay, Bisexual, and Transgender People and their Families*; and *In Our Family: Portraits of All Kinds of Families*.

For information about how to bring any of these exhibits to your community, please contact:

Family Diversity Projects, Inc.
PO Box 1246
Amherst, MA 01004-1246
Phone: (413) 256-0502
Fax: (413) 253-3977
Email: info@familydiv.org
Website: www.familydiv.org

National Association of School Psychologists (NASP) promotes educationally and psychologically healthy environments for all children and youth, by implementing research-based, effective programs that prevent problems, enhance independence, and promote optimal learning. This end is accomplished through state-of-the-art research and training, advocacy, ongoing program evaluation, and caring professional service. 4340 East West Highway, Suite 402, Bethesda, MD 20814 Phone: (301) 657-0270 Web: www.nasponline.org

National Association of Social Workers (NASW) is the largest membership organization of professional social workers in the world, with more than 150,000 members. NASW works to enhance the professional growth and development of its members, to create and maintain professional standards, and to advance sound social policies. 750 First Street N.E., Suite 700, Washington, D.C. 20002-4241 Phone: (202) 408-8600 or (800) 638-8799 Web: website@naswdc.org

National Depressive and Manic-Depressive Association (National DMDA) works to educate patients, families, professionals, and the public concerning the nature of depressive and manic-depressive illnesses as treatable medical diseases; foster self-help for patients and families; eliminate discrimination and stigma; improve access to care; and advocate for research toward the elimination of these illnesses. National DMDA has a nationwide grassroots network of chapters and support groups. 730 N. Franklin Street, Suite 501, Chicago, IL 60610-7204 Phone: (800) 826-3632 or (312) 642-0049 Fax: (312) 642-7243 Web: www.ndmda.org

National Mental Health Association (NMHA) is the country's oldest and largest nonprofit organization addressing all aspects of mental health and mental illness. NMHA works to improve the mental health of all Americans, through advocacy, education, research, and service. 1021 Prince Street, Alexandria, VA 22314 Phone: (703) 684-7722 Fax: (703) 684-5968 Web: www.nmha.org

National Institute of Mental Health (NIMH) prioritizes their work in four broad areas: (1) fundamental research on brain, behavior, and genetics; (2) rapid translation of basic discoveries into research on mental disorders; (3) research that directly impacts the treatment of individuals with mental disorders, including clinical trials and studies of treatment and preventive interventions in "real world" settings; and (4) research on child development and childhood mental disorders. 6001 Executive Boulevard, Room 8184, MSC 9663, Bethesda, MD 20892-9663. Phone: (301) 443-4513 Fax: (301) 443-4279 E-mail: nimhinfo@nih.gov Web: www.nimh.nih.gov

Obsessive-Compulsive Foundation (OCF) is an international organization composed of people with OCD and related disorders, their families, friends, professionals, and other concerned individuals. The mission of OCF is to educate the public and professional communities about OCD, to provide assistance to individuals with OCD, and to support research into the causes and effective treatments of OCD and related disorders. 337 Notch Hill Road, North Branford, CT 06471 Phone: (203) 315-2190 Fax: (203) 315-2196 E-mail: info@ocfoundation.org Web: www.ocfoundation.org

Substance Abuse and Mental Health Services Administration (SAMHSA) is the federal agency charged with improving the quality and availability of prevention, treatment, and rehabilitation services in order to reduce illness, death, disability, and cost to society resulting from substance abuse and mental illness. 5600 Fishers Lane, Rockville, MD 20857 Phone: (301) 443-0001 Fax: (301) 443-1563 E-mail: info@samhsa.gov Web: www.samhsa.gov

BOOK LIST

Children's Books about Mental Illness (Grades K–6)

Hamilton, DeWitt. *Sad Days, Glad Days.* Morton Grove, IL: Albert Whitman, 1995.

In this book, Amanda wants a kitten, but her mother, who is clinically depressed, says caring for it would take too much energy. As Amanda feeds a stray cat, she learns to accept her mother's condition.

Hanson, Regina. *The Face at the Window.* New York: Clarion, 1997.

In this book, Dora is frightened walking to school past Miss Nella's house because the old woman seems to see things that aren't there and has "such strange and scary ways." Teachers will find this an interesting stepping-stone to discussions of mental illness.

Torney, Carrie Lyn. *What's Wrong with Nick.* P.O. Box 972, Claremont, NH: Friend of Nick's. Available by mail for $3.95.

By means of a story about two boys, one of whom has schizophrenia, this book explains mental illness to young children. Written by a counselor, it has the mother explain that her son often doesn't leave his house to play because he sometimes hears voices.

Books for Young Adults

Bennett, James. *I Can Hear the Mourning Dove.* Boston, MA: Houghton Mifflin, 1990.

This tale follows the painful, introspective progress of a teenage girl through years of mental illness. Devastated by the recent death of her father and recovering from her own suicide attempt, Grace tries to pick up the pieces of her shattered world.

Cobain, Bev. *When Nothing Matters Anymore: A Survival Guide for Depressed Teens.* Minneapolis, MN: Free Spirit, 1998.

A guide to understanding and coping with depression, discussing the different types, how and why the condition begins, how it may be linked to substance abuse or suicide, and how to get help.

Naylor, Phyllis Reynolds. *The Keeper.* New York: Atheneum, 1986.

This is a story about a middle-school boy, Nick, coming to terms with his mentally ill father. The story is written from Nick's point of view.

Vonnegut, Mark. *The Eden Express.* New York: Dell, 1998.

The author describes his three severe schizophrenic episodes in the early 1970s. He recovered and became a physician.

Adult Books about Mental Illness

Adamac, Christine. *How to Live With a Mentally Ill Person: A Handbook of Day-to-Day Strategies.* New York: John Wiley & Sons, Inc., 1996.

Amador, Xavier, and Anna-Lisa Johanson. *I Am Not Sick, I Don't Need Help! Helping the Seriously Mentally Ill Accept Treatment: A Practical Guide for Families and Therapists.* Peconic, NY: Vida Press, 2000.

Backlar, Patricia. *The Family Face of Schizophrenia: True Stories of Mental Illness with Practical Advice from America's Leading Experts.* Los Angeles, CA: J. P. Tarcher, 1995.

Baron-Faust, Rita. *Mental Wellness for Women.* New York: William Morrow and Company, 1997.

Carter, Rosalyn, and Susan K. Golant. *Helping Someone With Mental Illness: Compassionate Guide for Family, Friends, and Caregivers.* New York: Times Books, 1996.

Casey, Nell. *Unholy Ghost: Writers on Depression.* New York: William Morrow/Avon, 2000.

Copeland, Mary Ellen. *The Depression Workbook: A Guide to Living with Depression and Manic Depression.* Oakland, CA: New Harbinger Publications, 1992.

Cronkite, Kathy. *On the Edge of Darkness: Conversations About Conquering Depression.* New York: Dell, 1995.

age thirteen, addresses the facts, fears, and fictions of depression. Interspersed with lively graphics and music, the video teaches adults and children to recognize symptoms, understand treatment, and work together to overcome this serious disorder. An accompanying handbook is also available. Mental Health Association of Summit County, P.O. Box 639, Cuyahoga Falls, OH 44222

Families Coping with Mental Illness is a video in which ten people share their experiences of having a family member with schizophrenia or bipolar disorder. The Mental Illness Education Project Videos, 22-D Hollywood Avenue, Hohokus, NJ 07423 Phone: (201) 652-1989 or (800) 343-5540 Fax: (201) 652-1973 Web: www.miepvideos.org

Invisible Workforce features a diverse group of over twenty-five employers, job developers, and employees with psychiatric disabilities. Through personal interviews, they speak of their experiences and offer sensitive and practical suggestions to help others achieve joining or rejoining the workforce. The Mental Illness Education Project Videos, 22-D Hollywood Avenue, Hohokus, NJ 07423 Phone: (201) 652-1989 or (800) 343-5540 Fax: (201) 652-1973 Web: www.miepvideos.org

I Love You Like Crazy: Being a Parent With Mental Illness illustrates how consumers balance the challenges of mental illness with the needs of their children. Eight articulate mothers and fathers with a wide range of serious disorders discuss their sense of disempowerment and invisibility at the hands of well-meaning social, legal, and familial systems. They poignantly express their grief about how their illnesses have affected their ability to parent. The Mental Illness Education Project Videos, 22-D Hollywood Avenue, Hohokus, NJ 07423 Phone: (201) 652-1989 or (800) 343-5540 Fax: (201) 652-1973 Web: www.miepvideos.org

Mental Illness: The Family's Story offers insight into schizophrenia as it focuses on a variety of issues that face the families of those with mental illness. This video is available for bor-

rowing or viewing at more than 2,000 public libraries throughout the United States. National Alliance for the Mentally Ill/Southwestern Pennsylvania Phone: (412) 366-3788

Stigma . . . In Our Work, In Our Lives showcases interviews with people from mental health and substance abuse communities: consumers, families, providers, educators, and administrators. Created by the antistigma project "On Our Own." Video available through the Massachusetts Department of Mental Health, 25 Staniford Street, Boston, MA 02114 Phone: (617) 727-5600 Fax: (617) 727-4350 Web: www.state.ma.us/eohhs/agencies/dmh.htm

The Stigma of Mental Illness features Dr. Ken Duckworth, medical director of the Massachusetts Mental Health Center. He confronts the ways in which stigma has a powerful impact on people who struggle with psychiatric disorders. This excellent video is available through the Massachusetts Department of Mental Health. 25 Staniford Street, Boston, MA 02114 Phone: (617) 727-5600 Fax: (617) 727-4350 Web: www.state.ma.us/eohhs/agencies/ dmh.htm

Straight Talk About Mental Illness features teens asking questions and sharing their feelings about mental illness with a psychiatrist. The tape is designed to teach students and teachers how to recognize the symptoms of depression, manic-depression, and schizophrenia, and how to get help for these disorders. It is accompanied by teaching materials and can be purchased from the National Alliance for the Mentally Ill. Phone: (888) 780-4167

The Touching Tree is the story of Terry, whose feelings of fear and isolation interfere with his daily activities. A special teacher takes an interest in him, helping him understand his illness and begin to recover. The focus of the tape is obsessive-compulsive disorder, but many of the situations are typical of those experienced by children with other mental illnesses. Obsessive-Compulsive Foundation, P.O. Box 70, Milford, CT 06460 Phone: (203) 315-2190

The Visionaries is a television series on PBS, which features a segment on Gould Farm, a community of more than 100 people—farmers, gardeners, cooks, forestry managers, weavers, social workers, musicians, grandparents, parents, and children—which provides psychiatric rehabilitation for mentally ill guests. The entire community cares for a hundred acres of farmland and gardens. The Gould Farm film, hosted by actor Sam Waterston, was awarded the National Educational Broadcast Media Award by the National Mental Health Association in Washington, D.C. Gould Farm, Monterey, MA 01245 Web: www.gouldfarm.org

Unlabeled is a vital tool to use in dismantling negative perceptions of people diagnosed with mental illness. Through the inspiring stories of leaders of the self-help and advocacy movement, *Unlabeled* documents how individuals with mental illness have taken charge of their illness and, in the process, discovered empowerment. This video portrays the inception, evolution, and future direction of the consumer empowerment movement. Created by Leonard Lies, of Dream Catchers, Inc. Pennsylvania Mental Health Consumers Association (PMHCA), 4105 Derry Street, Harrisburg, PA 17111 Phone: (717) 564-4930 Fax: (717) 564-4708

OTHER RESOURCES

Channing L. Bete, Inc., publishes scriptograph pamphlets on many topics related to mental health and illness. Phone: (800) 628-7733

The Expressive Arts Network of the New Jersey Alliance for the Mentally Ill (NJAMI) emphasizes common interests in creative activities that foster networking, outreach, advocacy, and community involvement. This network provides opportunities for individuals to communicate through alternative means, supportive environments, relationships and/or opportunities based upon similar interests. 1562 Route 130, North Brunswick, NJ 08902 Phone: (732) 940-0991 Fax: (732) 940-0355 E-mail: aminj@sprynet.com

Families for Depression Awareness is a website created by Julie Totten, the founder of this nonprofit organization. Its mission is to raise awareness of depression and to reduce the associated stigma. On their website, they publish "Family Profiles" and have reports on topics such as how to find good medical help, support groups, and books. Web: www.familyaware.org

The Journal is a magazine produced by the California chapter of the National Alliance for the Mentally Ill. It features a different theme in each issue. 1111 Howe Avenue, Suite 475, Sacramento, CA 95825 Phone: (916) 567-0163

The Mental Illness Education Project, Inc., seeks to improve the care and prognosis of people with psychiatric disabilities through video-based programs for those with disabilities, their families, mental health professionals, students, and others. P.O. Box 470813, Brookline Village, MA 02147

The National Alliance for Research on Schizophrenia and Depression Artworks (NARSAD Artworks) sells products that showcase museum-quality art by talented artists who share the common bond of mental illness. NARSAD Artworks provides self-esteem and income for artists who suffer from mental illness while promoting public education and destigmatization of mental illness. P.O. Box 941, La Habra, CA 90633-0941 Phone: (714) 529-5571

Project S.O.S.: Stamp Out Stigma of Mental Illness, affiliated with the National Alliance for the Mentally Ill, provides complimentary lesson plans to elementary schools, middle schools, and high schools for the purpose of educating youth about brain disease and fighting the stigma that surrounds mental illness. P.O. Box 766, Berea, OH 44017 Phone: (216) 572-5016

Psychotoxic Drugs: Legal and Illegal is a booklet by Jean K. Bouricius, a member of the Alliance for the Mentally Ill of Western Massachusetts. This booklet provides information about how illegal drugs and alcohol can adversely interact with mental illnesses and with medications. 717½ Main Street, Agawam, MA 01001 printed the photographs for both the exhibit and the book. We also appreciate the skill of Michael Ledgere, formerly of R. Michelson Galleries, for his work framing the photographs for the *Nothing to Hide* exhibit. Will Baczek, the owner of the Fine Arts Gallery in Northampton, Massachusetts, donated his glorious sunlit space for the local premiere of the exhibit. We are thankful for this meaningful gesture.

The members of the Advisory Board for the *Nothing to Hide* project have been our allies from the project's inception. They include: Steven E. Arnold, M.D., Assistant Professor of Psychiatry and Neurology, University of Pennsylvania; Marilyn Benoit, M.D.; Ellen Hofheimer Bettmann, Director of Research, The Anti-Defamation League's A WORLD OF DIF-FERENCE Institute; Jaime Campbell, mental health consumer advocate; Edwin H. Cassem, M.D., Professor of Psychiatry, Harvard Medical School and former Chief of Psychiatry at Massachusetts General Hospital; Laurie Flynn, Former Executive Director of the National Alliance for the Mentally Ill; Penny Frese, PhD; Fred Frese, PhD, Director of Psychology, Western Reserve Psychiatric Hospital; Kay Redfield Jamison, PhD, author of *The Unquiet Mind* and *Night Falls Fast;* Michael A. Jenike, M.D., Associate Chief of Psychiatry, Director, Psychiatric Neuroscience Program, Massachusetts General Hospital; Ann Madigan, former Anti-Stigma Coordinator, Massachusetts Department of Mental Health; Jay Neugeboren, author of *Imagining Robert* and *Transforming Madness;* Clea Simon, author of *Mad House: Growing Up in the Shadow of Mentally Ill Siblings;* Lesley Stahl, News Correspondent for *60 Minutes;* E. Fuller Torrey, M.D., Executive Director, Stanley Foundation Research Programs, NAMI Research Institute, and author of *Surviving Schizophrenia* and *Out of the Shadows: Confronting America's Mental Illness Crisis;* and Carolyn Villarrubia, M.D. Our thanks to them all for their support.

We gratefully acknowledge the financial support of the Tsunami Foundation and the Icarus Foundation, both of which made the publication of this book and the creation of the exhibit possible. In addition, we are indebted to the National Alliance for the Mentally Ill (NAMI), the Massachusetts Cultural Council—a state agency—the Gill Foundation, the Sopris Foundation, the Art Angels, Gilbert E. Jones, Jean J. Beard, Gregory Gillespie, and Lynn Glenn, all of whom contributed generously to this project.

Those whom we have acknowledged here have nurtured and encouraged us in our journey along the way. Their visionary spirit, commitment to social justice, and belief in our work continue to inspire us.

— JEAN J. BEARD,
PEGGY GILLESPIE, AND GIGI KAESER

My best friend, Anson M. Beard, Jr., and my sons Anson and Jamie have given me unconditional support and encouragement all along the way. My daughter, Ashley, has been my beacon of light and my constant source of inspiration. Without my family, I could not have stayed the course, and I am honored we took this journey together.

A special thank-you to my sister, Lee, whose generosity of spirit and love have been gifts for as long as I can remember. I am also indebted to my daughter-in-law, Veronica Beard, and my former brother-in-law, Sam Beard, for enveloping Ashley in their lives and keeping her there.

My loving appreciation to Kristi Nelson, who reminds me to breathe, and who nourishes my soul. My heartfelt thanks to Caryn Markson, PhD, for her understanding and wise perspective.

I am blessed by many friends, too numerous to mention here, who have made a difference in my daughter's life for many years. I am especially grateful to Pam Pressley Abraham, Psy.D., and Gunther Abraham, PhD, who ushered Ashley into the maze of the mental health system over twenty years ago. They helped us make sense of what, at the time, made no sense at all, and their support and responsiveness to her and our family brought relief beyond words. I also appreciate the caring staff of Gatehouse Cottage, both past and present. They have created a "home away from home" for my daughter, and they understand the importance of a white picket fence.

Peggy Gillespie is exceptionally good at pulling chestnuts out of the fire. She guided me through the labyrinth of the various stages of this project, and gave me the tools to do the work. Her imaginative and creative approach to the editing process was inspirational, and her unfailing sense of humor added to the joy of our collaboration. Most importantly, when I got testy, she did not. Thank you, Peggy.

And finally, my gratitude to Gigi Kaeser, who shares my appreciation of old cemeteries, funky bookstores, and Oklahoma City. The integrity of her photographs makes this book come alive, and that is a wondrous thing.

— JEAN BEARD

First, I want to thank Jean Beard and Peggy Gillespie. Jean made this project possible. It was her inspired vision that led us to the subject of mental illness in the family. Her wisdom has guided the project all along. And Peggy has always been the engine that made the project go. I offer special gratitude to her.

My husband, Jim Maraniss, has always been encouraging, even as I elbow our domestic life with this demanding project. My children, Michael, Ben, Lucia, and Elliott, inspire me and are trusted photo editors. Thanks also to my brother-in-law, Dave Maraniss, who has given us his essay "Uncle Phil's Brain," a great insight into the time of Phil's illness and the out-of-time agony of any parent facing mental illness in a child. And to Mary Maraniss and Jean Chulak, Phil's sisters, thank you for finding the perfect picture to illustrate Dave's story.

— GIGI KAESER

Above all, I want to thank my two Nothing to Hide colleagues. My coeditor, Jean Beard, who brought the idea of creating an exhibit and book about mental illness to Family Diversity Projects, has been incredibly generous in so many ways. Living with her daughter Ashley's mental illness led her to want to improve the lives of all individuals and their families affected by psychiatric disorders. Jean not only had the desire to create Nothing to Hide, she also had the vision to make it happen. I will always appreciate her hard work, excellent editorial skills, and dedication to all aspects of this project. Most of all, I'll never forget the wild sense of humor we shared during the very long process of editing the texts. Thank you, Jean, for making Nothing to Hide possible. It truly wouldn't exist without you.

Working with photographer Gigi Kaeser on our third book has been a pleasure, as always. She is steadfast, incredibly reliable, a great listener and advice-giver, and a rational thinker. As my codirector at Family Diversity Projects, I value her day-by-day support over the many years we have collaborated. Thank you, Gigi, for always being so present, patient, and honest.

My goddaughter, Ashley Beard, the inspiration for Nothing to Hide, is a shining star, living every day with astonishing courage. I have always been amazed by her kind and loving spirit, her laughter, and her beautiful smile. Thank you, Ashley, just for being the exquisite person you are.

In my family, I especially want to thank my fifteen-year-old daughter, Jay Gillespie, who has lived and breathed this project along with me. She has grown to understand mental illness in a compassionate way that is beyond the scope of many people her age. I am also extraordinarily grateful to my late husband, Gregory Gillespie. His loving support made it possible for me to take the time and have the energy to work on this project for many years. He had experienced mental illness in his immediate family, so he knew this topic intimately and cared deeply about Nothing to Hide.

Numerous dear friends supported me through the lengthy process of editing this book, as well as during times of personal challenge when my husband died in the midst of this work. Among those who have been there when I needed them the most were: Adi Bemak, Alexa Birdsong, Epi Bodhi, Alyse Bynum, Sophy Craze, Robin Freedenfeld, Ruth Harms,

Marsha Humphrey, Amy Kahn, Sue Leibowitz, Cathy O'Connell, Rob Okun, Susan O'Neill, Jeff McQueen, Penny Rhodes, and A. J. Verdelle. All of these caring friendships helped birth this project and I extend my heartfelt thanks to each of these nurturing people.

And finally, I wish to honor the never-wavering love and guidance of my three closest long-time allies and dearest sisters in spirit. Carla Brennan, sweet friend and spiritual seeker, your intense single-minded passion for freedom has given me the courage to face my own leap into the unknown. Your nonjudgmental kindness sustained me (and still does), and helped me find my way back to a path of clarity. Caryn Markson, you have *always* been there, traveling alongside me in times of sorrow and in times of hilarity and joy. I am so grateful that we walk together on the groundless path of the awakened and open heart, as we continue to fine-tune our understanding of how to live peacefully and lovingly. Nan Niederlander, you are a steady, kind, truthful, and loving presence in my life. Together, we laugh at our mistakes, celebrate our moments of insight, and help each other grow lighter and lighter in all ways. All three of you are beacons of compassion and wisdom in my life. Each of you, in unique ways, has helped me grow stronger, making it possible for me to complete this work. Thank you.

— PEGGY GILLESPIE

Peggy Gillespie, Jean J. Beard, and Gigi Kaeser *(photo by Jay Gillespie)*